W9-BLP-068

365 WAYS TO LIVE CHEAP

YOUR EVERYDAY GUIDE TO SAVING MONEY

365 WAYS TO LIVE CHEAP!

TRENT HAMM
FOUNDER OF THESIMPLEDOLLAR.COM

AVON, MASSACHUSETTS

This 2011 edition printed for Barnes & Noble, Inc. by F+W Media, Inc.

ISBN: 978-1-4351-3289-4

Printed and bound in the United States of America.

1 3 5 7 9 10 8 6 4 2

Library of Congress Cataloging-in-Publication Data
is available from the publisher.

CONTENTS

A QUICK QUIZ

WHERE DOES YOUR MONEY REALLY GO?

Do you know where your money goes? Are you really aware of every red cent you're spending, or does a lot of it slip right through your fingers, leaving you wondering at the end of the month how you're going to make ends meet? Knowing where every penny goes is one of the key principles of living cheap. Take this quick quiz to find out how your dollars stack up.

1.	**When you look at the receipt after leaving the grocery store, you:**
A.	Feel shocked at the total and express disbelief that you could have spent that much.
B.	Feel alarmed at the rising grocery prices, but feel that you made sensible purchases.
C.	Smile happily at your tiny total, knowing that you got the food you needed for the week at a minimal cost.
2.	**When you sit down to pay bills, you:**
A.	Hope that there will be money in your account to cover the checks.
B.	Get through the task as quickly as possible, but don't worry about having enough money to pay the bills.
C.	Look for ways to trim a few dollars off every bill you pay.

3.	**When an unexpected bill comes in the mail, you:**
A.	PANIC!
B.	Calmly take a little out of savings and a little out of the checking account and pay the bill, then use the credit card to cover regular expenses for the next week.
C.	Fire off that payment without thinking twice thanks to cheap living and an emergency fund.
4.	**It's Sunday afternoon and time to go grocery shopping. You:**
A.	Jump in the car and head straight to the supermarket.
B.	Make a grocery list.
C.	Use the grocery store flyer to plan your meals for the week and then make a list from that meal plan.
5.	**How much money is in your checking account right now (without peeking!)?**
A.	I have no idea.
B.	I know within a few hundred dollars.
C.	I know within a few dollars.
6.	**How much money did you spend on entertainment and hobbies last month?**
A.	I don't know—a lot?
B.	I know pretty close to the amount, but it's more than is probably healthy.
C.	Ten bucks or so.

7.	**A friend calls up and wants to do something fun. You:**
A.	Go out with your buddy and drop at least $100—or whatever the evening requires to "have fun."
B.	Go out with your buddy, but just spend $20 or so.
C.	Suggest twenty or so different things to do, none of which cost much of anything at all.
8.	**Your kids are bored. You:**
A.	Load 'em up and take them to the mall.
B.	Load 'em up and take them to the park and then out for ice cream.
C.	Pull out board games, play catch in the yard, and spend the afternoon together at home.
9.	**When you open up your cell phone bill, you:**
A.	Grumble loudly about overage charges, extra text message fees, and out-of-plan-area calls, but pay the bill anyway.
B.	See a few small additional costs, but pay the bill without sweating it.
C.	Rarely see an extra cost, but if you do, call up the cell phone company and make sure it doesn't happen again.
10.	**You see a new toy/gadget/clothing item you really want. You:**
A.	Whip out the plastic and buy it immediately.
B.	Don't buy it right then, but go home and plan how you can afford it, then buy it next week.
C.	Go home and see if it fits in your budget. If it doesn't, put it off until a later date when you really can afford it—if you still want it then, that is.

Scoring

For every A answer, give yourself 3 points.

For every B answer, give yourself 2 points.

For every C answer, give yourself 1 point.

Do you know where your money goes?

25 TO 30 POINTS: Your money flutters through your fingers and blows away in the wind. Time to buckle down and learn how to live cheap.

18 TO 25 POINTS: You know some of the tactics for living a financially sensible lifestyle, but too much of your cash still slips through the cracks. Time for a tactics refresher.

10 TO 17 POINTS: You're a thrift machine who knows how to save money—and knows the usefulness of discovering new ways to save a penny.

THE TEN BIGGEST TIP$ FOR LIVING CHEAP

1. Take Little Steps, Not Big Ones

Making changes to your everyday lifestyle is hard—that's why so many people try diets and eventually fail. They start off believing that they can make dramatic changes to their life and it works—for a while. Eventually, though, they fall off the wagon and all of that weight they lost comes right back. Cutting back on your spending is much the same. If you go at it with a high level of intensity at first, eventually you'll rebound and go on a spending spree. The best route to success then is to take little steps, not big ones. Find one tactic in this book and focus on just that tactic for a few weeks, incorporating it into your life. Then try another, and then another. Soon, you'll have made that big change you dream about and it will fit as naturally as a glove.

2. Realize That You're Not Alone in This Journey

Some people spend money like it is going out of style, racking up five figures in credit card debt, multiple vehicle loans, student loans, and mortgages, too. If you're struggling with debt and making ends meet, know you're not alone in this experience and that there are people out there who can help you through this, whether it is your family, your friends, or people online who are sharing their experiences. Don't give in to the sense that it is hopeless—there is hope, and there are people who want to help you.

3. Spend Less Than You Earn

Your primary goal each month should be to spend less than you bring in. If you do that consistently, over and over again, your financial situation will improve. There are a lot of ways to make sure you're doing this—an old-fashioned budget, complete abstinence from credit cards, putting some of your income into savings immediately before you even begin to spend it—but they all come down to one rule: Spend less than you earn. The tips in this book will help you with spending less so that you can achieve this goal every month.

4. Calculate How Much You Really Make

Many of the tactics of living cheap seem like a waste of time to many people. "I'm not doing that to save five dollars!" is a common thing to say. If you feel that way, try this experiment:

- First, calculate how many hours you work in a year. But that's not all . . . add to that the hours spent driving to and from work, the hours spent working on stuff at home, the hours spent entertaining and supporting coworkers, the hours spent shopping for work supplies, and so on. If you spend even a sliver of time on a task for your job, count it.
- Next, calculate how much money you earn in a year, including your benefits (you can get that off your paycheck stub). From that, subtract taxes, the cost of commuting (gas, oil changes,

wear and tear on the car, and other maintenance), the cost of work clothes, the cost of child care, the cost of other supplies you need to purchase, and so on. Anything that you buy for your job, subtract it here.

- Then, divide the amount you actually earn by the number of hours that you really work. This can be a painful process.

What does that number mean? You can use that as a comparison for everything that you do.

Thinking of buying an expensive gadget? Use that real hourly rate to figure out how much of your life you're giving to your job to get that gadget. Wondering if a money-saving task is worth it? See how much time it will take and how much money it will save.

You'll be very surprised—things like making your own laundry detergent (tip #18) end up earning far more in savings for the time spent than actually going to work will earn you.

5. Record Every Penny You Spend for a Month

Money slips through our fingers in simple and subtle ways. We spend a little here on something forgettable, spend a little there on an unimportant thing, and at the end of the month, it's panic time—we're left with very little money. Spend a month keeping track of every penny that you spend, noting exactly how much you spent and what you spent it on. At the end of the month, go through it and note which expenses were actually essential and which were frivolous. You'll find two things: The need to write your spending down makes you more vigilant against wasteful spending, and the end-of-month review of your records will surprise you when you see how much of your spending was nonessential. Use that information as a springboard to see what you need to work on.

6. Master the Ten-Second Rule

Want to curb that leaky faucet of unnecessary spending? Here's a great tactic. Whenever you're in a store and you pick up an item, hold it for ten seconds. During those ten seconds, ask yourself if you really need it and also if that money wouldn't be better used somewhere else. You'll almost always find yourself putting that unnecessary item back on the shelf and walking away, quite proud that you didn't waste your money on something so unnecessary.

7. Master the Thirty-Day Rule, Too

It's useful to use a similar approach with bigger purchases as well. Whenever you pick up an expensive but not immediately essential item (anything that costs more than $20) and decide after using the ten-second rule that you do want to buy it, put it back on the shelf and wait thirty days. If you still remember and want the item in thirty days, then go back to the store and buy it. Most such purchases will float out of your mind long before then. Using this tactic keeps you from making impulsive buys of expensive things that manage to get past your ten-second filter.

8. Keep Track of Your Progress

Each month, figure out how much you earned, how much you spent, and how much you saved that month and record it. Then, try to match that number the following month. This is, in effect, the simplest form of budgeting—you're merely trying to keep your spending under control from month to month. It also lets you see your continual progress. If you were able to live a bit cheaper and put just $50 a month into savings for six months, for example, you now have $300 saved up, showing you that your little changes are really adding up to something big.

9. Talk about Your Money, Especially with Your Partner

Many couples and families have a chaotic approach to money, with each person doing their own thing financially without understanding their partner's goals, desires, and challenges. Often, this results in partners hiding information from each other, such as high credit card statements and other debts, and this not only damages a family's financial situation, but can also damage a marriage. Take the time to sit down for an hour every month or two and go through your complete financial picture with your partner, including both your successes and mistakes. Plan goals together, and actively support each other. If you're single, identify a "money buddy" whom you can be similarly open with. You can support each other in making good spending and financial choices and offer each other advice in difficult situations.

10. Automate Your Savings

One nice thing about saving money is that you end up with more in your checking account over time—the savings slowly build up. For many people, the problem with that is that the extra money is a temptation to spend on unnecessary stuff. The solution is easy—just save automatically. Have your bank set up an automatic transfer of a small amount each week from your checking to your savings—say, $25 for starters. As you get more adept at saving money, increase that transfer amount, and keep saving. That money can help out in emergencies, help with a big payment, or provide the starting material you need to begin investing.

CHEAP TACTIC$ FOR APPLIANCES

11. Do the Research

The biggest mistake you can make when purchasing a new appliance is to head right down to the local appliance store and open your wallet. Do some research into different models and find out more about them. How reliable is the model? Does it do a good job at the task you want? Is it energy efficient? What's a reasonable price for that model? You can find the answers to all of these questions on the Internet. Spend half an hour studying archives of *Consumer Reports* or other consumer publications and find out what they say about the appliance you're considering buying. Just find an article covering the appliance that you're looking at, see what the study has to say, and find a few models that are appropriate for you—not whatever models the salesperson at the shop wants you to buy.

12. Reliability Is the Most Important Feature

The number-one feature that you should look at when buying a new appliance is reliability. Paying a bit more now for an appliance that will last twice as long is a great way to save money over the long haul. A $500 washer that lasts ten years is a far better deal than a $350 washer that lasts only five years. Neat features are nice, but reliability is the one feature that will help keep money in your pocket over the long haul.

13. Look for the EnergyStar Logo

After reliability, the most important feature is energy efficiency. Look for appliances that are EnergyStar certified. These appliances use less energy than those without the certification. Also, compare the energy use numbers among models. They're usually stated in kilowatt-hours per year. Every kilowatt-hour costs you about ten cents on your electric bill, so if you can get a model that uses one hundred fewer kilowatt-hours per year, you'll save $10 per year owning that model over its lifetime. That can really add up over the lifetime of an appliance.

14. Consider Last Year's Models

When you're shopping for appliances, most of the models that you'll be shown are the current year's models, but most appliance stores often have last year's models still available in the back, still new and often at a discounted rate. Research last year's models as well (using older issues of *Consumer Reports*) and if you find one of those for sale at a discounted rate, snap it up.

15. Shop Patiently

In order to find the best price for the appliance model you want, you may have to shop at several places. Take your time with this purchase. You're far better off shopping patiently and finding a good price on the model you want than just buying that model at the first place you go, or buying whatever model is on sale at that first store you visit. *Another tip:* When you know you're about to make the move to replace a major appliance, watch the flyers for appliance sellers in your area. If you've done your research, you should know the expected price on the models you want. A sale on that model can really pay off.

16. Use Cold Water for Most Clothes Washing

The Alliance to Save Energy reports that using cold water for most of your clothes washing saves up to $63 per year. That's because 85 percent of the energy used when washing your clothes is used not by your washing machine, but by the water heater. Most clothes that are not intensely dirty are made just as clean in cold water as in hot water, so give it a try, particularly on your underclothes and towels. If you feel like cold water isn't giving your clothes an appropriate cleaning, use a warm pre-soak—just fill your washing machine with warm water and let your clothes soak in it a bit before they're properly washed.

17. Clean Out Your Dryer Lint

Does your dryer seem to not work as well as it once did? Do you sometimes have to run a dryer load a second time because the clothes are still damp? That's not only time consuming, but it's also expensive, and the cause is usually dryer lint. It's easy to take care of the problem—just make sure your dryer's lint trap is clean (use a vacuum cleaner to clean out the lint trap slot) and also make sure that there's no lint caught where the dryer's exhaust leaves your home. You can also pull your dryer out from the wall, disconnect the exhaust pipe, and make sure that it isn't clogged anywhere (and also vacuum inside the dryer through the exhaust hole).

18. Make Your Own Powdered Laundry Detergent

Laundry detergent costs as much as twenty cents per load, but you can easily make your own powdered detergent at home for as little as two cents a load. Just take a bar of unscented soap and grate it into flakes using a box grater, then mix those soap flakes with one cup of washing soda and a half cup of borax. You can also add one half cup of an oxygen cleaner like OxyClean, but it works fine without it. You can make multiples of this mix and store it in a large tub. All you need for a load of laundry is two tablespoons (or ⅛ cup) of this mix. Leave a small measuring cup right in your storage tub.

19. Air-Dry Your Clothes Instead of Using the Dryer

An old-fashioned clothesline is one of the best cost-cutting items available to you. At current energy costs, the average dryer eats up forty cents worth of energy each time you run a load. Hanging your clothes on a clothesline reduces that cost to zero. Over many loads, that adds up to a real savings. Don't have an outside clothesline? Hang one across a spare room in your home, or spread the clothes out to dry. The clothes smell better and you save for every five dryer loads you hang up.

20. Don't Use the Stove When the Microwave Will Do

For many simple purposes, the microwave oven is much more energy efficient than the stove, often using 75 percent less energy for the same task and adding far less heat to your house. Use your microwave for tasks such as boiling water, steaming and browning vegetables, cooking rice, and other water-intensive applications. It can reduce your cooking costs by up to 20 percent.

21. Turn On the Oven Light While Cooking

Whenever you open the door on your oven, as much as 25 percent of the heat inside is lost and a significant amount of energy is used building that heat again, likely extending your cooking time. Instead of losing heat that way, turn on the oven light while cooking and use a meat thermometer in your food. This way, you can look through the glass on your oven and visually inspect the food inside without opening the door and losing significant heat.

22. Only Wash Full Loads of Dishes or Clothes

Instead of just washing clothes or washing dishes when it's most convenient, wait until the loads are truly full before running a cycle. Appliances are designed to handle full loads, so running partial loads is a sure way to let money float out of your pocket. According to the Rocky Mountain Institute, an average washing machine costs $155 per year to use. Reducing the number of loads you wash can add up to real money over time. Want something clean right away? Wash that item individually by hand.

23. Use the Short Cycle

Similar to the idea behind washing only full loads, consider using short cycles on your dishwasher and washing machine, especially when the items that you're washing aren't particularly dirty, such as work clothing that you may wear in an office. Using the short cycle can reduce the cost of an individual load by up to 50 percent depending on the model, so get in the habit of using the short cycle for most of your machine washing needs.

24. Make Your Own Dishwashing Detergent

Dishwashing detergent can be made at home with common cleaning supplies. Just mix one cup of borax and one cup of baking soda in a tub. Some harder water situations may require the addition of a cup or two cups of powdered purchased dishwashing detergent. Just put in two tablespoons of the powder mix (1⁄8 cup) into your dishwasher for each load and save about fifteen cents per load. *Another tip:* Instead of using Jet Dry in the rinse cycle to make your dishes dry, use a couple caps full of vinegar instead. Much cheaper, same effect.

25. Don't Install Your Refrigerator Next to Your Dishwasher or Oven

Many kitchens have this as the default layout, but if you can avoid it, your energy bill will thank you greatly. The natural heat produced by your dishwasher or oven can add heat to the refrigerator if it's placed nearby, causing the refrigerator to run more frequently to maintain the low temperature. If you can, look for a kitchen layout that places the refrigerator far away from the dishwasher or the oven, allowing your refrigerator to be significantly more energy efficient—and thus easier on your wallet.

26. Set Your Refrigerator to the Warmest Setting; Adjust from There

Many people have their refrigerator and freezer settings much colder than they actually need them to be to keep their food chilled. Instead of keeping your dials turned to the coolest settings, try the opposite—turn them as high as they can go and see how it meets your needs. If you need to, slowly adjust the temperature downward. A reasonable setting on your refrigerator and your freezer can save significant money over time, as your compressor will kick on much less often and thus save money on energy costs. *Another tip:* Pull out your refrigerator every six months and vacuum out the back of it, making sure to clean dust from the coils. This will keep your refrigerator running as efficiently as possible.

27. Invest in a Deep Freezer

If you have space (in your kitchen, garage, or basement), invest in a deep freezer. A deep freezer allows you to buy your food in bulk, saving significant amounts of money. For example, by contacting a meat locker directly, you can purchase meat in large quantities directly from the provider, filling up your freezer with meat discounted at 30 percent or more compared to what you'd pay at the meat counter at the grocery store. See a great deal at the store? You can stock up big time, putting the excess in the freezer for later use. The use of a deep freezer can save approximately 15 percent on your annual food bill without a major increase in your energy use.

28. Start an Automatic Appliance Replacement Fund

One of the "sneaky" expenses that often starts people sliding down a slippery slope into debt is the unexpected failure of an essential appliance, often at the worst possible time. This usually means that people run out and buy a new appliance on credit without having the money to pay the bill. They are then running short for the next year or so as they pay off that extra bill—and hoping nothing else goes wrong while they're paying it off. Here's a better solution: Take tip #10 and put it to use. Put aside a tiny amount, $10 a week, toward appliance replacement. You've probably already saved that $10 a week by using other tips in this book. If you start doing it now and your refrigerator fails in a year, you'll have $520 already in hand to pay that bill. If the water heater fails two years after that, you'll have $1,040 in hand to cover that bill. All it takes is $10 a week, and if you set up the transfer to be automatic, you'll never notice it—until you need it, that is.

CHEAP TACTIC$ FOR AUTOMOBILES

29. Focus on Reliability and Fuel Efficiency

It's easy to get excited about all the latest features when you're considering a car purchase, but instead of focusing on the DVD player or leather seats, focus on these buying tactics instead:

- Do your research before you go near a car dealership. Examine the most recent car-buying issue of *Consumer Reports*, for starters, and carefully study their findings on reliability as well as their overall conclusions. Cars marked as highly reliable have significantly lower expenses for repairs over the lifetime of the car, directly saving you cash.
- Focus on buying late-model used cars, as they often have the best long-term value for the dollar.
- Put a high emphasis on fuel efficiency. Over 75,000 miles of driving, a 15 mpg car guzzles 5,000 gallons of gas, while a 20 mpg car only uses 3,750 gallons. At $4 per gallon, that's a savings of $5,000—and that's if gas prices hold steady.
- Know your numbers before you go. Use the Kelley Blue Book (*www.kbb.com*) to find out the value of your current car (if you're planning on trading) and the value of the car you're looking at. You will then have a sense of how fair the offer is.

30. Read the Manual

Your car's manual is a treasure trove of tips and bits of information that can save you a lot of money over the long haul. It should be your primary source for information about how to care for your car and maximize its lifespan. Most of the information available through popular culture about automobile care and maintenance is placed there by organizations wanting to maximize their profits by convincing you that you need maintenance, replacements, and upgrades far more frequently than you actually need them. Read the next few tips and see how often the car manual comes into play to save you money.

31. Don't Buy a Service Contract or an Extended Warranty

When you try to make an automobile purchase, the dealer will often try to encourage you to purchase a service contract or an extended warranty on your new vehicle. Say no. If you're interested in such plans, you can shop around for a low-cost service plan. If you're concerned about a warranty, you can purchase one directly from a warranty provider such as Warranty Direct without paying the additional dealer markup. Plus, it gives you time while your basic warranty is in place to do the research and pick out the warranty that's right for you—and it will be far cheaper than what you'd buy at the dealership.

32. Air Up All of Your Tires

Airing up a car tire is a very simple free procedure that takes only a couple of moments, yet can save you a bundle over time. According to the Car Care Council, a mere 1 PSI drop in air pressure in all four tires can reduce your gas mileage by 0.4 percent, and your car can easily be 10 PSI low without even noticing it—a 4 percent reduction in gas mileage. Over 10,000 miles in a 20 mpg car with gas at $4 a gallon, you can save yourself $80 by just airing them up. Look inside your car's manual to find out the recommended maximum pressure for tires on your automobile and also to find out details on the exact procedure to follow.

33. Buy the Cheap Gas

The idea that you need high-octane gas for your car is mostly a relic from the days of older cars that could actually maximize the use of higher-octane gas. Today, most cars run just fine on low-octane fuel. Check your owner's manual to see what the recommendation is for your car and buy the cheapest you can within that recommendation. If buying cheaper gas saves you ten cents per gallon on a 20 mpg car, over the course of 10,000 miles, you'll save $50 in lower gas bills.

34. Don't Get an Oil Change Every 3,000 Miles

The mantra for oil changes is that you should get one every 3,000 miles, and most car owners quickly run off to get that oil change right on schedule. You might be surprised to find that the owner's manual suggests an oil change every 5,000 miles or, on some models, even less frequently. In fact, 5,000 miles is the recommendation from *Consumer Reports* as well as the guys from NPR's *Car Talk*. If you drive your car for 60,000 miles while you own it, just following the factory recommendations saves you eight oil changes.

35. Use the Manufacturer's Maintenance Schedule

Let's get this straight: Regular maintenance on your automobile is very important for keeping your car reliable and reducing repair costs, and it should be done exactly in accordance with the schedule that the manufacturer recommends. When you buy a car, most dealers will attempt to get you to subscribe to a maintenance schedule through their dealership and will tell you with dead seriousness that you need to follow that schedule to a tee. Often, that's not true—most dealer maintenance routines get you into their auto shop far more often than you need to be. Again, flip open that owner's manual, find the maintenance schedule information, and follow it yourself for all aspects of your car, from brake pad replacement to tire replacement.

36. Minimize Your Load

When you're driving on the highway, most of your engine power goes toward overcoming air drag—the resistance that the air is putting on your car. When you have extra items on your car, such as stuff bundled to the roof or even a ski rack, you're reducing your gas mileage by as much as 5 percent. Similarly, excess weight in your car reduces your gas mileage, so if you're using your trunk as a storage unit, you'll save yourself a significant amount by getting that stuff out of the car.

37. Practice Good Gas Conservation Habits

It's often the little things that really add up, and with gas at more than $4 a gallon, it adds up to big money fast. Here are five more fuel conservation tips that individually won't save a significant amount, but over time and done in combination can save quite a bit of gas expense.

- Tighten the gas cap as tightly as you can when you finish filling up. Gas evaporates rather quickly, and a loose cap allows that evaporated gas to simply drift out of your tank.
- Don't top off the tank. When you do, you dramatically increase the chance for gas to slosh out, and when gas prices are high, even a bit of sloshing is money gone from your pocket.
- Don't rest your left foot on the brake while driving. Even a slight accidental bump of the brake will cause some drag and some additional gas use—plus it'll increase the wear on your brake pads.

- Turn off the air conditioning as you approach your destination. When you're ten or fifteen minutes away from where you need to be, turn off your air conditioning. This will improve your car's mileage and the cab of your car won't get warm enough during that period to cause any discomfort.
- Use appropriate tires for the weather. Snow tires in the summer significantly reduce your gas mileage.

38. Use Public Transportation

If you live in an area where you have easy access to public transportation, use it. Use it to commute to work, to attend social and cultural events, and to run errands. The cost savings of using public transportation is tremendous if you get into a habit of using it consistently. If you can use the bus or the rails to take a trip for $2 when you would otherwise have to drive your car, burn two gallons of gas, pay for parking, and add extra miles onto the car that push you closer to maintenance, the choice is pretty easy.

39. Carpool

If you have an opportunity to share a ride to and from work with someone, jump on it. The cost savings of carpooling is tremendous. If your commute causes you to burn two gallons of gas and put forty miles on your car, just two days a week of riding with someone else can put the savings per month well over $100. Carpooling can also add some time savings to the picture as well if you have access to the

HOV lane. If you work in a large organization, it's pretty easy to get a carpool started. Send out an e-mail to as many coworkers as you can stating that you're interested in starting a pool from your area and see how many responses you get.

40. Use a Bicycle

Most nearby trips, such as a trip to the post office or a trip to the local grocery store, are very short—just a mile or two each way. They're also full of stop-and-go driving, which is the least efficient kind of driving for an automobile. Instead of driving, get a used bicycle and use it for these short little trips. Install a small basket on the front so you can easily carry a couple bags of groceries or a package to be mailed. It's a free mode of transportation, doesn't take much longer than a car over a short trip, and is a good way to get a bit of exercise, too.

41. Eliminate One of Your Cars Entirely

If you find yourself using your bicycle and public transportation frequently, you'll likely find that one of your automobiles is being used less and less. Consider selling it. Not only will you make some money from the sale, but you'll have a smaller car insurance payment and no license costs to worry about either, plus you may free up some garage space that can be put to better use in other ways. This is a big step, but it's one that can save you a ton of money on a monthly basis.

42. Don't Speed—Instead, Use Cruise Control

It's tempting to speed when you're driving somewhere, particularly when the commute is long, but speeding is an incredibly expensive tradeoff. It reduces your fuel efficiency, making the trip itself cost more. It puts more wear and tear on your automobile, increasing the chances of a necessary repair. It also increases the chance of an accident, as speeding gives you less time to react. If that's not enough, you also run the danger of being issued a speeding ticket, which has not only a direct cost but can raise your insurance rates as well. The costs of speeding, both potential and real, just to save a few minutes on a trip aren't worth it. Instead, just set the cruise control to the speed limit for long driving stretches; this will keep you from being tempted to speed.

43. Don't Get Optional Stuff During Maintenance

Often when you take your car in for maintenance, the workers inside will attempt to sell you additional products and services, such as replacement windshield wiper blades or a new air filter. Never buy them there. The cost they charge you for a new blade or a new filter, plus the cost for the minute's worth of work to install them, is far beyond reasonable. Instead, go to a discount auto parts store and buy these items yourself, then use the car's manual to install them. You'll not only save a lot on the part itself, but you'll save on the labor cost.

44. Shop Around for Car Repairs

When your car needs repairs, don't simply take it back to the dealership. Pull out the yellow pages (or check out Google Maps) and call several nearby auto repair facilities. Look for those that are ASE (Automotive Service Excellence) certified. You should also consult any of your friends who have knowledge about cars and ask if they have any recommended repair shops. If your car is under warranty, make sure the repair shop will honor that warranty. This will go a long way toward getting you a quality auto repair for a much cheaper price.

45. Pay for Car Repairs with a Credit Card

When you get your car repaired, pay for the repair with a credit card and then pay the credit card balance off immediately. Why? Credit cards offer significant consumer protection against fraud. If your car repair is faulty, you can contact your credit card company and have them deal with it rather than trying to fight it yourself—and likely coughing up more dough for more repairs.

46. Plan Ahead for a Car Replacement

If you want to replace your car as cheaply as possible, the best time to start thinking about it is the day you purchased the previous model. Start putting a small amount away each month automatically (see tip #10) and forget about that amount until your next car purchase. Putting $50 away each month into a 3 percent APY savings account gives you $4,000 toward your next car purchase after six years. That, plus a trade-in, is enough to let you drive off the lot with a very tiny loan. Putting away $100 a month will give you $8,000 after six years, likely more than enough to allow you to trade in your current car and then drive off the lot with a late-model used car without taking out a loan—no car payments at all.

CHEAP TACTIC$ FOR

BANKING AND INVESTING

47. Get a Bank Card with a Very Large Fee-Free ATM Network

Ever stood at an ATM and seen that dreaded message "This bank charges a $2 fee for use of this ATM"? If you have, blame your bank. In order to cut corners, they've decided to exclude ATMs from their network. Your bank should always have the widest ATM network possible. If you find yourself seeing those messages regularly, that adds up to significant cash straight out of your pocket. Talk to your bank and make sure that you at least have a debit card with a MasterCard or Visa logo on it so you can use it as a credit card. Often you're able to use it as a debit card in the checkout lane and use it to get cash back.

48. Get a Checking Account That Offers More Than 1 Percent Interest

If you keep your checking account at a bank that does not offer any interest on your checking account, or offers far less than 1 percent interest, look elsewhere. Many banks offer 1 percent or higher interest rates on their checking accounts, meaning they'll actually pay you money for just having your account there. Ask if your bank has an interest checking account and switch to that account. If not, you may want to look at tip #52.

49. Get a Savings Account That Offers More Than 3 Percent Interest

Similar to tip 48, if the savings account your bank offers doesn't offer at least 3 percent interest, ask them if there is one available that offers that much. Many banks offer rates at 3 percent or above, particularly banks that focus on online services. If you can't get a savings account at your local bank offering rates that high, consider switching to one that does and include online banks in that decision. See tip #52 for more details.

50. Don't Tolerate These Four Fees

Check your most recent bank statement. Do you see things like maintenance fees, mysterious monthly fees, check cashing fees, minimum balance fees, or other fees that seem inexplicable to you? These fees are unnecessary and cost you money. Call your bank and ask to have them waived. If they refuse, then it's time to start looking for a bank that respects you as a customer (see tip #52).

51. Make Sure the Bank's Hours Match Yours

If your schedule makes it difficult to conduct business with your bank and they don't offer online services to help out with basic tasks, then your bank is costing you money. Every time you can't get a check cashed, can't get a transfer set up, or can't do any other business you might want to routinely do, your bank's business practices are interfering with your financial life. Don't accept it. Your bank should have hours that match your schedule and/or online services that help you out with most of these basic tasks.

52. If You Can't Get These Features, Start Shopping for a New Bank

So, the last four tips identify basic features you should be expecting from your bank. Without them, your bank is costing you money. Most likely, your bank doesn't have all these things, but there are many banks out there that offer most if not all of these features. Here are some tips for finding a new bank and making the move to a new account.

- Use Bankrate.com to identify banks with good services. Bankrate.com identifies banks that offer high-interest checking and savings accounts. Click on the "Checking and Savings" tab there to find out all the info you need about your local banks.
- Consider online banks like INGDirect.com. An online bank doesn't offer a brick-and-mortar place to do your bank business, but they generally offer all of the services that a bank can offer through their online services or through ATMs. Even better, since they don't have to pay for a physical location, they can offer great interest rates and no fees.
- If you decide to move to a new bank, leave your old account open for a while to help with the transition. You may have many automatic deposits and other transfers that you may have for-

gotten about, so leave the old account open for a while to catch these. When you're confident that all of your business has been switched to the new bank, you can close the old bank accounts that were draining your pocketbook and move on with your life.

53. Opt Out of "Courtesy" Overdraft Protection

Many banks offer a "courtesy" overdraft protection service where they offer to cover any overdrafts you might make, which sounds like a good deal at first. It's not. You're usually better off bouncing the check. The program at many banks usually charges you a sizable overdraft fee (usually $35 or so), then charges you a daily fee for each day you're over ($2 to $10 a day). An overdraft check can quickly rack up as much as $135 in fees if you don't cover it in ten days. It's usually much cheaper to just deal directly with the business that you wrote the bad check to. They may charge you a small fee, but if you make it right with them, it'll usually be far cheaper than paying the fees your bank will charge you.

54. Learn How to Use Online Banking

Many banks are now offering online banking services that allow you to use your computer to track your account balances, check your recent transactions, and pay bills directly without writing a check. Learn how to use this service, as it can save you money in many different ways.

- If you're unsure of your account balance, you can log in and check your current standing and recent transactions, which can save you from an accidental overdraft.
- If your bank offers online bill pay, you can save money on stamps. If you can move ten monthly bills from paper checks to online bill pay, that's a savings of $4.20 every month.
- You can avoid late fees by scheduling your regular bills to be paid automatically. No more remembering to pay a bill on time.

55. Balance Your Checkbook as Often as Possible

If you're not ready to make the move to online banking, you should definitely make sure to balance your checkbook every month, as it can save you from a potentially devastating bounced check or overdraft fee. It's really quite simple; just make sure the statement your bank provides matches your own records. Find a point where you're sure both are right and work forward from there, making sure each payment is accounted for by both you and by the bank. As long as your records and the bank's records stay in alignment, you can be much more confident that you won't "accidentally" overdraft.

56. If You Do Overdraft for the First Time, Ask for the Fee to Be Waived

Everyone makes a mistake once in a while; sometimes that little mistake can result in an overdraft. If you're a regular customer, this is a fee that should easily be waived if you handle it appropriately. First, make sure that you have sufficient funds in the account to fully cover the overdraft check (and any others that may be outstanding). Then, call the bank's customer support line, confess your mistake, and ask that the fee be waived. If they say no, do not get upset. Ask to speak to a supervisor. If that person won't waive it, try the same procedure at your local branch office. Start by asking the teller, then moving up to the supervisor if you hear a negative answer. Be polite, dress well, and don't get angry if you still hear a negative answer. Quite often, one of the four people you talk to will waive your fee, and like that, you've saved yourself $35. Variations on this approach work well for any kind of fee.

57. Open Up a 401(k) or 403(b) Now

If your workplace offers you a 401(k) or 403(b) retirement plan and you haven't signed up, do it now. Don't wait another second to do so—it can save you far more money in the long run by starting now than by putting it off. A few pointers:

- If your employer offers to match your contributions, contribute as much as you have to in order to get that full match. This is free money from your employer that you don't have to pay taxes on until retirement. Take it if they're giving it to you!
- If you're worried that your paycheck can't take a 5 percent or 10 percent hit, don't worry—a 10 percent contribution won't actually

reduce your paycheck that much. This money comes out before taxes, meaning that the percentage of your check that goes toward income taxes right now will actually go down. If you start contributing 5 percent of your check, for example, you'll only actually see a 3½ to 4 percent drop in your actual take-home pay.

58. Use a Simple Method to Choose Investment Options

When signing up for a retirement account, the choices can be overwhelming. Keep it simple; here's what you need to know to get started now (you can always learn more later on).

- If you have the option of choosing a plan that targets a specific retirement date (often called something like Target 2040), choose the one that comes closest to the year you expect to retire and put everything into that one fund.
- If you don't have such an option available, take your estimated retirement age (if you don't know, use 70), subtract your current age from that, and multiply that by two. Put that percentage in the stock fund with the best returns and the rest in a bond fund with the best returns (ask for help if you don't know). For example, if you're 30 and you want to retire at 70, you should put 80 percent into stocks and 20 percent into bonds. If you're 50, you should put 40 percent into stocks and 60 percent into bonds. Then, every five years, adjust the amounts by refiguring

how your split should go. This is a simple rule of thumb that will put you on the safe side.

59. Contribute Regularly to That Retirement Account

When you first sign up, you'll be asked to put down a percentage contribution. Choose a realistic amount. Don't pledge more than you think you can easily swallow. When you've signed up, don't interrupt the contributions. The little sacrifices you make now to keep the contributions going will enable you to have a happy life in retirement instead of having to scrape by on a small Social Security check.

60. Automatically Build an Emergency Fund

At some point in your life, disaster will strike. Your car will break down. You'll need a medical procedure. Someone will break into your house. These can be bad news, and financially costly, too, especially if you have to use a credit card to get through it. During those times, you need to have some extra cash on hand. The solution is pretty simple: Start an emergency fund to help you resolve these types of problems. Simply instruct your bank to automatically take a tiny amount out of your checking account each week (say, $20) and put it into a savings account for you. Let the money sit in that account; then, when the going gets rough, you have that cash available to you. It's probably earned a bit of interest, too, which is a bonus. Planning ahead just a little bit right now can make an enormous difference later on.

61. If You Have an Unexpected Windfall, Put It into a CD

If you're in a situation where you have a significant amount of cash on hand—winnings, a settlement, an inheritance, or anything like that—don't touch it at first. Give yourself time to carefully consider what to do with that cash. A smart thing to do is put it into a certificate of deposit at the bank for six months. It'll earn some significant interest there and also give you the hands-off time you need to carefully come up with a plan for your newfound money. Spending it immediately is usually the worst option, particularly if you're not using it to eliminate debt or build your personal wealth.

62. Ignore Freebies Given Just for Signing Up for Financial Accounts

One tactic that many banks like to use to entice you to switch to their bank is the free gift. "Sign up with us and you'll get a free blender!" "Switch to our 'free' checking and you'll get a $75 signup bonus!" Those initial freebies are often hiding something about the account, something that will help them earn their money back over the long haul. Look very carefully at the account they're offering you with that bonus. Often, there are clauses like minimum balances, hefty overdraft fees, no interest at all, a poor ATM network, or other "features" that will cost you more in the long run. If you're going to switch to a new bank, switch because the account itself is good, not because of a welcoming prize. You'll be better off in the long run.

CHEAP TACTIC$ FOR CHILDREN AND FAMILIES

63. Start Saving for College as Early as Possible—Even Before the Child Is Born

If you're not saving for your child's college education now, get started right away. The amount of money your family will save over the long haul by socking a few twenties away each month starting now can be tremendous. Here are some options to consider:

- Make the savings automatic. Set things up so that even a small amount is put into a separate account for your child. Even $10 a month, started at birth and earning just a 5 percent annual return, adds up to $3376 for your child's college education. That amount can make a huge difference if your child attends a local school or a state institution.
- Look into a 529 savings plan. These plans allow you to earn a good return on your savings, allow you to automatically put away a specific amount each month, and protect your savings from taxes. Use Google to find out about the 529 plan available in your state or other 529 plans available to you.

64. Use Cloth Diapers

Most people, when they think of cloth diapering, imagine a horrible mess of plastic pants, washer loads full of stinky diapers, safety pins, and other such images, so they stick with disposable diapers. The only problem is that disposable diapers are a continual cost. You have to keep buying more and more diapers, and they're not all that cheap—often at least a quarter per diaper change for disposable. Modern cloth diapering can be quite simple and can save you tremendous money, especially if you plan to have multiple children. *Tip:* Ask for high-quality cloth diapers, like bumGenius as a baby shower gift, so that you're spared the start-up cost.

65. Make Your Own Wipes

Baby wipes are another common parenting expense when you have small children in the house, and it's another item you can make yourself for much cheaper. Just mix two tablespoons of baby soap, two tablespoons of olive oil, and two cups of water. Then, cut a roll of paper towels in half the long way and put the paper towels in a baby wipes box; pour the solution on top and swish it around. Alternately, you can just fill a spray bottle with the solution and use small pieces of cloth as baby wipes, which works well if you're cloth diapering as you can just store and wash the diapers and wipes together. Alternately, if you're adept at sewing (or know someone who is), a much more environmentally sound solution is to head down to your local fabric store and buy a large piece of flannel cloth. Take it home, cut it into wipe-size pieces, then sew the edges so that they don't fray, and you have a ton of excellent cloth wipes that you can continually reuse. Just keep a spray bottle with a solution of witch hazel and water in equal amounts to spray down areas, then wipe them down and wash the cloths. It's environmentally friendly and far cheaper than buying bundles of disposable wipes.

66. Shop Yard Sales for Young Children's Clothing

Many children, particularly young ones, outgrow clothes so rapidly that they wear them only a few times before they're too small. Many families deal with this phenomenon by selling these clothes at a yard sale. That's where you can clean up on baby and toddler clothes that have only been worn a few times. If you have a young child, hit the yard sales hard. If you find one with a lot of clothes, offer to buy everything that will fit your child at a reduced price as a bundle. *Tip:* Clean these clothes at a Laundromat before taking them home just to be sure you don't bring home any unwanted pests.

67. Take Advantage of Hand-Me-Downs

Similarly, if you have family members with older children, consider asking them to participate in a family hand-me-down cycle, where clothes are handed down among extended family members from child to child, and then offer to hand down your no-longer-wanted clothes to other younger children in the family. You can go beyond clothes for this, handing down items like bassinets, cloth diapers, and other useful child-rearing materials.

68. Buy Fewer, Higher-Quality Childhood Toys

Many families are often flooded with toys of various kinds for very young children, particularly when fueled by the desire to have "the best" for those kids. In fact, though, the opposite is true: Young children are far better off with only a small number of toys rather than an overwhelming abundance. Minimize your own spending on toys, leaving most of the toy-buying to relatives who may buy your children Christmas and birthday gifts. Encourage them to focus on only one high-quality toy rather than an abundance of cheap toys, as this minimizes health risks and ensures that the toys your child plays with are sturdy and long-lasting.

69. Focus on Buying Open-Ended Toys

Hand in hand with the idea of fewer toys is the idea of open-ended toys—those that encourage creative and imaginative play. Instead of focusing on electronic toys with limited interactivity, look at toys that offer plenty of room for creativity, such as art supplies and quality building blocks. Again, not only are these toys widely considered to be better for your child's cognitive development, but they're also often less expensive, meaning you can either save money or purchase items of high quality for the same price you might spend on "gee whiz" toys. *Tip:* Look for toys that match these criteria at yard sales when you're shopping for the clothes; just be sure to wash the items well when you bring them home.

70. Participate in Babysitting Exchanges Instead of Hiring a Babysitter

Do you have friends who also have children? Consider discussing a baby-sitting exchange with them in order to save money on babysitters.

Offer to watch their children on their anniversary night, for example, in exchange for the same treatment on your anniversary. Or offer to alternate weekends. Do you like to go out with other couples or other parents? Get a cycle going where two or three parents or couples enjoy an evening together while the other couple watches all of the children. This enables you to have many evenings of fun with a reliable parent watching your children—at no cost to you.

71. Encourage Art Skills with an End Roll of Newspaper

One of the best undiscovered secrets in many towns is on sale at the office of your local newspaper. Many newspapers often have a few hundred square feet of blank newspaper left over at the end of a large roll, and they will sell this roll of paper to the public for just a dollar or two. Buying one of these rolls can provide a huge amount of paper for your children to draw on to their heart's content for just a fraction of the cost of buying such paper at the store.

72. Extend the Life and Value of Crayons

If your children love crayons, they can often wear crayons down to unusable nubs. One great solution to this problem is to collect all of the nubs, then put several of them into an inexpensive small mold (you can get a nice one at the dollar store) and bake them in the oven at a low heat. You can easily make candy cane–shaped crayons that are made up of bits of old crayons, and this new crayon will change colors as you draw with it. If you save up a bunch of nubs and do this with many crayons at once, it can save you the cost of buying a fresh big box of crayons, plus create memorable and unique crayons for your child to draw with.

73. Make Your Own Playdough

Playdough is a wonderful children's toy. Instead of buying it at the store in overpriced containers, though, why not try making it at home (and getting the kids involved, too)? Just mix two cups of flour, two cups of warm water, one cup of salt, two tablespoons of vegetable oil, and one tablespoon of cream of tartar (found in the spices section at the grocery store) in a pot. Warm it up over low heat and keep stirring it until it begins to feel like playdough in your hands (if it's sticky, keep cooking it). Then scoop out a small ball of the dough and knead it in your hands until it's smooth. Want to make it colorful? Make a small hole in the ball and add a few drops of food coloring or a quarter of a tablespoon of a colorful drink mix, then close the hole and knead the ball again. If you want a brighter color, add a bit more—keep trying until you get what you like. Very quickly, you'll have a cheap and very fun toy for your children to play with and it's entirely edible (though it tastes rather salty).

74. Turn Supplies You Have on Hand into Toys

Almost every item in your home can be turned into a compelling toy for children with some imagination at almost no cost to you.

Here are three suggestions:

- Turn an old newspaper into a paper airplane contest. Give everyone a few sheets and see who can make the best paper airplane out of the sheets.
- Turn pots and pans and wooden spoons into a drum kit. Sit several pots and pans out on the floor, then hit them all on the bottom with a wooden spoon and observe the different noises they make.
- Turn strips of waste paper into a piñata. Cut any waste paper you have into strips. Blow up a balloon, tie it off and put a paper clip around the tie-off point, then tie a piece of string to the paper clip. Mix two cups of flour and ten cups of water, then boil the solution for a few minutes until it becomes paste. Start pasting the strips to the balloon, letting it completely dry overnight every four or five layers. After a few days of putting on strips, you'll have a piñata! Color it carefully with markers, then hang it up and let the kids break it.

75. Read Together as a Family

Reading is one of the most inexpensive and fulfilling hobbies that a person can have. Encouraging a love of reading in your own children is a great way to put them on the path to economic success. Plan a family reading hour each day, where everyone gathers in the same room to read independently. Then, once every few weeks, go to the library together and have everyone pick out a few books to read during that reading period. Reading time can be an hour a day where your family relaxes, improves themselves, and doesn't spend a dime.

76. Minimize Television Time

Where can that hour for reading come from? Take it away from time in front of the television. Not only does television gobble electricity (the average television uses about 150 watts, and the average cable box uses about 70 watts, meaning that it eats a dime's worth of electricity every four and a half hours of use), but it's also laden with advertisements and product placements that encourage you to go out and buy things you don't really need. Replace that time spent in front of the television with other activities.

77. Go Outside

One good replacement for television use is to simply go outside. Go on a walk together as a family. Play a game of catch in the yard, or try playing tag or touch football. Go to the park together. Go on a hike. Explore. Catch lightning bugs. Wade in a creek. These are all fun things that you can do together as a family in the great outdoors—and they're all free.

78. Utilize Community Resources

Extend that recreational exploration outside your home by looking for free resources and activities offered by your local community.

Take advantage of the public parks, basketball courts, tennis courts, swimming pools, and playgrounds in your neighborhood. Check out the organized recreational activities as well. Find out if there are any free or nearly free community events of interest. Stop by city hall or your library and ask for a community calendar. Often these are updated monthly. Join a local volunteer group. Your community is full of free entertainment for your whole family if you expand your horizons a bit.

79. Segment Their Allowance

Many families dole out allowances to their children, often giving them a few dollars once a week followed by a pat on the head. The only problem with this is that it doesn't guide children down a healthy path of managing their own money and often parents wind up supplementing a little. Instead, segment their allowance and teach them how to manage on their own. Break their allowance into four pieces and keep it in four separate jars: one for spending now, one for saving for a long-term goal (like an expensive toy), one for sharing with others (like buying a present for Mom's birthday), and one for charity. Not only does this teach them the basics of how to budget, but it also saves you money because they're fully in control of their own spending decisions based on the rules for each jar. You don't need to "slip" them money anymore, because budgeting is part of their learning experience.

80. Share the Thought Process Behind Your Purchases

Whenever you make a significant purchase, show your children how you came to the decision behind that purchase. Not only is it an opportunity to teach your children how to buy sensibly, but it saves you money as well because it keeps you honest about why you're buying stuff. In other words, if you do the research and pick the item with the best value, you're not only buying the best deal, but you're also creating an opportunity to teach your children how to find the best deal.

81. Resist the Temptations of Soda and Fast Food

Junk food is a common expense for children in American homes today. It's easy to see why: Junk food is convenient, tasty, and often makes kids happy. Resist that urge to take the easy route, though. Instead, buy inexpensive and healthy snacks to keep on hand. Buy yogurt instead of candy. Buy rice cakes instead of potato chips. Not only are healthier options often cheaper, they're also better for you, reducing health care costs over your child's lifetime (and probably improving your own health as well, since there aren't unhealthy snacks sitting around the house tempting you).

82. Involve Children in Frugal Projects, Like Gardening

Quite often, projects that can save a household a significant amount of money take a significant amount of effort. Take gardening, for example. A well-tended garden can easily save a lot of money in reduced food costs. The only problem with a garden is that it requires almost daily effort to tend it well. That's where the whole family comes in. Take everyone out in the garden and have them all weed, plant, fertilize, and water. Teach your children how it can be fun, and at the same time you'll spend quality time with them. You can also challenge them to weeding contests. Or show them how to make little trenches for watering around plants. Let them take charge of certain plants. The key to getting their interest is to get them personally involved with it. Not only will the effort pay off in terms of food costs, but if you can make it exciting, it also becomes a very inexpensive source of entertainment.

83. Be a Frugal Example

Whenever you are together as a family, put extra effort into showing your children that you don't have to spend money to enjoy yourself. Resist the urge to buy impulse items at the grocery store. Don't stop along the trip for a quick treat on the spur of the moment. Don't declare that you have to buy new clothes every month or two. Use the library for books and movies. Show them how you save money in your day-to-day life and they'll naturally do it, too. Not only will this save you money throughout their teen years, but it will save them money throughout their lives.

CHEAP TACTIC$ FOR CLOTHING

84. Avoid Clothes That Require Washing Separately

If at all possible, avoid clothes that require specific methods when washing. Every separate load requires the full cost: the water, the cost to run the water heater, the cost of running the washing machine, the cost of the detergent, and the cost of the other cleaning supplies you use. This can amount to as much as fifty cents for a load, and for a single item that can add up to some serious cost. Instead, avoid individual wash items and instead focus on those that can be washed together.

85. Focus on Clothes That Match Well

If you select modular clothing, items that go well with many other items in your wardrobe, you can easily get away with a much smaller wardrobe. For men, choose jackets, shirts, ties, and pants that easily mix and match. With five items of each, you can have 625 different dress appearances, more than enough to appear well dressed. This permits you to wash all of your clothes at once each weekend, then carefully remix your options for the week. This drastically reduces the amount of clothing you need to own.

86. Shop at Consignment Shops and Outlet Stores

When you do need to shop for new clothes and need professional and stylish options, start at consignment shops and outlet stores before hitting the mall. Outlet stores sell out-of-season, recently discontinued, and very slightly flawed clothing items at huge discounts, so shop carefully and you can find some amazing deals on excellent items. Consignment shops often contain the wardrobes of people with more money than sense, who empty out their closets after wearing clothes once or twice (or not wearing them at all). Again, it's a great place to look for nearly new items at extremely cheap prices.

87. Hit Thrift and Secondhand Shops in Upscale Neighborhoods

If you're willing to dig a little deeper for bargains, try hitting up secondhand shops and thrift shops in upscale neighborhoods. Look for the most upscale neighborhood around you, then find any such shops in their commercial area and see what's available. You can often find unbelievable bargains on top-quality and rarely worn clothes at such shops. Expanding your horizons a bit can save you a ton of money.

88. Focus on Quality Brands That Hold Up over Time

When you make the active choice to buy fewer clothes, it becomes much more important to buy individual clothes items that hold up well over time. This requires you to do some research. Identify the brands of the sturdiest clothes in your closet, and also do research online to identify fashionably appropriate brands that are also sturdy. If you're unsure about brands you should be looking for, visit the websites of stores that you would ordinarily buy clothes from and identify the brands they sell. Take that knowledge with you when you go thrift shopping.

89. Wear Old Clothing Around the House

When your clothes do begin to show signs of wear and are no longer appropriate to wear professionally or on social occasions, relegate them to clothes around the house. That's right, wear old, beat-up dress shirts when you're mopping the floor or working in the garden. These clothes are well made and sturdy and have a lot of life left in them. Keep wearing them until they really are ready to fall apart. That way, you don't have to spend much at all for casual clothes, either—you can keep that cash right in your pocket.

90. Buy Clothes Off Season and on Tax-Free Holidays

If you must buy new clothes, do some careful planning for those purchases. Buy summer clothes for the following year at the end of summer, and do the same for other seasons. Also, plan your clothes shopping for tax-free holidays, where stores compete for the customers that they know will be out and about by offering strong sales. Careful planning can save you a tremendous amount of money on clothes purchases.

91. Swap Clothes with Similar-Size Friends

Another useful tactic if you like new clothes to wear but don't want to spend the money for more clothes is to swap a portion of your wardrobe with a friend or relative who has similar sizes and tastes as you. Swapping several shirts or pants can make your wardrobe feel fresh and new again, cement a friendship, and save yourself a surprising amount of money.

92. Rotate Clothes Seasonally

Another trick to keep clothes seeming fresh and new for years is to rotate your clothes on a strong seasonal basis. Each spring, box up all of your winter clothes and put them into storage, then unbox your spring and summer clothes. Then, after the season is over, box up your spring and summer clothes and unbox your fall and winter ones. They'll feel fresh and new and make it appear to the people around you that you have a fresh new wardrobe. Not only that, but careful storage and clothes rotation can also extend the lifespan of your clothes significantly, allowing you to keep items seeming new for years.

93. Sell or Donate Clothes You No Longer Wear

For many people with an overstuffed closet, clothes are merely another thing to collect, and collections are almost always directly opposed to living cheap. If you have more clothes than you actually wear on a regular basis, consider getting rid of some of your clothes.

Sell some, or donate some to a charity, making sure to get the receipt for tax deduction purposes. Cleaning out your closet by figuring out what you actually wear and what you don't can both earn some money and also help you get more in touch with the clothes you own. You might realize that you do have plenty of clothes and don't need to buy more.

94. Don't Buy Clothes Simply for the Emotional Rush

For many people, it can feel very good to buy a new article of clothing. It provides something of an emotional rush. That emotional rush is dangerous, as is any strong positive feeling related to buying something. If you get excited at the thought of buying clothes and it gives you a big rush to get something new, recognize that this is a problem and it's extremely unhealthy for your long-term financial shape. Focus instead on other positive experiences that don't revolve around money. Realize that buying something new is merely an exchange of your hard work for a material item when that money could be used to buy your freedom from debt.

95. Don't Wash Clothes That Aren't Dirty

If you wear an item of clothing all day that doesn't get dirty, why wash it? Washing it reduces the lifetime of the clothes item and has a cost in terms of energy use, water use, and cleaning agent use as well. When you get undressed, inspect your outer clothes for cleanliness and, if they're still clean, hang them up for future use. One technique to use is to separate your clothes into "fresh" and "worn once" groups—if you use an item from the "worn once" group, it's time to wash it.

96. Learn Basic Sewing Skills

If you know how to hem a pair of pants, sew a button back into place, and repair a small breaking seam, then you've got the skills you need to fix most of the minor clothes repair issues that might occur. Fifteen minutes with a needle and thread to repair a shirt or make a pair of jeans fit your child can save you $20, so it's well worth your while to learn basic sewing. Don't know where to begin? Look for tutorials online that explain how to do this step by step.

97. Use Household Items You Already Have to Remove Stains

Most minor clothes stains can be fixed with just a few items from around your house. Try this simple solution for stains on furniture, carpet, and light-colored clothes: Make a paste by mixing ¼ cup hydrogen peroxide with ¼ cup baking soda, then spread the paste on the stained area liberally and rub it in deep. Let it sit for fifteen minutes, then rinse the area thoroughly. This procedure can take out sweat stains, mud stains, bloodstains, and many others and is a great (and cheap) first action to take before breaking out more expensive cleaners (or throwing the clothing away). On darker clothing, take a stick of clear underarm deodorant and rub it vigorously on sweat stains. On other stains, try rubbing the area briskly with a slightly damp bar of soap before washing it. These techniques will eliminate the vast majority of stains that you might face without having to buy expensive washing machine additives or pretreatment solutions.

98. Cut Dryer Sheets in Half and Reuse Them

Dryer sheets are a great way to reduce static cling and make your clothes smell fresher when they come out of the dryer, but a single dryer sheet can actually help with four loads of laundry, not just one. Just cut the sheet in half and use one of the halves in a load. Then, leave that used dryer sheet on top and use it again for a second load. This can cut down greatly on the cost of dryer sheets while still getting almost all of the laundry-freshening effect.

CHEAP TACTIC$ FOR CLUTTER

99. Realize That Clutter Itself Is a Giant Money Sink

Clutter accumulation is one of the biggest money sinks in a house. Unused objects and items, merely saved for "someday" or for faint nostalgic reasons, not only make your home or office appear cluttered and unfriendly to outsiders (reducing the value of your property), but also contain within them value that you're not using elsewhere. A $5 trinket shoved onto a shelf with dozens of other $5 trinkets is $5 that could be used to pay down your debt and make your environment look better at the same time. It's a way to simultaneously earn a profit while decreasing the cluttered look of your home.

100. Sell Specific and Individually Valuable Items on eBay

The first place to start in the clutter battle is looking at your collections. What do you collect? Where do you keep those collections? Do those collections provide genuine value to you, or do you keep them for reasons you can't really explain? Go through your DVDs, your CDs, your clothes, your collectibles, your video games, and so on, identifying items that you don't have a specific and clear attachment to. Clean out your closets and see what's in there that you actually need. Identify the valuable individual items in those collections and sell the individual items online on eBay or Amazon. Just focus on the items with significant individual value—the bulk, ordinary DVDs and CDs, won't earn you enough to make it worth your while.

101. Sell Bulk Entertainment Items at a Secondhand Entertainment Shop

What about the remaining bulk items, the unwanted collections of DVDs you'll never watch again and CDs that went out with the '90s? Box them up and take them to your local used media shop. You'll generally get a dollar or two a pop for these items, which you can then use to start saving or pay down your accumulated debt. Even better, your home will have less clutter in it, meaning less maintenance time for cleaning and less effort to make it presentable for guests.

102. Have a Yard Sale

Still got items left over? Have a yard sale and price everything to sell. The best yard sale tactic is pricing everything at the same price, then lowering that price at regular intervals throughout the weekend. So, start your yard sale on Friday evening with every item for $2. On Saturday morning, lower it to $1 an item then in the afternoon, go down to fifty cents. On Sunday morning, go down to twenty-five cents; then on Sunday afternoon, go down to ten cents. This will not only help you move all your stuff, it will attract repeat visitors who will elect to come back and try to get that item at a cheaper cost later. This can eliminate a lot of clutter and earn you some extra money as well.

103. Donate to Goodwill

If you're still holding leftover items, donate them to Goodwill or the Salvation Army. Get a receipt and use that on your income tax next year—even a small donation can get you a financial benefit. Plus, those unwanted items will wind up with someone who wants them.

104. Put a "Sell By" Date on It

If you have some items that you're thinking about getting rid of, but aren't quite sure, put them in a box and label the box with a date six months or a year in the future. If that date passes and you've never even looked at the items, it's safe to sell them. After all, at that point the items are no longer an active part of your life and are just taking up space and holding value that you could be putting into saving for the future or reducing debt.

105. Don't Replace Clutter with More Clutter

When you finally do get rid of all of the excess stuff, your home will feel emptier. Don't use that as an excuse to fill it with more stuff just for the sake of having stuff. Instead, enjoy the space. Spread out some projects that you've been thinking of working on. Enjoy more free time now that you don't have to deal with the clutter. Perhaps you'll even realize that you don't need all of the space that you have and look at downgrading your living space, or perhaps bring in a roommate to help share the costs of the rent or the mortgage.

106. Avoid Printed Documents

Many people get several different statements in the mail, often taking up pages and pages of space. These printed documents come at a price. They take up more space in the trash, increase chances for identity theft, and require more time to deal with. Find out whether you can switch to electronic copies of many of these statements. It'll reduce the amount of mail you have to deal with (which can decrease trash pickup costs), reduce the potential threat of identity theft, and perhaps also save you the cost of stamps if you can switch to electronic payments as well.

107. Trim Your Magazine Subscriptions

Another great way to reduce clutter and save money at the same time is to reduce your magazine subscriptions. If you find that you're not keeping up with a magazine subscription and old issues are stacking up, unsubscribe from the magazine and focus on those you actually read. Not only will this reduce clutter around your home, but it'll also save you money to invest elsewhere. *Another tip:* If you hold on to old magazines, go through them and just remove the material from each issue you might use again, then get rid of the issue. It'll free up space and make it easier for you to find information.

108. Borrow Stuff You'll Only Use Once or Twice

If you're considering buying an item that you'll only use a few times, look seriously into borrowing opportunities. Not only will this save you money in terms of buying the item, it also doesn't require the space to keep it around. For media sources, like books and movies and CDs, check out the library. Need some equipment or tools? Ask around the neighborhood (but be willing to lend your own stuff out in return). If you're close with another person in the area, you can even consider "sharing" significant purchases that you won't be using simultaneously, like lawn mowers.

109. Every Time You Buy an Item, Get Rid of One

This is a clever clutter-reduction tactic that keeps you from accumulating stuff and also saves you money. Every time you buy a nonessential item, commit to getting rid of another item you already own. For example, if you decide to buy a nifty new kitchen knife, commit to eliminating another similar knife. If you buy a new book, get rid of a book you already have by giving it to a friend or taking it to a used bookstore. This makes you carefully consider a new purchase and helps to eliminate clutter when you do decide to bring home something new.

110. Start a "Mail Basket" and Process It Weekly

Clutter can sometimes cause additional problems, such as misplacing a bill in the clutter and having to pay a late fee even though you had plenty of money to pay it. The solution is simple: Get a "mail basket" that collects all mail that you receive, then go through it completely once a week and process everything in it. Throw away any junk, pay any bills, handle any correspondence, and so on. If you successfully empty that mail basket each week, you'll never accidentally fall behind on a bill again and you'll never be caught up in a clutter of unhandled mail. *Bonus tip:* Start a filing system for your papers when you start a "mail basket" and handle all filing each week when you go through the basket. That way, you'll always be able to find important papers that may be costly to replace.

111. Go Through the "Clutter Attractors" Regularly

Every home has a few "clutter attractors," spaces where things seem to clutter over time. Like the catch-all drawer, the table near the front door where you toss your keys after a day at work, the bedside table, and the downstairs closet. These places almost always wind up catching little important things, things that you should have acted on, like bill statements or checks to be cashed, and sometimes these things can be forgotten in our busy lives. The remedy for this is to check those clutter-attracting areas regularly. Go through the items you find there and see if there isn't anything important you may have missed. This can easily end up saving you money if you discover a bill that needs paying or a check that needs cashing or a rebate form that needs filling out.

112. Read Your Favorite Newspaper Online

If you get a newspaper delivered every day, consider canceling the subscription and reading it online. Not only does this directly save you money by cutting out the cost of subscribing, but it also cuts down on the clutter in your home and the amount of trash you have to throw away. Many newspapers earn significant revenue from their websites today, so don't worry about hurting the newspaper's bottom line if you unsubscribe and replace it with regular viewings of the newspaper's site.

113. Unsubscribe from Catalogs

Catalogs are just collections of temptations. A catalog in the mail will do nothing more than encourage you to buy things that you wouldn't have otherwise purchased, and an unnecessary purchase is the mortal enemy of living cheap. Unsubscribe from any catalogs that you receive by calling the number in the catalog and requesting removal from their mailing list. Not only will this save you money, but it's also a useful way to reduce the amount of clutter that your house catches.

114. Unsubscribe from Charity Mailings

Another effective method of reducing temptation in the mail is to unsubscribe from charity mailings, particularly those that you do not intend to pledge to in the future. Call their number and ask them to stop their mailings to you, informing them that you'll be planning your charitable giving on a regular basis and will send them gifts of your choosing without the mailings. Giving to charity is a powerful thing, but it's something that's worth the time to carefully plan and budget for, not write out an unplanned and unbudgeted check on a whim. Not only does this reduce the costs for that charity, since they're no longer sending out wasteful mail, but it reduces your clutter and also reduces the chance that you'll send out a check without giving it the thought that charity deserves. Instead, plan your charitable giving well in advance and focus your gifts on charities that really matter to you, not on the charity that happens to send you something in the mail that week.

115. Sign Up for the Do Not Mail Registry and the Do Not Call Registry

Another effective way to simultaneously reduce clutter and also reduce the potential temptation of direct marketers is to sign up for the national Do Not Call registry, which informs telemarketers that you do not wish to be contacted by telephone regarding their direct marketing efforts. Visit *www.donotcall.gov* to get started. Similarly, there is an ongoing push for a Do Not Mail registry, which you can find out more about at *http://donotmail.org*. At that site, you can sign a petition to enact a national Do Not Mail registry, plus request that participating direct mailers no longer send junk mail to your home (many are happy to oblige because it cuts down on their costs). Both efforts will save you time in the long run and quite possibly save you money, too.

116. Don't Upgrade Your Living Space to House More Stuff

One of the biggest reasons that people consider upgrading their home is that they simply don't have room for all of their stuff. That's the single worst reason to lay out a huge amount of money for a space upgrade you don't actually need. If you're considering upgrading because your stuff is starting to fill up all of your space, take a hard look at that stuff around you and ask yourself how much of it you really need. Then, instead of shelling out a lot of money for bigger housing, put some money in your pocket by getting rid of that unwanted stuff using the tips in this chapter. The less junk you have, the less space you need to live, and the less your housing bill will be.

CHEAP TACTIC$ FOR CREDIT CARDS AND DEBT

117. Find Your Motivation

Bad spending habits, the kind that result in ever-increasing debt and credit card problems, are usually the child of a bad routine. Humans are beings of habit. We fall into certain routines and it takes a powerful force to knock us out of that routine. To break the habit of consistently overspending and putting things on credit, you need to find that powerful force that motivates you to change. Whenever you go to use the plastic or take out more debt, think about that motivator. Some suggestions: your children (and their future), your dream home, the ability to retire and still have some time to enjoy active life, the shame of having to declare bankruptcy, or the ability to quit your job and chase the career of your dreams. Find that one thing that you want so badly that it hurts, then recall it every time you pull out the plastic. *A great tip:* Glue a picture of that motivation to the front of all of your credit cards, so you have to see it each time you head to the checkout.

118. Know What You Owe

The first step is to get a grip on your total financial situation. Create a master list of every debt you have, including the total balance on that debt and the interest rate you're being charged. List everything, including credit card debts, student loans, mortgages, car loans, furniture loans, and personal loans. You need to get a complete picture of what you owe before you can start getting rid of your debt. Remember, every dollar you pay in finance charges or interest is a dollar lost. To truly live cheap means to pay no finance charges or interest at all.

119. Consolidate or Refinance Any Debts

Are there any debts on that list that you may be able to consolidate with others at a lower interest rate? Outstanding student loans are usually a good place to start looking, as consolidation can sometimes significantly reduce your overall interest rate and lower your monthly payment. You may also be able to refinance your home mortgage to a lower rate (if you can lower your rate more than 1 percent in the first five years of your mortgage, it's well worth it), or consolidate many of your high-interest credit card debts into a home equity line of credit. You may even want to look at transferring credit card balances to new cards with a 0 percent balance transfer offer. Your goal should always be to move the highest interest rate debts first; the bigger the gap between your old interest rate and your new interest rate, the better. Remember, though, these are solutions to make repaying your debt easier, not a tool with which to get more easy credit to charge up those cards even higher.

120. Visit Your Local Credit Union

If you don't know where to begin, the place to start is your local credit union. Explain your situation in detail and tell them that you're seeking to move your high-interest debt to something with a lower rate. Credit unions often have many options available and typically have the strongest rates in your local area, plus they often provide free financial advice for a person trying to deal with debt. Consider your local credit union as the first stop when thinking about how to fix your debt situation if it's starting to get out of control.

121. Confront the Credit Card Companies

If you still have high-interest credit card debts left after such consolidation, it's time to actually start confronting the credit card companies. This isn't unusual, particularly with younger people who don't have many accumulated assets. The first step is to flip your credit card over and call the number on the back. When you get someone on the line, state very clearly that you would like the interest rate on this card reduced because the rate is making it difficult to pay off the card, and that you are considering transferring the balance to another card. If the first person says no, ask to speak to a supervisor, and keep escalating until you hear a positive answer. Rinse and repeat for all of your cards and your finance charges will be greatly reduced, meaning you'll have smaller minimum payments and more breathing room each month.

122. Resist Temptation to Use Your Card Once You Pay It Down

All of these efforts are nice in that they reduce your monthly bills by reducing the interest rates, and likely you'll be able to start paying down your cards faster. If you did some balance transferring, it's also likely that you have a lot of free credit available already. Don't use it. Using credit cards beyond your means is what got you into credit card trouble in the first place. It's not merely a method to allow you to keep living beyond your means. It's an opportunity to get out of the hole and not worry about your debt ever again.

123. Switch to Using Only Cash and Checks for a Year

One method to keep your hands off the credit cards is to switch to using only cash or checks (or a debit card) for all of your purchases for a year. This forces you to get in touch with your money again. Without plastic, you're forced to carefully consider each purchase that you make and verify that you do in fact have enough money for that purchase before you make it. Some ideas:

- Don't destroy your credit cards, but instead freeze them in a block of ice. Just pour a small pan about a third full of water and freeze it. Then toss your credit cards on top of the ice and pour on some more water, then freeze it again. Your cards will be frozen in the middle of that cube, inaccessible unless there's a real emergency; any time you think about getting them, you'll have a long time to consider it as you melt (or break) the ice.
- Remove your credit card numbers from any online sites you use regularly. If you use your credit card for billing on iTunes or on Amazon (or anywhere else), remove your credit card number

and, if you must, replace it with a debit card number instead so the money comes straight from your checking account.

124. Construct Your Debt Repayment Plan

The next step to take to get your debt in order is to construct a plan for getting rid of it. Each month, you'll need to make minimum payments on all of your debts, as well as a larger payment on one of the debts. A debt repayment plan is mostly just a decision on the order of debts you'll repay and the amount you'll pay extra each month. The key to the plan is that you'll need to do this without racking up additional significant debt. Here are some ideas:

- The "debt snowball" method was made popular by personal finance radio host Dave Ramsey. With that plan, you always focus on paying off the debt with the lowest balance, so you can feel the success of eliminating debts on a regular basis. When a debt is paid off, you "roll" the payment you were making on that debt (the old minimum plus the extra you were making) into extra payments on the next debt on the list.
- The mathematically optimal method is to focus on paying off the debt with the highest interest rate, regardless of balance, and then "snowballing" the minimum payment onward once you pay off a debt. This method is the best in terms of the amount of money you have to pay overall, but is harder to follow because successes can be few and far between.

125. Try Using the Snowflake Method

Snowflaking is a spinoff of the "debt snowball" method described in #124. A snowflake is merely an opportunity to add a little bit more to your extra debt payment each month. For example, let's say that you usually go to the coffee shop on Monday mornings, but one Monday you decide to skip it. Instead of spending that $7 on a coffee and a bagel, instead you add $7 to your extra debt payment. Did you find $5 in the parking lot blowing in the breeze? Use it as a snowflake and add $5 to your debt payment. Sell something on eBay? Return some aluminum cans (or sell some for scrap metal)? Get a rebate? Receive an "economic stimulus" check or an income tax rebate from the government? Snowflake them all!

126. Know Your Credit Report and What It Means

Countless businesses utilize your credit report to assess how trustworthy you are. From the obvious (car loans, home mortgages, credit card rates) to the surprising (insurance rates), your credit report (and scores calculated based on the content of your report) has a great deal of influence on the amount you have to pay on almost everything. Even worse, errors on your credit report can cause all of your rates to go up, costing you a lot of money. Fortunately, it's easy to find your credit report for free, check for and correct errors on it, and ensure that it remains strong in the future by following these tips:

- You can get your credit report for free, no strings attached, from the federal government at *www.annualcreditreport.com*. This site allows you to exercise your legal right to check your credit report from each of the three major credit reporting agencies once a year. Use this site and download your report so you can know where you stand.
- Correct any errors on your credit report—debts you paid off that aren't reported, stuff that you have never seen before, and so on. Contact the organization that's claiming a debt (their phone number is usually on the report) and get the issue straightened out.
- Don't be late with payments and don't open up credit cards unless there's a good reason for it. Check your credit reports once every year so that you can quickly find out if anything false has popped up on your report.

127. Pay Off Your Whole Credit Card Balance Each Month

The best tactic of all with credit card usage is to avoid finance charges in their entirety, and you can do that on most cards by paying off the entire balance each month. Every time you carry a balance forward on your card, you're essentially agreeing to hand over money to the credit card company in exchange for nothing more than their permission to not pay the debt until next month. Don't pay that fee—pay off the whole balance instead. If you're spending within your means, this should be easy. It should only be challenging if you're pushing the limits of what you can afford or spending far beyond it.

128. Use a Credit Card That Actually Benefits You

Once your credit is in good shape and you're not overrun with debt, a credit card can become a tool to make regular purchases much easier and earn some useful rewards. If you get into a healthy routine of paying off your credit card debt each month, then a solid rewards card can be as good as money in the bank. There are many good card offers out there. Look for those that offer mileage bonuses to people who drive a significant amount, or cards that offer strong bonuses at the businesses you already use the most, like specific grocery stores or gas stations. A solid rewards card can earn you 3 to 4 percent in rewards or rebates on your everyday purchases. The key, though, is to pay off your balance every month. If you fail to do that, then you lose the benefits of a rewards card.

129. Don't Sign Up for Store Credit Cards Just for That One-Time Bonus

Many stores have an in-store credit card that is offered to you at the register, usually with some intriguing pledge like 10 percent off your current purchase. While it's tempting, it's not worth signing up for several reasons. First, the interest rates on in-store cards are often incredibly high, some approaching 30 percent annually. That means that for every $100 you leave on the card, they charge you $30 a year for that service. Second, the card itself tempts you to go back to the store, as it has the store's logo loudly branded on it. When you see it in your wallet, you'll think you can go there and buy more things and not have to actually pay the bill, but the bill comes around later and it's expensive. Third, every time you open a new credit card, you not only get a small negative impact on your credit report, but you also slightly increase your chances of identity theft. Add them up and a store credit card simply isn't worth the $10 or $20 you might save right then.

130. Be Accountable—Use Your Family and Friends

Recovering from debt is a challenge, and it's very easy to slip back into old habits. To keep yourself in check, utilize your family and friends to help you through these challenges. Tell them what you're going through, talk to them when it's tough, and have them help you steer yourself away from spending temptations. The support that family and friends can offer you is tremendous. Look to them as a valuable resource as you learn to truly live cheap.

131. Ask about Fees When Shopping for Loans

If you're in a situation where you're about to acquire a new debt, make sure you understand all of the fees you'll be charged when you get that loan. Many loans are saddled with lots of little fees—ask about all of them. Better yet, ask for them to be waived. If you can get even one or two of the hidden fees removed from your loan, it's worthwhile, and the worst they can do is say no. Take the time and challenge all of those little fees, it can really pay off.

132. Sign Up for Automatic Repayment Plans for Student Loans

Upon entering repayment, many student loans offer a small rate reduction if you sign up for an automatic payment plan. Do it, without hesitation. Not only does it directly save you money (remember, 0.25 percent of $40,000 is $100), but it also helps to ensure that you're never late with a payment, saving you from the cost of late fees. This is one of those rare opportunities where jumping on board with an offer from the company can save you real money, so don't miss out on it.

CHEAP TACTIC$ FOR ELECTRONICS

133. Never Be an Early Adopter

It's always a big temptation to be the first person on your block to be the proud owner of the latest hot item. It's fun to show off that gadget a little, but what's easy to forget is that the privilege of showing off that new item is incredibly expensive. You'll pay a huge extra amount up-front to be one of those early owners, plus the item is much more likely to be fragile and to wear down quickly if it's one of the early versions of the item, meaning it'll have to be replaced that much faster. Instead, if there's a hot new item you're tempted to have, exert a little bit of patience. You'll save yourself the "early adopter fee" and likely have a more reliable version of the item, which will save you even more.

134. Consider Whether You'll Actually Use the Item in a New Way

It's easy to see an item used by someone else and quickly convince yourself that the item will in fact change your life. But step back a minute and ask yourself how this device will actually improve your situation from the current condition. Will this device enable you to do something tremendously new compared to what you can do right now? Or is it just a minor change, like a small increase in display quality or a touch-screen improvement on a device you have right now? If it's just a little change, ask yourself whether that little feature is really worth the high price tag, particularly if it requires you to upgrade lots of other things as well (like the upgrade from videocassettes to DVDs) or requires you to start paying for a service for what you were getting for free (like the upgrade from AM/FM radio to satellite radio).

135. Pick the Model Now, Then Wait Six Months

If you're still convinced that you want a particular item, agree that you will purchase the item in six months if you still want it. Spend that time researching the item, considering whether or not you'd actually use the item, and waiting for the price to come down or a newer version to come out. If you decide that you're going to buy a newer model, start that six-month clock over again. The most likely result of this six-month wait is that you'll either forget about the item or realize that you don't actually need it, in which case you'll have saved yourself a significant amount of money by being patient.

136. Know the Features You Need Before You Shop

If you're about to sink some money into a new electronic item, know what features you actually need before even beginning to shop. List exactly what you're looking for before you even start looking at research materials. This is much the same psychology as preparing a shopping list before you go to the grocery store. It keeps you focused on exactly what you need instead of being distracted by something else that might come along. Before you even begin to research your purchase, know exactly what you want.

137. Avoid the "Feature Creep"

When you do begin to research your purchase or shop around, you'll often discover nifty features that show up in the higher-end models (often thanks to promotional materials, the overtures of a clever in-store salesperson, or a gadget-loving friend who extols the virtue of some minor, expensive, and nonessential feature). Ignore them. These neat features are not features you need, they're merely features you're being lured into wanting on the spur of the moment. Look for the core features you're interested in and let the rest steal the money from someone else's wallet.

138. Shop Around, Both Online and Off

If you're being patient about your purchase, you'll have plenty of time to shop around very carefully for the item. Look at retailers both online and offline and find the best prices, the best return policies, and the best assistance for questions that you may have about the item. Quite often, online retailers have better prices, but offline brick-and-mortar retailers can have better service and return policies, so consider the value of service and return policies in your purchase. If an item would be difficult to return or may require some service or assistance to install, consider that a valuable premium for buying the item in a store, even if the price is a bit higher. The key is to find the best overall value for your dollar, and that may be online in some situations and offline in others, depending on what you are trying to purchase.

139. Look at Refurbished Models

Many stores offer refurbished models—items that were originally sold and then returned with a minor defect that has now been repaired. These items are often as good as new, but are sold at a discounted price. Do some research into refurbished models available for the item you're looking for. Quite often, you can find refurbished models with the same warranties and benefits as buying new but with a significant discount on the purchase price. If you don't know where to begin, ask. A timely question can often save you money.

140. Ask about Retail Returns or Open-Box Items

Many shoppers will buy an item, take it home, rip open the box, then discover that it's not exactly what they wanted or that it's not compatible with their other equipment. They return it to the store and get their refund, but then the store is often left holding a perfectly new item in a beat-up box, which they're obligated to sell at a discount. If you're about to buy an item in a store, ask about retail returns or open-box items, particularly if what you're looking at isn't the latest and greatest version of the item. You'll often be surprised at how much of a discount you can get on a good-as-new item in a cardboard box with a torn flap.

141. Check for Discontinued/Floor Models

Another way to save on electronics is to check out discontinued models. Many stores will steeply discount brand-new products simply because a product line is being discontinued by the manufacturer, often for reasons that have very little to do with the quality of the item. You can also often find a steep discount in retail stores by buying floor items—those that sat out in the store on display for customers to look at. If you're certain of your feature list and find items in either of these categories that match the features you want, don't hesitate to jump on board, especially if the warranty on the item remains valid (be sure to ask).

142. If You Get a Rebate Form, Fill It Out Immediately

It's very easy to get lured in by a stellar price on an electronics item, only to discover that the low price is only that low due to a rebate. Retailers and manufacturers love to use the rebate as a method to make a price appear lower than it really is, because shoppers sometimes fail to send in their rebate form. Quite often, it's because they simply forget about it. It's another little task to do, one that's easy to toss in a clutter attractor and forget about. The solution to that problem is simple: Fill out that rebate form as soon as you can, even in the car before you leave the store. Make it your goal to get it in the mail by the end of the day or else the likelihood that you'll forget about that money will vastly increase, and a rebate form discovered after the expiration date is not worth anything at all.

143. Send in the Registration Form Immediately—But Don't Fill It Out Completely

Most electronics products (and many other products) include a registration form that they ask you to send in. Quite often, you're required to send it in to activate the warranty, and it also gives the manufacturer your contact information so they can notify you of product recalls or other important information about your product. However, there's a trick—the form usually includes the basics (your name and address and the product type), but it also often includes a lot of other unnecessary stuff, like questions about your buying preferences and other products you're interested in, for the sole purpose of filling your mailbox with targeted junk mail. Only fill in your name, address, and product identification unless you're specifically required to fill in more to get the warranty, but get that card sent in, as that warranty and other information about the model can be vital.

144. Keep Your Warranty and Receipts

Inevitably, you'll buy an electronic item and it will break. When that happens, it's essential that you have the warranty on hand to know who to contact in order to fix the problem. When you do that, you'll also need to demonstrate when and where you purchased the item. The best way to do that is to keep files on every significant item you buy. Keep a small filing box containing a folder for each major purchase, and within each folder keep the product manual, a copy of the warranty, and the receipt. Whenever you buy a new item, add a new folder to the box with that material inside. That way, when a problem occurs, you'll have all the paperwork you need to take care of the problem in one easy-to-find place.

145. Keep It Clean and Minimize the Dust

One of the biggest dangers to home electronics is dust and dirt. Dust is full of small amounts of metal, and home electronics use metal to store information and transmit data. Thus, it's unsurprising that dust buildup is one of the most common reasons for electronic failure. You can fight that hazard and extend the life of your equipment by keeping it clean and dusting it regularly. If you have a home computer, carefully open the case on occasion and use compressed air to blow out any dust that's built up inside. With other devices, keep the external areas clean and make sure no dust is building up near any ventilation areas, and also make sure the device has plenty of ventilation space (for example, don't move the vents up against a wall). Simple moves like these can vastly extend the life of your home electronics.

146. Use a Surge Protector

Most homes receive unexpected electrical surges occasionally, and these surges can damage home electronic devices if the devices are not properly protected. Invest in a surge protector for your most expensive items, preferably one with a switch that you can easily access. This surge protector will prevent your electronics from being damaged during an electrical surge, plus if you have a switch that's accessible, you can utilize it to cut power to all of your electronic devices before you go on a trip, potentially saving you money on energy use as well. A good surge protector is well worth the money. It only takes one prevented surge to make your investment pay off.

147. Read the Manual Carefully, Especially on Rechargeable Items

Whenever you open up a new electronic item, it's well worth the time to give the manual a reading, as there may be less obvious tweaks and settings that can maximize the value and usefulness of the product. Reading the manual is particularly important when it comes to any device that uses an internal rechargeable battery, as such devices often have different optimal ways to charge the battery in order to extend its life. Some devices last longer if completely discharged (used until there is no more juice), while others are better off being charged as often as possible and not allowed to run down to minimal energy. Know what works best for your device and take the steps to ensure a long and healthy lifetime for your new equipment.

148. Use Rechargeable Batteries

Rechargeable batteries have come a long way since the nearly unusable battery chargers of a generation ago. Today, top-quality rechargeable batteries, such as the Eneloop batteries available from GE and

Sanyo, don't become weaker after each charge and hold a charge for a very long time, maintaining 85 percent of their charge after a year of sitting on a shelf. An investment in a top-quality battery charger and a sufficient number of rechargeable batteries can keep your home equipped with ample batteries to keep your electronic devices going while saving you significant money over the long haul.

CHEAP TACTIC$ FOR ENERGY USE

149. Install a Programmable Thermostat

A programmable thermostat allows you to automatically raise and lower the temperature in your home at certain times of the day. For example, it can be set to raise the temperature in your house by 10 degrees while you're at work, keeping your air conditioner from running all day, then cooling the house all at once in the early evening just before you arrive home. Instead of just kicking on and off all day, burning energy, your air conditioner would just run for one somewhat longer session in the early evening, saving you significant energy. The reverse would be true with your furnace in cold weather. Your home temperature would automatically drop during the day, warming up again just before you arrive home. You can accomplish this automatically by installing a programmable thermostat in your home, available at your local hardware store for a fairly small price. You can often earn back the cost of the thermostat in just a year due to the energy savings.

150. Use LED Bulbs in Certain Places

Compact fluorescent lamp bulbs (CFLs) are currently all the rage for saving energy in your home, but they have their disadvantages—warm-up time, cold light, and cleanup challenges are among the common complaints. LED (light-emitting diode) bulbs, on the other hand, use very little energy and provide directional light (like a flashlight), perfect for lighting needs in small spaces, like closets. One way to get the energy use advantage of CFLs and LEDs without some of the disadvantages is by using a mix of bulbs in your home. Try a three-tiered lighting strategy: normal incandescent for general family areas, CFLs for hall lighting and infrequently used spaces, and LEDs for closet lighting, with a shift toward more LEDs as the technology improves. This will reduce energy use throughout your home and also increase the lifespan of most of your installed bulbs.

151. Put Your Home Electronics on a Switch-Based Power Source

Many home electronic devices continue to eat electricity even when turned off. The truth is that they often switch into "standby" mode, which means that they slowly consume energy even though they're not in use. Some devices can consume as much as 40 watts in standby mode, which costs you a dime a day at current energy costs. You can solve that problem by putting many of your devices on a single surge protector, then plugging that device into an outlet in your home powered by a switch. When you're done with the equipment, flip the switch. No more lost juice and instant energy savings. Don't have a switch like this? You can get a remote-controlled surge protector that will provide much the same functionality, or other devices that can do the same thing.

152. Turn Off Lights You're Not Using

A typical incandescent bulb uses 60 or 75 watts. That means that every fifteen hours or so, it consumes a kilowatt-hour of energy, costing you a dime at current average energy rates. Going through your home to turn off lights before you leave, or even flipping off switches as you wander through your home, can save significant money over the long haul. Got a strip of lights in your bathroom eating 60 watts each? Leaving them on for just a few hours eats a dime, and flipping off that switch before you leave for work can save you thirty cents or so. A minute's worth of walking through your house to turn off lights can be an extremely cost-effective use of your time.

153. Unplug Electrical Devices You're Not Using

Don't leave devices that you rarely use plugged in. Many electrical devices use a very small amount of energy from the outlet, called the "phantom load," even when unplugged. Unplug devices like cell phone chargers, laptop chargers, other electronic chargers, and small home electric devices and appliances that you don't use every day, like a toaster. Even with a phantom load of four watts—very common in household devices—you'll end up burning more than a quarter's worth of energy every month (at current energy rates) for each device you leave plugged in without reason. Unplug it and save.

154. Put All Device Chargers on One Power Strip

Create a power strip that has all of your chargers on it. Get one with a switch at one end for easy convenience. Whenever you need to charge a device, just attach it to the appropriate cord, then flip the switch to turn on the juice; when the device is done, flip the switch to cut the energy. This gives you the convenience of keeping your chargers plugged in and in a standard place along with the energy efficiency of eliminating the phantom power load that slowly adds to your energy bill. You can even get creative and put this strip and charger in a small box with just the switch and the ends of the various chargers exposed. This is an excellent craft project that makes your chargers look a lot neater while also cutting down on your energy use.

155. Turn Down Your Water Heater

The correct temperature setting on your water heater is just hot enough so you can get the heat you actually need when turning on your faucet on full heat. If the water coming out of your faucet is too hot when you've turned it on full blast, turn down your water heater. It'll save you on energy use (and likely save you from a burn from touching water that's too hot). Most water heaters have a very easy temperature adjustment—turn it down a bit and see how things are, then turn it down a bit more if it's still too hot.

156. Insulate Your Water Heater

Another useful tactic for reducing energy loss is to insulate your water heater. Many modern water heaters are already well insulated, but not all are, and even a well-insulated heater can use a little extra help. The Iowa Energy Center reports that a properly installed blanket can reduce energy loss by 25 to 45 percent on a water heater. If you lose even a dollar's worth of energy from your water heater, the blanket will pay for itself in just a few years (and likely you lose even more energy than that). Go to your local hardware store and ask about a water heater blanket.

157. Install Low-Flow Showerheads

The average price of water in the United States is about $1.50 per 1,000 gallons. The national average water flow for showerheads is about 2.6 gallons per minute. You can buy a low-flow showerhead with a switch that reduces the water flow to 1.2 gallons per minute without a noticeable difference in the shower. If you take an average of ten minutes in the shower and you and your spouse take a shower every day, that's 730 showers a year for a total of 7,300 shower-minutes. A low-flow showerhead can save you 1.4 gallons per minute, a total of roughly 10,000 gallons a year. Thus, a low-flow shower-head can save you $15 a year, and modern low-flow showerheads are indistinguishable from normal ones in terms of shower quality.

158. Take Shorter Showers

The average showerhead uses 2.6 gallons of water per minute, and water costs about $1.50 per 1,000 gallons used. If you dawdle in the shower and use five minutes' worth of extra water flow each time you take a daily shower, you waste 4,745 gallons of water each year. That adds up to about $7.50 in lost water for time just spent dawdling when you could be doing something else. Practice taking timed showers. See whether or not you can get in the habit of doing your showering business in just seven minutes, or even just five. Another tactic is to install a showerhead (preferably a low-flow one—see tip #157) with a switch and get in the habit of turning off the water while you lather up, scrub yourself, or put shampoo or conditioner on your hair. If you can stop the water flow for just three minutes while doing these tasks, you save $4.50 a year in water use and help the environment, too.

159. Air-Seal Your Home

Many homes, especially older ones, lose energy to the outdoors almost constantly because of drafts and other air leaks. Blasting cool air outside during the summer, or warm air outside during the winter, can be a significant energy cost. The U.S. Department of Energy states that two simple steps for air-sealing your home, caulking and weather-stripping, will pay for themselves within a year, leaving you with substantial energy savings for years. Visit the Department of Energy's Energy Efficiency and Renewable Energy site to find out more, including a guide to caulking and weather-stripping your home. You can find this information online at *www.eere.energy.gov/consumer*.

160. Adjust Your Home's Temperature Seasonally

Many people find an acceptable temperature in their home and never adjust it again, leaving it at the same temperature year-round. This can eat up significant energy, as your home heating and cooling equipment work year-round to maintain this steady temperature. Instead, adopt a seasonal temperature strategy. If you know what your "standard" temperature is, raise it up 4 degrees in the summer and lower it by 4 degrees in the winter. So, if "normal" is 71 degrees, set it to 75 in the summer and 67 in the winter. This will significantly reduce the effort put forth by your heating and cooling appliances and save you energy money over the long run.

161. Use Heavy Drapes and Blinds

Drapes and blinds serve to minimize the amount of heat transferred through windows by adding an extra layer of insulation. The heavier the drapes and blinds, the better insulation they will provide, thus they'll save you more money on both heating and cooling costs. The larger the window, the more important it is to use heavy drapes and blinds to cover it most of the time, as large windows lose far more energy than small ones.

162. Open and Close the Blinds/Curtains in Tune with the Weather

In the summer, keep the drapes closed, as they'll help block out the sunlight and help keep your home cool. In the winter, keep the drapes closed except when sunlight is directly on the window, then open the drapes and enjoy the "free" heat. In spring and fall, though, when the temperature outside is much the same as it is inside, open up those drapes and open the windows on pleasant days, allowing the air to flow in and out freely. Doing this habitually can save a lot of money on your energy bill, as it allows you to take advantage of external heat when it's beneficial and block it when it's a hindrance.

163. Use the "Hibernate" Mode on Your Computer

"Hibernation" mode, if available on your computer, is the best possible balance of intelligent energy use and convenience in powering up. Putting your computer in "hibernate" means that it copies your current computer state to the hard drive, then powers down the computer entirely, just as if you had turned it off. When you power up again, though, the computer reads the stored state and returns your computer to the exact same situation that it was in before you put it in hibernate mode. Many people do not like the inconvenience of going through a computer's lengthy start-up. "Hibernate" mode allows you to take advantage of the huge energy savings from powering down your computer when you're not using it coupled with most of the convenience of a quick start-up.

164. Close Off Unused Rooms

If there are rooms in your house that are rarely used, close them off so that you're not wasting energy heating and cooling those rooms.

Pull the blinds tight, close any vents in the room, and then close the door tightly, even stuffing any significant gaps under the door. This room will typically be warmer than the rest of the house in summer and cooler than the rest in winter due to the reduced energy used to heat and cool that room, and that reduced use goes straight into your pocket in the form of a smaller energy bill.

165. Clean Out Your Air Vents

Over time, the air vents in your home will slowly get clogged with dust, especially dust that's not visible at a glance. Once every year or two, spend the time to take a duster to every vent in your home, remove the cover, and dust deeply inside the vent to make sure there's no dust building up in there. Also, ensure that none of the vents in your home are covered up or obstructed—for instance, by a chair or bed—as blocked vents are incredibly inefficient. Rearranging a room to unblock a vent is well worth the effort in terms of money saved.

166. Install Ceiling Fans in Every Room You Spend Time In

Ceiling fans are brilliant tools for reducing energy use in every season, but you have to be a bit clever to maximize their value. In the winter, set the fan to run in a clockwise direction, which pulls the warm air from the ceiling and pushes it down toward the floor, subtly raising the temperature in the room and causing the heating system to work less. In the summer, have the fan run in the opposite direction, which maximizes the circulation benefit of a fan. Air circulation can make the room feel as much as 8 degrees cooler, and combined with a temperature-adjustment strategy it can save you as much as 30 percent on your cooling bill.

167. Do an Insulation Inspection

Unsurprisingly, having good insulation in the attic can make a huge difference in the amount of energy you expend in the winter keeping your home warm. In most modern homes, it's easy to check this. The attic is mostly loaded with insulation on the floor, so take a peek up there and see what you notice. Are there any bare areas? That's going to be a heat leak, so make sure you have insulation placed in that area. Also, if you're able to, note the resistance rating of the insulation in your attic. It's usually noted with the letter R followed by a number. Ideally, you want insulation between R-21 and R-30. If it's low, like R-10, you should consider installing some higher-resistance insulation on top of the existing insulation without pressing down the existing insulation. Your local hardware store will be glad to offer advice and suggestions.

168. Do Proper Maintenance on Your Furnace and Air-Conditioning Unit

Home energy use often revolves around your furnace and your air-conditioning unit, which is why so many of these tips focus on improving their efficiency. Efficiency doesn't matter, though, if your units aren't functioning well, and the best way to maintain their functionality is by performing regular maintenance on the devices. Make sure their vents are clean. Replace the filters in your air-handling system regularly. Make absolutely sure that you haven't stacked anything on or around your outside air-conditioning unit. These little tips will go a long way toward keeping your heating and cooling units running efficiently, and might even extend their life, putting money right in your pocket.

169. Plant Shade Trees

Planting shade trees on your property not only increases property value, but a well-placed shade tree can block direct sunlight from hitting your house, providing a direct reduction in the amount of energy you'll need to use to keep your home cool. Find a fast-growing tree that can provide ample shade for your home in your climate and plant it to the east or to the west of your home. Not only does a shade tree add property value and reduce energy use, but it also provides enjoyment for the family, like a great place to lounge on a lazy day.

CHEAP TACTIC$ FOR FUN AND HOBBIES

170. Cut Back on Hobbies That Constantly Require Buying More Stuff

Hobbies that require a constant influx of money—golf, for example—are dangerous to your financial well-being. In order to enjoy the game, you have to pay for greens fees, cart rentals, balls, clubs, and so forth, and playing regularly can become a serious drain on your money. Many collections are the same way. In order to increase the size of your collection, you often have to spend additional money. Cut back on these hobbies, which require constant money and resources, and instead find other hobbies that don't require that money influx.

171. Check the Community Calendar

If you're looking for free or low-cost entertainment in your community, look for a community calendar that provides a listing of all of these events. You might have to do a little footwork to track one down. Try visiting city hall, the chamber of commerce, the visitor's center, the library, or the post office, or visiting the city's website. They will list lots of free activities going on in your town, many of which you likely aren't aware of. If you start choosing an evening activity or two a week from the community calendar, that's time you're not out and about spending money.

172. Visit the Post Office

Most communities have a vibrant community bulletin board at the local post office. Stop in and see what's on the board. You'll often see notices of interesting community events, notices of people selling items extremely cheaply (many times just before a move), new local businesses and organizations, job opportunities, and countless other items of interest. Whenever you're in your local post office mailing a package, it's worth your time to take a serious look at the bulletin board. You might just save yourself some money or find something useful for cheap.

173. Read the Local Newspaper

Another venue for finding out about local activities and organizations is the community newspaper. Newspapers often include announcements of upcoming events, descriptions of the activities of local organizations, and countless other little things that you can use to get involved in your community. Even better, many alternative local newspapers are free on the newsstand. Check near the entrances of community centers and local grocery stores for a free copy. These papers are a treasure trove of engaging and interesting activities of all kinds that won't pinch your wallet.

174. Stop By Your Town's Visitor's Center

Towns and cities often have an interesting cultural or historical heritage that many residents are only remotely aware of. Spend a few minutes at your town's visitor's center to find out about these interesting local resources, and spend an afternoon or two visiting them. You might be surprised at the genuinely interesting and engaging historical and cultural elements around you. Many of them can be enjoyed without spending any money at all.

175. Check Out the Library—Not Just for Books

The local library has become an absolute treasure trove of entertainment options. Beyond the enormous collection of books, most local libraries have extensive CD and DVD collections that can be checked out for free or at low cost, and many have extensive magazine collections so you can catch up on your interests. Many community libraries also have movie nights, where you can watch a film in a theater setting for free. Libraries are also often hubs for all sorts of special-interest groups, from gardeners to people who enjoy playing bridge. In many communities, libraries are also a source of free Internet access. Most communities give out a free library card to anyone who lives in the community and often give free memberships to anyone living in adjacent cities and towns as well. Take the time to visit your local library. You might be genuinely surprised at all they have to offer.

176. Have a Money-Free Weekend

Transform the idea of living cheap into something fun. Challenge yourself and your friends to spend this entire weekend without spending any money. Look for free activities to do as a group. Eat using the stuff you already have in the cupboards. Engage in personal activities that don't require you to spend money, like curling up with that book you've had for a while that you've been intending to read or going through the junk in the downstairs closet. Get into a routine of having money-free weekends once a month, or even once every other weekend, and you'll find your entertainment expenses (and expenses in other areas) will go down rapidly.

177. See What Your Local College or University Has to Offer

If you live near a local college or university, particularly a large one, there's almost constantly a string of interesting speakers and activities happening on campus. Visit the school's website (or call their general information number) and find out what's on tap in the near future, then attend a meeting or a lecture on a topic that's compelling to you. Many student organizations are open to the community at large and often welcome people who are not students to participate, so if there's a group focusing on an area of interest to you, don't be afraid to dive in and get involved.

178. Start a Natural Collection

If you enjoy collecting things but are finding that your collections are costing you a lot of money, start a new type of collection. Spend your time collecting things that can be found in nature, like rocks of a particular color or type, leaves of particular trees, or pictures of birds. Think about what interests you, then look around in your natural environment for examples that you can collect.

179. Dig Through Your Media Collection

Many people have extensive collections of books, magazines, DVDs, CDs, and so forth. You can utilize these resources to earn some extra money, but you can also use them for a great deal of entertainment as well. Whenever you find yourself bored and itching for entertainment, go through your collection and pull out a few items that you may have forgotten about and dig in. Usually, you'll find an item or two that, when you see it, will make you feel a bit excited and think, "I'd forgotten all about that! Cool!" When you have that feeling, you have instant entertainment in your hands without any cost at all—a great way to save money on entertainment.

180. Shop for Used DVDs, CDs, and Books

When you decide to make an addition to your DVD, CD, book, or video game collection, start by looking in the used stores—particularly if what you're looking for is not the latest release. If you can find the item you're seeking in a used form, you'll save yourself money versus buying it new. Even better, if you're browsing for inspiration, start off browsing in the used section so that if you do find something, it won't cost you nearly as much. Used selections often include items that you'll have a difficult time finding new, such as out-of-print books and obscure CDs and DVDs. Start there, and you might find a cheap gem.

181. Swap Your Used DVDs, CDs, and Books Online

One way to keep yourself awash with fresh material to read, watch, or listen to is to participate in online clubs for swapping these items. PaperBackSwap (*www.paperbackswap.com*) is an excellent resource for swapping books. Just list the books you're willing to trade on the site and when someone requests the book, you send it out and earn a credit. You can then spend that credit on the site to have a book shipped to you. Swap-A-CD (*www.swapacd.com*) and Swap-A-DVD (*www.swapadvd.com*) offer very similar services online for CDs and DVDs. It's a great way to give yourself something fresh to listen to, watch, or read on a regular basis without leaving the comfort of your home.

182. Play Games for Free Online

If you enjoy playing classic games like chess, checkers, bridge, canasta, and so forth, there are many places where you can play the games for free against an opponent in another town over the Internet. Just sign up at Yahoo! Games (*http://games.yahoo.com*), make up a username, and join the game. The site offers a wide array of games that you can play against online opponents for free. If you like playing video games, try Kongregate (*www.kongregate.com*), where you can sign up and play a huge variety of games of all kinds, from puzzle games to action games and strategy games. These games cost you nothing and can provide nearly endless hours of entertainment if you have a home PC with Internet access.

183. Learn a New Card Game

Card games are another incredibly inexpensive way to enjoy an evening with friends or a rainy afternoon at the kitchen table. Spend some time to learn a new game, or call some friends and invite them over for an evening of playing an old familiar card game. In either case, you've got hours of fun, social entertainment for just the cost of a pack of cards. Cards can also be a social opportunity to meet new people. See if your community has a bridge, canasta, or pinochle club. Such clubs can be a very inexpensive way to meet new people, have a great deal of fun, and stretch your mind a bit, too.

184. Teach Yourself a Skill You've Always Wanted to Learn

A lazy afternoon is a perfect time to teach yourself a new skill. Why not spend an hour learning how to knit a scarf? Perhaps you can spend an afternoon learning how to play that musical instrument in your closet, or maybe you've always wanted to tackle making an egg soufflé. Don't put such ideas off. Learning a new skill, especially with friends, can be fun, and many skills can also end up saving you a lot of money over the long run.

185. Go Exploring

Another great way to spend time without spending money is to go exploring, even in your own neighborhood. Visit areas that you've never been to before, just to see what sorts of interesting things are there. This can be a great family activity. Take a "wandering walk" in your neighborhood by merely going out your front door and going in whichever direction looks the most interesting. Alternately, visit the nearest state park and spend some time exploring the wonderful outdoors, going on trails, and admiring the beauty of nature.

186. Read More

Reading is perhaps the cheapest hobby you can have. The library provides a nearly infinite supply of reading materials for free, plus the time invested in reading costs only as much as the energy cost of the light bulb over your head (or nothing at all, if you read outside). Even if you've never read much before in your life, try picking up a book that looks interesting and start digging in. You might surprise yourself and find something truly compelling. If you already read regularly, try trimming some time away from other expensive hobbies and devote a bit more time to reading. It's a healthy and mentally invigorating hobby.

187. Watch Less Television

According to the South Dakota Department of Health, the average adult watches television for 31.5 hours a week. That's a lot of time lost, but it's also expensive; the average cable/satellite bill runs around $50 a month. That's not all. The average television uses about 75 watts of energy and the average cable box uses 15 watts. That means in an average year, television usage eats up $15 worth of energy, too. And we're not even including the cost of buying the television. Even more problematic is that television is laden with commercials encouraging you to buy more stuff, both during the commercial breaks and via product placements in the programs themselves. Do yourself a favor and cut back on television viewing. You'll not only cut back on your energy use (saving money), but you'll also find yourself having more time to do the things you wish you had time to do, like talking to a relative or an old friend or taking care of an unfinished household task. Turn the television off and you'll have time to turn some of your life back on.

CHEAP TACTIC$ FOR GROCERIES AND SUPPLIES

188. Don't Eat Out as Often

Eating out on a regular basis can get very expensive. Aside from low-end fast food, there's almost no meal you can eat outside the home that's not far more expensive than a virtually identical dish you can prepare at home. You can usually prepare it much faster and with healthier ingredients. The only way to get good at this, and to really reap the cost benefits of eating at home, is to do it all the time. Reduce eating out (and ordering delivery or take-out) to special occasions only and start busting out the pots and pans more often. Not only will your wallet thank you, but your taste buds will, too. As you gain more practice at cooking, your dishes will become more delicious.

189. Go Grocery Shopping Once a Week at Most

Think about your average grocery store trip. You wind up buying mostly stuff you need, but a few odd and unexpected items always wind up in your cart. You've usually got enough fortitude to keep the items to a minimum, but they wind up in there each trip. The simplest way to curtail those extra items, and to save on gas and time as well, is to get into a routine of going to the grocery store less often. You should go once a week at most. Not only will you save time and gas this way, but you'll also cut down on the number of extras you dump into the cart.

190. Eat Before You Go Grocery Shopping

One of the most dangerous expenses in the grocery store is the impulse buy, and impulse buys are often directly caused by hunger. When you're in a grocery store and you're feeling hungry, many more items are going to look tasty to you and are thus much more likely to sneak their way into your cart. There's a simple way to suppress this grocery shopping impulse: Eat a small meal just before you leave to go grocery shopping. That way you're not hungry, but you're also not bogged down with a heavy meal in your stomach. This will allow you to keep your energy up and get finished with shopping quickly, but not be tempted to throw extras into your cart just because you're hungry and impulsive.

191. Plan Your Meals Using the Grocery Store Flyer

Another effective way to manage those weekly grocery store trips is to start off with a plan for what you'll eat in the coming week. The cheapest way to get started is to pull out the flyer from your local grocery store (often included in community flyers or in the Sunday paper) and see which items are being sold very cheaply to get you in the door. Identify a handful of these, then use them to plan your meals for the week by using those items as the core ingredients in most if not all of your dishes. For example, if you notice that chicken is discounted highly, as is broccoli, look for dishes that utilize both and plan one or two of them for the week. Not only does this reduce your cost, but it also encourages diverse meals when you base your meals on what's on sale instead of eating the same old tired thing you buy on every grocery trip.

192. Make a Grocery List Before You Go

Once you have the meal plan ready, make a list of all of the ingredients you'll need for those dishes that you don't have on hand and any other staples you might need in a pinch. Take this to the store with you and use it. That means focus on nothing but gathering the items on the list and getting them into the cart. With a focused list like this, you know everything you need is on the list, thus you don't have to wander down the aisles or through the produce section hoping to stumble upon an idea for a meal to prepare. Everything you need is on that list. This not only saves you time in the store, but it also greatly reduces impulse buying.

193. Get Comfortable with Cooking

One major challenge that keeps many people out of the kitchen is a fear of cooking. The easiest way to get comfortable with cooking is just to try it, starting with simple recipes. You don't have to match the latest amazing creation you saw on television. Just try beating some eggs and a dash of milk with a spoon and cooking it in a pan over medium heat, scraping the eggs away from the side until it tastes right. With only ten minutes, three eggs, and a pinch of salt, you have a delicious meal for just thirty cents or so. When you start with simple recipes and do them over and over again, you start mastering the little techniques, and eventually the things that seemed impossible before may not seem so hard—eventually they may even seem easy. The biggest step, though, is the first one. Get out there in your kitchen and try something.

194. Avoid Frozen and Prepackaged Meals

On the surface, these seem like good deals—complete meals for just a few dollars! But once you read the ingredient list, then open up the package and see what you actually get for your dollar, it becomes a pretty poor deal, indeed. You should cut frozen and prepackaged meals out of your buying habits. If you like the convenience of just pulling a meal out of the freezer, popping it in the microwave, and chowing down, prepare a bunch of individual frozen meals in advance, like handmade frozen burritos and the like. Your cost per item will drop and the food will be healthier, too.

195. Make Recipes with Inexpensive Base Ingredients

One quick way to start saving serious money in the kitchen is by learning how to cook inexpensive staple foods very well. Learn the art of preparing beans and bean dishes, for starters, and focus on other inexpensive staple foods: fresh vegetables and fruit in season, eggs, pasta, tuna, and oatmeal are all inexpensive places to start. Coupled with a strong assortment of basic spices, you have the backbone of many wonderful meals just with those basic items in various combinations—fresh fruit in oatmeal, pasta with tuna, pasta with tuna and fresh vegetables, beans with fresh vegetables, beans with eggs, and so on. If you learn to master these basic staples in the kitchen, it'll be much easier to move on to more advanced recipes—and you'll save a ton of money as you learn.

196. Start a Garden

If you have a bit of space where you live to break ground, gardening can be an extremely cost-effective hobby and can be as good as putting money in your pocket. You have to make some up-front investments—the cost of seeds and starter plants, the cost of a hoe or other equipment to break ground, and the time investment needed to tend to your plants—but you'll earn a nice harvest at the end of the summer. You'll have spent a lot of time in the garden on a very frugal activity, time you might have spent elsewhere engaging in expensive hobbies. In some fruitful seasons, you'll more than break even with the value of the produce you grow, and you have the freedom to grow the foods that you like. Don't have space? Try starting a window garden or a box garden. You can grow a small amount of food in one of these in even the tightest of spaces.

197. Learn to Love Leftovers

Many people turn up their nose at the idea of leftovers. The mere thought of reheating food originally prepared a day or two before convinces many that the food will be bland and rubbery, not worth eating. This assumption sadly results in a lot of good, quality food hitting the trash can before its time. The truth is that with a little bit of careful planning, leftovers can be a delicious and highly inexpensive meal. Some ideas:

- Add additional spices that you have on hand to leftovers just before you serve them. This will create a fresh snap to the flavor of the food.
- Use the leftovers as the basis for a second meal. For example, take leftover spaghetti and sauce, chop up the spaghetti, put it in a bread loaf pan, sprinkle some mozzarella cheese on the top, and bake it in the oven. Or take the leftover chicken breasts from the grill, dice them, and add them to a rice and vegetable skillet meal.
- Freeze the leftovers. This especially works well if you've made a large batch of soup and have plenty left over. Freeze it in portion-sized containers.

198. Buy Staples in Bulk

Buying in bulk can save you a great deal of money, but not if you wind up wasting part of your purchase by letting it grow old before you use it. Focus on buying only nonperishables and key staple foods that you use all the time in bulk. If you use a bulk purchase in its entirety, you'll almost always save money.

199. Freeze Extra Staple Foods

Another tactic for effectively using freezer space, especially if you have a deep freezer, is to freeze any extra staple foods you are able to purchase or make. For example, loaves of bread can be frozen and kept fresh for a short while, as can many fresh vegetables. This isn't a long-term solution for food storage as freezer burn can be an issue, but if you hit upon a big bargain on fresh vegetables, don't be afraid to take advantage of the sale and stock up, freezing the excess in portion-sized bags to thaw and use later on.

200. Cook in Advance and Freeze Complete Meals

Many busy families resort to eating out regularly simply because of time constraints, even though this maneuver costs them considerable money over the long haul. A much more sensible tactic is to prepare complete meals in advance and freeze them so that when the time comes to use the meals, they can be pulled out of the freezer and tossed into the oven. Spending time preparing meals to be frozen in advance is a great way to spend one day every month or two, especially when the cost savings of eating such prepared meals adds up so quickly when home-cooked meals replace those eaten out.

201. Prepare Extra Batches of Other Meals

Preparing a casserole for supper? Why not simultaneously prepare two or three casseroles, then pop the extras in the freezer for future use? This not only saves you a great deal of time later, but it actually saves you money now because it allows you to buy the ingredients of meals in bulk and use them immediately. For example, preparing three identical tuna noodle casseroles instead of one takes a bit of extra time up-front, but it saves a huge amount of time later on as you can just pull one out of the freezer. Better yet, because you're making so much at once, you can buy the large bags of noodles and the large cans of tuna, reducing the cost of each casserole by a noticeable amount.

202. Master the Art of the Slow Cooker

The slow cooker often creates visions in people's heads of mushy, tired, and bland food, not interesting to eat at all. That's a stereotype that's quickly being relegated to the dustbin of history, as modern slow cookers with timers are able to turn on when you want them to, creating perfectly cooked meals that finish exactly when you've specified. A slow cooker is a perfect way to cook a stew, a soup, a casserole, or a large cut of meat while you're at work, allowing you to walk in the door to a perfectly prepared meal. The slow cooker can be a massive time-saver, allowing you to eat at home on a highly pinched schedule and thus enjoy the cost savings of eating at home with the in-a-pinch convenience of eating out. Dig out your slow cooker and try some recipes—you'll be pleasantly surprised. Don't have a timer? Stop by your local hardware store and ask about an outlet timer, a device that plugs into an electrical outlet and only turns on power at a specified time. This can allow your slow cooker to turn on a few hours before you get home, creating a perfectly cooked meal just as you walk in the door.

203. Cut Down on Coffee, Soft Drinks, and Bottled Water

Not only are drinks such as soda and coffee generally unhealthy for you (creating a caffeine addiction and often loading your body with sugars and high fructose corn syrup), they're also far more expensive than water. Even if you spend as little as $1 on average per day brewing your own coffee, that adds up to $365 a year; a daily Starbucks habit can easily add up to $1,700 a year. Try replacing parts of your beverage diet with cool, clean tap water (or filtered water). Bottled water, on the other hand, is just a way to pay a significant premium for convenience. Get a refillable and reliable set of plastic water bottles and keep them filled in the refrigerator yourself from your own tap. If you prefer filtered water, you're still saving big money—most filtered water units pay for themselves in just a few weeks as compared to the cost of bottled water. Eliminating just a few beverages a day can easily save you $100 a year and help you live healthier, too.

204. Look into Joining a Community-Supported Agriculture Group

A community-supported agriculture group is a system in which a number of customers who use lots of fresh produce get together to financially support a farmer to grow vegetables and fruits for them.

You can think of it as a large number of households getting together to mutually hire a fruit and vegetable gardener. The typical cost of a CSA is $300 to $500 a share for eighteen to twenty weeks, and the food produced for a share is enough to handle the vegetable and fruit needs for two people. In other words, you pay roughly $20 a week in advance to get fresh produce delivered to you each week for most of the summer and early fall. If your diet is already heavy in fresh produce, a CSA effectively functions as bulk buying of vegetables. They're substantially cheaper than buying the same quantity of fruits and vegetables at the store, plus the produce is much, much fresher as it's grown locally and is usually just a day or two from being in the ground when it arrives at your door. If you eat a lot of fresh produce, a CSA can be a tremendous bargain.

205. Shop at a Farmers' Market

Many communities hold a weekly farmers' market where individual producers of vegetables, fruits, and other goods go to ply their wares. Often the prices are reasonable and comparable to the prices you'd pay at the grocery store, plus the produce is fresher and you have an opportunity to talk with the producers to find out suggestions for preparing the food and so on. A good food preparation idea can be more valuable than the food itself. *Another tip:* Try shopping late in the session, when farmers often cut their prices to get rid of unwanted produce. Although you may have to pick through some of the lesser produce you can get a substantial bargain at the end of a farmers' market.

206. Buy Generic Brand Products

Generic and store-brand products are often shunned by shoppers simply because of the unfamiliar label. It's often "safer" to buy a name brand than the generic. This line of thinking is nonsense. Often, the generic version is identical to the name brand except for the label and the sticker price. Not sure? If you discover that it's not up to your standards, switch back to the name brand. You'll likely be surprised, though, not just by the level of quality, but by the money you save in buying generics.

207. Try a More Value-Oriented Grocery Store

Most areas have a number of grocery stores that serve different levels of buyers. Some, like Whole Foods, cater to high-end buyers who are willing to spend more for organics and other such items. At the other end of the spectrum are grocery stores focused on economical foods. These stores usually use minimal advertising and find other ways to reduce costs for the customer. Give one of these value-oriented grocery stores a try. You might be pleasantly surprised to find that you can buy the exact same items at the value-oriented store as at the other stores, except significantly cheaper.

208. Master the Concept of Cost per Use

Cost per use is a tremendously useful way to compare all sorts of different items that you might buy, from breakfast cereals to shoes. The cost per use of an item is the cost of the item divided by the number of times you'll use it before it wears out, and the lower the cost per use of the item, the better value it is and the more money you'll save by buying it. Take, for example, two pairs of shoes. One costs $50 but is guaranteed to stand up to three years of wear. Another pair is $10 and will likely last only six months or so as it is cheaply made. The $10 pair might seem like the better deal, but the cost per use of the $50 shoes is significantly lower. For each month of use, you'll save twenty-eight cents automatically with the $50 shoes. In other words, it's often more cost-effective, and thus cheaper over the long haul, to buy the more expensive version that's guaranteed to last longer. You can apply this principle to virtually anything you might buy, from washing machines to toothpaste, and the principle holds up. The cheaper you can get the cost per use to be, the cheaper the item is overall, regardless of the sticker price. Give it some practice and you'll be surprised how quite often expensive things are actually cheap and cheap things are actually expensive.

209. Get Maximum Use out of Supplies Like Baking Soda and Vinegar

Baking soda, vinegar, and water are pretty much all you need for most cleaning situations in your home, and considering you can buy these items cheaply at the grocery store, consider switching to them for your cleaning needs. Need to scrub something down? Make a paste out of a spoonful of baking soda and a spoonful of water and use that paste to scrub the dirty dish or spot on the floor. Want to mop? Dilute a few capfuls of vinegar in a bucket of water and use that to mop things down. Got some foul odors? Sprinkle some baking soda on the source of the stench, or dilute some vinegar in water and use a spray bottle to spray a mist around the room. Got greasy dishes? Use some vinegar with the hot water to cut right through the grease. Baking soda and vinegar alone can take care of the chores you might have originally used a large array of unnecessarily expensive items for. Want more ideas? Search online for "baking soda uses" or "vinegar uses" for many more tips.

CHEAP TACTIC$ FOR HEALTH

210. Exercise Regularly

Over the long term, regular exercise is one of the most cost-effective ways around to live cheap. Exercise can be very inexpensive, lifts your energy level (improving your earning potential), and improves your long-term health (reducing health care costs). Consult your doctor and begin a simple exercise plan. No matter what shape you're in, a bit of exercise can do a great deal of good for you now and for your long-term health as well.

211. Find an Exercise Buddy or Two

With a packed schedule and many distractions, it's very easy to simply not exercise. Turn both of those around by finding an exercise buddy or two, people with whom you feel comfortable exercising multiple times a week. Use exercising as a social occasion and motivate each other to get into better shape. A morning walk or jog with a friend or a half hour after work playing basketball with some buddies can make it much easier and more enjoyable to actually get in better shape.

212. Slowly Substitute Healthier Food Options

Another cheap way to better health is to improve your diet, but as with anything, it's often hard to make a radical change to your diet and stick with it. Instead, improve your diet by slowly substituting inexpensive but healthy food options for unhealthy items. For example, choose to order a salad instead of an entrée at a restaurant. Not only will it be less expensive, but it'll be healthier, too. Try slowly substituting water for coffee and soda. It's less expensive and substantially healthier. Swap out your ice cream for some frozen yogurt or try making it yourself.

213. Eat a Balanced Diet

Another effective way to manipulate your food consumption to save money over the long haul is to keep it balanced. Make vegetables and fruit the largest portion of your diet, but keep it varied. Focus your food spending on whatever produce is on sale that week, then get something completely different that's on sale the next week. This keeps your diet varied, balanced, and inexpensive, resulting in better health over the long run.

214. Use your Flexible Spending Account

Many employers offer a flexible spending account to accompany their health insurance plan. This flexible spending account allows you to pay for some medical expenses with pre-tax money, saving you on your income tax. Take advantage of this if it's available to you, particularly if you have any maintenance prescriptions, ongoing health situations, or dependents who may have medical concerns. In fact, your flexible spending account can make it cheaper to go to your own regular medical checkups, which will go a long way toward keeping you in good health.

215. Wash Your Hands

The common cold destroys countless hours of productivity each year, causing people to miss days at work and miss out on income and other opportunities as well. If you're self-employed, a cold can be utterly devastating, resulting in lost work hours, missed contract opportunities, and other negative effects. These lost opportunities can often be prevented by doing the simplest of things to prevent the common cold: washing your hands regularly. Wash them every time you use the restroom and just before you handle food. Doing both will go a long way toward reducing your chances of getting a devastating cold.

216. Practice Good Hygiene

Along with washing your hands, you can not only prevent illnesses but also improve your appearance to others by practicing good basic hygiene. For many, this is common sense, but it only takes one whiff of a person with bad breath to see how devastating that poor hygiene can be and one look at a person with bad teeth to see how costly poor hygiene can be. Take a shower daily. Brush your teeth at least once a day. Use deodorant. Keep your clothes clean. The key is to keep yourself presentable and avoid germs that could bring on illness.

217. Drink More Water

Drinking adequate amounts of water improves your energy, increases your mental and physical performance, removes toxins from your body, reduces the chances of a heart attack, and helps you lose weight. Pretty amazing what a few more glasses of water can do each day, isn't it? The average American drinks far less than the appropriate amount of water each day. You should be drinking eight 8-ounce cups of water each day at a minimum (approximately five tumbler glasses full of water). Not drinking that much? Try drinking a tumbler full of water each time you begin to feel hungry during the day, making sure that you drink your minimum of five a day. You'll find your hunger lessens (saving you money on food) and after a while you'll begin to feel genuinely better both physically and mentally (improving your earning potential). That's not even counting the other health benefits. A glass of water is the best cheapskate deal of all.

218. Eat Breakfast Every Day

Eating a low-fat breakfast each morning, such as a bowl of healthy cereal or a piece of fruit, not only has a tremendous positive effect on your late-morning energy level and mood, but it also improves mental performance throughout the day. Even better, it keeps you thin by getting your metabolism going earlier in the day. Not only that, it also has the effect of subtly reducing your appetite at lunchtime and later in the day, resulting in lower overall food costs if you eat an inexpensive breakfast. A quick banana on your way to work can end up making your workday easier and save you money on lower food costs over the long run.

219. Eliminate Smoking and Minimize Drinking

Drinking and smoking, especially when done with any frequency, can be incredibly expensive habits by themselves, never mind the high health care costs they can bring on later in life. If you're a regular user of either, work hard to break the habit and you'll find yourself with substantially more money in your pocket and better all-around health, both now and in the future. If you're having trouble breaking the habit, ask for help from your friends and family. They'll help you work through breaking a difficult habit.

220. Sleep More

Sleeping more by itself doesn't directly save you money, but inadequate sleep can certainly cost you money. Lack of sleep can reduce your mental sharpness, costing you money when you make silly mistakes. It can also cause you to spend money on convenience because you're tired, and it can also make you more susceptible to advertising and coercion because your mental defenses aren't sharp. Make sure you get an adequate amount of sleep each night, seven to eight hours at least, to ensure that your mind is sharp and you don't lose money in such preventable ways.

221. Schedule Regular Medical and Dental Checkups

Many medical and dental conditions can be easily and inexpensively treated if caught in the early stages, but can be very expensive to deal with if caught in later stages. The solution to this conundrum is simple: Get regular medical and dental checkups. Such regular checkups are covered by almost all health insurance policies, as it's far cheaper for the insurance companies, too. So regular checkups often incur only the smallest of expenses while avoiding some potentially monstrous expenses down the road. Regular medical and dental checkups are an incredibly cheap deal compared to the huge costs you might face without them.

222. Talk to Your Doctor about Independent Steps

If you discover that you have a medical condition, ask your doctor about independent steps you can take to minimize the effects no matter what the condition is. Almost every condition can be improved by making certain choices in your life, and making those choices can almost always reduce your potential future medical bills. So, if you're diagnosed with a condition, always ask what you can do to help minimize the effects or damage of that condition.

223. Consider Traveling for Surgeries or Other Medical Care

One medical option that many people don't consider is the possibility of traveling to another country for expensive medical care, such as major surgeries or lengthy treatments. Depending on your insurance, you may be able to save a significant amount of money out of your own pocket by exploring these opportunities. If it appears as though a surgery or other major medical procedure is in your future, call your health insurer and ask if there are any available options for reducing the overall cost, including traveling to another region of the country or traveling abroad for the procedure. Many insurance companies are quite happy to send you to another country for medical work, then send you back, in order to save a significant amount on the procedure, as it can be done in other areas at the same level of quality for much less. If you find out that you are going to have a major medical procedure, don't panic. A bit of planning now can save you a ton of money later.

224. Ask Your Doctor for Prescription Samples

Whenever you're given a prescription, ask your doctor if they have any samples of the prescription available that they can give you. In many cases, the sample may be enough to eliminate a prescription refill, saving you money. It can also tide you over until you can go to a lower-cost pharmacy to get your prescription filled, saving you money merely by giving you more freedom to choose your pharmacy.

225. Ask Your Doctor about Generics

Now that many pharmacies are offering $4 generic prescriptions, you can save quite a bit of money merely by asking your doctor whether or not there is a generic version of your prescription available that will work for your condition. In many cases, the generic is a perfect equivalent of the name-brand prescription, and thus substituting the generic for the name-brand prescription can save you a great deal of money at the pharmacy. Always ask your doctor about generics when you're given a prescription. It can save you a lot of money, particularly on a maintenance prescription that you'll refill many times.

CHEAP TACTIC$ FOR HOUSING

226. If You're Planning on Moving in the Next Five Years, Rent

Considering buying a home because it's a "good investment"? That idea is conventional wisdom, but there are many cases where it simply isn't true. For example, if you're intending to move away from the area within the next five years, it's more cost-effective to rent rather than buy. Why? During the first five years of your mortgage, almost all of your payment will go toward interest in the property, not toward equity. In fact, when you consider the closing costs from buying the house, plus the realtor fees when you sell the house, that will eat all of the equity in the house and more in almost all housing markets. Instead, look for an inexpensive place to rent in the area until you're ready to move on, as rent is almost always far cheaper than house payments. Sock away that difference for the future.

227. If You Don't Have a Down Payment Yet, Rent

It's tempting to go ahead and buy a home as soon as you feel ready, regardless of whether you have the money or not. However, diving into buying a home without a full down payment can be a huge financial mistake that will cost you for decades. Most lenders expect you to have 20 percent down when you buy a home. Buying without that down payment usually gives you several options, none of them pretty: a second, smaller loan with a much higher interest rate, or private mortgage insurance to ensure that the lender will be protected against the mistakes of an unprepared home buyer. Both options will cost you a lot of money that you won't get back. Instead, get into an inexpensive rental situation and get serious about saving for a down payment. Use the other tactics in this book, live as cheap as possible, save up that 20 percent, and then buy. You'll save yourself a tremendous amount of money by exercising some patience.

228. Consider a Cheaper Neighborhood

It's wise to be the richest person in a cheaper neighborhood than to be the poorest person in a rich neighborhood. In the cheaper neighborhood, you won't be surrounded by peer pressure to constantly spend more to keep up with the Joneses. In the expensive neighborhood, you'll constantly be surrounded by temptations to spend money that you don't really have. Look to buy in a less expensive neighborhood at first, and if you're still tempted to move up, save the extra money you're not spending trying to keep up and eventually upgrade. You'll save a ton of money by keeping the expensive Joneses at bay.

229. Consider a Cheaper Part of the Country

Many areas of the country have prohibitively expensive housing costs that can singly devour any extra income that can be made from living in that area. Look at living in another region of the country, even if it means a reduction in salary. If you can buy a house for $200,000 in Des Moines that would have cost nearly a million in San Francisco, you'll be substantially ahead even if you take a lower paying job. Also, don't merely assume you can't find work in your area of expertise in those other areas. Take a serious look at the job markets in some of the less expensive areas and you might just be very surprised at what you'll find.

230. Get a HUD-1 Form and Know What Lenders Will Be Looking At

When you start to think about buying a home, request a sample copy of a HUD-1 form at *www.hud.gov*. The HUD-1 form explains in very clear detail exactly what you'll be expected to pay during the process of buying a home, and many people are often surprised by all of the extra fees. Get a copy of this form and learn about each of the items and what you should expect to pay for them. Doing this will help to ensure that you're not hit with some unpleasant surprises when you go to sign the papers, which could cause you to lose an escrow payment or have to take on significant credit card debt to cover things. If you don't understand something, ask questions of any lender that you approach so that you do know what's going on, and also ask for estimates on all of these numbers. Information is key here. Know what you're going into, and you can save a lot of money.

231. Get a Shorter-Term Mortgage with a Lower Interest Rate

The most important number concerning your mortgage isn't the number of years you'll have to repay it or the amount of your monthly payment, it's the interest rate you'll be paying. The lower the interest rate, the less money you'll be losing to interest payments over the life of your loan and the more money you'll be able to keep in your pocket. When you begin to look at your mortgage options, look seriously at shorter-term options with lower interest rates, like a fifteen-year mortgage. While the monthly payments may be higher, you'll fully own the home in half the time, and by applying many of the other tactics in this book, you'll be able to handle those larger payments.

232. Know Exactly What You Can Afford Before You Look

Before you even start looking at the real-estate listings, sit down and take a long and serious look at your finances. What sort of monthly payment can you realistically afford, especially when including homeowner's insurance, property tax, and upkeep and maintenance costs in the mix? Be realistic in your calculations and know what you really can afford before you even start looking at homes so that you don't waste your time (and tempt yourself) by looking at houses that are more expensive than you can possibly handle. Doing this sort of serious gut check before you even look will save you a lot of money and heartache throughout the buying process.

233. Buy on the Low End of What You Think You Need

When you're out looking at houses, it's very tempting to push what you can afford and get one of the nicer houses. Don't—you'll just be putting the whole thing at risk. Instead, get the less expensive house, which will give you cheaper mortgage payments. Sock the extra money you saved toward home improvements or extra mortgage payments and enjoy the extra breathing room you get from owning a less expensive home. Then, if you're tempted to upgrade later, you'll have improved the value of the house, giving you more leverage to easily handle the leap to a better home.

234. Look for a Fixer-Upper but Avoid Homes with Problems You Can't Fix

One great way to save money when house-shopping is to look for fixer-uppers, homes with minor problems that can be fixed with some effort and time. You can often find great bargains by looking at this category of house, but be realistic about your limitations. Don't buy homes with serious structural integrity problems or problems that involve demolishing pieces of the house to fix properly. If you're looking at options with these kinds of problems and feel like you're up to the task, you're probably better off just building the entire house yourself.

235. Know the Total Cost of the Move Before You Jump

There are many, many hidden costs in moving. Be sure you do an adequate calculation of all of your costs before you make the move, and know what financial resources you'll need so that you're not caught putting thousands of dollars' worth of expenses on a credit card without being able to pay it off easily. Have you considered all of the closing costs listed on your HUD-1 form? Have you considered moving costs? What about the costs for any items you'll need as soon as you move in, such as furniture or other necessary items that you won't be bringing into the house with you? What about the fuel costs of the many trips you'll have to make during the move? How about a small emergency fund to deal with any of the little issues that could happen during the move? These expenses can and will add up, so it's best to be prepared up-front. Make sure all of the costs you can think of are covered by your savings, plus have a small additional emergency fund to handle things you didn't think of. This way, you're not tossing tons of stuff onto a credit card and having to pay high finance charges as you pay them off. Planning ahead saves money, particularly when moving.

236. Ask the Seller to Pay Closing Costs and Other Fees

When you begin to negotiate the closing price of your home, one very useful tactic is to ask the seller to cover your closing costs. This has several benefits. First, it allows the seller to claim a higher sale price for their home, making them feel that they got a better deal (and they can tell their friends that they did). Second, it gives the buyer (you) some breathing room during the expensive closing proccss. Third, it's often the perfect thing to break an impasse in negotiating, when there's still a gap remaining between what you're willing to pay and what they're willing to offer. Having the seller pay the closing costs can often bridge that gap. In many cases, the end result is that the closing costs are effectively wrapped into the mortgage at a low interest rate, leaving you with cash in hand to take care of the moving costs instead of having to use the cash to cover closing costs and putting your moving costs on credit, which can be incredibly expensive. Paying for closing costs can be a great way for the buyers to keep some cash in their pocket right now while the seller gets the deal done.

237. Shop Around for a Mortgage

When shopping for a mortgage, particularly your first one, it's often tempting to stick with the first friendly person you talk to out of familiarity and nervousness. Don't. Instead, take the time to shop around at several places, including your local credit union. If you can shave an extra 0.5 percent off your mortgage now, it can save you thousands of dollars over the lifetime of your mortgage. There are times in life when doing the legwork really pays off and puts money in your pocket. Shopping around for a mortgage is one of these times. Use *www.bankrate.com* to find out national mortgage rates as well as the rates in your area and use their tools to help you find potential lenders, and don't be afraid to talk to several different lenders to try to find the best deal for you. Be sure, however, that you're not just chasing interest rates. Ask each place for a good faith estimate so that you know how many fees will be tacked on, as a lot of fees can eliminate any interest rate benefit.

238. Attend the Home Inspection Yourself and Ask a Lot of Questions

Most home sales today are contingent upon a successful home inspection. While it might be convenient for you to just have the home inspector visit the house while you're at work, don't do it. Go along on the trip, keep your eyes open, and ask lots of questions about everything you're unsure about. Go online and search for a "home inspection checklist," print it, take it with you, and make sure the home inspector goes through each step on the list. Take note of everything the inspector observes and points out to you and follow up on everything, regardless of whether it's your responsibility or the responsibility of the seller. Your home inspection is one of the best opportunities to have someone fully examine your potential home and point out problems. Knowing those problems now can save you tons of money later or possibly even indicate problems severe enough that you back out of the home purchase. Go along, take notes, and pay attention.

239. Be Aware of Any Homeowners' Associations or Covenants You'll Have to Adhere To

In many neighborhoods, there may be homeowners' associations or covenants that you have to follow and perhaps even pay fees to join. Know what these are before you close the deal or else you may have a nasty financial surprise waiting for you when you move in that may involve home improvements, other requirements, fines, and monthly fees that you didn't expect at all. If you don't know about such arrangements with the home you're buying, ask about them and get a copy of any covenants or agreements that will apply to this home. Any fees or other costs that you're subject to as the owner just add to your housing cost, and they may be enough to tip the scales against buying the property. Find this out up-front so that there's no confusion later on.

240. Practice a Monthly Home Maintenance Schedule

If you already own your home, one way to keep it in good shape (and thus maintain property value and reduce repair expenses) is to start and maintain a monthly home maintenance schedule. Make yourself a checklist of tasks to execute each month in order to keep your home in good shape. Simply do the ones that apply for your home or property.

- Check for squeaky doors and oil them as needed
- Check and clean range hood filters
- Check and replace furnace filters
- Check and replace other ventilation system filters
- Check and replace humidifier filters

- Remove grills on forced air system ducts and vacuum inside the ducts
- Examine the foundation for any cracks
- Examine exposed wood (for instance, in the attic) for insect damage and do any insect preventive maintenance that needs to happen
- Test all ground fault circuit interrupters
- Check all vents (inside and outside) and make sure there are no obstructions
- Remove screens, clean window wells, and dry them
- Examine all outdoor items and see whether any seasonal maintenance needs to be done
- Drain off a pan full of water from the clean-out valve at the bottom of your water tank (removes sediment and maintains efficiency)
- Check your sump pump for any issues
- Test all fire / smoke / carbon monoxide detectors in the house
- Check all window and door locks to ensure they're all in working order
- Check your fire escape plan and make sure that furniture additions haven't changed this
- Check all faucets for dripping water and change washers if needed
- Run all sinks, toilets, baths, and showers to ensure no problems (mostly just the ones not used frequently)

- Check the gauge on all fire extinguishers and replace if needed
- Use a pipe cleaner and baking soda to clean all drains
- Check all gutters for blockage and clean as needed (bird's nests, leaves, and so on)
- Check all visible pipes for leaks (don't forget under sinks)
- Check and clean refrigerator and freezer coils (once every six months is sufficient)
- Check all caulking and repair as needed

241. Learn How to Do Simple Home Maintenance Tasks

There are countless little tasks around your home that you can do yourself instead of hiring an expensive handyman to take care of them, such as installing a ceiling fan or fixing a faulty light switch. Pick up a general book on home repairs and when a minor issue develops at your home, such as a backed-up drain or a leaky faucet, try repairing the issue yourself using this guide. Most of the time, the fix is incredibly simple and doing it yourself is quick and easy, saving yourself the cost of having a repairman come in and fix it.

242. Don't Overspend on a Lawn Mower or Other Home Maintenance Equipment

When you first move into a home, particularly for the first time, you'll be hit with many obvious home and lawn maintenance tasks that need to be handled. Your first tendency will be to go to the local hardware store and pick up equipment to handle the task, but that would not be a cost-effective plan. Instead, hit yard sales and look for this equipment on the cheap. Many people upgrade to riding mowers while push mowers still do the job and will get rid of their older push mower for just a few dollars. If you can get just a year or two of use out of such an old mower, you're ahead, and then you can upgrade your mower on your own terms with proper research to find the best deal. The same policy is true for other maintenance equipment, like weed removers and leaf blowers. Look for them used for your first purchase and upgrade later on when you can do adequate research and get the best bang for the buck.

243. Build Relationships with Your Neighbors

Put in time and effort to build a relationship with the people who live around you, and the relationship will pay off in many ways. A good neighbor will lend you stuff in a pinch, keep an eye on your property when you're traveling, and help you out when you need a hand. If you put effort into cultivating that relationship by being friendly and taking the initiative to do those little things for your neighbor, you will almost always be repaid in kind, and little things like that can subtly save you time, money, and worry over and over again.

244. Consider Building Yourself

A more intense option for people who are looking to upgrade their living space with an eye toward the bottom dollar is to build your home entirely yourself, starting with just a piece of land. In effect, you would serve as your own general contractor, doing the pieces of work that you're most comfortable with and paying others to do the pieces that you're less confident about. This is a huge cost-saver for anyone who is into home repair and doing things themselves. If this is intriguing to you, visit the library and look for books on building your own home. There are many resources available to help get you started on this big project.

245. Consider an Alternative Living Situation

If you're looking to own your own home but simply don't have enough money to do it, consider an alternative living situation. Offer to split costs with close relatives, such as siblings or parents, and have them share the house with you. Consider a group living environment, particularly if you're single and are primarily focused on building your career. If you're living rurally, look into buying a large property with one house on it, then share that home with another family while you build a second home on the other end of the property. Think outside the box a little when it comes to living situations and you can save a great deal of money on your housing costs.

246. Rent Out Unused Rooms

If you live in a home with significantly more space than you need, you can recoup some of your costs by renting out an unused bedroom or other rooms in your home to a student or another person looking for temporary housing. Not only will you be able to earn some income this way, but that person can also help with household chores by reducing the amount of space that needs to be maintained. This can be an excellent option for a person with extra space who could use some help keeping things in order.

247. Downgrade Your Home

Another option to consider if you have more space than you need is downgrading your home. Put your home up for sale and buy a smaller home in a less expensive neighborhood, and not only will you have a house that's more manageable for you with lower bills and upkeep costs, but you'll also have significant proceeds from the sale that you can use to pay off debts or save for the future. Downgrading is a powerful way to live cheap. You can reduce your housing costs while also earning some money from selling the larger house.

CHEAP TACTIC$ FOR INSURANCE

248. Know Your Reasons for Insuring

Many people buy insurance on their home, their car, and other things simply because they think they're supposed to do it. With that mindset, you're probably not insuring some things enough and overinsuring other things, resulting in a hodgepodge of policies that aren't adequately protecting you and could be costing you more than they should. Whenever you buy or renew an insurance policy, ask yourself what sort of worst-case scenario this policy is covering, and make sure that scenario is fully covered and nothing more. Investment options and other bells and whistles are unnecessary, just make sure that the things that you need covered are covered. Using this tactic with any insurance you buy will always save you money in the long run while ensuring that you are adequately covered.

249. Buy Term Life Insurance

For life insurance, your long-term concern should be that your family is taken care of in the event of your passing. Buy a term life insurance policy with enough value that if you do pass on, your family is financially in good shape. Beyond that, however, avoid other bells and whistles. Don't pay extra to turn your life insurance into a mediocre investment. Instead, use that extra money to keep yourself and your family on a strong financial path.

250. Buy a Longer-Term Policy

When you buy term life insurance, you'll often be given several options with different terms. A shorter-term policy may have lower payments now, but over the long haul, a longer-term policy is a much better deal. Why? In ten years, when the short-term policy runs out, you'll have to get term insurance again, and then you'll be ten years older with the possibility of some health issues that may have arisen between then and now. Buying a policy then, no matter what the length, will be more expensive than buying one now. You're much better off buying a long-term policy now and making slightly higher payments than saving a few bucks now only to pay a lot more later on. The cheap method is to go for the long term.

251. Consider Long-Term Disability and Long-Term Care Insurance

Similar to the logic behind life insurance, take a serious look at long-term disability and long-term care insurance, particularly if your family relies on you as a wage earner. This insurance will protect you in the event that you're injured and left unable to perform your previous job. Look into an appropriate long-term disability policy to help replace lost income in the event of such an accident, and match that with a long-term care policy that will pay for any long-term care that you might need if you have medical conditions that require long-term medical care. This insurance covers an unlikely situation, but if something should happen to you, you'll be extremely glad you have this coverage. This is one case where it's often cheaper to spend a little more, just in case.

252. Drop Collision and Comprehensive Coverage on Very Old Vehicles

If you're driving a very old vehicle, particularly one you're only keeping for emergencies or for future trade-in value, drop comprehensive and collision insurance on that vehicle, keeping only liability coverage. The cost of just a couple years' worth of collision and comprehensive coverage will usually be more than an old car is worth. Making this change will save you money each month that's not being put toward insurance that you almost certainly won't use. With just liability insurance, your car will not be covered if you get into an accident or it needs repairs, but if the car is already near the end of its useful life with many small, impending problems, this isn't a major concern. Save money—go with only liability insurance on very old cars.

253. Shop Around for Automobile and Homeowners' Insurance

When you first got your insurance, you may have been getting the best deal around, but is that still true today? It's useful to shop around for rates once every few years just to see if you can save money through another insurance company. Get quotes from several different companies, and use resources like *Consumer Reports* to evaluate their customer service. Remember, though, that if your current insurance company has treated you well so far, it's worth a small premium to stick with them, because a combative insurance company can cause you a great deal of financial hardship.

254. Know Your Discounts

When you sign up for insurance, there are often many discounts that you may be eligible for that are stated in the fine print of the policy. Do the research and find all of these discounts and make sure you're getting the ones you're eligible for. Common discounts include a good student discount, a safe driving record (without tickets or accidents), and so on. If you've met the criteria for these, call your insurer and ask for a discount.

255. Try Bundling Your Policies for a Discount

Many insurance companies offer many different types of insurance—homeowners' insurance, auto insurance, disability insurance, and more all tend to be sold by the same group. Because of this, many insurance companies will offer you a discount if you sign up for multiple types of policies through their organization. Consider doing this, particularly if your current insurer won't offer a bundled package. Any time you need new insurance is a great time to shop around for your existing insurance packages, too, so that you can take advantage of bundled discounts in your calculations.

256. Increase Your Deductible

Tired of paying high premiums all the time, particularly if you're a safe driver? Look into increasing your deductible—the amount you'll have to pay out of pocket if you do make an insurance claim. Even a slight increase can make a big difference in your premiums. If you don't drive much, consider raising your deductible significantly, as your chances of having severe issues with your car are much lower than if you're a frequent driver.

257. Pay All of Your Bills on Time

Insurance bills are incredibly important to keep on top of. Don't be late on a single payment or else a domino effect of negative ramifications may occur: An increase in your premiums, a gap in your coverage, and potential penalties from driving uninsured can all occur, as can a true disaster if you're in an accident or have a breakdown while your insurance has lapsed. Many insurance policies have a grace period for late payments, but don't even push that, as it may still have a negative effect on the premiums that you pay. Don't let your insurance bills get behind or else you'll put yourself at significant risk and also potentially raise your premiums as well.

258. Drive Carefully

Defensive driving is important because it keeps you and your passengers safe, but it has the added benefit of keeping your wallet safe as well. Defensive driving can help you avoid accidents, helping you save on repair costs and potential traffic tickets and fines, and also keeps your driving record clean, which helps with insurance costs. Keep your eyes on the road when you're out and about. Avoiding the huge expenses that you can incur by making a mistake pays for the attention you give to driving.

259. Know What Your Real Rebuilding Costs Are and Provide Proof

Have a good idea of the total cost to replace everything that would be destroyed in the event of a disaster. How much is your property worth and how much would it cost to replace it? Make sure you've figured this up with plenty of breathing room before you purchase your policy, and make sure that the amount listed on the policy covers it. *Another tip:* Make a detailed list of all of the contents of your house, with specific descriptions and serial numbers when needed, and keep this in a safe place. You might also want to take a walkthrough video so that other things are captured as well, so you can demonstrate the property that was damaged and needs to be replaced. A bit of preparation now can save you a huge amount of financial heartache later.

260. Make Your Home More Disaster Resistant

Take some simple steps to decrease the likelihood of devastating disaster in your home, such as adding storm shutters, installing fire alarms, or updating your plumbing and electrical systems. These simple steps will each reduce the likelihood of disaster befalling your home. You can also earn some direct value from actions like these by obtaining a list of disaster resistance tactics from your home insurer along with an estimate on premium reductions you might earn by following these tactics. If you can make a few simple changes to your home to both make it safer and reduce your homeowners' insurance costs, that's a double financial benefit.

261. Combine Health Insurance with Your Spouse

If you're recently married, look into the possibility of combining your health insurance policy with the one held by your spouse. You might find that your partner has a better policy with smaller copays, plus it may be more cost-effective to have both of you served on the same policy. Similarly, when you add a new member to your family through birth or adoption, look at the various insurance options available to you, including family plans. You may find that a family plan will save your family a substantial amount over individual plans.

262. Bypass Agents and Buy Policies Directly from the Companies

If you're looking to buy your own insurance policies of any kind (life, health, homeowners', auto, and so on), try contacting the insurance company directly via their website instead of dealing with a local agent. Quite often, you can get a much better deal by bypassing the agent and his referral fees, though the process for signing up may take longer. Use the Internet to your advantage and shop around for different rates directly from the insurance companies themselves, then sign up for that insurance directly.

263. Raise Your Credit Score

One major factor in determining how much you pay for your insurance premiums is your credit score, which insurance companies will use to estimate how reliable and trustworthy you are. Thus, one quick and effective way to reduce the premiums on your various policies is to raise your credit score. Get a copy of your credit report, review it carefully, and eliminate any problems. Pay all of your bills on time. Keep your credit card debt under control and don't sign up for new cards all the time. Following basic steps for personal finance success will not only help you manage your money better, but it can also result in a nice deduction in your insurance premiums.

264. Use a Payment Option That Lets You Pay the Least Amount Total over a Year

Most insurance providers give you many ways to pay for this insurance: Monthly payments, quarterly payments, and annual payments are among the common offerings. Don't pay any attention to the option that gives you the smallest individual payments. What's really important is the option that enables you to pay the least amount per year. Multiply the annual payment by twelve, the quarterly payment by four, and the semiannual payment by two in order to make a fair comparison among them, and sign up for the plan that makes you pay the least each year. If you're worried about bills sneaking up on you, start saving automatically for that future bill, taking enough out of your checking each month to make sure you can easily cover that bill when it comes due. The less you pay annually, the less you have to take out of your account each month.

CHEAP TACTIC$ FOR LOVE AND MARRIAGE

265. Don't Spend to Impress

Many people tend to want to shell out the cash in order to impress a date right off the bat. That's fine, but if you're spending money solely to impress your date, particularly beyond the first date or two, you're creating an image of yourself that will be difficult to live up to over the long haul. Look for sincere and authentic ways to show your interest that don't involve throwing cash around and creating bogus expectations. Instead of going to the most expensive restaurant in town, ask around and find a great undiscovered place with much more reasonable prices. Instead of just picking something impressive, pay attention to what you know about him or her (and ask friends) to find out what your date genuinely enjoys and focus on doing something related to that. Be real and authentic. Don't let your wallet do the impressing or else you'll make an expensive impression you won't be able to live up to.

266. Give Gifts of Sincerity

When a relationship begins to grow and gift-giving occasions occur, the best option is to always go with a sincere gift from the heart. For example, let's say the person you're dating loves to read. An easy gift idea might be a book that someone at the store suggested that she might like, based on her tastes. A better idea would be a book that is genuinely powerful to you that somehow connects with your relationship. The best gift of all, though, is that book with a note folded up inside explaining just why that book was powerful to you and how it connects to the relationship. Just a little more effort takes an ordinary and unremarkable gift and turns it into something sincere and special that can help build the connection between the two of you. A bit of extra effort and sincerity can make something inexpensive into something truly profound.

267. Plan a Romantic Free Date

If you're committed to living a frugal lifestyle, get your date involved and plan a romantic free date where you don't spend money beyond what you'd ordinarily spend. Pack a backpack full of food, a candle, and some matches and go on an evening hike. Have a movie night where you each pick two films from your own collection and watch all four together. Go on a daylong bicycle ride out in the country together. Spend a Saturday together involved with a volunteer project. Dating doesn't have to be an expensive situation. It just has to be something that you both find value in, and that value doesn't have to cost money.

268. Take Walks Together

No matter what stage your relationship is in, there are a few things you can do to build a long-term bond, such as taking a long walk together and talking about life, problems, and everything else in between. Relationships are built on a bedrock of communication, and taking a long walk together and giving plenty of open air to revealing things about yourself and getting to know each other on an intimate level can be a big part of that foundation. Communication is the glue that helps people stick together and the best part is that it's free.

269. Write Love Notes

To some, this tip might seem very corny, but it's one of the best little things you can do to help keep a relationship alive and vibrant. Every once in a while, when the person you're with least expects it, take a few minutes to write a note simply stating how important that person is to you and then put that note in a place where it will easily be found by the recipient. Little token reminders of your love and affection like this are great, inexpensive ways to refresh the bond between you.

270. Be Attentive

While it's easy to get caught up in the big things in a relationship, it's often the little things that matter. Pay attention to what your partner is saying and doing, even if it doesn't directly involve you, and use that information to make little choices to make your relationship stronger. For example, instead of plotting a big surprise birthday party for your partner, pay attention and listen to what she really wants. You might find out that the big surprise bash you were thinking about is the last thing on earth that your partner wants and instead she'd rather have a simple and intimate evening alone with you. Another example: If you routinely go out on the town together, an attentive partner might notice that the other person is getting tired of the old routine and thus it might be good for both of you to build a different routine, perhaps one that involves going out less and staying home more. Attentiveness not only builds a relationship, but it often prevents you from throwing away money based on your own preconceptions.

271. Find Areas of Mutual Interest That Don't Involve Spending Money

Most relationships are built around some areas of common interest. What areas of common interest do you have with your partner? Which of those areas don't require a great deal of money to enjoy? Put some effort into finding areas of common interest, particularly those that don't require financial input. For example, perhaps you both enjoy bicycle riding or going on nature walks, or perhaps you're both happy to curl up with a good book. The more time you spend getting to know each other as people, the more likely you are to discover common interests that don't require throwing money to the wind.

272. Build a Financially Equal Relationship from the Start

Obviously, no relationship will start off with both partners on exactly equal financial footing, but that doesn't mean that a healthy relationship revolves around one person covering all of the necessary bills while the other member is a spendthrift. Instead, both partners should take responsibility for some part of the financial situation and both partners should also get to reap some of the reward in terms of financial flexibility and spending money. You can start this early on by having both partners occasionally paying for date expenses, or by going Dutch regularly. Later on, agree to have one person cover a few of the bills while the other person covers the rest. For example, one partner might pay for rent while the other one handles the other expenses. Eventually, you'll want to merge finances with some basic agreements and rules on how things work for both partners. Doing this now will save much pain and needless expense later on, as both partners are committed to and involved with the financial success of each other.

273. Get on the Same Page Financially

Beyond merely working together to get the bills paid, it also helps to talk about long-term goals and what you both can do to reach these goals together. What do you both dream about? Where do you see yourselves in ten years? Set some big goals that you both have an interest in achieving, and then offer each other positive encouragement toward reaching those goals. Encourage each other to reduce spending and make intelligent purchasing decisions. Talk about the temptations that you each have, and confess your fears and challenges to your partner as well. Put everything out there on the table—everything you're worried about, everything that makes you uncomfortable, everything you dream about. Work together to break down those worries and move toward those dreams. Knowing that you're both on the same page with similar goals and pushing each other in a loving way toward those goals will save both of you a tremendous amount of money over the long run and will also help cement a lifelong relationship.

274. Plan a Wedding Centered Around Loved Ones, Not Stuff

Many wedding plans grow completely out of control, costing the bride and groom and their family many thousands of dollars for one over-the-top day. In the end, though, memories aren't made of a ten-foot cake or of the perfect flower arrangement or of the expensive bridesmaids' dresses. The memories are about friends and family coming together to celebrate. Your wedding plans should focus on the people you love and care about, not on some giant fairytale wedding fueled by bridal industry marketing. Instead of asking how big your wedding cake should be, ask whether or not the wedding and reception will be accessible to everyone. Instead of picking out the "perfect" dress for the bridesmaids to wear, pick them out together and make a price-conscious choice that reflects the financial realities of everyone involved. Another option is to drastically shrink the entire wedding plan and have an incredibly simple ceremony, surrounded only by the people you care about the most.

275. Plan a Romantic Honeymoon, Not an Expensive One

Many marriages start off with a pricey honeymoon that goes far beyond what the new couple can rationally afford. While a honeymoon can be a truly memorable experience, it doesn't have to come at the expense of financial reality. Instead of planning an expensive "destination" honeymoon, plan something simple that you'll both deeply enjoy. Love wine? Tone a trip to Paris down to a week-long driving tour of the Napa and Sedona Valleys. Enjoy the outdoors? Spend your honeymoon together in a stunning national park, enjoying natural beauty during the day and each other at night. Just want to get away? Spend it away from everyone in a small, quiet town in your favorite area of the country where you can enjoy yourself deeply on a shoestring. Your honeymoon doesn't have to have five stars or a five-figure bill. Step back from that concept and look at what you're both really passionate about, and ask yourself how you can share that passion together in an intimate setting. You'll find your answer there, and it'll likely save you a lot of money over the usual honeymoon ideas.

276. Don't Get Married if You're Still Having Doubts

If you're nearing your wedding day and you're still feeling intense doubts about the whole idea, don't get married. For starters, if you're unsure about the whole idea, there's a strong chance that once you're married, your marriage will fail and you'll have to face the deep financial and emotional cost of divorce. For another reason, if your partner is committing with his or her whole heart and you're not doing the same, you're being truly unfair to that person, taking their hopes and dreams and passions and not giving the same in return. If you feel doubts, take the time and space you need to work through them, but don't commit to marriage unless you're truly ready to give it your all. Marriage isn't easy and ending a marriage can be incredibly expensive. Don't make that commitment unless it's with your whole heart.

277. Give Your Marriage the Care and Feeding It Needs

Once you're settled into married life, don't abandon the things that made your relationship work to begin with. Spend time every day, or as often as you possibly can, with your partner just talking about your cares and concerns. Engage in activities together as often as you can, and if you notice you're starting to do more things apart, make a concerted effort to steer that ship back in the right direction by suggesting things to do together. Forgive your partner for little mistakes. Your partner's not perfect and neither are you. Putting forth the regular effort to keep your relationship strong will not only make your marriage last, but it will save you the money and heartache of counseling and potentially the money and heartache of a painful divorce.

278. Realize Money Doesn't Heal a Marital Problem

Many people try to repair rifts in relationships by throwing money at the problem. A big bouquet of flowers, a wonderful gift, and a kiss on the cheek and suddenly everything is better, right? While a gift might appear to be a good patch, it's just superficial—the real problem often goes much, much deeper. If you find yourself in a situation where you're plotting to "fix" things by buying a gift, ask yourself honestly whether you're actually trying to fix the problem or if you're just hoping to smooth things over without really fixing anything at all. If you're just trying to smooth things over, a different approach might be in order. Instead of buying an expensive gift, set aside some time to talk with your spouse about the problem and listen to what your spouse says. Take it seriously. If passions are on display, then it's because something is important. Don't just buy something. Not only is it a waste of money in the end, it does nothing at all to actually heal the problem.

279. Be Completely Honest with Your Partner about Money Issues

When you're dealing with finances, complete honesty is always the best policy. It's far better to show your partner that bill you're hiding now than to hold on to it until later when months of dishonesty have built up around it (and a higher balance has likely built up as well). If you're ashamed to tell your partner about a purchase you've made, you're better off talking about it now than convincing yourself that it's really fine and opening the door to a Pandora's box of spending. Whenever you spend money, you should be willing to tell your spouse about it, and if you are truly open, it will encourage your spouse to be equally open.

280. Have Regular Talks about Your Financial Situation

Once every month or so, sit down with your partner and talk about your financial situation. Go through your bills together, allowing your partner to see exactly what you spend and you to see exactly what your partner spends. Talk about your progress toward your big goals and encourage each other to keep making good moves all the time. Doing this regularly encourages you both to make better financial moves on a daily basis, reducing unnecessary spending and thinking more about the big goals that you share, which in the long run is an incredibly financially strong way to live.

281. Encourage Your Partner's Frugality

Make a regular effort to encourage your partner to spend less money on frivolous things and make smarter buying decisions. If your partner made a tight grocery list, went to the store, and cut your usual grocery store bill in half, compliment him on the good move. If your partner is trying to choose between different items, encourage her to choose the less expensive one. If you're evaluating a new appliance together, look for energy-efficient and reliable models on sale and point these things out to your partner. Suggest activities together that don't require money and be optimistic and positive when your partner does the same. Rely on each other for living cheap and you'll both do much better.

282. Show Your Love Frequently Instead of Something Big Once in a While

Culture has taught us that big gifts on certain occasions are the way to go, but those gifts are often put up on a pedestal, far out of proportion as a symbol of love. Instead of focusing on a diamond ring or an absurdly expensive set of golf clubs, once every few years, look for smaller things that you can do more often to show your partner that you care. Don't worry about the expensive diamond necklace. Just put a note on her pillow every once in a while, give her a kiss and an "I love you" when you see her for the first time in the evening, or stick a bar of her favorite chocolate in her purse to surprise her sometimes. Don't focus on the amazing new gadget. Instead, make him his favorite sandwich and bring it to him when he doesn't expect it, encourage him to spend an afternoon just twiddling around by himself out in the garage when he's feeling restless, or surprise him with your passion at an unexpected moment. Those little things don't cost much at all, take the pressure away from an over-the-top "big" gift that could push some financial buttons, and helps keep your marriage alive and happy, all in one swoop.

283. Make Sure That You're Both on the Same Page When It Comes to Children

A final tip about relationships: Address the question of whether to have children openly and deeply, and only commit to having children if you're both ready and committed to it. Children can be incredibly expensive and also incredibly demanding of your time, but the emotional and personal rewards of parenthood are many. Even knowing this, it's not a tradeoff that some people want to make, and others may hide their reluctance in an effort to please their spouse. A child born into a situation where both parents aren't committed to the child can create an uncomfortable situation for everyone, one that might lead to separation and divorce. Not only would this be financially and emotionally devastating to you, but it's also wholly unfair to the child, who wasn't involved with the choice at all. Carefully consider the child question, be open about it, and listen to what your partner has to say. It's perhaps the biggest decision you'll have to make—only make the leap when you're both on the same page.

CHEAP TACTIC$ FOR SOCIALIZING

284. Join a Community Organization

Your best opportunity to meet up with a group of people who share your common interests is to join a community organization, such as Toastmasters, the Lion's Club, and so forth. Stop by city hall and ask if you can find a list of active organizations in your community and request contact information for those groups to find out more. Try visiting the websites and attending the meetings (if allowed) of a few groups to find out about them, then look into becoming involved with any organizations that do click with you. Most organizations provide a great positive way to get involved with your community, meet new and interesting people, improve yourself, and do it all for a very low cost.

285. Attend Community Events and Actively Participate

There are also many events held in communities every week that are open to the public where you can not only get involved in what's going on in your community, but you can also meet many people who are interested in the community as well. Check the community calendar and find out what sorts of community events are going on in your area this week, then dip your toes into any that might be of interest to you, from local politics (city council and school board) to cultural festivals. Introduce yourself to people and don't be afraid to ask questions. If an event doesn't "click" with you, try something else until you find a community event that does.

286. Get Involved in Youth Activities

Another approach for meeting new people in your community, particularly if you're a parent, is getting involved in the organization of youth activities. Volunteer to coach a youth sport. Participate in the PTA. Volunteer to help out with youth camps or to be a group leader in a youth organization. You'll not only get the opportunity to be involved in a productive effort that helps out young people, but you'll also get the social opportunity to get to know many parents whose children are involved in such activities. If you have children of your own, it can also provide an opportunity to get to know many of the parents of your child's peers, people you will naturally have common interests with.

287. Join a Volunteer Organization

Another angle to take on the whole socialization-through-involvement tactic is to join a volunteer organization that works in your community or in neighboring ones. Get involved with your local soup kitchen or food pantry. Volunteer to participate regularly in any Habitat for Humanity projects in your area. Volunteer your time at the local animal shelter. Get involved in efforts to maintain gardens in local parks. Get involved in encouraging people to vote, or join a political campaign as a volunteer. There are volunteer efforts for almost any interest you might have, and every volunteer effort is a collection of people passionate about the same thing, meaning you immediately have something in common. It's a way to meet new people, spend some time doing something personally compelling, and best of all, it's free.

288. Join a Book Club

Enjoy reading, but also value interacting with other people? Look around for community book clubs and join one. Start your search at the library. Most libraries have at least one book club, and many have several book clubs spread out over many different areas of interest. Many library book clubs have enough books (through interlibrary loans and so on) so that all members can check out the books, so there's usually no cost involved—plus you can meet interesting people who are genuinely enthusiastic about reading and sharing their thoughts on books. Book clubs are an incredible social opportunity for avid readers.

289. Take Leadership Positions

If you find an organization that really clicks with you, volunteer within those groups to take on leadership positions. This opportunity will not only give you more activities to spend your time on, but it will also provide many opportunities for additional social interactions, give you an opportunity to build strong relationships with other people who care deeply about the organization or the cause, and possibly provide a résumé builder, all for free. If you're involved, don't hesitate to get on a committee, head up a task force, or run for an office within the group.

290. Host a Potluck Dinner

Potluck dinners are a great way to get a group of friends together and enjoy a meal and a social evening with minimal cost for all involved. Just call up your friends, invite them over to dinner, and have them bring a side dish or some other element of the meal. Not only does this provide an inexpensive dinner for all involved, but it also sets the stage for a fun social evening. Better yet, get a regular potluck dinner going on a rotating basis among a group of friends.

291. Host a Game Evening

Don't want to mess with a meal? Host an evening where people come over to your house to play cards or a well-known game, such as Pictionary. Ask people to bring beverages and you have an evening's worth of fun with a group of friends for free. Keep the idea fresh by having different people host the event with different games, and make an effort to keep the games simple and open to everyone but still intriguing enough to reward repeat play. Some ideas and examples: trick-taking card games, Pictionary, and Monopoly.

292. Host a Sporting Event Party

Another great way to get a social crowd together without a great deal of expense is to host a sporting event party. Invite a long list of people to come and bring a beverage and/or a finger food and the expenses become minimal, plus the environment at such events is almost always upbeat, festive, and fun. Sure, you probably have some cleanup effort afterward, but if you host one party, you'll likely be invited to many others, which gives you a long chain of inexpensive or free social events to enjoy.

293. Host a Block Party

One effective way to get to know your neighbors better is to host a block party, where you invite over all of the people who live near you. Usually, this can take the form of a potluck, where everyone who attends brings a side dish, while the host provides a central dish or beverages. While this can be a bit of an expense, it also provides a stellar opportunity to get to know the people who live around you and can also provide the initiative for a series of such parties. Hosting a block party can initiate friendships, plus encourage others to do the same, both of which open the door to many other social opportunities.

294. Build Friendships with Parents of Your Children's Friends

If you're a parent, you'll be interacting with your child's friends and, inevitably, their parents. It's a good idea to make a social effort to get to know the parents of your children's friends. One way to do this is to simply invite their family over for dinner, which they can reciprocate later on. This allows the children to play together and the parents to get to know each other a bit. If a friendship takes hold, it can be a tremendously useful thing for both families, giving them each a known safe place for their children to go, plus a potential strong friendship. In the worst case, you find out more about your child's friends with only the cost of a few home-cooked meals, but in the best case, you begin to build a lasting friendship. That's an incredibly valuable investment.

295. When Making a Major Purchase, Tap Your Social Network

If you've put effort into hosting some social events, you'll likely have built a social network without spending money like crazy. Once you have that social network, it can pay off time and time again. For example, if you're about to make a major purchase, like a new appliance or a new automobile, call around and ask your friends for advice. What appliances work for them? Do they have any sellers that they recommend? Not only will you get honest and useful advice, you might also find that a friend of yours had a friend who can get you a great deal on what you're looking for, saving you a ton of money. Even if that doesn't happen, you'll have built upon the trust of your friendship simply because you asked for their help, plus you'll have some good advice to work with when moving forward with your big purchase.

296. Offer to Trade Skills with Your Friends

Another effective way to save money with your friends is to offer to trade skills with them. What skills do you have to offer? Perhaps you're good with computers, while you have a friend who's good at electrical wiring—you're a systems support specialist and your friend is an electrician. Offer to tune up your friend's computer in exchange for his assistance in installing a ceiling fan—both of you save money. Making this successful is easy: Know what your friends do professionally and what their primary hobbies are, and let them know that you're willing to help them out by providing whatever skills you have. The likelihood is that over the long run you'll both save money by sharing your skills.

297. Organize "Work Parties" Where People Gather to Help with a Task

Do you have a major task that needs to get done, like laying new cement for a basketball court or re-shingling your roof? Utilize the social network you've built and invite a group of your friends over to help out. Provide refreshments and be willing to offer your help to them if they need it for similar large projects. You can transform a large, arduous task into a fun social event for a large group of people. The key is to be willing to do the same for the people you invite; in fact, if you hear about a friend who is organizing such a "work party," volunteer to help out. You're much more likely to get people involved in your task if you show a repeated willingness to help others out. In either case, a "work party" can be a very inexpensive and fun way to spend an afternoon, plus it can save you a lot of money if it helps you get a major task done with minimal expense.

298. Share Purchases of Equipment with Neighbors and Friends

Do you have a large yard and need a riding lawn mower? Are any of your friends in a similar situation? Look into sharing the cost of a major purchase, then sharing the use of the item equally. Doing this gives you full use of the equipment that you need with only half the cost and half of the repair expense when it breaks down, or even less if you get a third or a fourth friend involved in the purchase. *A tip:* If you do enter into this type of an arrangement, clearly specify between you what the ground rules are for use, who will store it, how the other person can easily access it, and so on. Be a bit flexible and you can wind up saving yourself thousands of dollars.

299. Share Money-Saving Tips with Your Friends

If you discover a clever way to save some money, share it with your friends. Tell them about the great idea you've implemented and how much money it's saved you. Then, when they discover a clever way to save money, they're likely to share this idea with you, which you can then implement to save money as well. Sharing such ideas can be a great way to touch base with friends while at the same time discovering new ideas for reducing your bottom line.

300. Buy in Bulk with Friends

Bulk buying can save you a lot of money, but it's hard to get through all of the material that you purchase before it begins to go bad.

You can solve that problem by arranging bulk purchases with your friends, splitting the cost of the item and the purchase itself. For example, if you can save 20 percent by buying an enormous box of cereal, split the cost with a friend, then divide the box in half (with half remaining in the box and the other half in a container) when you get home. That way, you each have the contents of a normal-sized box of cereal with a 20 percent discount. You can do the same thing with almost any bulk purchase that you both agree on. Visit a warehouse store together and select items as a team.

301. Host an All-Day "Cook Ahead" Party

Eager to try cooking meals in advance but the time investment seems tremendous? Want to take even more advantage of bulk buying of ingredients? Host a "cook ahead" party at your house, where each person brings a huge amount of a few ingredients, then you all work together to assemble a bunch of meals that can be frozen for future easy cooking. Casseroles work really well for this, as do soups and stews. Figure out some recipes, call up some friends, assign some items for each person to get, and have a giant cooking party. It can be social fun while saving you all money on food and time later on, when evenings are busy.

CHEAP TACTIC$ FOR SHOPPING

302. Don't Shop for Entertainment's Sake

One of the biggest social temptations that people face is the idea of shopping for entertainment's sake. Heading out to the mall with friends, credit card in hand, or hitting the golf or electronics shop with your buddy are sure ways to convince yourself to spend extra money. If you don't have a distinct purchase you need to make, don't go to a shopping center. Instead, find another activity to do, one that doesn't constantly encourage you to bust out the plastic for things you don't really need.

303. Discover Craigslist and Freecycle

If you're unfamiliar with these services, get familiar. They're both tremendous ways for you to save money on items. Craigslist (*www.craigslist.com*) is essentially a giant free online classified ad service that often lists items at tremendous discounts or for free if you'll just come and get them. Freecycle (*www.freecycle.com*) is a series of local listings where people list things that they're wanting to get rid of, while others list requests for items that they'd like to receive. Visit these sites, browse the listings, and get a feel for the stuff that's available. You'll likely find some tremendous bargains, as well as a way to get rid of your unwanted stuff and find a happy home for it.

304. Get into Free Customer Programs

If a store you frequent regularly has a free customer rewards or a frequent buyer program, sign up for it. First, before you go to the store, sign up for a free Gmail account (*http://gmail.google.com*) to give yourself a free address with which to collect the e-mails they may send out. Then, sign up for any free programs at any stores you visit. Always list this new e-mail address in the email field. Then, on a regular basis, check that e-mail address and see what offers have been sent to you. Always check it if you're about to head to that store with a specific purchase in mind—you may have an appropriate discount just waiting for you.

305. Try Warehouse Shopping

Another effective way to save money is to try warehouse shopping at one of the many warehouse "members only" clubs, like Costco or Sam's Club. Call your local store and see if you can get a guest pass (some clubs offer these; others do not), then take your old grocery receipt in there with you to compare prices. Compare the prices you regularly pay with the regular prices in the warehouse club—some may be the same, but many may be lower. Depending on your purchasing habits, you can easily save $10 to $20 per shopping trip at a warehouse club, and if that's the case, a membership in such a club will quickly pay for itself.

306. Use the "One Month" Coupon Strategy

The coupon section in your Sunday newspaper can be a treasure trove of savings, but only if you use it effectively. Many items that you see coupons for are in the midst of a promotional campaign that will often include in-store sales as well at a later date, usually a month or so later. So, to maximize the value of these coupons, clip the good ones now and hold onto them for a while. Compare your coupon hoard with the store flyer each week to see if any of them match up, then add that item to your grocery list and take the coupon with you. Doing this as a regular habit can get you many items for mere pennies, particularly if you check the flyers from drugstores (like Walgreen's and CVS) and discount grocery stores for good coupon matches.

307. Use the Internet for More Coupons

Many websites offer coupons as well. Some of the more popular coupon sites, such as Coupons.com (*www.coupons.com*), offer a bevy of coupons for all sorts of products. Go through those sites, looking for coupons for products you already use or coupons that seem to create a tremendous discount on the product, and print them out to add to your coupon hoard. You can also directly visit the website of your favorite stores, as many of them offer in-store coupons to save even more money on specific products.

308. Double Savings with Manufacturer and Store Coupons

If you find a manufacturer coupon and a store coupon for the same item, you're in luck. Almost all stores will honor both coupons, meaning you can often double your savings with little effort. Thus, checking on both manufacturer and store coupons can be incredibly valuable, sometimes netting you free and almost-free items. If you're doing coupon searches online, open up two browser windows, one with a manufacturer coupon site like Coupons.com, and another with the website of your favorite retailer. Compare the coupons on both, and print out any coupons that appear in both forms, as quite often these add up to a free or nearly free item.

309. Wait on Purchases Until Sales Appear

If you're considering a larger purchase, particularly of an item that's not a hot new release, practice a bit of patience before you make your purchase. Shop around and wait for a sale to crop up. For example, if you're considering buying a DVD player, don't just run down to the store and pick one up. Be patient and wait for the DVD players to go on sale. Waiting a month or two won't be the end of the world, particularly if it saves you some cash.

310. Use Store Flyers to Identify Those Sales

The easiest way to find these sales is to hit the store flyers each week. Pick up a Sunday paper (which usually has dozens of store flyers inside) and examine each one for the item you're considering buying. If you don't find the item you're thinking of purchasing, wait until next week. This saves you the effort of searching in multiple stores for a particular item over and over again. Instead, let the sale come to you via the flyers.

311. Use a Price Book for Your Regular Purchases

Most people fall into a routine of buying thirty or so items on a very regular basis, sometimes during every shopping trip. Items like milk, eggs, laundry detergent, toothpaste, and bread are common purchases for most people, and many people often have a preferred choice or two within these items. One way to subtly save yourself money on these regular items is to start a price book, a brilliant tactic made famous by Amy Dacyczyn in her *Tightwad Gazette* newsletter in the 1990s. All you do is make a list of all of those items you buy regularly, then write down the price for that item at each of several different grocery stores in the area. You'll usually get a clear picture of where the discounts are, and it can help you select the cheapest store to shop at by default as well as a tool to compare your shopping list with, because there may be a cheaper store to shop at depending on the exact items you're buying that week.

312. Shop Alone

Unless you're shopping specifically to split purchases with a friend, try to shop alone. The more people you have along on a shopping trip, the easier it is for impulse buys to slip into the cart, as there's many more opportunities for impulsiveness with multiple people than there is with one person. A single person equipped with a planned shopping list has the least chance to slip an impulsive purchase into the cart, so go alone to save some money in the checkout aisle.

313. Set a "Time Goal" When You Walk in the Door

If you're entering a store where you know you're likely to be distracted (like a clothing store, an electronics store, or a bookstore), set a time goal when you need to check out and leave the store. This will reduce the opportunities you have to be distracted by impulsive buys and keep you focused on the items you're intending to purchase. One effective way to do this is to set the alarm clock on your watch or on your phone, so that it beeps loudly, reminding you that it's time to get out of the store and making sure you're not dawdling.

314. Only Buy the Specific Item(s) You're Shopping For

If you go into an electronics store specifically to buy a particular cable for your home entertainment system, don't walk out of the store with anything but that cable. If you go into a bookstore looking for a particular Stephen King novel, don't walk out the door with anything in your hands other than a Stephen King novel. When you enter a store with one or two purchases in mind and walk out with anything more than that, you're falling for the trap of impulse buying, which subtly eats your money and leaves you with nothing but stuff you really didn't need and a big fat bill. If you spy something that you want while in a store, take note of it, but don't buy it. Instead, use tip #7 and see if you even remember the item at all in thirty days. You more likely won't remember anything other than the money you saved that stayed in your pocket.

315. Don't Buy Any Item in the Checkout Aisle

Stores love to load their checkout aisle with impulse buys. Candy that's attractive to both children and adults, magazines aimed at tickling your fancy by shocking and surprising you enough to pick them up and add them to your cart, small overpriced versions of very common purchases such as batteries that you might see and exclaim, "Oh, I forgot, I needed those," and so on. The easiest rule of thumb for protecting your wallet is to not buy anything at all in the checkout. Make it a hard-and-fast rule. Once you head for the checkout, nothing else goes in your cart unless it's on your list. If you see something in the checkout that you remember that you needed (like those aforementioned batteries), don't just grab those. Either head back to the battery area and look at a more well-rounded selection of options or simply add batteries to your list for your next shopping trip.

316. Shop on Your State's Tax-Free Holidays

Many states offer tax-free holidays, where you can buy certain items such as clothing or books without paying sales tax on those items. Not only that, many stores have sales on those days, because they know that people will tend to go out and shop on those days more than on other days. If you have any purchases that you know you need to make, such as clothing purchases, find out if your state has an upcoming tax holiday and hold off on your purchase until then. When the day approaches, find out about sales on the items you're looking at and find the best opportunity to get the items you're looking for with both the benefit of a sale and without the cost of sales tax.

317. Shop Online for Better Price Comparisons

Whenever you're looking to buy any nonperishable item, particularly one that costs more than a few dollars, always do price comparisons online before buying. Utilize the websites of your preferred stores as well as the websites of online retailers and seek out the best price for the item you want. The more expensive the item, the more valuable this comparison shopping can be. You can often save 10 to 15 percent off the purchase price of an item (or even more) with just a few moments of comparison shopping. For just a few minutes' worth of footwork, that can be a very solid return.

318. Don't Store Your Credit Card with an Online Shopping Site

If you get into the routine of buying items online, it's very easy to store your credit card number there, making it incredibly simple to buy things with a click and ship them to your home, no fuss, no muss. The convenience, though, is a clever trap. The quicker you can go from selecting an item to having bought it, the less time you have to actually think about what you're buying and the more likely you are to just go ahead with a completely impulsive and unnecessary purchase. The easiest thing you can do is simply not store your credit card number on a retail website, so that you have to re-enter your number each time you make a purchase. Doing this effectively works like the ten-second rule (tip #6). It makes you pause for a bit and think about what you're actually buying, and that's often enough to make you realize that you're making an impulsive decision. You'll put your credit card away and happily realize that you just made the frugal choice.

319. Don't Buy "Just One More Thing" to Get Free Shipping

Online shopping sites commonly offer free shipping if you spend beyond a certain dollar value, and when you're close to that amount it's often tempting to just find one more item to buy to push yourself over that threshold. Don't. Buying an item just to fill up a slot in your cart means that you're spending more money overall just to get an item you don't really want. Instead, just pick the low-end shipping (since that's what free shipping is) and be glad that you didn't waste $8 on some item you didn't really want just to get "free" shipping. In the end, free shipping isn't really free at all if it makes you spend more money to buy more stuff you don't need.

320. If Prices are Equal, Buy at Your Local Store

If you do a price comparison between online stores and local retail shops and find the prices to be the same, buy at your local retail shop. Why? There's extra value at your local retailer. Salespeople who can answer questions and help with setup, and the store is a place to easily return a faulty product, for starters. In terms of customer service, you get much more value from your local brick-and-mortar retailer than you do from an online service because you can actually communicate face to face with the retailer, tap their knowledge, and take advantage of their return policy and other services they might offer. Buying local puts more value with your product than buying online, so when all else is equal, buy local.

CHEAP TACTIC$ FOR UTILITIES AND BILLS

321. Eliminate Any Monthly Services You Don't Use

Take a look at all of your monthly bills. Are any of those bills going to cover services that you don't use or that you use only once in a while? Ask yourself some hard questions about your services. Do you rarely watch television? If so, why are you paying a cable bill? If you don't use your landline telephone at all, scratch that service. Similarly, if you don't use a cell phone, scratch that. Perhaps you can replace a bill with a cheaper alternative; for example, if you've got both an Internet bill and a landline bill, ditch the land line and use a VOIP (voice-over-Internet protocol) phone service like Skype or Vonage at a cheaper rate.

322. Take a Hard Look at Club Membership Fees and Gym Fees

Are you a member of the local country club or gym? Do you use that service, or is it something that you keep open because you might use it someday? If it's just a "someday" service, take the initiative and cancel the membership, because it's just eating at your money without providing you any benefit in return. If you do change your mind and decide to utilize the service, you can always sign up for the service again, but most likely you'll walk away happy knowing that you're spending significantly less each month on something you didn't really use.

323. Take a Hard Look at Entertainment-Oriented Monthly Bills

Are you subscribed to a DVD rental club? Do you pay for premium movie channels? Are you involved in a book-of-the-month club in the mail? Regular bills for entertainment purposes are great places to look for areas where you can reduce spending. Ask yourself how much you honestly use these services and whether or not the monthly bill you pay is really worth it. Explore alternatives for the same thing. Perhaps you can rent a few videos locally each month for less money, or maybe a trip to the library once a month might sate your reading desire as well as or better than a book-of-the-month club. If you're paying a bill every month just to entertain yourself, ask yourself if there's not a better option available that isn't a constant drain on your budget.

324. Clean Up Your Remaining Bills

After you've eliminated some of your regular bills, look for options to clean up your remaining bills. Go through those bills and look for optional services that you rarely or never use. Don't text message? Eliminate buying text messages for your phone. Don't use Internet access? Eliminate that service. Don't watch channels outside of basic cable? Downgrade your cable or satellite package. Paying an arm and a leg for child care? Look for another provider, or see whether or not you can change your schedule to reduce the number of days you're paying for. Pay for a session at the salon every few weeks? Cut it back to once every other month and get a less maintenance-heavy cut. Simple moves like these cut down your bills, giving you more breathing room each month. Just downgrading some services can move you from treading water to making progress against your debts.

325. If You Go over Your Cell Phone Minutes, Upgrade Your Plan

If you're ever over on your cell phone minutes during a "normal" month (not one with a particularly exceptional event that won't be repeated), call your cell phone provider and upgrade your plan to include more minutes. An overage during a normal month is often a sign that future overages will occur in the coming months as you're beginning to use your cell phone more than you used to. Don't get eaten alive by overage fees. Get a plan that covers your actual cell phone usage and don't sweat it.

326. If You Rack Up "Out of Calling Area" Charges, Upgrade Your Plan

If you begin to rack up regular "out of calling area" charges on your cell phone bill (more than once or twice a year), then it's time to upgrade your cell plan from a small region to a larger one—or perhaps to a nationwide plan. It only takes a few calls outside your calling area each year to eat up the entire difference in the cost of the plans, so if you find yourself beginning to make out-of-area calls on a regular basis, look at another plan. It will save you money over the long haul.

327. Avoid Long-Term Contracts

Many services you sign up for, particularly cell phones, gyms, cable, and satellite radio and television, require that you sign a contract to use the service for some specified length of time. While it might seem like a better deal to sign a long-term contract because of a slightly lower rate, don't. Keep your contract short. This gives you the freedom to cut your relationship with them much earlier if you're not happy with the service or you're not using it regularly enough to justify the expense. Plus, with shorter contracts, you have more freedom to jump to other providers and enjoy very lucrative introductory offers. Long-term contracts are only a good deal if you're very happy with the service that a particular company offers and you know you'll be happy with that company more than with other companies for a long time to come.

328. Ask for Introductory Deals, Even if You're a Regular Customer

Whenever you're shopping around for services from vendors, look at the introductory deals available to new customers, particularly those that also apply to shorter-term contracts. Introductory deals can often save you a bundle. Don't stop there, though. If you discover a new introductory deal offered by a company you're already with, call them and ask for that same introductory deal for yourself. This works best near the end of your contract with them, as the introductory deal can be applied to a renewal of your previous contract. Don't be afraid to ask. The worst they can do is say no, and if they say yes, you save a bundle. Don't know how to find introductory deals? Do some online searching on occasion to see what's out there by searching for the name of the provider and the phrase "introductory offer."

329. Leverage Competing Deals

Similarly, if you're about to sign a new contract or renew an existing one, shop around beforehand for offers from various companies and try to use them for leverage. Bring in an introductory offer or advertised rate from another company and ask your current company to match or beat it. Either they do agree to match the price, which means you save money and get to continue with the service and equipment you already have, or they refuse, which opens the door to you to switch to that better offer. You may have to be upfront about this in order to achieve success. One strong tactic is to ask to talk to a supervisor if you hear an initial refusal to match the offer. Many companies will try very hard to keep you as a customer, so use an opportunity to switch companies as an opportunity to save some money.

330. Ask about Termination Fees

Whenever you're about to sign a contract, make sure you're very clear on the termination fees associated with that contract. Why? There may come a situation, particularly early in the contract, where it's more cost-effective to terminate the contract, pay the termination fee, and move to another contract with another group. Also, know about the situations in which the termination fee doesn't apply, for example, if you move to an area without adequate service for your phone or if they change your contract (which should give you a window of opportunity to terminate the contract). Knowing when you can terminate without a fee can save you a bundle, particularly when it enables you to quickly sign up for an introductory deal elsewhere.

331. If You Receive Large, Irregular Bills, Save for Them Automatically

Many of the regular bills people face don't come on a monthly basis. Tax bills often come annually or semiannually, as do insurance bills. For most people on a tight budget, bills like these are devastating. They force you to buy regular things on credit and then get saddled with finance charges on the credit card as you pay it down. The most effective method to handle bills that come irregularly is to automatically put away a fraction of the cost of that bill every month. Contact your bank and ask if you can set up automatic deposits into a savings account each month. For an annual bill, put away 1⁄12 of the bill amount into a savings account each month (just divide the bill total by 12). For a semiannual bill, put away ⅙ of the bill amount into a savings account each month. If you have your bank do this automatically, you'll barely notice that the money is gone, but when the bill comes due, you'll find you have the money already in a savings account, saving you the pain of having to scrape together the money for the bill. Even better, it will have likely earned a few dollars' worth of interest—an extra bonus for being smart about your bills.

332. Know What Every Fee Is on Every Bill

Take a recent copy of each of your regular bills and go through them all, item by item. Try to figure out what every fee is. If you don't know what the fee is, call the company and ask what it is. Quite often, you're being assessed a fee or two that do not apply to you and your situation, and identifying them now means a few dollars each month that you get to keep in your wallet instead of needlessly sending to a company. Knowledge is money, particularly when it comes to fees.

333. Always Ask for Fees to Be Waived

Even if you know what a fee is, if you're uncertain as to the necessity of a fee you're being charged, whether it is on a monthly bill, in a contract you're about to sign, or in a bank transaction, always ask for that fee to be waived. Your bank statement is usually a place where many useless fees stack up, but many other needless fees crop up on telephone bills, cable bills, energy bills, and so on. If you don't see the purpose of a fee, call and ask it to be waived. If you don't get a clear answer as to why it can't be waived, ask to speak to a supervisor. Getting even one fee waived, particularly a recurring fee, usually pays for the effort put out for several fees.

334. Pay Your Bills on a Weekly Cycle, Not a Monthly One

Move to a cycle of paying your bills every week instead of every month. At the end of a week, collect all of your outstanding bills and pay them all at once. This serves two purposes. First, it allows you to entirely avoid late fees and missed grace periods, which can stack unwanted charges on future bills. Second, if you find yourself a little short during one session of bill payments, you can easily hold the bill until the following week without worrying about whether it will be late and incur more charges. A weekly cycle of bill paying can save you a great deal of money, particularly if you're consistently late with bills and have faced late charges before.

335. If You Know You're Going to Be Late on a Bill, Call Them

If a situation ever arises where you know that you're going to send in a bill late, call the company and describe the situation to them, and ask for the late fee to be waived just this once. Quite often, particularly if you're a long-term customer and have consistently paid your bills on time, they'll gladly waive a late fee if you can get your bill in within a certain number of days past the due date. In a pinch, a simple phone call can often save you a penalty, keeping that money in your pocket right where it belongs.

336. Learn How to Use Online Bill Pay

One of the most effective tools available to you for paying bills is online bill pay. If your bank offers this for your use, take advantage of it, particularly if it's free. Such services are typically very easy to use. You just enter the account information for your bills once, including the address where you send the bill to and your account information, and save it in their system. Then, you basically just fill out your payments electronically on their website, entering the amount you intend to pay and identifying which company you wish to make the payment to. Click your mouse a time or two and the bill is paid immediately. No need to waste a stamp or an envelope on the bill—it's already done. If you pay six bills a month with this method, you can easily save $30 a year just in stamps and envelopes using online bill pay.

337. Schedule Regular Bills to Be Paid Automatically

Another particularly useful feature of online bill pay is the ability to schedule payments. For example, let's say you pay the same fixed amount each month for your mortgage and for your student loans. With online bill pay, you can set up these bills to be paid automatically each month a few days before they're due. Not only does this save you stamps, but it also saves you time and ensures that you won't ever be late on that particular bill, avoiding any nasty late fees that you might incur. Automatic bill payments are easily the smartest and cheapest way to take care of regular bills. Set them up once and you don't have to worry about remembering to pay the bill ever again.

CHEAP TACTIC$ FOR VACATIONS

338. Plan *Far* in Advance

The best time to plan a summer vacation is during the previous summer. Not only do you have plenty of breathing room to figure out exactly what you want to do, but you can often get stellar rates reserving things far in advance as compared to reserving closer to the dates you wish to travel, and it gives you more time to keep your eyes open for good deals along the way. Plus, locking things in stone far in advance gives you much more leeway to get the time off from work and make any other necessary plans you need to make—it not only saves money, but saves you a lot of headaches, too.

339. Do Your Own Travel Planning

Instead of relying on someone else to plan a trip for you, get involved and do the planning yourself. Organize your own transportation, lodging, and tickets to any events you want to attend. With the many online tools available to you, it's easy to find good rates on these options without having to pay the expensive fees that a travel agent might charge you just for a bit of planning convenience. Make a list of what you need on your trip and take care of each category yourself, acting as your own travel agent.

340. Be Flexible When You Plan

If you're planning far in advance, you have lots of flexibility when it comes to the dates and locations that you'll be traveling. The more flexibility you have, the better—find out what all of the restrictions are before you even begin planning by checking on the dates that everyone can get away from their work and other commitments. Don't commit to a specific plan too quickly. Instead, ask around and gather ideas before committing to a specific plan. Tap the social network you built and see whether your friends have any suggestions or valuable resources (like, perhaps, a cabin owned by a friend of a friend) that you can utilize. Look at lots of potential options within your plan and get the whole family involved in the details. Vacation options may open up that you didn't know existed. The more flexible you are about your plans as they come together, the more likely you are to plan a vacation that everyone will thoroughly enjoy while also saving quite a bit of money on the trip.

341. Consider Camping

One often-overlooked option is the idea of camping while traveling, particularly if your mode of transportation is a lengthy car trip. Instead of spending your vacation money on a hotel during your car trip, instead rent a campsite for the night and cut some serious expense out of your trip. You can often spend four nights or more in a tent for the cost of one night in a hotel. Don't want to camp out for your entire vacation? Go ahead and mix the two by spending a few nights camping in one place, then stay in a hotel the rest of the time.

342. Consider All Forms of Transportation, Including Train and Bus

Don't just immediately rule out all options besides flying or driving. It may be much more cost-effective to take a train or a bus to your destination and rent a car when you arrive instead of burning gas and putting wear and tear on your car during the long trip to your destination. Trains and buses can also be a low-cost alternative to airfare, particularly if you're traveling as a family. They may take a bit longer, but the cost savings can be tremendous. Include services such as Greyhound and Amtrak in your travel planning and you may just save your family some significant cash on your vacation.

343. Stay Away from Tourist Traps

While it's tempting to see the "touristy" sites when you visit a place, including all of the famous landmarks and amusement parks, you're much better off if you get away from the tourist traps and instead observe how the locals live. Spend some of your trip hitting the must-see tourist sites, but then get off the beaten path and find some of the undiscovered things on your trip. Get out in the countryside and view the natural beauty of the region you're visiting. Go to some of the smaller cities and towns and enjoy some of the truly local fare. Not only will they make the trip less expensive, but going away from the tourist traps will also give you an interesting and unique vacation that goes far beyond the same old things you find in guide books.

344. Pack Food and Beverages

If you're about to embark on a long car trip, you'll always come out ahead if you pack a cooler full of beverages, snacks, and meals before you leave. Doing this enables you to stop at a park and enjoy an inexpensive meal instead of stopping at a restaurant along the way. It also allows you to dip into the cooler for a cold beverage instead of stopping at a gas station and spending your money on their expensive fare. You can do the same when returning home as well. Stop at a grocery store before you depart and stock up on food and drinks at low prices before you leave. You can even do this while you're there—eat simple meals in your hotel room or at the campground instead of bearing the big expense of dining out. Doing this even part of the time can really reduce the cost of a family vacation.

345. Explore Your Local Area

Instead of spending a lot of money on big, exciting trips, spend some of your vacations exploring your local area. Visit historical and cultural sites that you can reach and fully enjoy over a weekend. Instead of planning one megatrip, you can do three or four of these short trips in a summer and still save significant money. Don't know what to look for? Get a map and draw a circle around your area that includes everything that's two hundred miles away or less. Everything within that circle is worth looking into. Do some Internet searching on these states and counties. You'll be surprised how many interesting things you'll find, even in the most rural areas.

346. For Hotel Rooms, Call the Local Branch and Negotiate

If you're booking hotel rooms, don't just pop onto a website and book a room at a hotel, particularly if you're reserving well in advance. Instead, get the phone number of the hotel you'd like to stay at and call them. Ask to speak to a manager (as you'll likely be unable to negotiate with the person who first answers the phone), ask what their rate is for a hotel room far in advance (providing the dates), then negotiate. Flat-out ask for a lower rate than that, and suggest you'll try a competitor. Managers usually have the flexibility to adjust rates and thus you can often end up with a discount just because you did your footwork. This works particularly well in more rural areas where the hotels rarely fill to capacity. They'll negotiate because they need the business.

347. Do Necessary Currency Conversions Before You Leave

If you're heading to a country that uses a different currency than you, convert some cash long before you head out on your trip. Your bank may provide this service for you for a very low fee or no fee at all, and if that doesn't work, there are usually currency exchanges available in most large towns and cities. Don't ever use currency exchanges at airports, hotels, or tourist information sites. They universally have very high rates. You'll get a far better deal if you do the legwork yourself in advance of your trip.

348. Know the Rules When You Use Your ATM Card When Abroad

Your ATM card is usually the best method you have of getting a good exchange rate when traveling abroad. Call your bank well before you travel and find out about any extra fees you'll be charged for using the card in your country of destination, particularly if you use the card as a credit card. There will probably be some fees involved, but if the fees add up to a significant amount or there are a lot of hoops to jump through, do some shopping around for a checking account at another bank that has better fees and service abroad, then put enough cash in that checking account so that you'll have plenty on your trip. A bit of legwork now can save you a pile of fees and headaches abroad.

349. Plan the Backbone of Your Vacation Around Inexpensive Stuff

Instead of just hitting tourist attraction after tourist attraction, space them out and fill in the gaps in between with more inexpensive activities. Find out about natural attractions and state parks in the area. Are there free museums, zoos, and other such things in the area where you're going? Build up a long list of things to do in the area you're visiting that have little or no cost by reading up on the area and the resources available there, both on the Internet and at the library. A long list of inexpensive activities means that there will surely be a few things that intrigue most of the people on the trip. Use this list as the primary tool for selecting activities on your trip, maximizing the inexpensive stops and minimizing the expensive ones.

350. Avoid Typical Souvenirs

It's easy to just grab the typical souvenirs when you're traveling. A quick stop in a gift shop and you have something ready to go. The only problem is that the typical gift store item is not only overpriced, but it's also not something that would fill your recipient's heart with joy. Instead, take a serious look at the area where you are and get something local that the recipient would particularly enjoy, and that includes you. Skip the gift shop. Instead, get a bottle of the local wine, hot sauce, barbecue sauce, jelly, or another local treat (which will be far cheaper than the typical gift shop item, anyway). Get a few simple postcards and drop them in the mail instead of worrying about some "perfect" souvenir. The real purpose is to show you care, is it not? For yourself, keep a travel journal. Write down your thoughts each day in a little notebook. That little notebook will bring back many more memories than a pile of T-shirts ever will.

351. Use a Digital Camera with a Large Memory Card Instead of Film

Never travel without taking along your digital camera. Invest in a huge memory card and feel free to snap plenty of pictures. If you have a huge memory card, you can snap pictures of anything that looks interesting. Later, you can just toss out the pictures that didn't turn out well and the rest will provide a wonderful record of your memorable trip. It's also another brilliant substitute for expensive souvenirs. Instead of buying everyone back home junk that they really didn't want, spend some time taking pictures of things you think people at home might enjoy, then send them those pictures when you arrive home, or post them on a website to share with everyone.

352. Use the "Peak-End" Rule

One particular trait of human psychology is known as the "peak-end" rule. Our memories of something are defined by the peak of that experience and also the end of that experience. In other words, when you think back to your vacation in a year or two, you'll likely just remember the best thing you did and the very last thing you did, along with a few other scattered bits. So, when you plan your vacation, instead of jamming each day with amazing things, just plan one peak experience, the real centerpiece of your trip, and one great experience near the end of the trip, perhaps on the next-to-last or last day. Fill the rest of the trip with inexpensive options and also relaxation, and you will create an incredibly memorable vacation without shelling out the cash for nonstop and exhausting memorable activities.

353. Align Vacation Trips with Visiting Family and Friends

When you're traveling, particularly on a long road or train trip, devise a plan that enables you to stop and see family and friends on the long legs of the trip. Not only will this usually amount to a free night's sleep while traveling, but it's also a perfect opportunity to touch base with people you may not get to see very often. It's often worth it to plan your travel in an unorthodox way just to make it to visit family and friends. The opportunity to catch up is personally worth it and the free night of sleep makes it financially worth it.

354. Don't Overload a Vacation with Scheduled Activities

When you're planning a trip, it's often tempting to pencil in tons of things to do on various days because there's so much you'd like to see. This often results in expensive tickets purchased in advance, lots of pressure to stay on schedule when you arrive, and a sense of wistfulness when you see things you wish you had time to explore, but don't. Instead of planning tons of activities in advance, just plan one or two and leave the rest of the trip entirely open, so that if you're out and about and stumble upon something interesting to explore, you can just detour at your own desire. Not only is this a less expensive method for planning a trip (as exploration and discovering new things is often the cheapest part of a trip), it's also much less stressful and more fun. Don't make a tight schedule, instead, just bring along a big list of inexpensive ideas that can fit in anywhere.

355. Vacation with Others

If you're still worried about vacation costs, plan a vacation trip with another family, so that many of the costs for various activities can be split. Thinking of renting a cabin somewhere? Invite another family to come along and split the cost. You can also split the cost of car rentals, boat rentals, and other expenses that might come up during a trip, plus a well-chosen traveling companion can increase the enjoyment factor of a vacation.

TEN TACTIC$ FOR STAYING CHEAP

356. Figure Out Exactly What You Saved

Whenever you use a tactic in this book to reduce your expenses, it's worthwhile to figure out exactly how much you're saving by using this tactic, as it can directly affect your budgeting for the month. Eliminated your coffee addiction? Figure up how much you used to spend on coffee. Dropped a subscription service? How much did it save you this month? If you have a good grip on your spending and know where your money is going, each frugal tactic you use will free up some amount of money that you can use for something else. Perhaps you can add it to your debt snowball if it's a recurring savings, or you can snowflake it if it's a one-time savings. The real benefit, though, is psychological. By figuring up how much you've saved by making a good choice, you'll directly translate your action into real dollars and cents, something that you can tell others about and something that you can be personally proud of.

357. Automatically Sock Away That Savings

Many people wonder what to do with their careful planning once their debts are paid off. The next step in living a life of financial freedom is not to start spending that money, but instead to start saving it. When you've paid off your mortgage, don't start spending that money; instead, start automatically saving that mortgage payment, or dabble your toes in investing. Eventually, that money will build up into something that can enable you to change your life. Maybe you've always dreamed of going back to school or trying another career. Perhaps the next time you buy a car, you can just pay cash for it instead of taking on a car loan. If you stick to your money-saving principles and sock away that money instead of spending it, you'll eventually have personal choices that you never dreamed of.

358. Handle a Raise Intelligently

When you get a raise at work, it may be tempting to celebrate and to use that money as a personal reward to buy something nice for yourself. Instead, think about the times where you were barely making ends meet and were scared of facing the next bill. Instead of using that raise to buy more stuff that you were happy not having before, use that extra money to get rid of your debt a little bit faster or to save for a big purchase, like an appliance or an automobile. Don't be tempted to spend more just because of a little bump in your income.

359. Handle a Windfall Intelligently, Too

What about a big bonus check or a nice inheritance? Surely, that's something you can use to live the high life, right? Think of it this way: A windfall is an opportunity to undo the mistakes of your past, not repeat them. When you receive a windfall, put it in the bank immediately. Buy a certificate of deposit at your local bank with the entire amount so you can't touch it. Then think carefully about what you can do with it. While it might be tempting to think about all of the fun you could have with the money, in the end you'll just be right back where you are right now, with the same problems and the same worries. Instead, consider using that windfall to eliminate any debt you might have, or sock it away in an investment somewhere for your children's education or for your own retirement. Sure, you might not get to have that fun you're imagining, but you'll no longer worry about that debt you've built up. Maybe you won't have to worry about how you'll pay for college for your kids, or how on earth you'll ever be able to retire and enjoy life. Instead of just spending it wildly, put that windfall to work for you.

360. Find Frugal Friends

It's hard to live cheap when you're constantly encouraged by your friends to spend money. How can you save money, after all, if your friends are constantly heading out to the mall? One way is to simply look for new friends who share your other interests. Try some of the socializing tips to find people who share your values. Look particularly for activities that might attract frugal people, like the film club and the book club at the library or at a volunteer project. Get to know people and suggest frugal social opportunities with them to build a friendship. It's a lot easier to be cheap if you have friends who share the same philosophy; you can constantly help each other and motivate each other to make good financial choices.

361. Think about Why You Want Something

We all have idle desires. We think about the things that we wish we had and we're often tempted to make choices to allow us to have these desires. Instead of just thinking about how much you want something, ask yourself why you want it. Did you see an interesting advertisement? Is that advertisement realistic? Maybe you saw someone else enjoying whatever it is you're thinking about. That person might be having fun, but would you really enjoy it? Use this tactic every time you start thinking about something you want, and you'll be surprised how often that idle desire is actually working to convince you to buy something you don't really need or even want when you think about it rationally.

362. Remember That Time Is Money

One of the most common complaints about living cheap is that many money-saving tactics also can eat up a bit of time. If you're wondering how you'll ever be able to live without paying for convenience (like when eating out instead of making food at home), look for ways to save time in your own life and tackle them as fervently as you tackle ways to save money. There are countless tactics for saving time: Cut down on your television viewing, reduce the number of activities you're involved with (particularly ones that eat into your personal expenses, too), and keep a sharp eye on your personal energy level.

363. Keep Trying New Cheap Tactics

Just because you're turning your financial life around doesn't mean that there's no longer anything useful you can learn about living cheap. Look online at various websites that offer frugal living tips and other good financial advice, particularly those that engage you in conversation (you can start by visiting my own site, The Simple Dollar, at *www.thesimpledollar.com*). Visit the library and check out books on frugal topics. Most important of all, actually try out the ideas you learn. You might find that the most surprising things work well for you.

364. Share Your Experiences and Frugal Tips

While it's great to find new frugal tips, it's also useful to share them as well. Talk to your friends and swap frugal ideas. Search online for frugal message boards and blogs to share your ideas. Perhaps you could even start your own blog to share frugal tactics. You can get a free one at *www.blogspot.com* or *www.wordpress.com*. Putting your frugal ideas out there not only helps inspire and motivate others to be frugal, but it often inspires others to share their own frugal tactics—a win-win situation, indeed.

365. Have Fun

This is the most important thing of all. Have fun in whatever you choose to do, and realize that living cheap can often be incredibly enjoyable. You'll never know how much fun frugality might be until you dip your toes in and give it a shot, so flip through this book, find a tactic or two, and get started today. Not only will you discover something new to do, but you'll also save money, and that will likely help relieve some of the stress you feel about money. What could be more fun than that?

ADDITIONAL RESOURCES

For more information on these tips, additional money-saving tactics, and suggestions for additional reading, please visit this book's free companion website at:

WWW.THESIMPLEDOLLAR.COM/365

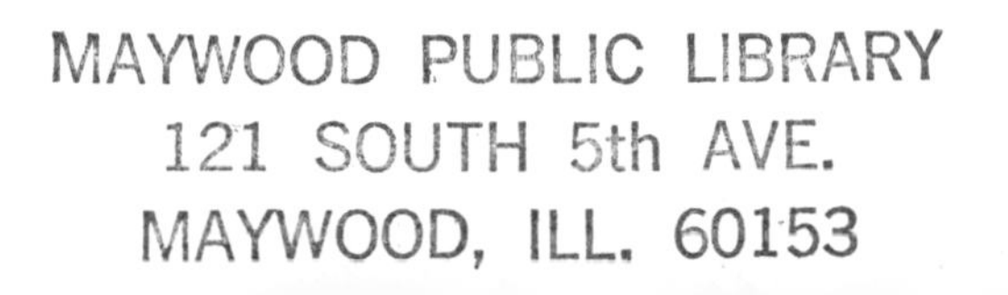

· S H O T S ·
in the Streets

· S H O T S ·
in the Streets

Violence and Religion in South Africa

David Chidester

Beacon Press • Boston

Beacon Press
25 Beacon Street
Boston, Massachusetts 02108-2892

Beacon Press books
are published under the auspices of
the Unitarian Universalist Association
of Congregations.

Printed in the United States of America

98 97 96 95 94 93 92 91 8 7 6 5 4 3 2 1

Text design by David Ford

Library of Congress Cataloging-in-Publication Data

Chidester, David.
Shots in the streets: violence and religion in
South Africa / David Chidester.
p. cm.
Includes bibliographical references and index.
ISBN 0-8070-0218-6 (cloth)
1. Violence—South Africa. 2. Violence—
Religious aspects.
I. Title.
HN801.Z9V53 1991
303.6′0968—dc20 91-12834
CIP

For Careena

Contents

Preface

ON 2 FEBRUARY 1990, South African State President F. W. de Klerk announced in Parliament that "the season of violence is over." This book is about the cycling, spiraling, persisting seasons of violence in South Africa. President De Klerk promised that political life in the country would be normalized. Political organizations were unbanned, prisoners freed, and a "New South Africa" waited to be born. In the meantime, however, South Africa remained a violent place. A "culture of violence" permeated the society. Violence had been normalized in political, social, and economic relations of power. South Africa seemed to be a model for the definition of politics provided by the sociologist C. Wright Mills: "All politics is a struggle for power; the ultimate kind of power is violence."[1]

While President De Klerk called for peaceful negotiations to bring an end to the violence of apartheid, other negotiations over power, violent negotiations, continued to be conducted in South Africa. Both domination and resistance were forcefully negotiated with weapons. They were also negotiated with religious symbols. This book examines the role of religion in the violent contests over meaning and power that have been conducted in South Africa. I focus on the recent, ancient history of the 1980s, a time of particularly intense conflict in South Africa. With the promise of a "New South Africa," the violence of that decade must not be forgotten.

It has been said that conquerors tell the history. The history of South Africa has been told by Afrikaner nationalist historians and public school textbooks as a triumphalist saga of white conquest in Africa. The story of white conquest began with the Dutch occupation of the Cape from 1652 to 1795. It continued under British rule during the nineteenth century. The emigrations of Dutch-speaking farmers into the interior starting in the 1830s, the formation of four white settler colonies, and the military subjection of African chiefdoms completed the military conquest. The discovery of diamonds in 1867 and gold in 1886 started a mineral revolution that enabled an economic conquest of the region. But diamonds and gold also brought conflict between Boers and Britains over control of that wealth, resulting in the Anglo-Boer War (1899–1902). The twentieth-century conquest of South Africa was fulfilled in the 1910 Union of South Africa, the 1948 victory of the National Party under the slogan of apartheid, and the social engineering of a country to enforce racial separation and white domination.

Like any nationalist history, however, this "progress" has been a project of selective memory, strategic forgetting, and self-interested interpretation. During the 1960s and 1970s, liberal historians in South Africa tried to recover what the nationalists had erased. They wrote instead a history of multiracial, multicultural, intergroup relations, recalling moments of both conflict and cooperation. But something was also missing in this liberal retelling—the influence of the rise of capitalism on the lives of South Africa's people. Thus, more recently, radical or revisionist historians have brought into their interpretation of the conquest of South Africa the economic incorporation of precapitalist societies into new commercial relations in the nineteenth century and the rise of industrial capitalism during the twentieth—a story of capital accumulation and labor extraction and exploitation.[2] In all these versions, South Africa's history is a history of violence. In this book, I have tried to recover some of the many, multiplying forms of violence that have appeared in the recent, ancient history of South Africa. Even if the seasons of violence should prove to be over, we would still need to find ways to remember and make some sense out of the violence of that past.

What is violence? Although we might think we know violence when we see it, the concept of violence is notoriously resistant to definition. In simplest terms, violence has been defined as harm to persons or property.[3] But the terms become less simple when we ask, "What counts as harm?" Particularly in cases of violence against persons, we need some standard—of human wholeness, or human integrity, or human dignity, or human rights—against which harm can be measured. That concern has given rise to a second definition of violence: violence is the violation of humanity. In this definition, violence harms because it violates, denies, or exploits human beings. Anything that violates humanity counts as violence. Defined as relational, structural, or institutional violations of humanity, however, violence becomes nothing more nor less than social injustice.[4]

Returning to a notion of violence as direct physical harm, a third definition makes a distinction between legitimate force and illegitimate violence. The American philosopher John Dewey, for example, argued that legitimate force is required to build bridges and maintain law and order. Violence, however, is force gone wrong. It is the force that blows up bridges, breaks laws, or defies public order. In other words, in this third definition, violence is always illegitimate. Unfortunately, this distinction between force and violence is easily employed by any state, including the South African state, to call its own violence "legitimate force" and the force of its opponents, "violence."[5] A fourth definition therefore defines violence as direct physical harm but insists that any act of violence must be immediately evaluated in terms of the ethical ends that it serves. In this fourth definition, the ends justify the means. In some cases, however, particularly in the colonial situation, theorists of violence have even claimed that violence can be a potentially liberating means in and of itself for recovering humanity from oppression. Here Frantz Fanon was certainly the greatest exponent of a revolutionary violence that promised to be a liberating, purifying, and humanizing force for the "wretched of the earth."[6]

Therefore, I start not with a single definition of violence but with four definitions: direct physical harm, the violation of humanity, illegitimate force, or legitimate liberation. These definitions can be taken beyond the realm of academic debate when we look at an incident that took place on the streets of Cape Town in early 1990. In January, a progressive organization of teachers and parents planned a peaceful protest march through the city to call attention to the dismal state of black education in South Africa. As teachers, parents, and students assembled, the police arrived and cordoned off the area with barbed wire. The marchers walked toward the wire. From an armored vehicle, the police turned their water cannon on the marchers. As people began running in every direction, police chased them, beating them with leather whips and shooting them with rubber bullets. At some point, a student running with other students through the downtown shopping area of Cape Town apparently shouted, "The windows!" Using bricks from a nearby construction site, the students broke shop windows and damaged cars as they ran through the streets. After about an hour, calm returned to the city of Cape Town.

The next day, a debate raged over the violence in the city. The local press interviewed people involved. As might be imagined, not everyone agreed on what had counted as violence in the day's events. First, a spokesman for the city council of Cape Town complained about the violent harm to property caused by rampaging students. The city council recognized that protesters had been provoked by the police but insisted on defining the violence as direct physical harm to property. Second, organizers of the protest march identified the violence of the day's events as the violation of the fundamental human and civil right to peaceful assembly and protest. That violation of rights was symptomatic of the more general structural violence of social injustice enforced by the South African state. As an extension of the state, the police committed violence by enforcing that fundamental violation of human rights even before they used their water cannons, guns, and whips. Third, for their part, the police claimed that they had merely exercised legitimate force to prevent protesters from violating laws that prohibited illegal gatherings. According to the police, the violence in the day's events was the illegitimate, forceful breaking of laws that they were charged to uphold with legitimate force.

Finally, unfortunately, no journalists interviewed any of the students who had damaged property as they ran from the police through the streets of Cape Town. We can only guess how they might have defined the violence of that day. If they acknowledged their destruction of property as violence, we might suppose they found that violence justified, or legitimate, or even liberating. We will never know. What we do know is that the definition of violence that day on the streets of Cape Town was relational, situational, and contested. Again, we are not left with a stable, simple definition of violence. Rather, we have power relations and confrontational situations in which fundamental interests are contested. At stake in these violent contests, I would suggest, is something as fundamental as what it means to be a human being.

The question of what it means to be a human being brings us immediately, directly, to religion. Religion might be described as ways of experimenting in being human. Through symbols, myths, rituals, and traditions, religion has generated a variety of ways of negotiating the meaning and power of a human world. But as we will see, religion has also been implicated in violent forces of dehumanization. Inherently ambiguous, religion has been interwoven with both affirmations and denials of humanity. The Christian religion has been particularly problematical in South Africa, operating as it has to justify domination and oppression, but also to mobilize people in struggles for liberation. That ambiguity reflects something important and fundamental about the way religion works in the world. Like violence, religion is relational, situational, and contested.

Part of my intention in this book is to explore this fundamental ambivalence in relations between religion and violence. But I will also be asking readers to think about religion in new, unexpected ways. Religion's symbols, myths, rituals, and traditions are not only found in the kinds of conventional religious institutions associated with the church, mosque, temple, or synagogue. Religion is a dimension of human experience that permeates networks of social relations. In this sense, religion can be found not only in the churches, but also in the classroom, the workplace, the courtroom, the prisons, the battlefield, the political arena, and perhaps most important for my purposes, even on the streets, as a meaningful, powerful dimension of human life. In those arenas, contests over religious meaning and power have been conducted.

As a way of reopening an understanding of religion, I have used the word "negotiation" in a specific, somewhat unusual way throughout this book. A religion, or a religious worldview, I will argue, is not a "thing," but a complex process of symbolic negotiation. Although "negotiation" has usually been used to refer to what officials do when they meet to agree on the terms and conditions of a treaty, or what people in business do in working out the terms and conditions of a contract, I will use the word to refer to the ways in which religious worldviews are worked out in the world. Like politics and business, religion is a negotiated reality. Through discourse, practice, and social relations, human beings continuously negotiate and renegotiate the meaningful contours and powerful relations of their worlds. If religious worlds are negotiated, then we cannot assume that religious meaning or power is simply "given" in the world. Meaning is not something waiting to be "discovered." Power is not something waiting to be "acquired." Both meaning and power, I suggest, are always emerging, changing, and "at stake" in the strategic, contested processes of religious negotiation. Sometimes negotiations over meaning and power are peaceful. Sometimes they are not. I will be paying attention to the violent negotiations that have been conducted in South Africa.

The chapters of this book follow a logic—perhaps what a reviewer of an earlier book of mine called "a certain kind of loony logic"—in raising questions about the relations between religion and violence. In simplest outline, I am concerned with three basic exercises of religious violence in South Africa—ritual killing, dehumanization, and the spiritual politics of armed religion.

Chapter 1 defines the concept of worldview that I use in this book and examines the religious motivations behind the violent acts of the self-proclaimed "White Wolf" Barend Hendrik Strydom, who randomly shot black people on the streets of Pretoria in November 1988. Justifying himself as a Christian and an Afrikaner nationalist, Barend Strydom tried to renegotiate the meaning and power of his worldview through violence. Arguably, it was already a violent worldview, not unlike that constructed and enforced in South Africa as apartheid. In the first chapter, therefore, I explore the religious underpinnings of the apartheid system of racist separation and domination. In particular, I look at the role of ritual killing as a sacrificial offering to a nationalist God. As an offering, ritual killing has been a form of violence especially linked with claims on superhuman power.

Chapter 2 examines the religious negotiations at stake when residents of the black township of Paballelo killed a municipal policeman in November 1985. While Barend Strydom's violent act can be understood as a sacrificial offering, this killing can be interpreted as a ritual killing that renegotiated the purity of a community by eliminating a surrogate victim. Here the work of René Girard on sacrifice, ritual killing, and scapegoating makes sense of the collective selection and elimination of victims. I also apply this line of analysis to the practice of capital punishment and other violent public systems of law and order in South Africa. Like mob violence, these public systems involve the ritual elimination of surrogate victims in an attempt to renegotiate the purity of society and the power of the state. Among other things, this chapter shows how a sacred order is defined not only by what it includes but by what it absolutely excludes. In this sense, ritual killing is a particularly violent ritual of exclusion for renegotiating a symbolic order.

Chapter 3 concludes the exploration of ritual killing by placing it within the context of symbolisms of evil. As a symbolism of evil in traditional African religion, witchcraft beliefs and practices have located violence as a superhuman, disruptive, defiling force in human social relations. This chapter examines two types of ritual killing associated with traditional African religion: the execution of alleged witches and the sacrifice of humans for "strong medicine" of power. The execution of witches is a ritual of elimination; the killing of human beings in order to acquire power can be regarded as a ritual of incorporation. Both, however, can be interpreted as strategies for negotiating within symbolic orders of purity and power. Similarly, the South African government has experienced its own threats to purity and power, its own "inner demons," perceived as the dangers represented by satanism, communism, or revolutionary onslaught. Chapter 3 explores the importance of the symbolism of evil for locating violence in dangers to and defenses of a sacred order.

Chapter 4 considers violence defined as the violation of humanity, locating violence in anything that dehumanizes, subclassifies, alienates, or exploits, thereby relegating persons to a subhuman status. To explore that definition of violence, I propose a tour through two modern versions of hell—the mines and the prisons. Referring to the work of Orlando Patterson on slavery and social death, I argue that black mineworkers in South Africa have endured the violent domination, dehumanization, and alienation that Patterson has identified as the defining characteristics of slavery. Living and working in a type of social death in South Africa's underworld, mineworkers have also advanced visions of freedom from bondage, strategies for recovering humanity from extreme conditions of dehumanization. In this analysis, torture can be seen as a state ritual practiced in the depths of a secret and officially denied underworld. This chapter imaginatively enters the underworlds of the mines and the prisons in order to see what might be revealed there about the truth of power in South Africa, a truth revealed at the intersection between the power of the mining industry, the state, and the power of the singular, living, suffering human body. Mines and prisons bring into focus crucial issues of superhuman power and dehumanization, but they ultimately clarify what it means to be human. Chapter 4, therefore, explores not only violent dehumanization in the underworlds of the mines and the prisons, but also the possible redefinitions of humanity that might emerge from those regions of social death in South Africa.

Shifting to the spiritual politics of armed conflict in South Africa, chapter 5 examines the religious worldview of the South African Defence Force. Although drawing considerable legitimation from more conventional Christian sources, the SADF has constructed a religious worldview of its own, a kind of armed religion, that has animated its exercise of military force in the region. This chapter explores the dimensions of that worldview with particular attention to the importance of sacred space. On the borders, in the townships, the South African military has been involved in violent negotiations over a world and a worldview. The symbolic and religious dynamics of those negotiations can be measured by the emergence in the 1980s of organized, articulate conscientious objection to military service in South Africa. In the face of this religious opposition, the South African Defence Force persisted in its armed religion all along the fluid, contested, and always potently symbolic battlelines of the region.

On the other side of those lines, chapter 6 examines the religious worldview of the African National Congress and its military wing, Umkhonto we Sizwe. In the 1980s, proclaimed by the ANC as the "Decade of Liberation," armed struggle against the South African regime was animated by worldview negotiations, particularly by symbolic negotiations in the idiom of sacred time. The ANC was engaged in armed symbolic contests over a mythic past, a revolutionary present, and a liberated future in a new, unified, nonracial, and democratic South Africa. Those negotiations were conducted not only in relation to the prevailing regime, but also in relation to other black political movements. Thus, while the military wing of the Pan Africanist Congress, known as Poqo, had distinguished itself in the early 1960s for deploying violence as a strategy of sudden, apocalyptic redemption of the people and their land, and while the Zulu nation alist movement, Inkatha, was widely perceived in the 1980s to be building up an ethnic, royal, and religious nationalism through violence and coercion, the ANC gathered considerable international support for what was seen as its reluctant use of force to achieve the legitimate end of destroying apartheid. This rational justification of means and ends, however, was also embedded in worldview negotiations over sacred meaning and power that assumed the dimensions of an armed religion. Chapter 6 outlines the spiritual politics of that armed religion in the discourse and practice of the African National Congress.

Finally, chapter 7 concludes this book with some general observations about the violent contests that characterize South African religion, society, and politics. As South Africa has entered the 1990s, symbolic negotiations—nonviolent as well as violent—continue to be conducted. Although President De Klerk has proclaimed an end to the season of violence, violence remains implicated in the strategic negotiation of worldviews in South Africa. As a historian of religion, I have tried to work out a redescription—a disciplined, interpretive analysis—of religion and violence that might contribute to our understanding of the seasons of violence in South Africa. In the end, however, if we are not merely to understand, but to change, much more than this remains to be done.

Obviously, South Africa has not been the only violent place on earth during the 1980s. Interminable conflicts have rent other regions, most notably Northern Ireland and Israel, where religion has played a significant role in violence. In offering explanations for the role of religion, analysts have tended to assume that it has operated as a disguise for more basic struggles over economic resources or national identity. But wealth, national identity, and political power, as we will see in this examination of religion and violence in South Africa, are inevitably contested in potently symbolic terms. Appearing in and through highly charged and contested symbols, myths, rituals, and traditions, religion has been more than a social institution in these conflicts; it has been a significant, powerful dimension of the battlefield upon which these conflicts have been fought. As a dimension of human action, rather than a particular social institution, religion has been directly implicated in violence all over the world. It is in these terms, therefore, that I propose a reopening of our understanding of religion, the better to understand the implication of religious discourses and practices in violent conflict, wherever conflict might arise, whether in South Africa, Northern Ireland, Israel, or even in a place like the United States of America.[7]

I arrived in South Africa from America in July 1984. Two months later, the country entered into a period of intensified, widespread violence, variously described as a time of "unrest," of "general uprising," of "total onslaught," or of "civil war," depending upon the political vantage point of the analyst. Unavoidably, living and working as a student of religion in such a "culture of violence," I was compelled to attend to linkages between religion, politics, and violence in ways that I probably would not have if I had remained in America. I cannot say that I brought with me what South African anthropologist Monica Wilson once called the "sharpness of a stranger's vision," but, as a displaced academic stranger, I have tried to pay attention and learn. This book is a product of my South African education. During seven years in the Department of Religious Studies, University of Cape Town, my colleagues have taught me much, even when they did not know I was learning anything from them. In gratitude, I acknowledge John Cumpsty, John de Gruchy, Jan Hofmeyr, Tom Leeuw, Welile Mazamisa, James McNamara, Gordon Mitchell, Ebrahim Moosa, Itumeleng Mosala, Gabriel Setiloane, Abdulkader Tayob, Charles Villa-Vicencio, and Charles Wanamaker, each of whom, in one way or another, has contributed to making this book possible. Thanks also to Darrel Wratten for his valuable editorial and research assistance. In addition to departmental colleagues, I especially acknowledge Martin Prozesky, Professor of Religious Studies, University of Natal, for his friendship, support, and critical conversation. Outside the discipline of religious studies, I thank historian Greg Cuthbertson and anthropologist Martin West for their critical readings of earlier drafts.

In America, I express my special appreciation to Ninian Smart of the University of California, Santa Barbara, and to Edward Tabor Linenthal of the University of Wisconsin, Oshkosh, for their friendship and ongoing support. Professor Linenthal, in particular, made this a better book by forcing me to give eleven lectures in seven days all over Wisconsin, lectures that had to make sense out of material in this book for diverse American audiences. At Beacon Press, senior editor Lauren Bryant improved this book, among other ways, by convincing me that less is more. As always, I must mention the invaluable support of the steadily expanding, increasingly international Board of Directors. Finally, to my wife Careen, I pay the highest tribute for the love and humor she demonstrated while together we lived through this book.

David Chidester
Cape Town 1991

CHAPTER I

White Wolves

•

I WANT TO enter the worldview of apartheid by considering an extreme act of racist violence that occurred in Pretoria in November 1988, performed by a twenty-one-year-old former policeman by the name of Barend Hendrik Strydom. Strydom claimed to be a member of a militant, underground, right-wing, Afrikaner nationalist, white-supremacist group called the White Wolves. Possibly, he was the only member. After Strydom committed his public act of violence, however, other right-wing activists adopted the name of White Wolves. In 1988, right wing, Afrikaner nationalist groups seemed to be proliferating in South Africa. Militant right-wing Afrikaner nationalists and white supremacists were demanding an all-white republic. They were threatening to fight for it. They were ready to kill and die for it. Strydom introduced a new twist into this militant rhetoric, however. He killed people. On 15 November 1988, Barend Hendrik Strydom loaded up a 9mm automatic pistol, put on a police uniform, and walked through the streets of Pretoria randomly shooting people. Barend Strydom was white; his victims were black. He was apprehended by an unemployed black taxi driver while stopping to reload.

Barend Strydom was charged with eight counts of murder, sixteen counts of attempted murder, and a charge that seemed absurd compared to the magnitude of his other crimes, one count of pointing a firearm. He stood trial in May 1989. First, the court had to decide on Barend Strydom's sanity. The state's expert witness concluded: "I cannot say he is completely normal and I cannot say he is completely abnormal." Therefore, Strydom was classified on the borderline between sanity and insanity. Second, the court had to decide on a verdict. Strydom was found guilty on all charges. Finally, the court had to decide on sentencing. Given the opportunity to testify in mitigation of his sentence, Barend Strydom argued before the court that his sanity or insanity, guilt or innocence, could only be decided on religious grounds. "From a Christian point of view," he informed the court, "the killings were justified." Although Strydom's acts were extremely and obviously violent, his justifications for killing were drawn from a religious worldview that had been fundamental to the justification of apartheid. The religious worldview of Barend Hendrik Strydom thus bears closer examination for what it might reveal about the religion, racism, and violence of apartheid.[1]

There have been many attempts to identify the worldview underlying the system of racial order, classification, separation, domination, and exploitation in South Africa that came to be known as apartheid. Many candidates have been proposed in efforts to define what animated Afrikaner nationalists in carrying out the apartheid project. Was it Calvinism? Was it civil religion? Was it an ideological class alliance for economic power and advancement through a *volkskapitalisme*? Was it the awakening, the mobilization, or the invention of an ethnic nationalism? Was it a political mythology? Or was it simply, bluntly, nothing more nor less than racism? As Jacques Derrida has suggested, apartheid is racism's last word, "the unique appellation for the ultimate racism in the world, the last of many. . . . the most racist of racisms."[2] Perhaps apartheid has been at one time or another all these things and more. But I hope to make some different suggestions about how we might understand the worldview of apartheid and the implications of that worldview for racism and violence.

We must first notice the particular, peculiar way in which apartheid itself has been named. In doing this, I do not merely want to recall that racial separation in South Africa has been disguised under many names: "separate development," "cultural autonomy," "self-determination," "multinational cooperation," or even the "good neighborliness" that under apartheid has required the building of very strong fences. Instead, I want to point to two important features of the way in which apartheid has been named in the English language. First,

English-speakers have persistently, stubbornly insisted on retaining the Afrikaans term, apartheid, instead of translating it as English "apartness" or "separation." The term thus sticks out as an unfamiliar, and even unpronounceable, word in the English language. Since apartheid does not belong in their language, English-speakers can assume that apartheid designates something that does not belong to them because it is unique to white, Afrikaans-speakers in South Africa.

Second, I think that apartheid has defeated this attempt at distancing by becoming an international, generic term for racism. If we are to use apartheid as a generic term, however, we must recognize that it does not merely define personal prejudice or bigotry. Apartheid designates a racism that is enforced by legalized coercion and maintained by military power. Apartheid is therefore a generic term for institutionalized racism. I propose, however, that we can go even further in using apartheid as a generic term. Apartheid, I suggest, is the name for any power that is based on domination and exploitation, any purity based on separation and exclusion. Beyond personal or even institutionalized racism, apartheid in South Africa has been woven out of inherently violent dreams of purity and claims to power.

Attempts to explain the worldview of apartheid have been frustrated by apartheid's own definition of worldviews. The apartheid approach to the study of worldviews looks something like this: There are many peoples in the world; each people has its own language, its own culture, and its own worldview; each worldview can be named and described as the separate, bounded, and coherent mental universe of a particular and separate group of people. The discourse of apartheid is perpetuated in any study of worldviews that defines "worldview" as the constant, shared mental framework of a particular group of people or a particular culture. Both "people" and "culture," it must be remembered, have operated as synonyms for race in apartheid discourse.[3]

Allow me some sweeping claims and indictments: In the nineteenth century, the study of worldviews served the imperial project. An imperialist study could discover that Africans had a static worldview, Indians had a passive one, Chinese an inscrutable one, Arabs an irrational one, but Europeans had a rational, dynamic, and expansive one. Not only false and racist, the imperial project created the very subjects that it studied in the interest of subjecting large populations to imperial or colonial domination. In the twentieth century, any study that describes worldviews as if they were "things" that belong to distinct groups of people, or distinct cultures, or even distinct religions, serves the apartheid project of separation, exclusion, and domination. No matter how well intentioned, any reification of worldviews perpetuates the discourse and practice of apartheid in the world.

A postimperial and postapartheid study of worldviews must therefore begin by resisting the reification of the many languages, peoples, cultures, and religions upon which the ideologies of imperialism and apartheid have both depended. Toward this end, I propose the following as a working definition of worldview: A worldview is an open set of discursive, practical, and social strategies for negotiating person and place in a world.[4]

I want to comment very briefly on some of the aspects of this definition. First, "strategies for negotiating person" refers to the process of classifying persons that is inherent in any worldview. Some persons are classified as being "like us." They count as human. Some are "not like us," however, because they are classified as either superhuman or subhuman. A worldview is in this way an ongoing experiment in being human. But that human identity is negotiated by factoring out superhuman persons, perhaps to be worshiped, and subhuman persons to be dominated, excluded, or eliminated. The subhuman classification might be applied to animals, vegetables, and minerals. But it can just as easily designate any persons who are excluded from the universe of morally protected entities to the extent that they are not treated with the mutual recognition or reciprocal regard owed to those classified as human. As we will see, subclassification inevitably leads to violence. But the subclassification of persons is already a violent act in the strategic negotiation of any worldview.

Second, "strategies for negotiating place" refers to processes of orientation in time and space that are also inherent in any worldview. These processes constitute a struggle against what the historian of religions Mircea Eliade once called "the vertigo brought on by disorientation." As we will see, strategies for negotiating a place inevitably get tangled up in dreams of purity and claims to power. Purity and power are not simply given in the world; they must be constantly negotiated and renegotiated through the strategic placement and displacement of persons. Strategies that negotiate place are often inherently violent, especially when they are deployed to uphold a purity based on exclusion and a power based on domination.

Finally, my use of the term "negotiation" indicates that the terms and conditions of any worldview are always emerging, changing, and contested in relations with other persons. Worldviews emerge through human interactions and transactions. They change under the pressures of historical situation and social circumstance. Their basic elements—person and place—are fought over by competing interest groups. Through speech, action, and social interaction, a worldview is negotiated. By directing attention to strategies of negotiation, I propose an understanding of "worldview," not as a fixed set of ideas, or a "view" of the world, but as a dynamic, multidimensional process, an open and ongoing work of creating and maintaining a world. The worlds constructed, deconstructed, and reconstructed through worldview negotiations are obviously plural. The plurality of worlds does not only result from people living in many different "life worlds." Human worlds are plural because plurality is inherent in symbolic negotiation. Relational and contested, the symbols, myths, rituals, and traditions at stake in worldview negotiations are always in flux because they are constantly being appropriated, owned, and operated by different actors. In this symbolic activity, worlds may rise and fall, but worldview negotiations continue. In short, then, worldviews are processes through which human beings negotiate meaningful, powerful worlds. Sometimes relatively peaceful, these negotiations can often be violent. In this chapter, I will be concentrating on the violent negotiation of an apartheid world.[5]

The Superhuman

According to his testimony, Barend Strydom went to the Voortrekker Monument in Pretoria, the most sacred place in Afrikaner nationalism, where he meditated, prayed, and made a vow to his God and his people. "I made a vow to my volk," Strydom said. "I prayed to God and asked him if he wanted to use me in any other way." Apparently, Strydom's God did not object to his plan of making a sacrificial offering of black people. "Something drastic had to be done," Strydom concluded, "and it was God's will that I protect Christian morals in South Africa." What were Christian morals? Barend Strydom derived his from a reading of the Bible. He read the Old Testament and identified with Samson, the hero of ancient Israel, the prolific killer of Philistines. He read the New Testament and found the key to Christian morals in the instruction, as he told the court, "You should love your nation like yourself." Replacing "neighbor" with "nation" in the biblical text, Strydom indicated that the superhuman power of his religious world could be located in a merger of God, nationalism, and the Bible.

Although Barend Strydom was by no means a typical or representative Afrikaner nationalist, this potent religious mix of God, nationalism, and the Bible has historically been important to Afrikaner nationalist projects. Beginning in the 1940s, theologians of the Dutch Reformed Church worked hard to bring the Bible into alignment with National Party projects of racial separation. They read the biblical injunction to "be fruitful and multiply" as "be fruitful and divide into separate groups." By 1986, however, the Dutch Reformed Church had officially renounced such biblical justifications for apartheid. Right-wing Afrikaners felt betrayed by the church and by a state that talked about "reform" and "power sharing." In the 1980s, they tried to revive a Christian, biblical justification for racial separation and white supremacy.[6]

The most visible right-wing group during the 1980s was the Afrikaner Weerstandsbeweging (Afrikaner Resistance Movement) led by Eugene Terre'Blanche, whose name, suitably, could be translated "White Earth." Barend Strydom was a member of the AWB. Their flag—three black sevens in a white circle on a red background—might have looked like a Nazi swastika, but Eugene Terre'Blanche insisted that it was the only flag in the world that was based on the Bible. The three sevens symbolized Christ in battle against the Antichrist—777 against 666. But the flag also represented the most sacred moment in Afrikaner mythic history—the Battle of Blood River, fought on 16 December 1838. According to legend, the ancestors of Afrikaners, known as Voortrekkers, prayed for seven days before fighting a battle in which they killed three thousand Zulus without suffering a single casualty. In this myth, the Voortrekkers sealed their covenant with God as the rivers ran red with the blood of Zulu warriors.[7]

Historians have discovered that the battle's legendary status was not invented until the 1870s. The legend of Blood River was revived in the 1930s by Afrikaner nationalists, mainly teachers and clergy, who tried to forge a class alliance that linked farmers, manufacturers, and white workers. On the centenary of Blood River, a former minister of the Dutch Reformed Church, and later prime minister of South Africa, D. F. Malan, made a stirring speech that celebrated the glory of the Afrikaner ancestors. "They received their task from God's hand," Malan declared. "They gave their answer. They made their sacrifices. There is still a white race." Shifting quickly to the concerns of 1938, however, Malan told his audience that "today black and white jostle together in the same labor market." Therefore, he concluded, "Your Blood River is not here. Your Blood River lies in the city."[8] Black warriors had been sacrificed in covenant with a nationalist God in 1838; black workers would be sacrificed in the urban labor market in 1938. In Malan's light, the Battle of Blood River would be reenacted. After Malan's National Party came to power in 1948, the nationalist covenant with God was enshrined in the Voortrekker Monument. Speaking at its opening, Malan declared that the Voortrekker Monument was "a symbol of that godly truth, so saliently affirmed by the Voortrekkers, that no great ideal can be achieved without its sacrifices, that it is along the way of the cross that victory is won, and that it is the dead from whom life appears."[9] The godly truth of sacrifice was a dual truth. New life appears out of killing and being killed, the two kinds of sacrifice demanded by the nationalist deity.

This "godly truth" was contested in the 1980s by competing groups of Afrikaner nationalists who claimed ownership of its sacred power. What was that sacred power? It is tempting to conclude that the power of the covenant, celebrated every December on the Day of the Vow and enshrined in the Voortrekker Monument, was the sacrificial, ritual killing of black people as an offering to an Afrikaner nationalist God. In starkest terms, that is precisely what its symbolism represented. On 16 December 1988, the 150th anniversary of the Battle of

Blood River, the National Party government conducted a celebration inside the Voortrekker Monument. But right-wing Afrikaner nationalists challenged their control of that ritual space by reenacting the sacrificial, ritual power of the Battle of Blood River on its original site, complete with authentic costumes, rifles, wagons, and the prerecorded sounds of Zulu war cries.[10] The month before, Barend Hendrik Strydom had reenacted his own Battle of Blood River in the city of Pretoria. "I saw my actions as a type of war," Strydom explained to the court. "I saw a group of enemy powers charging at me, and it was me or them. I decided to attack." Acting out a type of war, a type of sacrifice, Barend Strydom certified the authenticity of his claim on the Afrikaner nationalist myth by ritual killing. In his case, a violent act was a way of making myth real, of inscribing the terms and conditions of his worldview into the world by carving their design on real, living, human bodies.

The problem that needs to be addressed at this point is not merely the violence of Barend Strydom. Nor do I only want to point to the violent history of Afrikaner nationalism. What must be underscored is the nature of that violent religion, the most powerful religious force in the world since the nineteenth century, the inherently violent religion we call nationalism. Like most religious traditions, the religion of nationalism comes in different denominations. But it is in essence the same religion. In the eighteenth century, Baron d'Holbach recognized that nationalism always serves a violent God, "a God of armies, a jealous God, an avenging God, a destroying God, a God who is pleased with carnage, and whom his worshippers, as a duty, serve to his taste. Lambs, bulls, children, men, heretics, infidels, kings, whole nations are sacrificed to him." More recently, an American historian has noted that "the nation-state, including our own, rests on mounds of bodies." Nationalism is a religion of ritual, sacrificial killing.[11] The sacrifice of another or oneself, the scapegoat or the martyr, are two sides of the same nationalist sacrificial coin. As a religious worldview, nationalism is violent for at least two reasons: It serves a God who demands blood sacrifice and its symbolic terms for inclusion are also the symbolic terms for exclusion. Clearly, Barend Hendrik Strydom was a devotee of a religious nationalism based on sacrifice and exclusion.

The Subhuman

In South Africa, race has apparently been the dominant principle of exclusion. Racist exclusion has been legislated through population registration acts, land acts, group areas acts, separate amenities acts, mixed marriages acts, and a host of other legalized forms of racial discrimination. At the same time, racism has been entangled in religious worldviews that have tried to make sense out of the world by classifying persons. In his testimony before the court, Barend Strydom explained that he had been taught by his father that the white race originated in Israel, but that today's Jew was not really a white person. The black person, his father taught him, was an "animal." By classifying blacks as subhuman, Strydom's father removed them from the universe of morally protected beings. His son certified this symbolic exclusion through violent acts that made that myth real. But his father's denial of black humanity was itself already an act of violence.

During the 1980s, one of the more prominent defenders of this racist mythology was J. C. Schabort, a former biochemistry professor and leader of the Blanke Bevrydigingsbeweging (White Freedom Movement). Schabort's movement was the only white, right-wing organization to be banned in South Africa (to put that banning in perspective, the movement was banned in 1988 along with eighteen nonracial, anti-apartheid organizations). In February 1990, when President De Klerk unbanned the African National Congress, the Pan Africanist Congress, and the Communist Party, he unbanned Schabort's movement as well. Schabort described himself as a "positive racist based on love for my people." He insisted that the interests of his white, Christian people set the ultimate standard for morality. "What is good for the white man is the highest virtue," he said, "and what is bad for the white man is the ultimate sin." Schabort argued that his people had to be protected from those he called the "mud races." In Schabort's racist worldview, those people were less than human. Schabort represented them in symbols of impurity—as mud, dirt, or defilement—that had to be excluded from South Africa in order to create a pure national culture. "To develop a pure culture," Schabort argued, "requires a pure environment."

In developing his racist logic, Schabort proposed three ways of creating a pure environment. The "mud races" could be enslaved, exterminated, or removed. Enslavement would certify the dehumanization of the "mud races." As Orlando Patterson has taught us, slavery is a form of social death. But Schabort was not satisfied with the domination, exploitation, and social death of the "mud races"; he wanted them entirely excluded. Exclusion could be accomplished in two ways: extermination or removal. Schabort preferred removal, arguing that all blacks in South Africa should be given a two-year notice and then at the end of that period they should be removed in a matter of weeks. In this logic of exclusion, however, extermination could have worked just as well.[12]

In the 1980s, Schabort's racist obsession with purity was a marginal right-wing position, but in the 1930s and 1940s it had been at the center of the Afrikaner nationalist project. There were nationalists, particularly those under the influence of Nazism, who promoted a myth of purity based on total racial separation. According to defenders of "pure" apartheid, blacks had to be removed even from employment in white-controlled mining, farming, and industry. Some even proclaimed this logic of purity and exclusion as a Christian duty. Other Afrikaner nationalists argued that this ideal of complete purity was not practical. Purity had to be adapted to the realities of power. This was called "practical" apartheid. Its defenders in the 1940s argued that "it must be acknowledged that the non-white worker already constitutes an integral part of our economic structure, that he is now so enmeshed in the spheres of our economic life that for the first fifty to one hundred years (if not even longer), total segregation is pure wishful thinking."[13] Defenders of practical apartheid therefore combined the removal of blacks into segregated townships, group areas, or homelands with the enslavement of blacks as exploitable labor in order to balance the demands of purity and power.

In South Africa, I would suggest, racism has been a symptom of these conflicting demands. Although cloaked in racism, apartheid has not been essentially about race, but about the horrible logics of purity and power. Purity and power are inherently violent. Put simply, the symbolism of purity determines who is in and who is out; the symbolism of power determines who is up and who is down. Persons whose humanity is denied under these symbolic logics may be forcibly kept in their place, down or out. But even without violent reinforcement, a worldview embraces violence in the very act of subclassification that relegates persons to a subhuman status. Obviously, Barend Strydom enacted precisely such a violent classification of persons in the interest of renegotiating a particular kind of human purity and power in South Africa.

In renegotiating an apartheid worldview, however, Strydom did not merely practice a violent form of racism. He acted upon a claim to an authentic human identity that was defined in terms of a category less obviously violent than racism: ethnicity. Historically, apartheid ideologues have justified separation by the principle of "self-determination" for peoples, cultures, or ethnic groups. Ethnicity, not race, has been the bedrock of apartheid in South Africa. Identification with an ethnic group has been the primary symbol of apartheid. As Barend Strydom told the court, "I did not commit murder, but merely exercised my rights as a son of the Boerevolk." Strydom claimed that his human identity and human rights were based, not merely on race, but more importantly and specifically on an Afrikaner ethnicity.

The Human

In an apartheid worldview, ethnicity represents the basic condition for negotiating a human identity. Barend Strydom, like other right-wing, Afrikaner nationalists in the 1980s, located person in place by negotiating an exclusive, privileged, ethnic claim on the land. In strategic contests over land, the supreme symbol of human entitlement was blood. Blood was a dual symbol: It represented the ethnic purity of a shared, pure blood. But it also symbolized ethnic power, as the supreme, ultimate payment that entitled that pure ethnic group to its land.

During the Anglo-Boer War, F. W. Reitz, a defender of the Boer cause against Britain, wrote that "the territory had been purchased with our money and baptized with our blood." Money and blood fused into a single symbol of payment in negotiating an authentic ownership of the land. In the 1980s, Afrikaner nationalists fought with each other over the authenticity of their competing claims to an Afrikaner identity. For example, at a National Party political meeting in 1983, Marie van Zyl, the leader of a right-wing Afrikaner women's brigade called the Kappie Kommando, accused P. W. Botha of betraying the Afrikaner people and the land with his policy of "reform" and "power sharing." In this ethnic contest over person and place, Botha tried to reassert his own legitimacy in the symbolism of blood. "I was born out of a Kappie Kommando," he declared, "which really wet the African soil with its blood."[14]

Blood thus signified the supreme sacrifice, the greatest gift, the highest price that could be paid for the land. Like blood, sacrifice operated as a dual ritual symbol: It signified ritual killing as well as being killed. Eugene Terre'Blanche exhorted his followers to be prepared to kill for the land. Referring back to the Anglo-Boer War, Terre'Blanche reminded his followers, "22,000 British were killed by the volk for their land. The enemy must know this. Learn a lesson from it. Because we will kill people if they take our land from us." Terre'Blanche called upon his followers to become "arms carriers" for the volk in a "holy war" for the land.[15]

In his testimony before the court, Barend Hendrik Strydom insisted that the Afrikaner place in South Africa was in danger. First, that place was undermined by the very presence of black human beings. "Scientists have proved," he told the court, "there is less oxygen in this country as a result of all the blacks." Even his "breathing space," Strydom suggested, was threatened. Second, Afrikaners were threatened not only by those he classified as subhuman, but by superhuman demons, by a satanic enemy. South Africa was "going to the communists," Strydom told the court. Communism, he insisted, was a "Satan-inspired ideology." Strydom had a fairly broad definition of communism which included the archbishop of Cape Town and a leader of the Democratic Party. "If the communists such as Bishop Desmond Tutu and Denis Worrall are arrested immediately," he informed the court, "I will cooperate with the state."

Of course, since the Suppression of Communism Act of 1950, the South African government itself had operated with a very broad definition of communism. Legislation defined it so broadly that any opposition to the prevailing government was specified by law as "communism." Strydom's linking of communism and satanism was also widely made by defenders of the South African order. To cite only one example: In 1987 P. W. Botha's President's Council published a report on the dangers threatening South African youth. Among many dangers, the report exposed the connection between satanism and communism. The council's expert witness on satanism was a certain R. A. Seale, who ran an organization called "Manna for Youth." In particular, Seale was dedicated to exposing the satanic influence exerted over South African youth by rock 'n roll music, whether that music was played forward or backward. The council's expert on satanism was also its expert on communism. Seale identified eleven communist objectives for the report, all of which he got from a 1940s publication by the John Birch Society, *The Naked Communist*. Sounding vaguely pornographic, this text was used by the expert on Satan to expose communists as agents in a demonic conspiracy against South Africa. In these worldview negotiations advanced by the President's Council, satanists and communists represented antihuman forces. They were apartheid's inner demons. Defenders of the South African order looked out from their threatened place and saw those demons surrounding them in the form of the African National Congress. Throughout the 1980s, the government, the state-controlled media, and the Dutch Reformed Church continued to demonize the African National Congress as a black, revolutionary, and communist "total onslaught" against South Africa.[16]

Barend Strydom imagined that he lived in a place threatened by enemies he classified as subhuman and by those he classified as superhuman, demonic, or satanic agents of evil. These two enemies, however, were one and the same. Strydom had to have known that blacks were human, but he classified them as both subhuman animals and superhuman demons. In other words, blacks represented an anomaly in Strydom's worldview. By negotiating his worldview on the streets of Pretoria, Strydom tried to eliminate that anomaly by eliminating persons who violated his classification system by being simultaneously human, subhuman, and superhuman. He acted to eliminate that anomaly of person and place through an act of ritual killing. But he told the court that the forced removal of blacks from the place he claimed as his own could have worked just as well. "I grant blacks the right to live," he told the court, "but not in our country. They should not be seen in Pretoria, but in their own homelands."

Strydom thus invoked the grand apartheid design that called for the creation of ten ethnic homelands for the black population of South Africa. Each so-called ethnic group—Zulu, Xhosa, Tswana, and so on—was relegated to a different territory, ostensibly to preserve the purity of its own language, culture, and people. However described, it was an ethnic apartheid that served the interests of Afrikaner nationalists. Purity was served by excluding all blacks from citizenship in the Republic of South Africa; power was served by exploiting the homelands as reservoirs of cheap, subordinate labor. All this was enacted, not in the name of race, but in the name of ethnicity.

Since Barend Strydom justified his violence in terms of assumptions about ethnic persons and places, a brief digression on ethnicity is important at this point. Ethnicity has been a remarkably fluid category in South African history. Let me give three examples: First, in the nineteenth century the term "Malay" was used to describe certain people in the Cape, but it referred to Muslims, irrespective of "race." Less than 1 percent of people called Malay came from Malaysia. As British visitors in the 1850s noted, Malays included both blacks and whites. Under apartheid, however, "Malay" became a separate ethnic group. Second, "Arab" became an ethnic designation in the early part of this century in Natal. It was adopted by Indian merchants who wanted to distinguish themselves from indentured Indian laborers. In Natal, "Arabs" were upper-class merchants from India. Third, "Peruvian" became an ethnic designation that was inexplicably applied to eastern European Jewish immigrants in Johannesburg between 1888 and 1914. Even the Jewish Board of Deputies in 1904 said that these "Peruvians" were on the borderline between what they called white and colored. Therefore, South Africa has had Malays who were not from Malaysia, Arabs who were not from Arabia, and Peruvians who were not from Peru. Ethnicity therefore has not only been fluid, but arbitrary and entirely invented. Nevertheless, people have persisted in negotiating worldviews within the potent fictions of ethnicity.[17]

Proponents of apartheid, or separate development, tried to freeze ethnicity as a permanent feature of the human landscape in South Africa. The government found willing collaborators in this ethnic enterprise. A comparative illustration of a prominent political leader who negotiated power and purity in ethnic terms will be helpful in understanding the ethnic nationalism of a defender of apartheid like Barend Strydom. Among apartheid homeland leaders, the most successful was the Zulu chief Mangosuthu Gatsha Buthelezi. In 1952

Buthelezi worked as a clerk in the Bantu Administration of the apartheid ideologues H. F. Verwoerd and W. M. Eiselen. In 1954, as chief minister to the Zulu king, Cyprian, he introduced a new annual ritual of Zulu national unity, Shaka Day. He had King Cyprian dress up in a so-called traditional Zulu royal costume that neither Cyprian, nor his father King Solomon, nor for that matter any other Zulu king, had ever worn. A new, ancient tradition was born. In 1975, Buthelezi started an organization called Inkatha in which he claimed all Zulu-speakers were automatically members, whether they knew it or not. In 1988, Buthelezi exhorted his Inkatha followers at a Shaka Day celebration to defend their ethnic nationalism. While presented to the public of South Africa and the world as a proponent of nonviolence, his language implied the need to fight to preserve Zulu ethnic power. "Our nationalism is like a weapon," he declared, "we pick it up whenever we are threatened." This ethnic nationalism was to prove a particularly violent religion. On Shaka Day in 1990, King Goodwill reportedly warned dissenting Zulu chiefs that Inkatha members would find them and kill them. Zulu purity, Zulu power—these were the elements of an ethnic nationalism produced under apartheid and separate development.[18]

During the second half of the 1980s, Buthelezi's homeland of KwaZulu and the surrounding region of Natal became one of the most violent places on earth. In August 1990 the epicenter of violence shifted to the area around Johannesburg, when over 700 people were killed during a period of six weeks. Once again, Inkatha was at the center of the violence. Without benefit of explanation, we are left with the task of description. How do we describe that violence? The media resorted to racial and ethnic descriptions, thereby subscribing to the worldview promoted by Barend Strydom. *Time* magazine called it "black on black" or "black against black" violence. That is racist. It makes as much sense as calling the First World War "white on white" violence. It describes nothing real or human. *Time* also called it "ethnic" violence, a Zulu ethnic group fighting with a Xhosa ethnic group, as if it were the continuation of some old "tribal" animosity. This also is nonsense. There is absolutely no history in southern Africa of factional fighting between a Zulu ethnic group and a Xhosa ethnic group. In any case, Zulu and Xhosa ethnicity, like Malay, Arab, and Peruvian—or Afrikaner, for that matter—are modern inventions. They are imagined identities that are manipulated in the interest of dreams of purity and contests over power. Ethnicity also describes nothing that is real or ultimately human.

Should we then describe the violence as a political struggle? Inkatha's support had slipped in 1990 to as low as 5 percent of the black population. Was public violence a way to demonstrate its power? Supported by the government, Inkatha had an interest in sending a forceful message to the African National Congress. Violent acts communicated the message that Inkatha was a powerful player in the negotiations for a "New South Africa." Unlike race or ethnicity, communication *is* something real and human, because humans are communicating, symbol-using beings, often sending messages to each other through the medium of violent symbols. Sending a message, communicating something—violence can be interpreted as a kind of forceful discourse.

When Barend Strydom killed on the streets of Pretoria, as he later explained, he was making a statement. By his own account, Strydom used a violent act to communicate with two audiences. One was an audience that might be called the world at large. "I wanted the world to notice," Strydom explained. "There are Boers on the southern tip of Africa who are prepared to fight for survival and the maintenance of Christian, Protestant beliefs until the end." Sending a message to the world had long been an important part of the apartheid project. The architect of "grand apartheid," H. F. Verwoerd, frequently sent such messages as prime minister between 1958 and 1966: "We send this message to the outside world, and say to them . . . that there is but one way of saving the white races of the world. And that is for the White and non-white in Africa each to exercise his rights within his own areas." To work out that plan of salvation, Verwoerd insisted that South Africa had to be left alone. "If meddlesome people keep their hands off us, we shall in a just way such as behooves a Christian nation, work out solutions in the finest detail and carry them out."[19] P. W. Botha sent similar messages in the 1980s.

Strydom's second audience was more specific. He explained that he wanted to send a message to the African National Congress. "I would simply shoot blacks at random," he said. "I wanted to attract attention and show the African National Congress who we were." P. W. Botha's government sent similar messages to the ANC through cross-border raids, assassinations, death squads, torture in detention, and legalized executions—violent acts of communication, violent negotiations.

For its part, the African National Congress had been fighting since 1912 to reverse the classification of persons, along with the dreams of purity and claims to power, that Strydom tried to carve into the world. Speaking on the ideology of racism, ANC president Oliver Tambo observed that racists have tended "to enrobe [their] racist ideas and practices with the cloak of religion." Racists derived legitimation from "the God they dragoon to serve their interests and whom they claim to worship." Claiming a special relationship to the superhuman power of that God, Tambo noted, racists held the "view that the European was a higher being deposited on this planet to play God over 'the Natives.'" Racists reinforced their claims to a unique human status not only by invoking the superhuman but also by dehumanizing others in an inhuman system. "The arrogantly racist architects of the apartheid system," Tambo recalled, "thought the oppressed [were] not sufficiently human to rebel against the inhuman system they have imposed on our country." The apartheid system was violent in two obvious ways—it was a violation of humanity and it was reinforced by direct physical harm; it was violence reinforced by violence. The architects of apartheid, Tambo observed, "thought the subhumans could and would be kept in their place by brute force." Apartheid dreams of person and place, power and purity, were maintained by force. Tambo and the ANC concluded that those dreams could only be shattered by force. "By rising up in favour of justice," Tambo concluded, "we have turned these maniacal dreams into a nightmare."[20]

How is humanity to be recovered in the midst of that nightmare? The place to look for a recovery of humanity in South Africa is among those who have been dehumanized. New dreams have emerged. First, there is the vision of a multiracial humanity. In 1955, the African National Congress sponsored a Congress of the People that drafted a "Freedom Charter." The Freedom Charter announced a new dream of person and place in South Africa: "South Africa belongs to all who live in it, black and white." Although the Congress of the People was broken up by the police, its leaders charged with treason, and the Freedom Charter banned, this vision of a nonracial, democratic, and just South Africa continued to be proclaimed by the ANC. Second, there is the hope of an African humanity. In 1959, "Africanists" within the ANC formed an alternative movement, the Pan Africanist Congress, that insisted on "Africa for the Africans." In principle, however, "African" was a geographical location, not a racial or ethnic designation. Anyone who lived in and identified with Africa was in principle an African. Like the ANC, the PAC was banned in 1960. Third, there is the strength of a black humanity. Drawing some inspiration from North American developments, the black consciousness movement of the early 1970s redefined "black," again not as a racial or ethnic designation, but as a class location—the oppressed. Blackness became a potent, multivalent symbol of class oppression and human empowerment. Its meaning depended upon who invoked it. As a prominent South African black theologian noted in the mid seventies: "As long as somebody else says to you, 'You are black, you are black,' blackness as a concept remains a symbol of oppression and of something that conjures up feelings of inferiority. But when the black man himself says, 'I am black, I am black,' blackness assumes a different meaning altogether. It then becomes a symbol of liberation and self-articulation."[21] Like the ANC and PAC, however, the black consciousness movement was brutally suppressed by the government.

In the early 1970s, the leadership of the ANC initially resisted the redefinition of humanity advanced by the black consciousness movement. Oliver Tambo, for example, argued that the movement's psychological discourse lacked real force. "To be effective," Tambo insisted, "a break with the cultural and spiritual mode that the enemy has imposed on us cannot but be sharp and violent." Police action in Soweto on 16 June 1976 was sharp and violent, initiating a general uprising that continued with greater or lesser intensity throughout the 1980s. Declaring the 1980s the "Decade of Liberation," the ANC embarked upon an intensified armed struggle against the apartheid government. It referred to its campaign of military training, armed attacks, and acts of sabotage as "armed propaganda."[22]

"Armed propaganda" had two fundamental components: discourse and force. First, the armed struggle required a new way to speak about force. Reversing the terms by which the government defined violence, the ANC argued that its armed struggle was not violence;

it was legitimate force necessary to end the illegitimate violence of apartheid. Some South African theologians in opposition to the government embraced this new discourse. In 1985, for example, the theologians who produced the *Kairos Document* asked: "Is it legitimate, especially in our circumstances, to use the same word violence in a blanket condemnation to cover the ruthless and repressive activities of the State and the desperate attempts of people to defend themselves?" The kairos theologians suggested that legitimate force was in fact being exercised by those who defied the illegitimate, violent law and order of the state.[23]

Second, the ANC saw force as a kind of discourse, as a message, communication, language, or powerful voice. Since the early 1960s, ANC leaders have explained the content of that forceful discourse: force was a language of communication with the enemy; force was a letter of invitation to the government and the white minority of South Africa to come to a national convention; force was a tactic of pressuring the oppressors to open their ears and hearts to the demands of the oppressed; force was necessary to talk to the enemy in the language he understood best; force was the only language which Botha and his regime understood. Without the armed struggle, Oliver Tambo concluded in 1987, the ANC "would be a voice without force." As John Dewey once observed: "To be without force is to be without a foothold in the real world." Once again, violence made myth real; it realized a myth of redemption for human beings whose humanity had been violently denied in an inhuman system. Since all nonviolent means of communication had been closed by the government, violence was the only medium left for the ANC to make their myth real.[24]

Barend Hendrik Strydom was also trying to renegotiate the reality of a myth through violent acts. Strydom specifically chose Strijdom Square for his ritual killings because, as he later explained to the court, "Advocate [J. G.] Strijdom," who had served as prime minister of South Africa from 1954 to 1958, "signified the beginning of apartheid." Mircea Eliade used to argue that ritual often acts out a symbolic return to "the mythic time of the beginning of things."[25] Symbolically, Strydom conceived his actions on 15 November as redemptive. That is, he imagined that his dramatic mass murder of blacks in Strijdom Square would initiate the restoration of his country to the time of the beginning of apartheid, to that mythic, sacred time when the utopian (or dystopian) dream of an all-white nation was being implemented by the violent force of law in South Africa. By his own account, Strydom was the authentic, legitimate extension of that force. The violence of apartheid had been refracted through the long history of a nation under God in Africa, carving its cruel pattern into the lives of South Africans. Barend Strydom tried to revitalize the violent myth of apartheid by his ritual killings on the streets of Pretoria.

Although the myth of apartheid was obviously, violently racist, it was more than racism. It was a mythic worldview of person and place. Strydom tried to make that worldview real by enacting his classification of persons upon the world. He verified his human identity by factoring out those he saw as superhuman and subhuman—a superhuman power to be worshiped and served by sacrificial offerings and subhumans to be enslaved, removed, or exterminated. Locating person in place, Strydom tried to renegotiate a purity based on exclusion and a power based on domination. That is the apartheid worldview. Although Strydom claimed it as his own and tried to authenticate his claim by a violent ritual sacrifice in Pretoria, that worldview did not belong to him alone. Nor did it belong exclusively to the Afrikaner Resistance Movement, or Afrikaner nationalists, or the government of South Africa. If, as I have suggested, an apartheid worldview is any classification of persons into "us" and "them" that negotiates purity by exclusion and power by domination, then apartheid has not merely been the religious worldview of white South African racists. It has been the worldview of a violent world.

CHAPTER 2

Black Sheep

•

IN THE CASE of Barend Hendrik Strydom, we have seen an act of violence that can be understood as a sacrificial offering to a violent, nationalist God. In the next two chapters, I want to explore two other types of ritual killing in South Africa. Besides blood offerings, it can be argued that ritual killing has taken two other basic forms—elimination and incorporation. Already, we have seen that Strydom's offering was also a ritual elimination. Strydom acted to eliminate persons that he classified as subhuman. I have suggested as well that Strydom acted to eliminate what he experienced as an anomaly in his own, racist classification system. There was no room in his sense of order for those who were human but who at the same time were classified both as superhuman demons and subhuman animals. Like the apartheid worldview, this strategy of elimination was not peculiar to Barend Strydom. I will suggest that it is found in public systems of sacrifice that eliminate persons who have been perceived as violating the symbolic purity of a community. While ritual killing for elimination has been about purity, ritual killing for incorporation has been about power. In other words, sacrificial victims have not been killed in order to remove them from the world; they have been killed in order that their power can be incorporated or absorbed into the body of the sacrificer. In very simple terms, offering, elimination, and incorporation represent three basic types of ritual killing.

Let me briefly illustrate these three types of ritual killing by referring to ethnographies of Zulu traditional or ancestral ritual practice.

I do not cite these examples to suggest by any means that the types of ritual killing I have outlined are "primitive." On the contrary, I will be suggesting in this and the following chapter that ritual killing is a basic pattern of violence in the modern world. I refer to ethnography at this point simply to clarify my distinction of different types of ritual killing.

On some Zulu ritual occasions, the ritual killing of an animal, preferably an ox, was made as an offering to the ancestors or ancestor-spirits. The offering was not merely in the blood, the bones, the fat, and the meat of the sacrificial animal. It was also in the bellowing of the animal, which opened up contact between the living and the dead. In this ritual offering, therefore, human beings communicated their proper place between the subhuman animal victim and the superhuman ancestor-spirits.

On other occasions, however, a ritual killing was required to eliminate a condition of impurity that had resulted from some violation of the moral, social, or ritual order of the community. In ritual killings performed to remove the taint of impurity and restore a condition of purity, the preferred sacrificial victim was a black sheep. In particular, the ritual killing of a black sheep was employed as a strategy for warding off the evil, defiling effects of witchcraft or sorcery. As symbols of evil, witchcraft and sorcery represented fundamental anomalies in the order of the world. They were things performed by human beings, who drew on superhuman power, medicines, or techniques, to achieve antihuman ends. But witchcraft and sorcery also defined the very nature of violence. They caused violent harm to persons and property and violated the basic terms and conditions of a human world. That violence could be counteracted, however, by the ritual killing of a black sheep. The victim served as a scapegoat. The animal was treated with the respect owed a human being, but it was then suffocated and buried in the ground. The victim was entirely eliminated. The purity and order of a human world was thus temporarily restored through the ritual elimination of a symbolic victim that stood on the borderline between human and subhuman. The line between human beings and the antihuman forces of defilement, violation, and violence represented by witchcraft or sorcery could be redrawn and reinforced through an act of ritual killing. Ritual killing for elimination is in this way symbolic work that reinforces purity and order.[1]

In Zulu practice, the black sheep also appeared within another ritual context. Sacred specialists in the ritual art of making rain occasionally required the killing of a black sheep. They killed the sheep and skinned it. Out of the fat of the sacrificial victim, they made medicines to be carried, worn, or eaten for their superhuman power. They put on the skin of the sacrificed sheep, inside out, and kept an all-night vigil at a river or lake to commune with the spirit of the python in the depths of the water. By contacting that spirit, the rainmaker gained the power to make rain. In this ritual, therefore, the lines between human and superhuman were again redrawn. The human ritual specialist absorbed the superhuman power to bring rain that was associated with the black sheep, the python, and the cool waters of a river or lake. Ritual killing for incorporation, therefore, is a way of acquiring superhuman power.[2]

It has often been noted that one of the recurring features of ritual killing is symbolic substitution. For example, as the anthropologist E. E. Evans-Pritchard observed in his research on Nuer ritual, sacrifice required an ox as victim. Under some conditions, however, a cucumber could work just as well. The Zulu ethnographies I have referred to suggest that a black goat might be substituted for the black sheep. In extraordinary cases, however, only a human victim could satisfy the ritual logics of elimination or incorporation. I will be focusing below on the ritual killing of human beings, concentrating on rituals of elimination for purity and rituals of incorporation for power that have required human victims. Again, however, we cannot suppose that these practices are archaic, "primitive" rituals of a premodern world. Ritual killings for purity or power are also rituals of the modern world, and of the modern state.

Violent Unanimity

In chapter 1, I examined an act of ritual killing in which one person killed many. Here I want to examine an act of ritual killing in which many people killed one. In the early morning of Wednesday, 13 November 1985, in the black township of Paballelo, about five kilometers from the white town of Upington in the northeastern Cape, a young black municipal policeman by the name of Lucas "Jetta" Sethwala was killed. The killing took place out in the open, in front of witnesses, and apparently with the support of a crowd of about 120 people. Lucas Sethwala was killed by two blows to the head. After he was dead, his body was kicked, beaten, stabbed, doused with petrol, and set alight by members of that crowd of residents of Paballelo.

Many joined in this ritual-like desecration of the body of Lucas Sethwala, but relatively few were arrested and charged. Eventually, twenty-five persons were charged with the murder—and one with the attempted murder—of Lucas Sethwala, although it was established that only one person in the crowd had actually struck the blows that caused his death. The twenty-six accused, however, were charged under the legal principle of "common purpose," a principle in South African jurisprudence that was invoked to name the unanimous intent—and therefore the collective guilt—behind this violent act. After a long, complicated trial that lasted two and a half years, the court found all the accused guilty, to one degree or another, in the murder of Lucas Sethwala and sentenced fourteen of the defendants to death.

After sentencing, the "Upington Fourteen" became the focus of intense debates about the use of the death penalty in South Africa, particularly when its judicial exercise involved something as potentially nebulous as identifying the common purpose that united an otherwise disparate group of defendants. Although the court insisted upon the doctrine of common purpose as a legal principle, it also suggested that, at least in this case, common purpose had a more direct political implication. In passing the death sentence on the fourteen accused, Justice Jan Basson observed, "One cannot allow that people murder an innocent person if they have grievances against the state authority."[3] In reasserting the sovereign authority of the state over life and death, the court sentenced the largest group in recent South African history to hang for what the prosecution insisted was the political crime of wanting policeman Lucas Sethwala dead. Although many of those sentenced to hang had proven that they were not even present at the scene of the crime, all fourteen were condemned to death on the basis of an imputed common purpose.

During the long course of the Upington trial, the court operated on the premise that the killing had been an act of collective violence. Even when the defense established that many of the accused had not been present, this fact did not change the collective nature of the crime, nor did it alleviate the imputation of guilt. In the end, the doctrine of common purpose assumed mystical dimensions, binding all of the accused together as one in the eyes of the law. The court could have considered alternative explanations for collective violence by crowds, "mob hysteria," for example. This alternative reading of the event would have retained its collective definition, but it would have substantially diminished the individual liability of each of the accused. Instead, the court stuck with its collective definition of responsibility and guilt under the doctrine of common purpose.

A version of the "mob hysteria" explanation was presented before the court during testimony given in mitigation of sentencing after the convictions. The head of the Division of Experimental Psychology at the University of the Witwatersrand, Professor Graham Tyson, offered the court his expert testimony on the theory of "deindividuation." Professor Tyson addressed the accused as individuals. He noted that the accused Kenneth Khumalo, for example, had "no logical reason to participate in the murder"; likewise, he observed, the involvement of Elisha Matshoba was "totally out of character," suggesting that he was responding to "strong situational forces." These defendants, and others, Professor Tyson concluded, had been "deindividuated" in the crowd that had gathered outside the Sethwala home. In this process, members of a crowd did not become totally irrational, but they did suffer a decreased awareness of their personal moral standards. They were inclined to perform certain acts that they would not perform as individuals. The crowd in Paballelo on 13 November 1985, Professor Tyson submitted to the court, had suffered the situational forces of deindividuation. Therefore, they acted illogically, completely out of character. Tyson argued that the situational force of deindividuation should be taken into account as a factor that might diminish the personal liability of each of the accused standing alone before the judgment of the court.[4]

The judge, however, rejected the theory of deindividuation as a mitigating explanation for collective violence. The court found "that each of the 14 was acting with the specific aim of murdering the policeman and not as a 'deindividuated' mob." Ironically, judicial procedure in the case enacted its own systematic deindividuation of the accused. Not only did the principle of common purpose override any consideration of individual intentions, motives, or even direct participation in the actual killing, but the court replaced the names of the accused with numbers, the numbers one through twenty-six, by which they were referred to throughout the trial. On the day of sentencing, for example, Judge Basson called each of the accused by number. Basson called Kenneth "Pinkie" Khumalo, age thirty-three, the first mayor of Paballelo, married, with three children, to hear his verdict. "The accused," read the judge, "by his actions outside the victim's house, associated himself actively with the common objective of the group, namely to drive the victim out of his house and kill him. Accused no. 1 is found guilty of murder and is classified as an accomplice. The form of intention is dolus directus." Khumalo, however, had not assaulted the victim, nor had he been there when Sethwala was killed. When the day of his sentencing arrived, he was given, by number, the penalty of death. The judge read, "Accused number 1, 2, 4, 5, 6, 8, 10, 11, 13, 15, 18, 19, 20, 21 . . . I sentence you to death."[5]

One further example of judicial deindividuation should also be mentioned: When informed in court about the results of a survey of Paballelo township residents conducted by researchers from the University of Cape Town that found that most (nearly 70 percent) felt that the Upington Fourteen should not be punished at all for the death of Lucas Sethwala, the judge saw no relevance in these results because, he said, the township residents were "a bunch of faceless and uninformed people."[6] In the Upington murder trial, the judicial system found the accused to be nameless numbers, but, not altogether incidentally, they were nameless numbers that had been selected out of a faceless community to be punished for a collective act of violence.

Although this case could be examined from a number of different perspectives, the story of the Upington Fourteen is suggestive of the complex relations between religion and violence that are associated with what is usually referred to as the ritual killing of a scapegoat. In this respect, René Girard's theory of religious sacrifice is helpful in reexamining the events surrounding the killing of Lucas Sethwala, as well as allowing us to reread the trial that resulted in the conviction and sentencing of those who were found guilty of his murder. Among other things, Girard's theory of sacrifice includes the notion of unanimous violence, a collective violence that a social group focuses upon a sacrificial victim in order to deflect the potential, uncontrolled violence of the society itself. Furthermore, to anticipate a consideration of one of his contentions about ritual killing, Girard has argued that the sacrificial system that focused, deflected, and thereby contained violence in so-called primitive societies has been replaced in modern societies by the judicial system. In applying what Girard has called the "scapegoat mechanism" of ritual sacrifice to the Upington case, it may be possible to draw some useful conclusions about sacrifice, collective violence, and negotiations over the sacred in South African society.[7]

To place the killing of Lucas Sethwala in perspective, it is necessary first to recount the events that led up to the violence of November 1985 in Paballelo township. During the previous year, many similar townships in South Africa had been sites of "unrest." But Paballelo was described as a more conservative, quiet, relatively calm community, with a low crime rate and fewer "disturbances" than elsewhere. But the residents of Paballelo were beset by the same structural conditions under which blacks had to live throughout South Africa—high unemployment, low wages, overcrowding, and official harassment. They were described by anthropologist Martin West as "third-class citizens" who were subjected "to all the controls and restrictions placed upon black people." Even such a quiet community had limits to what it would tolerate, just as, West observed by way of comparison, police firing tear gas on the campus of the University of Cape Town had caused "normally sedate academics to hang out of buildings and heap abuse on police."[8] At Paballelo, normally sedate township residents had exploded under conditions of economic deprivation and police pressure.

Four days prior to the killing, on Sunday, 10 November 1985, a township meeting of youths and elders was held at J. Shimane Community Center to air grievances about high rents, beerhall drunkenness, and two municipal policemen who allegedly had been frightening street vendors and confiscating their goods. Apparently, Lucas Sethwala was named as one of those policemen. After the meeting ended, a dancing, chanting group disrupted a soccer game in progress on the nearby Eleven Experience field. Police arrived, stones were allegedly thrown, and tear gas was fired to disperse the crowd. Apparently, this was the first time that police had ever teargassed residents of Paballelo. During that night, about twenty-two incidents of arson, assault, and damage to property occurred in the township. The next day, a township resident was shot by the police. Residents said that the victim was a pregnant woman returning from shopping, but the official police report on the shooting identified the person as a troublemaker. On Tuesday, there was another shooting. This time a young boy was shot by the police, crippling him so badly that three years later he was still hospitalized. As a result of these three days of confrontation with the police, the township was in a state of considerable tension.

At the age of twenty-three, Lucas Sethwala had only recently finished his police training. A former Sunday school teacher, Sethwala had not wanted a career in law enforcement; it was apparently the only job he could find in the poverty-stricken township. During the trial, Sethwala was described as an "ordinary boy." "Some people thought he was a good person," the wife of one of the defendants testified in court. "I don't think they hated him."[9] As a policeman, however, Sethwala became a symbol of power, blamed for abusing the authority of his position by harassing vendors on the streets. After he had been mentioned at the Sunday community meeting, Sethwala stayed away from home for the next three days, only returning at about 3:00 Wednesday morning. He sat in his house, holding a loaded shotgun, until a crowd gathered around his house about four hours later, around 7:00. Sometime between 7:00 and 8:10, Lucas Sethwala was killed.

Precisely how that crowd arrived at the home of Lucas Sethwala has been a matter of some dispute. According to the judgment of the court, the crowd—acting with one mind—had converged on Sethwala's home in order to kill him. It was in the view of the court premeditated, collective murder. In other words, the court had to assume that the murder had been planned. At what point that collective intention had formed, however, has been difficult to determine, partly because the crowd that ended up outside Sethwala's house was only a small part of a much larger crowd that had started to gather on the Eleven Experience soccer field by about 6:00 A.M. At least some of that crowd was under the impression that the gathering had been called by the police to discuss township grievances. Apparently, some even thought that the police had called a meeting to apologize for shooting residents of Paballelo over the previous few days. Nearby, another group had assembled, elderly people lining up outside the J. Shimane Community Center, waiting to collect the pension payments that were issued every two months. As the police arrived with an armored vehicle, loudspeakers, and video cameras, some of the elderly joined the crowd on the soccer field.

Descriptions of the crowd on the soccer field have differed: There were about 3,000 people. Some witnesses claimed they were quiet and peaceful; the police insisted that they were aggressive and dangerous. In either case, the police announced over the loudspeakers, in Afrikaans and English, "This meeting is illegal in terms of emergency regulations. You have ten minutes to disperse." Those in the crowd who thought the police had called the meeting to apologize must have been surprised to find them breaking it up. The crowd responded by singing the African national anthem, *Nkosi Sikelel' iAfrika*. Song was followed by a prayer in Xhosa, which the police interpreted as a dangerous exhortation because they did not understand the language. Without warning, the police fired tear gas. People ran, fleeing in different directions. Some ran across the street to the beerhall, near where the police vehicles were parked, pushed down a wall, and tried to set the building on fire, while others ran away from the police, separating as they ran. About 120 people out of the original crowd ended up at a T-junction, some fifty meters from the soccer field. From that point, they could see the community hall, the clinic, a tarred road, and the home of municipal policeman Lucas Sethwala.

During the trial, Judge Basson insisted that "the meeting on that morning and the events after it were not a spontaneous hostile outburst but a semi-organized uprising."[10] If that "uprising" had been intentional, however, the intention to attack the home of Lucas Sethwala must have been formed at the T-junction, at the crossroads, because it was an intention formed, if formed at all, by only about 120 of the original 3,000 on the soccer field. The murder would have to have been decided on the run, over the short space of fifty meters, while fleeing the tear gas. Running away from the police, people ended up at the home of a policeman.

The Surrogate Victim

Inside the Sethwala home, Lucas, his mother, siblings, and other children were hiding. Outside, people in the crowd threw stones, broke windows, but no one actually tried to enter the property. According to later testimony, someone in the crowd yelled, "Let's get him out alive and give him the necklace." In this threat, at least some in the crowd seemed to have developed murderous intentions. Curiously, however, the crowd also included people who would not have been expected to want Lucas Sethwala dead—a colleague in the municipal service, a young man who was regarded as a son in the Sethwala household, and his best friend. Perhaps Sethwala referred to this friend when he looked out a window and exclaimed, "The man who is supposed to come and save me is come here to kill me!"[11] Sethwala fired his shotgun out the window—two, three, or four shots, depending upon the testimony of different witnesses—and wounded an eleven-year-old boy who was running down the street. Next, trying to escape, Sethwala went out his back door to a neighbor's house, but was turned back. He then ran around his own house, but instead of turning right and trying to run away, Sethwala ran straight through the crowd, firing his shotgun in the air. Continuing up the street, Sethwala, again, instead of turning right and running toward the community center and police, ran to the left into a vacant lot. There, one of the crowd—Justice Bekebeke, later found guilty of striking the fatal blows—caught up with Lucas Sethwala, took his gun, and hit him twice with it, killing him. At that point, people from the crowd joined in and desecrated the body.

The ritual character of that communal act of desecration holds the key to whatever religious significance the killing of Lucas Sethwala might have had for the residents of Paballelo township, as well as for the South African judicial system that tried and convicted them. In the context of the "unrest" that had erupted in South Africa in September 1984, the public execution of black collaborators, policemen, and other enemies of the people had been at the center of media accounts and public fears. The "necklace," placing a petrol-soaked tire around the head of the victim and setting it alight, became a ritualized method of both eliminating and desecrating perceived enemies. These "necklace murders" can be seen as ritual sacrifices of human beings.

In an important sense, I want to suggest, the killing of Lucas Sethwala was a ritual killing, a ritual act in which negotiations over the sacred were at stake. Clearly, the fact that the body of the dead Sethwala was desecrated suggests the importance of ritualized negotiations over sacred power in this event. Furthermore, the ritual character of this killing is also suggested in the interpretations of those who participated. Lucas Sethwala might have been known by the residents as an "ordinary boy," but as a policeman he had become implicated in the power of the state, a superhuman power that continuously reinforced the subclassification and oppression of the residents of Paballelo. No longer merely "ordinary," Sethwala could be identified as a symbol of the superhuman power of the system in and through which the people of Paballelo had been dehumanized.

For the residents of Paballelo, that system demonstrated its power by enforcing its own worldview—its classification of persons and its orientation in time and space—that dehumanized, displaced, and dispossessed those under its domain. The residents of Paballelo have been described as, for the most part, apolitical before November 1985; but they knew the pressures under which they lived. In the classification system of their world, Lucas Sethwala could be regarded as a symbol of the superhuman power of oppression. In the killing of Lucas Sethwala, as journalist Rex Gibson observed, "a symbol of the system had been demolished."[12] But in the person of Sethwala it was not merely demolished; it was desecrated, desacralized, and in the acts of kicking, stabbing, and setting the body on fire, that superhuman power was dramatically, symbolically disempowered.

As flames engulfed Sethwala's body, at least some of the crowd demonstrated that they knew that a dramatic contest over symbols had occurred, as they sang, "Hey, hey die hond is dood" ["Hey, hey the dog is dead"]. Sethwala's status was not only ambivalent—similar but, at the same time, different than that of other residents of the township—but he held a highly charged position at the heart of a network of classifications. If his killing was in fact a ritual sacrifice, it was enacted in the interest of renegotiating the ordinary, normalized classification of persons within which the participants lived.

Here I think that Girard may provide some help in understanding what was at stake in the killing of Lucas Sethwala. First, the killing can be understood as the deflection of the violence that had entered the community onto a single, sacrificial victim. Girard has referred to such a victim as a "surrogate," a single target for all the violence and conflict that might be active or endemic in a human community. "Any community that has fallen prey to violence," Girard has argued, "hurls itself blindly into the search for a scapegoat."[13] Clearly, Paballelo township had fallen prey to violence, which had assumed many, multiplying forms. It had found its way into the township in the structural violence of oppression; it stalked the residents in the violent interventions by the police. But violence also appeared in the internal tensions and conflicts over community resources extracted by the high rents charged by absentee landlords and dissipated by beerhall drunkenness. In the midst of this turmoil the community looked for a scapegoat. This violent response to violence emerged in the selection and elimination of a surrogate victim. The killing of Lucas Sethwala did not result from a premeditated design, as defined under the legal doctrine of common purpose; nor did it result from the deindividuation of participants in mob hysteria. I suggest that the killing of Lucas Sethwala should be seen as a momentary, spontaneous, violent unanimity achieved by a community when it identifies a surrogate victim. By eliminating that single victim, the community briefly defended itself from the violence that threatened to destroy it.

As Girard has observed, the perfect scapegoat tends to be a person that a community identifies as both familiar and foreign. The surrogate victim stands on the symbolic boundary that divides the inside from the outside of the community. According to Girard, "the victim must be neither too familiar to the community nor too foreign to it."[14] The perfect victim, therefore, would have to be a marginal, liminal, or borderline person who was both inside and outside the community. Lucas Sethwala occupied precisely such a borderline position in the Paballelo township. He was an "ordinary boy" from the township, but he was also a policeman who drew upon sources of power and authority that resided outside the township. If some of the residents of Paballelo did look for a surrogate victim on that Wednesday morning in 1985, they would not have looked for the landlords outside the community or the drunkards within; they would have looked for a victim on the margins, neither too familiar, nor too foreign, one whose position was nevertheless symbolic of the tensions in the community.

Lucas Sethwala was marginal in another sense that must have been important in his selection as a surrogate victim. We have seen that he held a peculiar position in a system of classification that was probably widely shared by residents in the township. He was obviously a human being, but he had drawn upon the superhuman power represented by the state in the pursuit of antihuman ends. But even before his ritual desecration, Lucas Sethwala was widely known in the township by the nickname, "the dog." This "ordinary boy," this "symbol of the system," was also "the dog," because, as many residents observed, "He bites like a dog." In this symbolism, therefore, Lucas Sethwala violated a widely shared classification of persons in the community by simultaneously representing the human, superhuman, and subhuman. He was a perfect surrogate victim because his elimination could renegotiate a pure, human place by removing a human anomaly that was symbolized as both subhuman dog and superhuman system. By the selection, elimination, and desecration of a single surrogate victim, residents of Paballelo temporarily renegotiated the purity of person and place in their world.

In such a violent ceremony of ritual elimination, Girard has noted, "the community itself is felt to be free of infection—so long, that is, as the cultural order within it is respected."[15] Because Paballelo township was absorbed in the larger economic, social, and political order of the South African state, the ritual renegotiation of its own, internal cultural order was not respected for very long. Residents themselves were soon selected for a different, yet similar, role as surrogate victims in the cultural order represented by the South African judicial system.

Public Systems

René Girard has made some sweeping claims for violent unanimity as the origin of religion. He has even insisted that "violent unanimity will reveal itself as the fundamental phenomenon of primitive religion."[16] Many commentators have expressed reservations about Girard's argument. According to Girard, however, violence is at the root of everything—religion, culture, society. In arguing that violence is endemic to human social relations, he has traced violence back to what he has called "mimetic desire." Simply, valued objects of social interest are not desired because they are intrinsically valuable; they are desired because they are objects of someone else's desire. In this logic of desire, conflict is not derived from some kind of libidinal, aggressive instinct, but from symbolic, dramatic imitation.

When conflicts over the objects of desire inevitably arise, those conflicts take on the character of reciprocity, a reciprocity of reprisal and revenge. In the cycle of revenge, every reprisal calls forth another, so that each reprisal feeds "an interminable, infinitely repetitive process." Instead of breaking the pattern of violence, every act of reprisal perpetuates it by becoming the occasion for a corresponding act. In Girard's analysis of human social relations, the reciprocal regard of mimetic desire inevitably results in an interminable cycle of reciprocal revenge. Revenge cannot break what it in fact perpetuates. Therefore, Girard has argued, "it is vengeance itself that must be restrained."[17]

How is vengeance—the cycle of reciprocal revenge—restrained? "Only violence can put an end to violence," Girard has insisted. That ultimate, final, terminating violence, however, must somehow stand outside of the cycle. The violence that stands outside—a superhuman, transcendent violence—can be located in those public systems that focus the internal aggressions, conflicts, and tensions of a community upon selected victims. Thus the sacrificial system in so-called primitive societies and the judicial system in so-called modern societies are in place "to avoid the vicious cycle of revenge" and "to break the symmetry of reprisal."[18] They represent a systemic, structural, or institutionalized monopoly on violence, ostensibly representing the violent unanimity of a community that focuses, deflects, and thereby restrains its own potentially self-destructive violence.

Both of these public systems, however, duplicate the structural violence that Girard has located in generative scapegoating, the selection of a surrogate victim who will be identified and killed through the violent unanimity of a community. The sacrificial system and the judicial system therefore might be understood as transcendent substitutions for the violent unanimity that constitutes a community whenever it channels its internal "bad" violence into the "good" violence that expels or eliminates its surrogate victims. These public systems of religion and law therefore involve ritualized substitutions that replace, yet duplicate, the kind of mob violence that results in the selection and killing of surrogate victims.

In his analysis of sacrificial ritual, Girard has insisted that "in every instance a mob murder is being reenacted, although the scenes will vary in detail." In spite of all the differences of detail in practices of ritual sacrifice, the killing of animal or human victims recreates the violent unanimity found in any collective murder of a surrogate victim. Girard has identified the connection between the collective killing of a surrogate victim and sacrificial ritual as a process of symbolic substitution:

> All sacrificial rites are based on two substitutions. The first is provided by generative violence, which substitutes a single victim for all the members of the community. The second, the only strictly ritualistic substitution, is that of a victim for the surrogate victim. As we know, it is essential that the victim be drawn from outside the community. The surrogate victim, by contrast, is a member of the community. Ritual sacrifice is defined as an inexact imitation of the generative act.[19]

Like the generative act of violent unanimity in the expulsion of a surrogate victim from the community, sacrificial ritual deflects and thereby restrains all the internal tensions, feuds, and rivalries that would otherwise disrupt a community. In other words, Girard has argued, ritual sacrifice breaks the cycle of reciprocal revenge by a process of substitution. That ritual substitution must have at least two characteristics: It must receive unanimous assent and it must focus the violence of the community upon a victim who is sacrificeable because it is drawn from outside the human community—as animals might be outside or, in the case of human victims, as slaves, enemies, or strangers might be outside. That is, the sacrifice must be a victim who may be killed without risk of reprisal. In a functioning sacrificial system, therefore, ritual killing breaks the cycle of reciprocal revenge by assuming a monopoly over the exercise of legitimate violence, a monopoly over the "good" violence that protects a community from its own "bad" violence by channeling all its internal conflicts into the violent elimination of sacrificial victims.

Like the sacrificial system, a judicial system operates to break the cycle of reciprocal revenge in a society. As part of the legal apparatus of a modern state, a judicial system is necessarily part of the organized, exclusive exercise of violence over a territory that defines what is meant by a state. In Girard's terms, a judicial system holds a "monopoly on the means of revenge." By maintaining that exclusive, legitimate exercise of violence in a society, a judicial system functions to interrupt any cycle of revenge that might erupt. Under a judicial system, "an act of vengeance is no longer avenged; the process is terminated, the danger of escalation averted."[20]

In order to work, however, a judicial system must disguise the tenuous grounds of its legitimacy and the arbitrary nature of its selection of victims. A judicial system must therefore operate with the functional equivalent of a theology in order to justify its exclusive monopoly on violence. Like a religious sacrificial system, a judicial system, if it is to maintain any sense of legitimacy, must employ a convincing symbolism of authority. "In the same way that sacrificial victims must in principle meet the approval of the divinity before being offered as a sacrifice," Girard has suggested, "the judicial system appeals to a theology as a guarantee of justice." Even without an explicit appeal to religion, a judicial system must draw on symbolic resources of superhuman power and sacred purity if it is to retain an aura of legitimacy. The transcendent authority of a judicial system is most obvious in its claims on sovereign power over life and death. However, the power invested in a judicial system to exact capital punishment also tends to be negotiated within a symbolic idiom similar to that articulated by the expulsion of the surrogate victim.

Clearly, the selection of a surrogate victim for elimination by residents of Paballelo township came into conflict with the state's claims to an exclusive, sovereign monopoly on violence through its own judicial system. To refer again to a statement made by Justice Basson, the court "cannot allow that people murder an innocent person if they have grievances against the state authority." Only the state, through its judicial system, has that transcendent, pure power to kill persons, innocent or otherwise. The work of René Girard has suggested that the power and purity of state violence is essentially religious. The state's monopoly on violence is asserted as "that transcendental effectiveness of violence that is holy, legal, and legitimate." Any exercise of violence outside of the control of the state is "a violence that is unjust, illegal, and illegitimate." In the ordinary workings of any judicial system, the transcendent and sacred dimensions of law and order remain hidden because they are unquestioned. As soon as the legitimacy, power, and purity of a judicial system are lost, however, they become conspicuous by their absence. "There are no longer any terms," Girard has noted, "by which to define the legitimate form of violence and to recognize it."[21] Without a legitimate public system to contain and restrain violence, the social order breaks under the strain of what Girard has called a "sacrificial crisis" and begins to identify and to eliminate surrogate victims in attempts to renegotiate the order of its world.

In the conflicts, tensions, and violence that beset South African black townships in the 1980s, one of the sites of struggle was the ideological power and purity of the state's monopoly on violence. In an important sense, the military and the police had set the terms for negotiation over the legitimate exercise of violence in South Africa. In defending the actions of the South African Defence Force in the black townships, Minister of Defence Magnus Malan told Parliament in 1986 that the state was in a contest against radicals and agitators who "seek the sole right to threaten, to intimidate, to terrorise, and to manipulate people in black areas."[22] Presumably, only the state held that sole right. In claiming that exclusive right to the exercise of violence over a territory, spokesmen for the military and the police justified their actions in terms of a holy, just, and legitimate violence that would restrain any violence defined, circularly, as illegitimate because it violated the established order of the state. As Brigadier Theuns Swanepoel was quoted in 1986, "You can only stop violence by using a greater amount of violence."[23] René Girard could not have said it better. But Girard has also insisted that for a public system—religious, sacrificial, or judicial—to work, the violence it exercises must be greater not only in quantity, but also in the quality of the unanimity it invokes. When a public system does not achieve the unanimity that allows its arbitrary construction to be disguised, it collapses, not only in what has been called a legitimation crisis, but also in the sacrificial crisis that inevitably results in the search for surrogate victims.

The state has had three basic mechanisms for the ritual killing of surrogate victims: capital punishment, extrajudicial detention, and death squads with a mandate to eliminate persons regarded as enemies of South Africa. The latter two mechanisms have been largely invisible, performed in secret, and veiled by official denials. Nevertheless, they represent important avenues by which the state has violently negotiated its own sense of power, purity, and order. Between 1976 and 1990, approximately eighty people died under suspicious circumstances while held in detention without charge or trial. The most widely publicized death in detention was that of Steve Biko, leader of the black consciousness movement, in 1977. The judicial system collaborated in Biko's death to the extent that it exonerated the police of any responsibility. It can be argued that Steve Biko was a sacrificial victim in a recurring state ritual of law and order. National Party Member of Parliament Frank le Roux spoke on behalf of many in the government for whom Steve Biko was a surrogate victim in a ritual killing that renegotiated the power and purity of the apartheid world. "In South Africa," Le Roux was quoted in the press, "when a man disturbs law and order in the way Steve Biko did, he should be killed." Announcing a common purpose in that ritual killing, he was quoted as concluding, "I would have killed him."[24] Although a martyr for the majority of South Africans, Steve Biko was a scapegoat for those who killed him. For the state, his killing symbolically reinforced a domain of law and order through violent ritual.

Long suspected of operating inside and outside the country, death squads came to the attention of the South African media at the end of 1989. Ironically, it was a prisoner on death row who broke the story by claiming that he had been a paid killer in a secret military death squad working for a government agency known as the Civil Cooperation Bureau (CCB). The CCB had apparently drawn up a long list of "enemies" of the state, identifying them as sacrificial victims for elimination. The first media account of a CCB operation contained many of the ritual elements that appeared in the Paballelo killing: It described a collective act, performed on a single victim, whose body had been ceremoniously stabbed, mutilated, and desecrated. The common purpose in the act apparently issued from the state, for the death squads allegedly operated under the auspices of the South African Defence Force. As a secret society, the CCB was involved not only in political violence but also in religious ritual. The religious interests of the CCB were certainly revealed in its targeting of prominent church leaders for surveillance and elimination. In the case of Archbishop Desmond Tutu, however, the CCB engaged in a curious ritual by placing a monkey fetus at Tutu's home. Although government agents in the past had been accused of killing pet dogs or cats to threaten and intimidate "enemies" of the state, the ritual manipulation of a monkey fetus was a bizarre twist in state sacrificial ritual. Like the sacrificial killing of animals, the selection of surrogate victims by death squads enacted a ritualized, sacred order of power and purity enforced by secret agents of the state. One of those secret agents, self-confessed CCB operative, Captain Johannes Dirk Coetzee, indicated that he had imagined his work as ritual killing by describing his attitude toward "enemies" of the state: "Let the bastards burn at the stake." Like the burning of heretics or witches, the killing of "enemies" was in the worldview of the Civil Cooperation Bureau a ritual elimination.[25]

While ritual killings in detention or by death squads were carried out in secret, another form of sacrifice was exercised in the public judicial system. Throughout the 1980s, South Africa maintained a notoriously high rate of judicial executions. During 1987, for example, South Africa executed more people than Iran (population 47 million) or China (population 1 billion). The 164 executions in South Africa, excluding the so-called independent homelands, stand in contrast to 25 in the United States and, more significantly with regard to changing perceptions of the death penalty, with the fact that since 1985 there had been no judicial executions in Western Europe.[26] General arguments against capital punishment have stressed the lack of evidence that it serves as a deterrent, the possibility of judicial error, and its irreversibility, allowing for no redress. In South Africa, however, two more specific problems with the state's use of capital punishment were identified—racial bias and absence of a mandate.

First, critics often alleged that the death penalty had been applied unfairly and arbitrarily along racial lines. In a 1985 report on the legitimation crisis of the South African legal system, Professor John Dugard criticized racial bias in sentencing in "interracial homicides and assaults, where the evidence suggests that whites found guilty of killing or seriously assaulting blacks are punished more leniently than blacks when they kill and assault whites, and in interracial sexual offences, particularly rape, where black offenders are punished more severely than whites." After a 1987 case in which a seventeen-year-old white youth was sentenced to six strokes with a light cane and a suspended five-year sentence for killing a black man with a baseball bat, Professor J. D. van der Vyver observed that in many cases "it would seem that our courts regard the racial element in a white-against-black violent crime as an extenuating circumstance and in black-against-white crime as an aggravating circumstance. This kind of racism in the administration of justice is most unfortunate." These interracial cases were merely the most visible instances of racial bias in the application of the death penalty in South Africa. In all capital cases, blacks were more likely to be sentenced to death than whites. Commenting specifically on the collective death sentence delivered in the Upington case, Brian Curtin, the national director of Lawyers for Human Rights, warned that "continued application of the capital system, particularly with murder convictions where judges have no discretion in the absence of extenuating circumstances and where the common purpose doctrine is applied—will inevitably result in the perception primarily in the black community, that judicial execution is nothing other than legalized genocide."[27]

Second, the South African judicial system was vulnerable to the criticism that it lacked a popular mandate to sit in judgment over the majority of the population. Representing the objection of the African National Congress to capital punishment, one critic observed that "the people of South Africa have never granted the regime and its judiciary the right to make laws on our behalf and stand as judges over us." Therefore, capital punishment was not only opposed for legal or humanitarian reasons, but on the more fundamental political ground that the South African judicial system lacked legitimacy. The selection of victims for capital punishment suggested that the death penalty was being deployed in a political conflict. By 1988, more than fifty people were awaiting execution for crimes related to political activity. Many of those on death row were claimed by the ANC as soldiers in their liberation struggle against the government. As prisoners of war, the ANC argued, they should be treated under the terms of the 1977 protocols to the Geneva Conventions of 1949, which the ANC had signed, but the South African government had not. By denying them POW status and executing these soldiers in the struggle, the judicial system was perpetrating what the ANC and its supporters regarded as war crimes under international law.[28]

Those who denied the judicial system's legitimacy, however, extended the argument over POW status in capital cases even to cover the defendants in a murder trial like the Upington case. In a discussion of a similar case in 1988, Mervyn Bennun argued that the trial of the Sharpeville Six revealed the crisis of legitimacy facing the South African legal system. "The South African regime is illegitimate," Bennun insisted, "and it is an atrocity and a war crime to put on trial those who strive to bring it down." Throughout the country, people had tried to bring down apartheid by killing town councillors, municipal policemen, and others perceived as collaborators with an oppressive government. In the Sharpeville case, a crowd had killed a town councillor and had desecrated the body. As in Paballelo, the victim, according to Bennun, had "identified himself with the regime, and was willing to enforce its oppressive laws." Since the legitimacy of those laws had been denied by international law, Bennun concluded that those captured in the Sharpeville case, and by implication those singled out for trial and punishment in the Upington case, should have been assigned the status of prisoners of war.[29]

During the 1980s, the legitimacy crisis of the judicial system was contested not only in terms of international law, but also by the creation of alternative judicial systems in the townships. Rejecting the "apartheid courts" of the state, "people's courts" emerged in many townships as an alternative mechanism for adjudicating conflict and enforcing law and order. While most cases before "people's courts" addressed domestic or neighborhood conflicts, in rare cases the courts claimed a popular mandate for carrying out rituals of capital punishment. As in Paballelo, the victims of these rituals were marginal persons—inside the community, but identified with the state outside—who were selected as sacrificial victims as a way of renegotiating the power and purity of the community. In the contest over sacred rituals of judicial violence, the state responded to the challenge to its legitimacy represented by these executions by reasserting its own rituals of capital punishment. As long as "gruesome and senseless killings like 'necklace' murders are committed," Minister of Law and Order Adriaan Vlok announced, "no one can claim pardon for such brutal killers."[30] In the state's myth of legitimation, the authority of its judicial system had to be reasserted through an uncompromising exercise of revenge by means of capital punishment.

Imbued with a sacred aura, the sacrificial killing of surrogate victims through capital punishment was a significant ritual of the South African state. That ritual served to enact certain important myths—a myth of revenge, a myth of deterrence, a myth of law and order, and even a myth of the immortality of apartheid. At Pretoria Central Prison, ritual attended the disposition of the bodies of the executed. Families were allowed to attend a brief service at the prison following the hanging, but were excluded from the burial. They were only provided with the number of the grave in the cemetery to which the body had been assigned. The dead were taken to the cemetery that corresponded to their racial group under the apartheid system of population registration. As Lloyd Vogelman has noted, "even in death apartheid lives."[31] Even the ritual disposition of the sacrificial victim's body, therefore, reinforced the power and purity of the particular, peculiar order represented by the South African state.

A countermyth emerged, however, in the midst of the state rituals of execution. Apparently, prisoners on death row circulated a myth of survival, a mythic expectation that when the noose was placed around their necks, and the floor dropped out beneath their feet, they would fall into the pit alive. Below the floorboards of Pretoria Central Prison, according to this myth, all those who were supposed to have been executed continued to live and work in the government mint. In the Upington case, state judicial ritual also generated a countermyth, not a myth of survival in the underworld of the South African economy, but of liberation in a free world. That countermyth was voiced by defendant Justice Bekebeke, who had been identified by the court as the one who had delivered the fatal blows, singled out, in that respect, as the state's primary sacrificial victim. As he heard his sentence of death, Justice Bekebeke announced a religious and political vision of liberation. Addressing the court, Bekebeke told the judge, "I would like the Lord to give you many years so that one day you can see me walking on the streets of a free South Africa—may the Lord bless you."

CHAPTER 3

Witches and Demons

•

WE HAVE seen ritual killing operating in two ways: as a violent offering and as the elimination of a surrogate victim. Certainly, those types of ritual killing have overlapped. In the case of Barend Hendrik Strydom, the ritual killing of black people was a sacrificial offering to a violent nationalist God. But it was also a sacrificial elimination of human victims that Strydom had classified as marginal persons in his racist worldview. In that sense, it was also an elimination of surrogate victims in the interest of renegotiating the order of a particular community. People who shared Strydom's worldview saw his actions as reinforcement of their unanimity. While Strydom stood trial for his crimes, supporters gathered outside the courthouse. One visible supporter was the leader of the Kappie Kommando, Marie van Zyl. She was quoted as claiming that nothing had unified her people, the Boerevolk, like the violent acts performed by Strydom on the streets of Pretoria. As both offering and elimination, therefore, Strydom's ritual killings became the focus for a violent unanimity among right-wing, white supremacists.

In chapter 2, we saw how the violent unanimity of those who suffer under apartheid could also be achieved by the collective ritual killing of a surrogate victim, a process duplicated and claimed by the state in its public systems for identifying and killing its own surrogate victims. This chapter continues the analysis of how ritual actors have dealt with those who are perceived to be violating the sacred purity, law, and order of a community. In traditional or ancestral African religion, the identification and elimination of people who challenged the unity of the social group was conducted in the symbolism of witchcraft. In addition to the elimination of witches, however, I also want to consider a third type of ritual killing, one that involves the incorporation of the victim as a symbol of power. Where the elimination of witches might be practiced to restore purity to a community, the killing of human victims for strong medicine has been performed and understood as a means of increasing the power of ambitious individuals. Often referred to as "medicine murder," or "*muti* murder," the ritual killing of human beings for power has been perceived as an antisocial, evil practice in traditional African religion. But symbolisms of evil have often provided the context for interpreting and exercising violence. In this respect, witches, demons, and as we shall see, even the evil forces of Satan have been important factors in the relations between religion and violence in South Africa.

Ritual Elimination

Traditional African religion has provided symbolic resources for negotiations and contests over sacred symbols of power and purity. The idiom through which those negotiations often have been conducted has been called witchcraft. Careless use of the term, however, has often blurred crucial distinctions, not only that between witches and sorcerers, but among witch finders, witch accusers, witch doctors, witch confessors, and many others who have participated in these African negotiations over sacred symbols. Furthermore, witchcraft beliefs and practices have comprised a highly charged symbolic idiom in and through which violence has been defined, exposed, and counteracted in human social relations. Whether violence is defined as harm caused to persons or property, or as any violation of humanity, witchcraft and sorcery have located violence in African religious worldviews.[1]

In his notes on African religion, J. C. Warner, a government agent in the eastern Cape in the 1850s, described the ritual practiced to identify the evil influences that disrupted a person, family, or community, a ceremony that was dramatically enacted by African specialists in the idiom of sacred symbols. Before describing this *umhlalo* ceremony—the ritual of "smelling out," in which a sacred specialist detected and identified evil persons as witches—Warner was careful to qualify his observations with two preliminary judgments that continue to distort perceptions of African religion up to the present. First, he noted that this ceremony for detecting witches was called the "witch dance" by white colonists. In that designation, the colonists obviously misunderstood a ceremony conducted to oppose witchcraft as an instance of the very thing it was designed to eliminate. This misunderstanding would have significant repercussions. Second, Warner insisted that the ceremony not only represented the practices of self-deceived deceivers, but demonstrated that Africans were "under satanic influence." The imposition of a Christian symbolism of evil on an African ritual also would reverberate throughout the South African history of religions.

According to Warner's account, the ceremony for identifying witches first required the permission of a chief. Political sanction was necessary for the religious, ceremonial purification of a person, family, or village of evil influences. Once a chief's permission had been obtained, those seeking assistance with some illness, crisis, or affliction went to a priest's homestead, hired the priest, and arranged for the ceremony. During the ritual, the people sat in two semicircles, one side comprising those who were seeking assistance, the other side made up by the priest and his supporters. Although a number of different techniques might be employed, one method for discerning the source of evil was a kind of group therapy session conducted by the priest. Making diagnostic statements about their crisis, the priest listened carefully to the responses of the clients as they indicated their assent by agreeing, humming, clapping, drumming, or striking spears against the ground. At some point, the priest retreated to his hut, while the humming and drumming continued. Emerging from the hut, the priest went into a frenzied dance, during which he was said to be possessed by or in communication with ancestral spirits. Finally, the priest named the witch, sorcerer, or evil person and identified the acts that had been responsible for causing the crisis under investigation. If the person was present, family, friends, and neighbors in the semicircle separated to leave the accused standing alone, exposed as an evil, disruptive, defiling influence in the community.

Apparently, the accused had a number of options at that point. If the accused confessed, the purity code of the ceremony required the offering of an animal sacrifice as a ritual cleansing. The power code required payment to the chief, a custom often alleged to have been abused by chiefs to appropriate the property of wealthy subjects. Once the symbolic demands of both purity and power were satisfied, the accused was at liberty to resume a normal life in the community. If this reincorporation did not take place, the accused faced the confiscation of property and banishment as punishment. In some cases, the accused might be interrogated and even tortured to confess and reveal the magic materials that had been used to exert evil influence over others; and in rare cases the accused, especially one who refused to confess, could be executed under the authority of a chief. Although the execution of witches was always a possibility, it is important to remember what a rare occurrence the killing of accused and convicted witches apparently was. As long as African polities were intact, confiscation of property and banishment of the witch could work just as well as execution to eliminate evil from the midst of a community.[2]

This complex of witchcraft beliefs and practices has often been credited with underwriting a certain moral order and social stability in traditional African societies. In an often cited passage, anthropologist Monica Wilson described the social function of this symbolism of evil among the Pondo she studied in the 1930s:

> The danger of being "smelt out" for witchcraft or sorcery is a sanction for social behaviour. Any who make themselves unpopular are liable to be "smelt out." The woman who is lazy and bad tempered will soon be accused of witchcraft by her co-wives. A man who is stingy and quarrelsome is accused by neighbors. Any who diverge widely from the social norm are in danger. In this way belief in witchcraft and sorcery makes for social stability.[3]

Besides maintaining the ethnographic present, this description of moral sanctions and customary stability was framed in the passive voice, obscuring the interests and agency of the actors in the ceremony. In this respect, it is important to remember that sacred specialists who acted against the violence of witchcraft and sorcery were not only representatives of chiefs and public opinion; they were also crucial counteragents against danger and defilement in their own right. To the extent that these counteragents were integrated in an African polity, they operated simultaneously in a power code under the auspices of a legitimate ruler and in a purity code of a religious symbolism of evil.

Accusations of ritual killing, human sacrifice, and cannibalism periodically recurred in nineteenth-century missionary propaganda about Africans in southern Africa, with a few missionaries even claiming to have found entire tribes of cannibals who feasted with grisly delight on human flesh. Certainly, these accusations must be subjected to skeptical critique, especially when African political discourse employed the expression "eat up" to signify the victory of one army over another on the field of battle, or to describe a chief's confiscation of the property of a subject convicted of some crime, but not to indicate the dietary consumption of human beings. While isolated incidents of eating human flesh might have occurred as a result of the disruptions of African subsistence economies in colonial wars, there is no convincing evidence that human flesh has ever been a regular part of the diet of any southern African community. In fact, the stereotyped figure of the cannibal appears in African folklore, always characterized by specifically antihuman attributes. For Africans, as well as for Europeans in South Africa, the motif of the cannibal must therefore be read with some caution, particularly when it operates in cross-cultural negotiations over claims to an authentic human identity that exclude some other as basically subhuman.[4]

Nevertheless, anthropologists working in South Africa have occasionally described human sacrifice as a feature of traditional African religion. As recently as 1950, the missionary and ethnographer François Laydevant insisted that many African communities in southern Africa had once included human sacrifices in their ritual practices that marked certain special occasions—the initiation of young men, the first hunt of the year, the first fruits festival, the founding of a new village, and the ceremony of rainmaking. Although Laydevant tried to make his case with reference to traditional practices of the southern Sotho, he argued, by extension, that human sacrifice had been an integral part of traditional African religion throughout southern Africa.[5]

The anthropologist had another, more proximate concern, however, in trying to show that human sacrifice was a traditional feature of African religion. Reports of ritual killings in Basutoland had been appearing in the press, shocking in their details of murder and the use of human flesh in powerful medicines prepared by witchdoctors. If the anthropologist could argue that ritual killing was a traditional African practice, then he could conclude that the recent "medicine murders" were nothing more nor less than the stubborn persistence of the same primitive patterns of thought that had operated in African religion for centuries. In that explanation, Africans could become explicable as an odd, but understandable, displacement of the past in the present, a past waiting to be replaced by a modern, westernized world and worldview.

I would argue, however, that the increasing incidence of ritual killing did not suggest a continuation of traditional practices at all. Instead, it represented new, innovative negotiations in the arena of sacred symbols that were only made possible by the separation of the purity and power codes that had been joined in the older African religious and political symbolisms of evil. This separation of power and purity was evident in two types of ritual killing that were often confused in public perceptions, media accounts, official condemnations, and legal prosecutions: (1) the sacrificial execution of accused witches to eliminate evil in the interest of restoring a symbolic order of purity, and (2) the sacrificial killing of humans to prepare medicines in the interest of symbolic, yet also tangible, gains in power. Both might be regarded as types of ritual killing. But the execution of alleged witches and the sacrifice of humans for medicine were two very different kinds of acts, one constructed in terms of purity, the other in terms of power, but both enacted in a social and political context in which those codes had been divorced and radically disrupted.

In several rare, but prominent cases in the 1970s and 1980s, alleged witches were executed. Characteristically, the execution was a public, ceremonial act. The witch was first identified by a sacred specialist as the evil, defiling agent responsible for the recent misfortunes of members of the community. Once the witch had been identified, the people who felt they had been wronged initiated the execution. But frequently, as accounts of these ritual killings noted, many other members of the community might be present as observers or participants. In a collective ritual, the designated victim was apprehended, stoned, killed, and finally burned, with the purifying flames signifying the total elimination of the defilement that had endangered the health, well-being, and order of the community. However, since that order had been fundamentally disordered by its absorption in the alienating political order of South African law, the witch accusers themselves became the accused and the condemned within a different symbolic order.

In some cases, one person could stand trial under South African law on behalf of a group. In 1971, for example, Mapela Daliwonga was sentenced to seven years in prison for the murder of a woman he believed to be a witch. On 2 April 1971, Daliwonga and seventeen other youths in the Mahlungulu location had hacked to death the alleged witch with axes and had burned her body because they had reason to believe that she had killed one of their friends by witchcraft and turned him into a zombie of the forest. Without invoking a principle like common purpose in this case, Justice Munnik only sentenced the one youth to prison. Explaining to the press that he kept telling people that there was no such thing as witchcraft, the judge complained that no one ever believed him.[6]

More frequently, large numbers of people were arrested. In December 1971, ninety-four people were arrested in the Maake township, near Tzaneen, for the stoning of two elderly people, both aged 60, who had been pointed out by a witchdoctor as the agents responsible for the deaths of two other people (and a pig) by lightning about ten days earlier. In February 1984, at Skilpadfontein, near Warmbaths, eight men were arrested following the killing of three members of a family—a man (aged 67), his wife (aged 45), and his brother (aged 47)—who had been designated by a witchdoctor as those who had called down the lightning that had recently killed a teenage boy. A large crowd—described in the press as a "mob of villagers"—had apprehended the three alleged witches, pelted them with stones, and finally burned them alive inside a car, before completing the ritual elimination of any trace of the witches by also burning down their houses. Upon conviction, the sentencing of these groups of people for the collective killing of alleged witches varied from case to case. In the 1971 Maake township case, for example, the ninety-four executioners were each given a two-year suspended sentence.[7]

The most widely publicized witch executions in recent times were the ritual killings that took place over a six-week period in 1978 in Lebowa, in and around a township near Pietersburg. Known as the case of the "Pietersburg Sorcerers," this series of executions accounted for the ritual killing of fourteen alleged witches. In the first incident, villagers consulted a *sangoma* to discover the cause of a car accident that had claimed the lives of three men returning from a football match the previous month. Apparently, the sacred specialist identified the source of that misfortune as a man (aged 60) and his wife. According to reports, villagers found the alleged witches, tied them up, and threw them into a fire. In a second incident, a man (aged 60) and two women (aged 44 and 45) were also pointed out as witches, locked into a hut, and burned alive while hundreds watched. Some days later, a third, similar incident resulted in the killing of a man (aged 58) and his wife (aged 50), also burned in their hut. The last episode concerned three men and two women who had been pointed out by a *sangoma* as the ones responsible for the death of a newlywed woman and her sister-in-law who had died on New Year's Eve when the wall of their hut collapsed after being struck by lightning. The five accused witches were locked in a hut that was then set alight, while hundreds of villagers watched. Their bodies were left in the charred remains of the hut because, as one of the villagers observed, "they were sorcerers and should not be buried decently." In the end, more than 150 people were arrested in connection with these executions; twenty villagers and one *sangoma* were eventually charged under the Suppression of Witchcraft Act.[8]

What are we to make of these witch executions? Clearly, they were ritual killings that acted out a symbolism of evil. Although they were made possible, certainly, by sacred specialists, they were ultimately enacted by members of a community, ostensibly on behalf of the safety and security of their community as a whole. In the interest of renegotiating the wholeness of a community that had been disrupted by some recent misfortune, ordinary people engaged in an extraordinary symbolic work that was designed to restore a pure, healthy social order by eliminating the defilement represented by the witches. In other words, these ritual killings were enacted in a symbolic purity code that required the expulsion of evil. In these cases, a sacred, pure order was restored by desacralizing or desecrating the witches, burning their bodies, burning their homes, burning their cars, and finally, completing a ritual exclusion of their remains that would prevent any reincorporation of evil into the purified community.

We know what the South African legal system made of these ritual killings, however. In arresting, charging, and convicting the executioners, South African law placed an entirely different symbolic construction on these events. Under the Suppression of Witchcraft Act, those who had thought they were detecting and punishing crimes were themselves charged and convicted as criminals, a reversal that, in the end, revealed the absence of any supportive power code strong enough to sustain the domain of purity that had been negotiated through the expulsion of witches. Moreover, the South African legal system was not alone in placing alternative symbolic constructions on the ritual killing of accused witches. For example, in response to the case of the "Pietersburg Sorcerers," the chief minister of the Lebowa homeland, Dr. Cedric Phatudi, made a public statement in which he blamed the ritual killings on illiteracy. Observing that only compulsory education could eradicate the superstition behind the killings, Dr. Phatudi not only tried to distance himself and his homeland administration from the recent events, but his interpretation also implied that the killings were residual survivals of a primitive, preliterate culture that must inevitably give way to modern, western education. In other words, the chief minister echoed a common assumption about these ritual killings: They were the result of primitive beliefs and practices that did not belong in a modern world.

But I have argued that these ritual executions of witches should be seen as modern innovations within the major, massive redistributions of purity and power that have occurred in the history of twentieth-century South Africa. To place these modern innovations in perspective, we need only refer to a different historical context, for example, that of the Xhosa-speaking communities of the eastern Cape in the 1830s. Among the Xhosa, the execution of convicted witches was an extremely rare occurrence. As one observer noted in 1837, the entire region might see no more than one execution a year, while some years would go by without a single execution for witchcraft. As the same observer continued, "Confiscation of cattle, and the facilities tacitly allowed the accused for escape, even when apprehended, diminish the list of public executions."[9] In short, as long as the purity code of witchcraft expulsion was embedded in the power relations of an independent polity, confiscation of property and banishment served as functional equivalents to execution in restoring the purity of a community. Only with the destruction of those independent polities did execution become the sole means available for eliminating a person identified and convicted as a witch.

Asked to comment on the ritual killing of accused witches in Lebowa, anthropologist Adrian Boshier, who had lived for seven years among the Pedi of Lebowa, suggested that it was the breakdown of political order that was responsible for the series of ritual killings. He insisted that the witchdoctors were involved in healing—especially the healing of "psychological disorders"—but not killing. Although Boshier apparently imagined that this medicalization and psychologization of the witchdoctor could stand free of any political grounding, he did recognize that it was the disruption of the political order that had made the ritual killings possible. During the time he had lived there, Boshier noted, "chiefs restrained the people from burnings and ritual murder."[10] What he did not suggest, however, was that the destruction of the polity had made killing not only possible but also necessary in any negotiations over the code of purity in African symbolisms of evil. Because the purity code had been torn loose from any power code sustained by an independent polity, the only avenue left for renegotiating purity was the elimination of evil through killing, burning, and desecration. Where purity could not be upheld by political power—the power to confiscate property and banish persons—it could only be achieved through violent rituals of elimination. Under conditions of political disempowerment, therefore, the ritual killing of witches emerged as a modern strategy for negotiating a sacred order of purity.

Ritual Incorporation

Witch executions represented symbolic negotiations over the sacred conducted by ordinary residents of a township or village. A different set of negotiations were undertaken by those who found themselves in the insecure positions of power, authority, or wealth within the new tribal politics of twentieth-century South Africa. We can trace the course of these negotiations in an examination of a second type of ritual killing—again rare, but highly sensationalized in the South African media—involving the sacrifice of human beings for the preparation of powerful medicine. These so-called medicine murders were also imagined to have had a long history in African traditional religions. Ethnographic literature on the subject of ritual murder suggests that human beings were sacrificed for two purposes—fertility and polity. If ritual killing was practiced in traditional African religion, its two purposes were defined as the doctoring of seed and the strengthening of chiefs. Since these two domains overlapped in traditional African sociocultural orders, however, they might be regarded as two aspects of a single power code that was reinforced by the ritual killing of human beings to strengthen the political interests of chiefs.[11]

The ethnographic evidence for human sacrifice in fertility rituals is actually rather meager. One Zulu case was reported in which a child was alleged to have been killed to make medicine for treating seed. Apparently, the medicine was made by mixing ingredients from plants, snake, rock rabbit, and the flesh and powdered bones of the child in order to make a compound that, when mixed with the seed, would protect against witchcraft and ensure a good crop. In a Swazi case, a young man was supposedly killed so that parts of his body could be used in a rainmaking ceremony. And in a case reported from Basutoland, certain chiefs apparently commissioned a sacred specialist to shed human blood in the fields when the maize was still green in order to ensure a good harvest.[12] It is difficult to draw any general conclusions from only three reports. However, if the planting and the harvest both came under the authority of a chief, we may assume that any killing of human beings for the purpose of making fertility medicine should be regarded under the same category as sacrifices made to strengthen the political power of the chief. In this light, there is slightly more detailed ethnographic evidence that ritual killing operated within a power code to provide strong medicine for insecure strong men.

Ethnographic examples of ritual killing to strengthen chiefs were all framed in terms of power. Extraordinary medicine derived from the taking of human life, flesh, and blood became a means to add strength to strength. Significantly, the earliest report of such a medicine killing suggests that the ritual code of power could be constrained by a communal purity code of social ethics. In 1874 a sacred specialist, a *ngaka* of the northern Sotho, with the complicity of his chief, killed his traveling companion and made medicine out of parts of his body to strengthen himself and his chief. Instead of realizing increased power, however, the *ngaka* was found out by his community and lynched for what must have been regarded as a crime against society. In addition, his wife was also killed, and his homestead destroyed, eliminating any trace of the sinister sacred specialist from the community.[13] Here the power code of ritual killing seems to have come up against and been constrained by a purity code that represented the moral standards of the community. In the ethnographic record, this earliest reported case of a ritual killing for medicine is also the only one that suggests that its practice was in tension with the moral order of an African community. Subsequent cases, particularly in the mid twentieth century, were quite clearly in conflict with the legal order that dominated South African society.

A Zulu case was reported in the 1930s in which a boy was allegedly killed, with the permission of his father, to make medicine that would strengthen Chief Nkunduzwa in the Nkandhla district.[14] But most of the cases in the 1930s and 1940s were reported from Basutoland. Earlier Basuto cases had also been reported. For example, a chief in the Pitseng district allegedly had an old woman killed, her flesh and bones powdered, to prepare medicine that would make him rich and powerful; and as early as the 1890s, rival sons of Chief Molopi of the Makholokoe district had supposedly committed ritual murders to obtain the chieftainship. They were believed to have consulted a Zulu sacred specialist by the name of Khokong, who was said to have used human flesh to make "medicine of power." Not altogether incidentally for the subsequent history of medicine murders in Basutoland, the witchdoctor Khokong was convicted under colonial law for his involvement in these symbolic, sacred negotiations over political power.[15]

In general terms, it was easy to observe in the 1930s and 1940s that ritual killings were performed by rival chiefs in Basutoland as a means of gaining power in the contests over status, prestige, and wealth in a shifting, changing political order. Chief Mahlomola Lerotholi required the body of a twin girl for medicine. With several allied chiefs, and the advice of the witchdoctor Seelso Motlatsi, Chief Lerotholi killed to obtain that medicine of power. Chief Tumahole Bereng ordered the murder of a certain Katse Phatela to use the victim's blood in a ritual to secure control over a disputed territory. His advisor in this matter, the witchdoctor Mosimo Kaphe, was subsequently arrested and died in prison. Chief Lehooe Letsikhoana killed a certain Lenkoe Motsotsoane in 1945 to use his body for medicine that would add to his strength. The chief himself was executed for this act by the colonial administration. In these three cases, medicine made from human flesh or blood was used to secure a chief in his position, to turn disputes in his favor, or to keep evil influences away. Nevertheless, the "medicine of power" obtained by ritual killing was not enough to counter the authority of the colonial legal system.[16]

By the end of the 1940s, it could be seen clearly that among the causes of these ritual killings were the political tensions created through colonial government policies that multiplied the number of chiefs, but drastically diminished their power. This analysis was developed with even greater precision in the early 1950s. In a report on the Basutoland medicine murders, G. I. Jones attributed the ritual killings to the instability of the political order that had resulted from the so-called reforms of 1938. In those reforms, the government had intervened directly in African politics by imposing two new systems. One was a placing system by which chiefs were often assigned arbitrarily to their positions. Sometimes minor chiefs were preferred to major chiefs, thereby disrupting hereditary or other prestige systems that had traditionally operated. The second was a money system, introduced particularly through the payment of salaries to chiefs, that disrupted conventional economic relations. As a result of these disruptions of African social, economic, and political life, chiefs—sometimes chiefs in name only—looked for sources of superhuman power under conditions of extreme instability. Of the ninety-three medicine murders that Jones was able to count going back to 1895, as many as seventy had occurred during the decade that followed the government interventions and reforms of 1938. The cause of this increase of ritual killings in Basutoland therefore could be specifically located in what M. D. W. Jeffreys called "a growing sense of insecurity among the minor chiefs because it is they who must resort to these murders to obtain human remains as a means of magically protecting themselves against adversity."[17]

In Basutoland, the "medicine of power" that required a human sacrifice was employed by insecure chiefs as an extraordinary strategy for negotiating their positions in the idiom of sacred symbols. By 1950, however, evidence had emerged that ritual killing for medicine might on rare occasions also be used by persons of lesser rank in the new tribal politics. In a case that came before the Native High Court in Durban in 1951, a village headman (*induna*) was tried for organizing a ritual killing in Zululand. According to the government witness Maqwangase Nzuza, an accomplice in the killing who was given immunity for his testimony, the *induna* Mhlopeni Koza (aged 46) had not only felt threatened in his position of authority, but had been beset by misfortune with the illness of his wife and children. The *induna* consulted two sacred specialists (*inyangas*), requesting powerful medicine that would strengthen his position as village headman. The specialists prescribed medicine mixed in the top of a human skull. Although a human skull was difficult to obtain, they advised Koza that he could buy one from a hospital. But the headman complained that he could not afford the expense of such a purchase.

At this point, tribal policeman Luhele Biyela (aged 50) apparently stepped in to suggest that they could acquire the skull by killing an *inyanga* by the name of Mgenge (aged 45). Proposing that they kill two birds with one stone, so to speak, the policeman Biyela suggested that if they killed Mgenge, Koza could take Mgenge's skull, while Biyela could take Mgenge's wife, whom he had been courting for some time. On 7 December 1950, the *induna,* policeman, and two accomplices invited Mgenge to join them in the Ongoye forest to search for monkey rope. According to the government witness, the *induna* also took along his son, allegedly with the intention of sacrificing his own child if the killing of Mgenge should fail. The witness Nzuza admitted that he had been the one to strike the first blow with an axe, but then described how he was joined by the others. The corpse was taken to another *inyanga*—not one of the original two sacred specialists who had given the prescription for "medicine of power"—and the body was cut up, its pieces distributed among the men who were present.[18]

This case illustrates some of the conclusions that anthropologist Harriet Ngubane has drawn about the practice of ritual killing for medicine. First, it was not the sacred specialist, the *inyanga,* who selected, let alone killed, the ritual victim. Receiving a demand for an extraordinary medicine of power, the specialist merely reflected back to his or her client the ultimate seriousness of that request within a traditional format of healing. Second, the ritual killing was not performed by an individual, but always by a group of people with some common set of interests. In most cases, that group was not defined by family or kinship, but by some set of political, business, or other interests that brought them together for the purpose of ritual killing. Third, the victim was selected because he or she had certain qualities required by members of the group to advance their position. In this case, those qualities ranged from the victim's symbolic power desired by the headman to the victim's wife desired by the policeman. But, in any event, the ritual victim was not chosen at random. In fact, the victim might have been a relative, a loved one, or as in this case, a child of one of the participants, who could be sacrificed in the interests of the group. Fourth, the demand for medicine of power came from relatively successful people who wanted to be more successful. In most instances, the demand for medicine derived from the ritual killing of a human being came from ambitious people who desired promotion, wealth, business advancement, or other symbols of power, but who felt blocked from achieving those goals through the ordinary means available to them within the traditional or modern society.

Finally, therefore, recourse to ritual killing for strong medicine was understood by sacred specialists and participants alike to be an extreme measure, a last resort, in symbolic, sacred negotiations over power. In apt imagery that deserves to be quoted at length, Harriet Ngubane has captured the extraordinary nature of both the theory of ritual killing in the traditional format and its increased practice in modern social settings.

> As I have tried to say, if we find that ritual homicide is no longer very rare we are certainly entitled to think that something is very wrong indeed; but what has gone wrong is not in any sense that the old and evil practices are being revived, rather that measures formerly reserved for exceptional circumstances are now evidently being used constantly. It is rather as though a man who kept a gun in his house lest violent thieves broke in at night found that he was bringing it along to the door every time anyone called; it would imply that normal conditions of security in everyday life had broken down. Anyone who thought that what was wrong was either the availability of the weapon or the readiness of the man to use it would obviously have misunderstood the whole situation.[19]

Ngubane has suggested a way to understand these practices of ritual killing. In traditional healing, the sacrificial killing of animals has been prescribed for two basic purposes: the expulsion of serious illness, disease, or evil through the sacrifice of a scapegoat animal and the restoration of health, purity, or order through sacrifice for the ancestral spirits. In exceptional circumstances, however, traditional healing might have prescribed a sacrifice to achieve both the expulsion of evil and the restoration of purity, for which an animal would not be adequate. Only a human victim would be sufficient for negotiating extraordinary purity and power in a single sacrificial act.

In that killing, sacrificial rules would have to be followed: After selecting the victim, the parts of the body required for medicine would be cut out while the victim was still alive. The victim's cries of pain—like the cries of any sacrificial animal, thought to summon the presence of supernatural forces—were required for the success of the ritual. Finally, the remains of the victim would not be buried, but would be left exposed in the open. In following these rules, the sacrificers obviously saw themselves operating in a traditional religious format. But those traditional religious resources, it is important to remember, were mobilized in new social, economic, and political situations, situations of intense insecurity and conflict over positions of power brought about by the government-enforced "retribalization" of African communities. As Harriet Ngubane has concluded, "the popularity among the ambitious of ritual homicide is due primarily neither to the wickedness of *inyangas* nor to the overweening greed of those who employ such means to attain their goals, but rather to the sickness of the society which induces them to believe that there is no effective alternative."[20]

Other conclusions, however, have been drawn by participants in the power struggles within which ritual killing has been employed. As already noted, the chief minister of Lebowa maintained that only modern, western education would put an end to the ritual killing of alleged witches. In the question of ritual killing for medicine of power, a similar argument was put forward by the chief minister of Zululand when he insisted that "only education and enlightenment can end such beliefs."[21] In other words, both homeland leaders concluded that the solution to the problem of ritual killing would be found in the very process of modernization that had disrupted social relations and thereby increased the practice of ritual killing. Along similar lines, officials in the government of Swaziland, where an estimated thirty ritual killings for powerful medicine had occurred during a five-year period in the early 1970s, appealed to chiefs, traditional healers, and the general public to replace these "primitive" rituals with "modern" forms of power. For example, the prime minister, Prince Mabandla, appealed to chiefs to cooperate with the power of the government and police to stamp out ritual killing and cannibalism. A national councillor, Lusendvo Fakudze, addressed a meeting of traditional healers, warning them against ritual killings for powerful medicine, but also invoking the power of the Swazi state by threatening them that if they refused to pay taxes they would be prosecuted like anyone else. The deputy prime minister of Swaziland, Zonke Khumalo, was reported to have been touring the country telling villagers, "You don't need human *muti* to make your crops grow. Look what I produce with fertilizer."[22] In these official responses to ritual killing, the "modern" power of the government, police, tax collectors, education, and even fertilizer was invoked as a stronger medicine to counteract the alternative negotiations on sacred power enacted through ritual killing. Ironically, it is in relation to that "modern" network of power relations that these desperate searches for strong medicine must be seen.

In the South African media, furthermore, different symbolisms of evil have been superimposed upon reports of ritual killing. Often, ritual killing has been represented in terms of the general, pervasive psychologization of evil that has been a common feature of modern worldviews. Thus it has been depicted as an insanity or mania endangering South Africa. Personifying that evil in psychological terms, one columnist declared, "In the past four years the mad '*muti* man' has struck nine more times." Another columnist employed terms from another symbolism of evil that reflected widespread public fears of these ritual killings by suggesting that they resulted from the demonic evil of satanism: "There is a dark, satanic side that has led to the wave of ritual murders."[23] Coincidentally, perhaps, this fear of satanism gained particular prominence among white churchmen, politicians, and the general public in South Africa at about the same time that ritual killings seemed to be on the increase. In doing battle against satanism, however, white South Africans demonstrated that they also could conduct witchhunts in their own negotiations over the purity and power of a sacred world.

Satanism

The headline of a 1974 feature story by journalist Norman West announced the danger: "Devil Worship Comes to South Africa." West described how this "new dangerous practice" had invaded the country, with its underground "Devil's Church" and "witches covens in old and derelict buildings where society's drop-outs live." The author had visited those derelict buildings in Cape Town in search of satanists, but, he complained, "None of the Satan-worshippers wanted to talk about the cult." Elsewhere, however, he did find a young man, described as a former university student, who was willing to talk. "Satan is for real, man," West quoted his informant. "I know many mates who are hooked on Satan. But it's a bad scene, real bad, man. Be a buddy and leave me out of the scene altogether. I'm a Jesus man now."

Although West was disappointed that none of the drop-outs, drug addicts, or street people wanted to talk to him about Satan worship, he did discover that many church leaders were eager to tell him what they knew about the dangers of satanism in South Africa. One Dutch Reformed Church minister in Cape Town told him that "many 'respectable' office workers go 'underground' at night and become ardent devil worshippers"; another in Johannesburg informed him that "devil-worshipping was becoming the 'in thing' among upper-income earners." Both of these informants disputed his earlier assumption that satanism was only a practice of society's degraded drop-outs. Apparently, it was also at work among decadent office workers and income earners. Cutting across class divisions, satanism also cut across the racial divisions that separated South Africans. "Satanism is also spreading," West discovered, "among non-whites in all the major cities." In the 1970s, satanism had come to South Africa. It continued to resurface periodically as a topic of public attention and concern throughout the 1980s.[24]

What are we to make of this symbolism of evil? It is tempting to conclude that, at least in one respect, satanism represented a blurring of class and racial distinctions embedded in the South African political order. In this view, satanism reflected a dangerous disordering of the dominant social, economic, and political order of South Africa. Perhaps the fear of satanism was nothing more nor less than a projection of white South Africa's inner demons.

This symbolism of evil was framed in highly charged imagery of defilement, danger, and superhuman demonic power. In claiming that satanism was widespread in South Africa, an exposé in the *Sunday Times* in 1974 revealed instead that the symbolism of evil associated with a particular kind of Christian demonology had considerable salience for many South Africans, both for the informants upon which the exposé was based and for its readers. Informants were cited to marshall evidence of the threat: A Johannesburg businessman, Mr. Neville Brown, explained that he had exorcised evil spirits from as many as 4,000 people in the past ten years; a former missionary worker by the name of Miss Winsom Schroeder exclaimed that "Devil worship is rife in South Africa"; a Presbyterian pastor was quoted as claiming that satanism "is the most dangerous and harmful cult in the country"; and a twenty-two-year-old woman by the name of Heather McLeod, described as a "devout Christian," recounted her spiritual battle against the forces of evil in which she exorcised a demon from a suicidal girl through prayer. "I believe she was genuinely possessed," Heather McLeod was quoted. "At the end of three days she vomited, had a final convulsion, and then relaxed. The demon had left her."[25] Of course, none of the testimony by these informants on satanism in South Africa actually presented any proof that such a cult existed. Rather, informants testified to their own appropriations of particular Christian symbols of evil in their own negotiations over sacred meaning and power.

The principal source of most media accounts of satanism in the 1970s was a self-proclaimed former satanist in his early forties by the name of Philip Botha. Claiming that he had been a member of a satanic church for seventeen years, until he converted to evangelical Christianity in 1969, Botha could say by 1975 that he had spoken about the evil of satanism to Christian audiences at over 650 churches throughout the country. He made many other claims: In February 1974, he stated that there were at least 20,000 satanists in South Africa; by September 1975 he was claiming that there were 40,000; and in May 1978 he seems to have been the authoritative source behind the statements made by Dutch Reformed churches—an editorial in the Nederduitse Gereformeerde Kerk's *Die Kerkbode,* a conference on satanism held by the Nederduitsch Hervormde Kerk—claiming that there were 90,000 satanists operating in the country. Showing a remarkable rate of growth over those years, the "Devil's Church" also seemed to be a curiously mobile organization. In 1974, Botha noted that there were seven satanic temples and forty-two satanic sanctuaries spread throughout South Africa, with most of the satanic cell groups meeting in "underground cellars, remote farmhouses, or disused warehouses." Questioned as to the whereabouts of those sites a year later, he explained that the satanists kept moving every three months so the police would not be able to trace them.[26]

According to Philip Botha, therefore, satanism was an expanding, mobile, underground force that threatened the Christian order of South Africa. Its central ritual, by his account, was the Black Sabbath, which systematically inverted Christian sacred symbols. Standing naked before an altar, the Satan worshiper sacrificed a black cat, bathed in its blood, spat out a communion wafer, saying, "I denounce Christ," and recited the Devil's Prayer, which began, "Our Father who art in Hell." In addition to specifying such details, Botha also revealed that Satan's priests were blond, blue-eyed, and tall, "something," he explained, "like fallen angels."[27] At this point, it might be argued, we have entered a realm of pure fantasy. Fantasy or not, it is important to remember both how widely publicized Botha's accounts were in South Africa and that satanism was real for those who negotiated the meaning and power of their sacred world against it.

For example, at a national youth conference of the Nederduitsch Hervormde Kerk, the Rev. Theunis F. J. Dreyer told his audience that satanism—with its 90,000 satanists—was a pervasive evil that threatened South Africa. "Satanism," Dreyer declared, "with its ritual murders, should be rooted from the country." Included in Dreyer's definition of satanism, however, were such things as the peace sign (because, he explained, it was actually a symbol of the devil, representing the horns of the goat), feminism, denim jeans, and the electric bass guitar that "stimulated sexual feelings."[28]

Certainly, these claims could be dismissed as the cranky fears of a particular kind of fundamentalist Christian worldview. Not so easily dismissed, however, was the seriousness with which satanism was addressed in South African newspapers. One editorial commented on the alleged wave of satanism in South Africa, not only arguing that its apparent increase was evidence of a society in violent turmoil, but also that it was a recent symptom of "primitive" man's superstitious misunderstanding of "hidden forces" that could only be understood by "modern" man: "Primitive man accepted that this world was full of hidden, mysterious forces which he did not pretend to understand. Modern man, looking inward, applying his intelligence, his will, and his understanding to some of these hidden forces, might well find himself; might find both the way out and the way to new life."[29]

Even this journalistic celebration of a "modern" worldview might be discounted if the issue of satanism in South Africa had not been taken up with such enthusiasm by the police. In March 1976, Minister of Police Jimmy Kruger promised strong government action against satanism. "We will stamp out this evil," Kruger declared, "with new and tougher legislation." The minister of police revealed that the government was looking into a revision of the Suppression of Witchcraft Act so that the "police can take more effective action against White satanists." "We don't take this lightly," Kruger warned. "We are determined to stop these satanic practices with every means at our disposal."[30] In 1990, the minister of law and order, Adriaan Vlok, made a similar pronouncement. The police would do everything possible to combat this evil. Merging with communists, terrorists, traitors, and other political criminals that Ministers Kruger and Vlok were committed to stamping out, satanists became another potent symbol of evil within South African law and order. To that extent, satanism was a reality in South Africa even if no satanists actually existed.

In September 1978, a Cape Town newspaper reported that a witchdoctor in the black township of Guguletu had predicted the outcome of the current battle in South African politics over who would become the next prime minister. Considering all the potential candidates, the witchdoctor consulted the spirits of his ancestors. "They said he was a strong man," the witchdoctor reported, "a leader of men, of soldiers and armies. It was Mr. P. W. Botha. He will be the new Prime Minister." Of course, the witchdoctor was right, but right or wrong, there were white, Christian South Africans convinced that any contact with an African sacred specialist was evil. One reader wrote to the editors, objecting to the story about the witchdoctor and P. W. Botha because "the scriptures totally forbid us to have anything to do with such things as witchcraft." Hinting at the latent violence of this Christian symbolism of evil, the author concluded, "As I understand it, we uphold Christian standards in South Africa. Then don't let us incur the wrath of God in resorting to heathen practices."[31]

In white South African demonologies, heathen, demonic, satanic, and other evil practices have registered the disorder that has seemed to threaten an ordered world. Another name for that disorder has been "native crime." In the early 1950s, "native crime" assumed an increasingly blatant political definition. Blending with the political, however, was a certain kind of body politics, or sexual politics, that reinforced the separation of the races, protecting the purity of white women from black men. The "black scare" in this particular white South African worldview was embedded in a politics that was simultaneously sexual, political, and religious. In this respect, native crime was defined as anything that defiled the purity code or disrupted the power code of the body politic.

This overlap between the sexual and the political in a symbolism of evil has often been explicit in white South African worldviews. In 1953, Dr. M. W. Retief, acting secretary of the Federal Missionary Council of the Dutch Reformed Churches, spoke to a church conference in Pretoria on the topic of "native crime." Revealing the symbolic character of the domain of law and order, Dr. Retief informed his audience that "native crime" was caused by "bad literature." As we might expect, "bad literature" was of two basic types—sexual and political. With respect to literature of an erotic nature, Retief maintained that some publications contained "photographs which had the effect of destroying the native's respect for White women." In this sexual "bad literature," Retief insisted, "subtle propaganda was made which led to the healthy relationship between the racial groups being harmed." One step in preventing "native crime" and protecting a "healthy" white purity and power, Retief insisted, was the censorship of any erotic literature, not because it was erotic, but because it symbolized a blurring of the distinctions enshrined in the racial classifications of South African law and political order.

Moving from sex to politics, Retief proceeded to attack political literature that he regarded as representing a similar danger to "healthy" race relations. In particular, Retief argued that communist literature held a "stranglehold on the imagination of the Bantu." Like pornography, communist literature was thought to endanger "healthy" relations of purity (based on exclusion) and power (based on domination) in the sacred world and worldview of apartheid in the early 1950s. Communist literature was also like religion because it promised redemption from the very world that apartheid reinforced in South Africa. Retief observed that "Communism held out the promise of improvement of the fate of those who possessed nothing." Ultimately, however, Retief attacked communism and communist literature on religious grounds. Communism, he complained, "promised a virtual heaven on earth." According to Retief, this promise was one of the two basic causes of "native crime." Like pornography, communist literature should also be banned in South Africa as part of a larger sacred process of worldview negotiation conducted in and through a highly charged symbolism of evil.[32]

By the time Dr. Retief addressed his church conference, communism had already been specified by the government as the dangerous, disruptive, disordering evil that threatened the sacred world of the South African regime. An identification of evil with any change in the prevailing order was made explicit in the Suppression of Communism Act of 1950. Included in the definition of communism were any doctrines or practices "which aim at bringing about any political, industrial, social, or economic change within the Union by the promotion of disturbance or disorder, by unlawful acts or omissions, or by means which include the promotion of disturbance or disorder." Communism was broadly defined as anything that disrupted power or disordered purity in a sacred, inviolable South African world. Furthermore, that sacred domain of law and order was obviously constructed on racial lines. Thus the definition of communism also stipulated that for purposes of law it would include doctrines or practices "which aim at the encouragement of feelings of hostility, between the European and Non-European races of the Union, the consequences of which are calculated to further the achievement of any object referred to earlier in the definition."[33] Although many other conclusions might be drawn from this distinctive definition of communism in South African law, it is important to recognize this strategic exercise as an integral part of the negotiation of a worldview.

In this respect, communism emerged on one side of South African racial lines as a demonic, satanic evil, in fact, as the single designation for an entire symbolism of evil. On the other side, it should not be surprising that for many people communism did not register as evil within the same symbolism of evil that dominated South African law, politics, and religion.

We have seen that the sacred order symbolized by white domination and capitalism has been defended by the South African state through ritual killing. The lives claimed in this reinforcement of South Africa's purity and power can be seen as offerings to a violent nationalist God and as the elimination of surrogate victims. But that sacred order has also been defended against what have been perceived as satanic, demonic evils—the evils of communism, the evil of revolutionary onslaught, the evil of black liberation—by means of rituals of incorporation. In maintaining the power of its own order, the state has "eaten" people. Thus, in response to brutal police repression of the Defiance Campaign in the early 1950s, South African communist and labor leader Moses Kotane declared that government authorities "are Christians but they eat people. . . . If they represent God they represent a false God."[34] In profoundly symbolic terms, state and capital in South Africa have exercised other rituals that have "killed" human beings by incorporating them in regions and regimens of social death. The mines have eaten people; the prisons have eaten people. In those underworlds, the superhuman power of the South African order has been reinforced. As we will see in the next chapter, the mines and the prisons have been regions of ritual incorporation, dehumanization, and social death. To enter those regions is to enter a modern hell.

CHAPTER 4

Tours of Hell

•

IN THIS chapter, I focus more directly on the relationship between religion and dehumanization in South Africa. I indicate some of the ways in which religion has been implicated in institutionalized denials of humanity. Certainly, religion has underwritten the "crime against humanity" that has come to be known as apartheid, the separation, exclusion, and domination of black human beings in South Africa. This is well known. But beneath the surface of the racist order of apartheid, the South African economic, social, and political system has produced what I call violent underworlds of social death. In the depths of the mines and in the tortures of detention, many black South Africans have entered those violent underworlds. Many have never returned. Those who have returned to the light of day have known that they have been through a modern tour of hell. The dehumanization of human beings, as practiced in the mines and prisons of South Africa, has not merely been the consequence of a racist order; it has been a feature of the modern state. In South Africa, as elsewhere, one place to look for a recovery of humanity is within those places of social death.

It might be argued that religion is the opposite of racism. Putting that opposition simply: religion is humanizing; racism is dehumanizing. According to this argument, religion represents human beings at their best, striving for fulfillment in relation to the superhuman or the sacred. Racism, on the other hand, reduces human worth, something of irreducible value, to the accidental attribute of skin color. To remove religion by definition from the processes of dehumanization, however, is not so easy. Historically, religion has operated in many respects like racism to subclassify and exclude persons from the circle of humanity.

In the study of religion, scholars have operated with two basic definitions. One definition, following the anthropologist E. B. Tylor, sees religion as beliefs and practices related to superhuman beings. The other, following the sociologist Emile Durkheim, views religion as beliefs and practices related to sacred things that provide a unified focus for a community. These definitions suggest that religion is either about superhuman transcendence or about sacred inclusion in a human community. What these definitions neglect, however, is the ways in which religion is also the opposite of these things. The good news about religion—superhuman transcendence and sacred inclusion—has also been religion's bad news.[1]

Religion not only relates humans to the superhuman; it also carves out a classification of persons as subhuman. Those persons might possess what a biologist would regard as human features—opposable thumb, bipedal locomotion, and increased frontal lobe of the brain—but they are nevertheless classified as not fully human under such terms as stranger, enemy, heathen, infidel, pariah, heretic, criminal, or crazy. If religion can be described as an experiment in being human, it is an experiment, as we have seen, that is conducted by factoring out superhuman persons, perhaps to be worshiped, and subhuman entities to be excluded, dominated, or exploited.

Thus, religion sets symbolic terms for inclusion in a community, providing what sociologists of religion like to call the sacred canopy, overarching umbrella, or social cement that binds a community together. But it is important to realize that the terms for inclusion are also the terms for exclusion. In fact, a religious community often identifies itself in terms of who is outside it. Rituals of exclusion include excommunication, confinement, banishment, execution, and genocide. If exclusion is not complete in this world, it can still be anticipated in the next, when, to cite an example from one religious tradition, there will be a dividing of the saved from the damned, the sheep from the goats, the wheat from the tares, and the light from the dark.

Therefore, I would argue, the projects of subclassification and exclusion are shared by religion and racism. They are also shared by the modern state. Although the modern state frequently has drawn legitimation from conventional resources provided by religious institutions, it has also assumed a superhuman power and a sacred aura that has lent it a religious character of its own. Like any religion, the religion of the modern state has reinforced its superhuman transcendence by subclassifying certain classes of persons as subhuman; it has defined a sacred circle of human inclusion through exclusion. In the religious ideology of the modern state, the principal symbolic terms of subclassification have been the "criminal" and the "crazy." The principal ritual of exclusion has been a confinement, whether in prisons or asylums, that should be regarded as a type of social death.

In South Africa, religion, racism, and the emergence of a modern state have been intertwined in establishing rituals of exclusion. Certainly, the power and authority of the state has been reinforced by means of the standard modern institutions of exclusion, the prison and the asylum. But the authority of the state has also been shored up by two other ritualized practices that have been enacted in regions of social death—labor in the gold mines and torture in the secret confines of detention without trial. I turn first to an exploration of the violent underworld of the mines.

Slavery

In February 1987, the president of the National Union of Mineworkers, James Motlatsi, addressed the fifth annual congress of the union. With over 360,000 members, the National Union of Mineworkers could claim to be the largest national union in South Africa. It represented the interests of black mineworkers involved in a system of labor extraction, exploitation, and control. That system was based on migrant labor. It separated workers from wives, children, and families, who remained for the most part confined within one of the so-called homelands that functioned as reservoirs of cheap labor. That system was also based on the network of social controls that confined workers on the mines in single-sex hostels or compounds and restricted their movements through pass laws. According to Motlatsi, that system could only be called slavery. "The mineowners," Motlatsi declared, "have kept us in conditions of wage slavery and oppression." Slavery was the world that the mineowners had made.

His use of the highly charged term "slavery" should not be taken lightly, as if it were merely a rhetorical flourish. Certainly, the link between slavery and wage labor has been a commonplace in the Marxist analysis of social relations. As Marx observed, "direct forced labour, slavery, or indirect forced labour, wage labour," are both embedded in social relations in which wealth confronts labor as a "relation of domination."[2] The links between slavery and wage labor on the mines, however, can be even more clearly drawn. Black mineworkers have lived under conditions that fulfill every requirement of the definition of slavery provided by Orlando Patterson in his remarkable, cross-cultural analysis *Slavery and Social Death*: "Slavery is the permanent, violent domination of natally alienated and generally dishonored persons." As Patterson has argued, we misunderstand slavery if we think that it only occurs in legal systems that allow certain persons to be classified as property. Slavery occurs whenever and wherever persons are violently dominated, alienated from nurturing and supportive family relations, and treated in ways that violate their dignity and deny their humanity. In these terms, slavery is not merely a relation of domination; it is a violent social death.[3]

James Motlatsi described the migrant-labor system, the hostel system, the compound system, and other worker-control systems as if he were referring directly to Patterson's work. Motlatsi reminded his union that "these systems have robbed us of our dignity and destroyed our family life. The empire of the mineowners has been built on the blood, sweat and toil of black workers. Workers' rewards have been low wages, unhealthy and dangerous working conditions. Many comrades have paid the ultimate sacrifice of death at the hands of this brutal capitalist system."[4] In the worldview from the bottom of the mine, therefore, the labor system of the mining industry, reinforced by the state, looked exactly like slavery, the "permanent, violent domination of natally alienated and generally dishonored persons."

From its beginning, the mining industry justified coercion as an instrument of labor extraction. One mining official was asked, "Is there any way short of compulsion to make [the black worker] go to a mine?" He replied, "Not one that I know of." The state and the mining industry cooperated by introducing coercive tax systems. In 1893 a report of the Committee of the Mine Manager's Association advocated raising taxes "to such an amount that more natives will be induced to seek work, and especially by making this tax payable in coins only." The state was eager to comply. By 1900 a worker might have to labor for a period of three months just to pay the tax for himself and his family. In 1903 the Transvaal Labour Commission bluntly explained that the purpose of the state's taxation system was to "force the Natives to work in the towns and on the mines." The tax system thus worked in concert with land acts, color bars, pass laws, and other legislation through which the state lent its support to the mining industry's exploitation of black workers.[5]

The church also helped to create and sustain the violent underworld of the mining industry. In 1912, for example, the General Missionary Conference, meeting in Johannesburg, formally expressed its thanks to De Beers Consolidated Mines for supporting Christian missionary work among mineworkers. The conference declared that by allowing Christian missionaries to enter the closed worker compound, with its single-sex hostels, barbed-wire fences, armed guards, and pass system, De Beers had helped spread a Christian gospel of "morality" and "loyalty."[6] In the nineteenth century, Christian missions in southern Africa had been directly involved in the advance of commerce and the extraction of African labor. By the 1870s, the missionary "gospel of work" had become a standard theme. An 1878 editorial in the missionary newspaper the *Christian Express* stated this clearly: "We want to see the natives become workers. We believe Christianity will be a chief cause of their becoming a working people."[7] During the rise of an industrial capitalism based on the mining industry, this Christian "gospel" continued to be proclaimed by leaders of English-speaking churches. In the 1920s, an Anglican bishop observed with respect to black South Africans that "it may be God's will that most of them should always remain labourers, herd men, domestic servants, and the like"; a Methodist periodical announced that the formula for success in South Africa was the "combination of white man's brain and organizing power, and black men's hands and sweat." In both cases, the church lent its ideological support to the subclassification and dehumanization of black workers.[8]

The mineowners not only required a cheap labor force, but also needed to keep that labor force under control. Here churches also played a significant role. One of the most remarkable Christian missionaries in Johannesburg during the 1920s and 1930s was the representative of the American Board for Foreign Missions, Ray Phillips. Just as the American mining expert John Hammond had engineered the world of the mines, the American missionary Ray Phillips tried to engineer the religious worldview of the mines. Phillips saw the mines as a perfect opportunity for missionary work. The mining industry had brought workers from all over the country and locked them in compounds as a captive audience for the missionary. According to Phillips, therefore, migrant labor and mine compounds were blessed institutions through which "the Almighty works to bring His will to pass in this great continent!" Ray Phillips preached a "social gospel" that was particularly suited to the demands of the mining industry. Instead of calling for improved working, living, and wage conditions, Phillips tried to defuse discontent with those conditions, which he and the mining industry argued had been stirred up by agitators, communists, and labor unionists. Toward this end, he called for "moralizing the leisure time" of workers. In the mining compounds, Phillips argued that the church had to "capture the physical and mental life of these young men during six days of the week besides preaching the Gospel to them on the seventh." On a mission of total social control, Phillips introduced sports and games such as football, volleyball, "hunt the thimble," and "who's got the ring." But he gained his greatest success by introducing movies, entertaining workers with regular film shows in the compounds. During the mineworker strikes of the 1920s, Phillips claimed that he defused worker discontent by showing Charlie Chaplin films. Impressed by this success, the mining industry helped finance other churches in conducting movie missions on the mines, arguably in an effort to make workers more docile in their dehumanization.[9]

The complicity of Christian churches in an exploitative system did not go unnoticed by black political leaders. The Methodist local preacher and leader of the Transvaal Native Congress S. M. Makghato was particularly adamant in the 1920s that Christianity had to be seen from the bottom of the mines, from the underside of the racist class system enforced by industrial capitalism. "The God of the white people was Gold," Makghato observed, "their heaven money." Christian missionaries had warned blacks about the fires of hell that were reserved in the afterlife for sinners against the God of

Gold. But Makghato replied that "black people in this land are in hell already."[10] Black mineworkers were enslaved in the lowest circles of a hell owned and operated by the white-controlled mining industry, with the support of the state and the complicity of the church. Although it was supported by conventional religious resources, I want to suggest that the mining industry also achieved its own religious authority. The mining industry demonstrated its superhuman power by the symbolic, yet also real and systematic, dehumanization of black workers.

First, the official discourse of the mining industry insisted on referring to black workers as permanent children. As the *South African Mining Journal* reported in 1892, "the position of [blacks] is in many respects like [that of] children." Significantly, such a classification has also appeared frequently in the history of religious justifications for slave systems. Slave systems have also justified the exploitation of forced labor through symbols of "fictive kinship." In South Africa, "fictive kinship" was invoked in claims to a Christian trusteeship or guardianship over blacks that was exercised by both state and industry.[11] But that symbolism of "fictive kinship" was canceled by the fact that the mining industry and the state also classified black workers as permanent aliens. A government commission in the 1940s made this permanent alienation explicit: "The Natives in our areas must be regarded as visitors who will never be entitled to any political rights or to social rights with whites."[12] The mining industry, however, by depending on the reserve or homeland system for cheap, exploitable migrant labor, had long operated with a classification of black workers as foreign visitors. In the worldview of the mining industry, therefore, black workers could be legitimately enslaved either because they were wards of the state or because they were foreigners with no rights of citizenship. Such are the classifications upon which slave systems have been built.

Second, the mining industry justified the natal alienation of mineworkers—that is, their forced separation from wives and families in the migrant-labor system—by claiming that this condition was natural or traditional for black people in southern Africa. In 1936 and 1937, the Chamber of Mines was assisted in trying to prove this case by the anthropologist H. P. Junod, who gave lectures on the "Bantu Heritage" to mining officials and compound managers. In 1938,

Junod's lectures were published as a book, complete with a preface by mining-industry spokesman William Gemmill. Gemmill recommended the book because it explained "the races whose work makes European life in South Africa, as we know it, possible." Although Junod covered many topics, it was probably what he had to say about the sex-life of the "Bantu" that was most relevant to the interests of the mining industry. Unlike other human beings, Junod claimed, a black migrant worker on the mines was perfectly suited to have sexual relations with his wife once a year when he returned home to his family in the reserves, because his "sexual life is more seasonal, more natural, than [that of] other people." In other words, according to Junod, the "Bantu" had a sexuality more animal than human, which was entirely fit for migrant labor, the single-sex hostel, and the closed compound. In this respect, black South Africans were supposedly unique: "One only needs to remember the 330,000 Bantu men working on the mines, most of them segregated in compounds, to visualize what the conditions would be from a sexual point of view if they belonged to other races." Other people might present a problem, Junod concluded, but black workers—more seasonal, more natural, and, by implication, more animal than human—were supposedly suited to those subhuman conditions.[13]

Third, even the language deployed in the mines was experienced by black workers as an instrument of domination and dehumanization. The dominant discourse replaced names with numbers, indicating, as many mineworkers observed, that "you are not human." White managers spoke to black workers in the mining industry's lingua franca, known as Fanagalo, a language developed specifically for command and direction.[14]

Above all, the mining industry asserted its superhuman power through the degrading working and living conditions on the mines. The mining compounds have long been recognized as subhuman environments. For example, in 1903 a government health officer's report found that food served to black miners was "not fit for human consumption." A government report in 1908 found worker hostels "unfit for human habitation." These reports, however, changed nothing. In 1945, the president of the African Mine Workers Union, J. B. Marks, specifically identified the mining compound as a hell on earth. "The workers are herded into compounds," Marks observed, "fed on cheapest food and made to sleep on cement bunks resembling coffins." The compound was a coffin, the mine was a tomb, and devils reigned there. As Marks concluded, "workers in the mining industry are subjected to systematic oppression and exploitation by a clique of human vampires."[15]

Where human vampires hold superhuman power, black mine-workers continue to be dehumanized in the underworld of the mining industry. As general secretary of the National Union of Mineworkers Cyril Ramaphosa noted in 1983, "Black workers in the industry have just been treated like dirt. Not only because they are miners or because they are workers, but because they are black workers."[16] In early April 1990, a delegation of 28,000 black workers marched on the main offices of their mines to present a list of demands. Among their grievances, mineworkers singled out a practice that seemed to epitomize the mine as a hellish netherworld. In accordance with regulation 10.12 of the Mines and Works Act, any mineworker who performed manual labor underground at temperatures over 27.5 degrees centigrade had to go through a process called "acclimatization." Although ostensibly designed to prepare workers for the underground heat, the process of acclimatization had all the characteristics of a rite of passage, marking a transition into an underworld of torment. First, the workers had to be stripped. "You have to be like when you were born," one worker reported. Then the workers were taken to an overheated room where they had to climb up and down steps for a period of four hours. Usually, acclimatization took five days, but workers who showed intolerance to heat might have to continue the process for ten days. Once the testing was complete, however, the workers were allowed to descend to the hot, dark underworld of South African labor in the mines.

Acclimatization was a ritual. Workers recognized that it was primarily a symbolic act. One worker observed that "a person can pass the acclimatization process, but still collapse underground, so the whole thing is useless." It was a rite of initiation, a rite of incorporation into the underworld of the mines. It was also a ceremony of degradation that reinforced the superhuman power and authority of the mining industry by dehumanizing black workers. Supervisors and team leaders did not go through the ritual. Since whites tended to occupy those jobs, it was unlikely that any white person would ever have to go through the process of acclimatization. Acclimatization thus reinforced a racial classification of persons by enacting the subhuman status of black workers in the official world and worldview of the mines.[17]

Rite of passage, ceremony of degradation—but I can suggest another name for this ritual. We can name it more simply and bluntly as torture. In South Africa, torture has also been a significant, powerful ritual practice. We will return to the violent underworld of the mines in a moment, but I want to turn now to a different, yet similar, tour of hell through the secret places of confinement where rituals of torture have been practiced by agents of the state.

Torture

In September 1988, a Roman Catholic priest, Father Smangaliso Mkhatshwa, testified in an affidavit that he had been tortured while held in detention without trial. Father Mkhatshwa was a prominent South African religious leader, secretary-general of the Southern African Catholic Bishops Conference. His affidavit told of the psychological and physical torture he had suffered while in police custody. It was read into the public record in Parliament. It was formally denied by the minister of police. But reports and denials of torture had become a familiar, recurring pattern throughout the 1980s in South Africa. Here is Father Mkhatshwa's officially denied report of torture:

> I was left standing on the same spot for at least 30 hours—with blindfold and handcuffs always on. My genitals and buttocks were left exposed for at least 29 hours. A watery substance was smeared on my legs and thighs—this together with the cold air caused much discomfort. A creepy creature or instrument was fed into my backside. From there it would crawl up and down my legs, thighs, and invariably ended up biting my genitals. When I cried with pain they would laugh. Twice during the interrogation shots were fired from behind and just above the back of my head.[18]

In a recent study, Martha Himmelfarb has pointed to some of the basic features of the underworld in the Jewish, Christian, and Islamic religious imagination: The freezing and fiery environments of hell, the calculated attention to specific parts of the body, the creepy creatures and infernal worms that never died, and the laughing angels or demons of hell who took pleasure in their sacred work of causing pain. "When I cried with pain," Father Mkhatshwa recalled, "they would laugh." The whole point of hell, of course, was the demonstration of divine power in the power to punish. Besides excluding and confining sinners in a violent underworld, hell translated pain into power. As Dante described the inferno, the sign above the gates of hell read: "Divine power made me." But that sign could also be read to suggest that hell—the power to enact punishment and exact pain—made and reinforced divine power. The divine comedy was supported by a divine economy of power and pain.[19]

By the seventeenth century, as the historian D. P. Walker has shown in his book *The Decline of Hell,* this infernal calculus of divine power and pain had fallen out of fashion among influential Christian theologians in Europe.[20] However, its terms and conditions have easily been transposed into the rituals of exclusion, confinement, and punishment that have defined the power of the modern state over human beings. Through rituals of pain, the state exercises control over the body of the victim to certify its claims to ultimate authority over the body politic. In this respect, I suggest, state rituals of torture are not essentially different than other rituals of punishment through which the modern state reinforces its superhuman power. Like these other rituals, torture is a ritual reproduction of the power of the state, "a process both constitutive of and expressing—although in a negative and debased form—the cultural meaning of the totalisation of society by the State."[21] Like the inferno, torture reveals the terrible truth of divine power, not perhaps the power of God, but the sacred superhuman power invested in the apparatuses of the state. In South Africa, reports of torture have revealed the violent underside of a modern state.

Accounts of police torture proliferated in the 1980s. Tales of physical and psychological abuse were circulated, the number of deaths in detention were counted, and the practices of torture that allegedly led to all this pain, suffering, and death were consistently denied by officials of the government. This discourse of reports and denials itself became ritualized in the 1980s. In 1982, the Detainee's Parents Support Committee published its findings that 77 percent of detainees had been beaten, kicked, suffocated, given electric shocks, suspended in the air, forced to stand for hours, kept naked, deprived of sleep, or had suffered genital assault while held in detention. The minister of law and order denied these allegations and attacked the Parents Support Committee for seeking sensational publicity. In 1985 researchers at the University of Cape Town published their findings on the extensive physical and psychological torture in police detention. The minister of law and order dismissed this report as "subjective, unscientific, prejudiced." In 1986 a group of medical doctors who had treated former detainees reported that 83 percent showed medical evidence of suffering some form of physical abuse. Out of that group, 90 percent had been punched, kicked, slapped, beaten with whips and batons, or hit with a rifle butt; 25 percent had been stripped and assaulted on their genitals; 20 percent had been given electric shocks; 20 percent were held in solitary confinement; 7.5 percent had been hooded and partially suffocated. In addition to all this physical torment, the doctors found that 95 percent showed signs of post-traumatic stress syndrome as a result of their ordeals in detention. In response to this report, a spokesman for the government's Bureau of Information stated that these allegations were "too vague" in this "so-called" study to warrant further investigation or comment.[22]

Officials of the government and the police, however, did not merely try to silence these reports through denials. They also tried to transform both reports and denials into a restatement of an official reality in South Africa. In that reality, the state and police always exercised their superhuman power in the interests of humanity. In 1982, Minister of Law and Order Louis Le Grange proclaimed the official position: "A detainee shall at all times be treated in a humane manner with proper regard to the rules of decency and shall not in any way be assaulted or otherwise ill-treated or subjected to any form of torture or inhuman or degrading treatment." The minister thus publicly recognized that state rituals of torture were inherently dehumanizing. In a more candid moment, however, Le Grange also observed, "You won't get much information if you keep a detainee in a five-star hotel or with friends." Therefore, on the pretext of gaining information, detainees had to be held in such a place and treated in such a way that they would know they were not among friends.[23]

This symbolic discourse of "friends" and "enemies" runs throughout official statements in response to allegations of torture. In the official version, friends of the government's enemies were also its enemies. The state was at war, detainees were enemies of the state, anyone who befriended them by calling attention to their treatment in detention was therefore also an enemy of the state. On these terms, the World Council of Churches was an enemy of the state. In April 1987, Minister of Law and Order Adriaan Vlok responded to WCC claims about torture in detention: "It was very clear that the claims of assault and torture of detainees were in most cases either willful lies or exaggerated distortions manufactured by political activists to vilify the police." On these terms, the South African National Medical and Dental Association was also an enemy of the state. In response to the association's call for an investigation into police torture, the spokesman for the Prison Service replied that "a well-known tactic used by ex-detainees is to make false and far-fetched allegations about the incarceration circumstances in South African prisons." Thus anyone who gave credence to the "false and far-fetched allegations" of the state's enemies was also an enemy of the state.[24]

More ingenious methods were also used to reinforce official reality and reempower the state. Ritualized reports and denials provided an opportunity for the state to redraw the lines between fantasy and reality. For example, when the Afrikaans novelist Breyten Breytenbach reported that he had been tortured in prison, the public relations officer for the South African Police explained that those allegations of torture had been "derived from an obvious background of fantasy." The official reality was that the police were "totally opposed to any illegal, cruel, or inhuman treatment of prisoners."[25] Ritualized reports and denials allowed the state to draw its own lines between what counted as the inside and the outside of the Republic of South Africa. For example, the deputy bishop of the Evangelical Lutheran Church, Simon Farsani, alleged that he had been tortured while held in detention in the South African "homeland" of Venda. In 1983, Reverend Farsani sued and was paid damages out of court. In spite of this apparent confirmation of his torture, the South African Police issued a public statement which read: "The South African Police deny that he was tortured or assaulted while in custody in the Republic of South Africa."[26] If misread, as the public was meant to misread this statement, the police were denying that Reverend Farsani had been tortured. What the state was actually claiming, however, was that the "homeland" of Venda, even though it was under the supervision and control of the South African government, police, and military, was not really part of South Africa. In these and many other ways, the reports and denials of torture presented occasions for the state to reiterate its official reality, even if that reality assumed an aura of fantasy—with victims jumping out of barred tenth-floor windows, slipping on soap in the shower, falling down flights of stairs, or dying suddenly, inexplicably while in police custody with no person or act found responsible by a police investigation, a government commission, or a court of law.

In the official reality, there was a central irony in the relation between ritual torture and discourse: Enemies of the state outside the prison were commanded to keep silent, but enemies of the state within the prison walls were induced to speak. In the official reality, the whole point of detention was to elicit a confession. Its purpose was to gather information. Even the most notorious torturers of the 1970s who worked for the Bureau of State Security, known under its fitting acronym as BOSS, claimed in public that their methods of gathering information were based on conversation, education, and psychological persuasion. For example, in response to allegations of torture in his interrogation cells, Major Fourie stated, "I don't know what you mean by interrogation. That was where we chatted." In Johannesburg, Colonel Swanepoel testified during a treason trial in the early 1970s that he never used torture; he used conversational methods to gain "the co-operation of the detainee." In that mutual pursuit of truth, Swanepoel concluded, the detainee then "tells us everything we want to know." Through conversation, education, and psychological persuasion, Colonel Swanepoel insisted that he was able "to win the confidence of detainees, even that of the most fanatical communist." Detailed, documented reports of physical and psychological torture under interrogation accumulated throughout the 1970s and 1980s. Officials of the state did not merely deny these reports. They did not merely use them as occasions for restating the official reality. They used them to claim their own human motives and humane methods in the gathering of information.[27]

In her brilliant analysis *The Body in Pain,* Elaine Scarry has shown that torture is not about gaining information. Nor is torture practiced to force its victims to make confessions. As a ritual practice, torture cannot induce any meaningful discourse from its victims, because their worlds collapse under the searing effects of pain. Torture is not a ritual that translates pain into meaningful speech—the information, the confession, or even the betrayal. Torture is a ritual that translates pain into power. Torture translates the pain of the victim into the power of the state. The power of torture, the unbearable pain into which the victim's body, mind, and entire world is dissolved, is nothing more nor less, as Scarry has noted, than the "deconstruction of humanness."[28] If we can regard torture as a religious ritual, symbolically negotiating a claim on superhuman power, then I would suggest that the "deconstruction of humanness" under torture ritually reinforces the superhuman power of the state.

Claims of transcendent authority were frequently made explicit by the police and security police during the 1970s and 1980s. American journalist Joseph Lelyveld noted that the South African security police was "probably the only secret police in the world to have created a branch specializing in theological matters." In the 1970s, Colonel Swanepoel testified in court that his special gift for psychological persuasion was God-given. "Well," he told the court, "the Lord endows certain people with certain talents. Perhaps this is one of my talents." Swanepoel was not alone in this presumption of divine endowment or empowerment. The head of BOSS in the 1970s, General Hendrik van den Bergh, was even more adamant that he was on a mission from God. Van den Bergh once told his counterpart in what was then Rhodesia a story of death and resurrection in which he had been restored to life by God so he could continue his divine mission in the world. It seems that one day while he was welding on his farm, Van den Bergh had grabbed a live electrical cable and had been electrocuted. While he was dead, Van den Bergh heard God speaking to him. "Hendrik," God apparently said, "your life's work is not finished—I need you back on earth." When one of the black farm workers switched off the electricity, Van den Bergh revived and continued his life's work. His friend from Rhodesia suggested to Van den Bergh that perhaps his life had been spared, not by divine intervention, but by a black laborer who had shown the presence of mind to switch off the electricity. Van den Bergh, however, disagreed: "How could any Bantu have had the sense to do what he did, unless God gave him the right instructions."[29]

During the 1980s, claims to superhuman power and authority continued to be asserted by the South African Police. Adriaan Vlok insisted that the police had "always maintained Christian norms and civilized standards." In 1988, the official history praised the contribution of the police "to the maintenance and expansion of the nation's common spiritual concerns." The official report on the police to Parliament in 1990 noted that the chaplain department provided the force with its "spiritual armament." But the South African Police and the security police did not really need chaplains. They had long claimed a spiritual armament of their own. Divine intervention, divine mission, divine gifts—these were essentially religious claims to superhuman power that were ritually enacted and reinforced in the violent underworld of detention.[30]

Recovery

How might humanity be recovered from these realms of dehumanization? How is humanity recovered from the depths of the mines, from the pain of torture in detention? Strategies have been advanced in South Africa to resist the power claimed by the state and demonstrated in its violent underworlds. Some have turned to religious arguments. In the 1920s, black religious leaders who saw the world from the bottom of the racial class system of industrial capitalism proposed two basic religious strategies for redemption. One strategy could be called "traditional," the other "apocalyptic." The "traditional" argument asserted a fundamental entitlement to the land because it had been given by the gods or ancestors of Africa. At a meeting of the Transvaal Native Congress, the journalist Selope Thema declared that the "God of our chiefs gave us this part of the world we possess." The "traditional" strategy, therefore, called for restitution of the land and its wealth to those who had been dispossessed.

By contrast, the "apocalyptic" promise proclaimed an imminent, sudden, this-worldly redemption through supernatural intervention. At another meeting of the Transvaal Native Congress, a black mineworker by the name of Mgoja called for labor organization and resistance to oppression. He observed that "the black race must know that white people are thieves and devils." If workers were imprisoned, they could draw strength from knowing that they were following God's will. "God did not want cowards," Mgoja declared. "They must look to the gaols as their homes. The mine natives must know they are producers of wealth and must get better pay." In conclusion, Mgoja foresaw redemption in a form that captivated the imaginations of many black South Africans during the 1920s and 1930s—the Americans would come. "America said they would free all natives and they will help," Mgoja declared. "America has a black fleet and it is coming."[31] Influenced by reports about Marcus Garvey, the Industrial and Commercial Workers Union in particular elaborated this vision of black American liberators coming in fleets of ships and planes raining fire from the skies.[32]

While the traditional strategy claimed the restitution of a past entitlement to the land, the apocalyptic strategy anticipated a radical inversion of social relations in the immediate future—the first would be last, the last would be first, and those at the bottom of the racist system would emerge from the underworld in which they had been tormented by white thieves and devils. Arguably, however, both of these strategies of redemption did little more than symbolize the predicament of black South Africans in the modern industrial state. To represent a predicament is important, but it does not necessarily constitute a recovery of the humanity that has been lost. Nevertheless, we must still look to the condition of dehumanization for a recovery of humanity in South Africa.

At the end of his analysis of slavery and social death, Orlando Patterson left us with an unsettling question: Without bondage, would the notion of freedom have any content? "The first men and women to struggle for freedom," Patterson wrote, "the first to think of themselves as free in the only meaningful sense of the term were freedmen. And without slavery there would have been no freedmen." In 1955, a multiracial "Congress of the People" sponsored by the African National Congress met in Kliptown, near Johannesburg, to draft and adopt a document called the Freedom Charter. The text of the charter was a general outline for a free, multiracial, democratic, and just South Africa. Police broke up the congress on its second day and confiscated all documents. Participants were charged with treason. The Freedom Charter was officially banned for possession or distribution. Even silenced by the state, however, the Freedom Charter assumed a sacred, canonical status for political movements aligned with the African National Congress in its struggle for liberation in

South Africa. The Freedom Charter was also embraced by many who had been dehumanized in the depths of the mines or through torture in detention. In 1987, Cyril Ramaphosa stated on behalf of his union that the "Freedom Charter in our view, and indeed in the view of workers, contains the minimum demands that have been put forward by the oppressed people in this country." Speaking for the Southern African Catholic Bishops Conference, Father Smangaliso Mkhatshwa claimed that the Freedom Charter was theologically and politically sound because "it forms the basis for a new society where all South Africans will have the right to be fully human." In contrast to the system defined by the apartheid state, monopoly capitalism, and international imperialism, Father Mkhatshwa concluded, the Freedom Charter "puts the human person right in the centre of the universe."[33]

But what does it take to rescue human persons from the violent underworlds of dehumanization and to place them at the center of the universe? Black mineworkers have not been at the center but at the bottom of the universe built in South Africa by the mining industry and the modern state. As I have suggested, the mines have been a region of social death. But they have also been a region of real death. The mining industry has reported annual deaths on the mines in such a way that death seems like a statistical loss to the industry. For example, in 1984 the mines claimed 1.15 deaths per thousand miners; in 1985, 1.05 per thousand. Those bloodless statistics translate into a total of 1,127 workers killed on the mines over that two-year period. In the way the mining industry reported those deaths—1.15 per thousand, 1.05 per thousand—it almost looked as if there had been only one death a year. A manageable loss. In the view from the bottom of the mines, however, even one death represents an unacceptable loss. As James Motlatsi observed, "we cannot accept this situation. One more death, is a death too many." The mining industry, like the modern state, rests on mounds of bodies—bodies exploited for labor, bodies sacrificed to the mines, bodies trapped in a violent underworld of dehumanization and death. The recovery of humanity from the bottom of the mines therefore requires a complete refocusing of attention upon the single, living human body. One death is a death too many.[34]

Furthermore, a recovery of humanity from the social death of detention, confinement, and torture requires a similar refocusing upon the single, living human body. Such a recovery and refocusing was undertaken by religious and political leaders in opposition to the government by organizing and supporting hunger strikes in South African prisons. In an important sense, the hunger strike was a strategy that escalated the struggle over the pain of the body that the state had translated into its own power. The hunger strike recaptured some measure of personal control over the body's pain. By going on a hunger strike, a detainee could redefine the meaning and power of his or her own body even while still in prison.

In February 1987, a spokesman for the minister of law and order complained before Parliament that large-scale, coordinated hunger strikes were being conducted at prisons throughout the country. He argued that "these so-called hunger strikes are mostly undertaken by large groups of detainees on an obviously orchestrated basis."[35] Government officials pointed to the organized nature of hunger strikes to discredit them. But the hunger strikes were effective precisely because they were organized. In early 1989, religious organizations played a dramatic, public role in the orchestration of hunger strikes. The World Conference on Religion and Peace organized services and vigils. The Southern African Catholic Bishops Conference issued a public statement that "the Catholic Church prays for the detainees in their suffering and hardship and wishes them to know that it stands behind them in love and solidarity." While on a fast in solidarity with the hunger strikers, the Rev. Allan Boesak sent an open letter to Adriaan Vlok. Boesak informed the minister that joining the hunger strike was what God wanted him to do. He asked Mr. Vlok if he knew what God wanted him to do. Archbishop Desmond Tutu declared that "a very significant thing has occurred through nonviolent action." The significance of the hunger strike was at least this: it had provided the occasion for a broad-based coalition of religious groups to refocus public attention on the violence of detention.[36]

But I would like to suggest that the hunger strike had a second significance for the recovery of humanity from the state's violence. The hunger strike signaled an alternative politics of the body. It drew public attention away from the official reality by refocusing on the irreducible value of each individual body in detention. In the hunger strike, each body became a powerful point of pressure exerted against the entire system of detention. Under that new pressure, public political discourse about detention shifted into the singular. Member of Parliament for the opposition, Helen Suzman, reflected this shift in body politics by insisting that "*one* death would be a disaster."[37] Although he tried to shift responsibility away from the government, even the minister of law and order had to recognize that politics had become more immediate and specific.

First, Minister Vlok blamed the detainees for any harm that might result: "If the government refused to budge and *one* detainee died, or permanent damage was done, [the detainee] would have only [himself] to blame." Second, he blamed "ringleaders" who had been orchestrating the hunger strike: "If unrest again flares up or if a *single person* dies as a result of the hunger strike these organizations and people who encourage these campaigns will have to accept responsibility for their devilish deeds." But in the end it was the government that had to assume responsibility for working out a compromise in order to avoid the public-relations disaster that would have resulted from the death of even one prisoner. As a journalist noted, "the specter of a hunger striker dying—thus becoming a martyr figure of the order of Steve Biko—is enough to convince the government of the need to compromise."[38]

In order to prevent even a single hunger striker from negotiating a superhuman martyrdom through a publicized death in detention, the government capitulated, even if only temporarily, to the pressure generated by this new body politics. In March 1989, the government released about 900 detainees who had been held in detention without charge under emergency or security legislation. As many as 700 of the released detainees, however, were immediately placed under restrictions that required them to report daily to a police station, remain indoors for twelve hours every night, and refrain from any political activity. Nevertheless, the hunger strike had achieved a certain degree of success, especially in recovering the value of the single, living human body. In that body politics, a different truth of power had been announced. It was not the truth of the power of the state, but the truth of pain, suffering, and death. All along, that truth had been hidden in the violent underworlds of South Africa. For a moment, the unveiling of that truth seemed to promise a human redemption.

CHAPTER 5

The Space of War

•

DURING the 1980s, South Africa was a space of war. On the borders, in the townships, a war was going on. That war was fought not only with arms, but also through the deployment of powerful religious symbols. In this chapter, I want to reflect on the role of religion in the military ideology and practices that transformed South Africa into a region of total warfare. I will suggest that religion was not only drawn upon to provide support or legitimation for the exercise of military violence by the South African government. Religion was directly implicated in the symbols, myths, and rituals of the military. In this sense, the religion of the South African Defence Force, supported by the South African Police, was an armed religion.

Historically, religion seems to have performed two different functions in relation to military violence: it has operated as either a resistant or a cooperative force. As a resistant force, religion has been invoked in support of a position of generalized, universal pacifism; and religious resources have been drawn into the formulation of certain restraints on the exercise of military violence, from ritual rules of conduct to the kinds of moral limits on declaring and conducting war that have appeared in ethical traditions such as the Christian theory of the "just war." But religion has also cooperated in military violence. Indeed, religion can be said to have cooperated with military violence whenever it has been relegated to a separate, privatized sphere of social life, allowing the state free reign to conduct warfare on its own terms. Most obviously, religion has functioned as a cooperative force in forms of nationalism that have surrounded military violence in a religious aura. In these ways—pacifism, restraint, separation, and legitimation—religious discourses, practices, and institutions have interacted with warfare.[1]

In the history of religions, however, religion has been more intimately entwined with warfare than this functional analysis might suggest. Religious symbols, myths, rituals, and traditions have infused the strategies and practices of military violence. Not merely resistant or cooperative, religion has animated warfare. In his useful, wide-ranging survey of religion and war, James Aho has explored how religious discourses and practices have been inevitably entangled with the violence of armed battle. Aho has identified two mythic orientations toward warfare, the "immanent-cosmological" and the "transcendental-historical."[2] Adapting his terminology and conclusions slightly, we might call the first orientation "sacred war" and the second "holy war."

Sacred war is more like play than work, a drama in which ceremonial costumes and weapons, customary displays of courtesy and respect, ritual rules of etiquette and restraint, and myths of cosmic order have contributed to a certain pattern of warfare found in the traditional military ideologies and techniques of, for example, India, China, and Japan. As an end in itself, sacred war has represented the ritualized, ceremonial enactment of a cosmic and social order. In simple terms, sacred wars are waged to protect that order from chaos. By contrast, holy war has appeared as a utilitarian, serious, self-righteous work under the authority of a supreme deity. Not a ceremonial end in itself, holy war has functioned as a means for working the will of a transcendent God in the world. Holy wars—Christian crusade, Islamic jihad, or ancient Israelite herem—have tended to define the purpose of that work as the elimination of evil from the world by eliminating evil persons. In short, then, holy war has operated to protect an "us" from a "them," emphasizing the prominence of a symbolic classification of persons in warfare, rather than the ritualized spatial orientation found in the assertion of a cosmic order in sacred war.

Certainly, these ideal types—sacred war and holy war—provide only a point of entry into the interpretive analysis of religion and military violence. They do suggest, however, that the violence of war might be engaged in vital symbolic projects, even if the point of war is as basic, as Elaine Scarry has insisted, as settling a contest by damaging and killing bodies. Through symbols of person and place, military violence inevitably has been entangled in worldview negotiations. In South Africa, particularly during the so-called uprising from 1984 to 1986, many agreed that the country was at war, not only on the borders, but also in the black townships. Attention to worldview negotiations might allow the potent symbolic dimensions of a world at war to emerge with greater clarity.

Sacred War, Holy War

By the 1980s, South African military theory and practice had succeeded in combining elements of sacred war and holy war in the formulation of a general strategy of military violence. If holy war was dedicated to the purging of evil from the world through the elimination of evil persons, then South African military strategy exercised a holy, self-righteous vengeance on enemies of the state. Consistent with the ideology of holy war, those enemies were demonized and depersonalized in the highly charged symbolism of the "total onslaught" against South Africa, primarily defined as a communist onslaught, but also as a black, revolutionary, and terrorist invasion of the country. In this strategic symbolism, the South African military not only sanctioned unlimited violence against its enemies but also reinforced its own classification of persons in South Africa.

Linked with the symbolism of "total onslaught" was the South African regime's prominent and much publicized "total strategy." In terms of a sacred war, this strategy represented the deployment of military violence—in concert with myths, rituals, and other symbolic instruments of power—in the reinforcement of a certain order in the region, an order of both political and cosmic significance for those who defended it. While this "total strategy" received some support from right-wing religious organizations, it is important to recognize that South African military strategy was itself a type of armed religion, appropriating basic elements of holy war and sacred war in its violent worldview negotiations over person and place.

The discourse of "total onslaught" was apparently first developed in the State Security Council in 1972. By the next year, P. W. Botha, then minister of defence, warned that the dangers faced by South Africa were not merely military but also ideological. In fact, the ideological threats to state security were perceived as having increasing effect. "Ideological attacks on the Republic of South Africa," Botha wrote in the Defence White Paper of 1973, "are progressively being converted into more tangible action in the form of sanctions, boycotts, isolation, demonstrations and the like."[3] In response, what might be called military idealism became a recurring formula in the state's discourse of total onslaught. The conflict over South Africa was first and foremost symbolized as a type of spiritual warfare, a battle in which ideological instruments of power—will, faith, belief, culture, and religion—were to be deployed against the forces of evil.

This military idealism justified a wide-ranging defense of the role of military power in the service of the South African government. For example, when as state president P. W. Botha initiated the Steyn Commission for the investigation of the media, he warned that South Africa was "entering a new phase in the total onslaught . . . manifested by malevolent efforts to question the very essence of military service." In 1983, Defence Minister Magnus Malan apparently issued a secret memorandum in the South African Defence Force instructing all personnel to minimize references to a total onslaught against South Africa, because such language was "exaggerated and fearful." Nevertheless, in 1986, the secretary of the State Security Council, Lieutenant General Pieter van der Westhuizen, was still using the phrase to represent the dangers to the security of the political, social, and spiritual order of South Africa.[4] Obviously, the discourse of total onslaught was invoked to justify the increasing militarization of South African society. But it also expressed perceptions of danger that were widely held by white South Africans.

This danger was symbolized as a depersonalized violence that threatened a white world in Africa. Although often specified as communist, the more pervasive, latent symbolism was black, even if the word was not actually used. A long history of symbolic discourse in South Africa had represented black Africans as a massive wave, crashing against a white world. In his survey of African tribes, the geologist turned ethnologist G. W. Stow characterized Africans as a "seething mass of equatorial life," a dehumanized, faceless mass that came into contact with "white faced men." In Stow's argument, this depersonalized mass of African life found the personalized men behind those white faces to be "still more invincible than they had imagined themselves to be," an invincibility demonstrated as "the tidal wave of rude barbarism beat in vain" against them. In the 1980s, as G. M. E. Leistner noted, many white South Africans continued to symbolize danger in terms of being "drowned in a sea of blacks." In this symbolic discourse, transposed into the formula of total onslaught, a particular classification of persons was at work that tried to create an island of white humanity in that sea.[5]

Against the tidal wave of the total onslaught, as the Defence White Paper of 1977 insisted, "the principle of the right of self-determination of the White nation must not be regarded as being negotiable." Rather, the nonnegotiable principle of a white, national humanity formed the basis for the military, political, social, economic, and ideological negotiations that comprised what we have described as the "total strategy." Whereas the symbolism of total onslaught enacted a classification of persons, the total strategy was designed to weave an absolute, fixed orientation in space into the social fabric of South Africa. The all-encompassing character of this orientation was formulated in almost endless lists of the various dimensions of public life in which the total strategy had to be enacted. In the 1977 Defence White Paper, for example, total strategy demanded "interdependent and coordinated action in all fields—military, psychological, economic, political, sociological, technological, diplomatic, ideological, cultural, etc." In circular argument, all this military, symbolic activity was required "to counter the multidimensional onslaught against the Republic of South Africa in the ideological, military, economic, social, psychological, cultural, political and diplomatic fields."[6]

Although only one catalog in the 1977 Defence White Paper explicity identified "religious-cultural action" as one of the necessary aspects of strategy, it should be noted that the very idea of an ultimate strategy carried an aura of the sacred. For a student of religion, the total strategy immediately calls to mind what Marcel Mauss referred to as the "total social fact," something particularly evident in the multidimensional character of ritual practice, in which "all kinds of institutions find simultaneous expression: religious, legal, moral, and economic."[7] In this respect, the total strategy represented a ritualized totalization of South African society. Whatever its practical consequences, the total strategy signaled a symbolic, ritual, and religious commitment to a sacralized orientation in southern African space.

From a variety of perspectives, attempts have been made to explain this orientation in the total strategy of the South African government. Perhaps the strategy represented a mystical, religious nationalism, transposing Afrikaner religious notions—chosen people, promised land—into a modern military defense of power and privilege in South Africa. However, for all its military and religious idealism, the total strategy cannot be understood simply as a continuation of traditional Afrikaner religious nationalism. It represented true innovation in the field of ideological, psychological, and symbolic warfare. In this respect, the media, not the Bible, were identified in the 1977 Defence White Paper as the "essential link in the total strategy." The religious worldview of the South African Defence Force, therefore, was not a persistence of Afrikaner nationalism. It was a new, modern armed religion devoted to a total strategy of anticommunism.

In some ways, the total strategy calls to mind the nineteenth-century frontier battle formation assumed by Boer trekkers when they drew their wagons into a circle, as Philip Frankel has noted, forming the "highly symbolic yet strategically effective *laager.*"[8] Certainly, the laager mentality might have been sustained in defense strategy. However, the military ideology of total strategy blurred and often dissolved the spatial distinction between inside and outside upon which the military and symbolic formation of the laager depended. The battlefield was everywhere in the total strategy. As we will see, the borders defended in this total warfare were extremely fluid because the battleground could appear anywhere.

One could argue that the total strategy reproduced the frontier commando system in which civil and military functions flowed into each other as white settlers formed a citizen army to enforce their common political, social, and economic interests against indigenous opposition. However, the total strategy was not designed as an egalitarian, communal coordination of citizens for their own temporary defense, but as a permanent, bureaucratic security system managed by specialists—"managers of violence"—who rose in prestige and power as they assumed increasingly comprehensive control of the society. In a moment of frankness, one military theorist acknowledged that "conventional organisations in democratic systems do not as a rule lend themselves to these procedures."[9] Furthermore, the total strategy blurred any temporal distinction between peacetime and wartime that was part of the commando system. A man might be a farmer before, a warrior during, and a farmer again after battle, but in the total strategy South Africa was defined as a region in a perpetual state of war. The spatial orientation of defense policy thus carved out a space of total, omnipresent, and eternal warfare in South Africa.

Dedicated to protecting South Africa physically and spiritually, the South African Defence Force was served by an armed religion. Illustrations of this orthodox military religion can be almost endlessly multiplied. In a 1975 South African Defence Force manual for "citizen training," the public was warned of the danger of the total onslaught through which the enemy was undermining the "military, economic, political, and moral strength of a nation." Emphasizing the vital role of military idealism in this spiritual warfare, the SADF manual instructed, "Believe in—Your God, Your People, Yourself." Frequently, publications of the SADF insisted that military power resulted from psychological, spiritual, or religious strength. For example, the monthly SADF publication, *Paratus,* consistently claimed that war was "waged in the minds of men"; it was fought for "the basic right to religious worship"; and it was conducted with the support and blessing of a militant chaplain service.[10]

The chaplain service of the SADF was particularly vocal in proclaiming an armed religion. In characteristic terms, one SADF publication announced: "When the men in uniform defy the Marxist danger with arms, they are assisted by the Chaplain with the weapon of the Gospel." Carrying that sacred weapon into battle against evil enemies in a holy war, "a man in uniform is made aware of his calling, to live and if need be to die for his country, South Africa." As this SADF publication suggested, the chaplaincy legitimized the religious mission of the SADF. In the words of the chaplain general, Major General C. P. Naude, the "Chaplain Services of the SADF is a direct extension of the Church of God and both the English and Afrikaans churches have to join forces in the SADF to serve the Kingdom of God." The South African Defence Force could thus claim its own religious justification, independent of any church, in the pursuit of God's will on earth. Recognizing the complicity of the chaplaincy in the armed religion of the SADF, the South African Council of

Churches, among others, called for its "demilitarization." Nevertheless, the chaplaincy continued as one potent source of legitimation for the South African military.[11]

Ultimately, therefore, the military idealism of the total strategy made warfare a matter of faith. This spiritual warfare demanded faith in God, but it also required the psychological faith of the people under its domain. Referring to the withdrawal of the Portuguese from southern Africa, Magnus Malan insisted that they did not lose the military battle over Angola and Mozambique, "but they lost the faith and trust of the inhabitants of those countries."[12] In the 1980s, the SADF conducted its own battles over hearts and minds on the borders and in the townships. In the military idealism of the total strategy, however, psychological warfare was not ancillary to the exercise of military force; it was conceived as the entire point of military strategy, a strategy for winning a war of will, faith, ideology, and spirit.

To win that symbolic warfare, a soldier's spirit had to be strong. As military journalist Willem Steenkamp declared, "it is the soldier's spirit that counts, whether he is equipped with machine-gun and mortar or the stabbing-assegai and oxhide shield." Of course, the history of the encounter between the machine gun and the assegai in South Africa has demonstrated this assertion to be highly questionable. After the brutal massacre of alleged Zulu rebels in 1906, John X. Merriman observed, "How thin the crust is that keeps our Christian civilisation from old-fashioned savagery—machine guns and modern rifles against knobsticks and assegais are heavy odds and do not add much to the glory of the superior races."[13] In the armed religion of the total strategy, however, advanced military technology registered as merely an outer sign of the inner strength of spirit that was necessary for victory. That spirit was cultivated through military discipline and training, but the spirit also had to be prepared to engage the battle against South Africa's enemies in every sphere of public and personal life.

In this total war in South Africa, educational programs in the public schools represented a significant dimension of military strategy. Schools introduced specific programs, such as the weekly lectures on Youth Preparedness, mandatory cadet training, and occasional youth camps for the instruction of pupils in military ideology and exercises. The militarization of white education was an important component of the comprehensive strategy. In the familiar discourse of military idealism, pupils were exhorted to prepare physically and spiritually to fight the total war. "We must be spiritually prepared," pupils were told in one youth camp lecture. "We must be like David against the Philistine Goliath, and SA will triumph against the Red Onslaught." Militarized curricula, programs, and camps were designed to prepare white youth for the red, black, total onslaught by the enemies of their country. As part of the total strategy, however, militaristic educational programs were not merely preparation for war; they were one of the fronts on which the war was already being fought. This blurring of the distinction between preparing for battle and engaging in battle was characteristic of the way in which warfare was defined as a permanent state of affairs in South Africa.[14]

Although the borders on which this total war was fought were extremely fluid, the major military and ideological border during the 1980s separated Angola from South African–controlled Namibia. On both sides of that border, the South African Defence Force was deployed. That deployment was not merely a military exercise, but also an ideological, symbolic negotiation of a particular spatial orientation. It represented the negotiation of a moral, psychological, and spiritual boundary in the armed religion upheld by the South African military.

Borders

Throughout South African military history, borders have defined highly charged, symbolic orientations. Shifting with military conflict and conquest, borders nevertheless have represented spatial orientations that symbolize both danger and security in the world. As early as the first European settlement in South Africa, Jan van Riebeeck tried to define a border for the Dutch East India Company station on the Cape by constructing a hedge around its perimeter. By planting that hedge, Van Riebeeck demarcated a symbolic zone of protection: On one side of that hedge, a white settlement; on the other, Africa. On both sides, however, the hedge represented an organic, yet constructed symbol of a new orientation in space. As an exercise in military world-making, Van Riebeeck's hedge served as a symbolic prototype for subsequent attempts to enforce borders in and around South Africa.[15]

Three hundred years later, the South African Defence Force was engaged in a different ecology of world-making in its occupation of Namibia/South West Africa. In 1981, 1983, and 1985, according to Magnus Malan, the SADF had used herbicides to eliminate vegetation in the operational area. Rather than planting hedges, the SADF deployed a military strategy of defoliation in order to make it easier to spot enemy crossing the border. If applied according to directions, Malan assured Parliament in 1985, the use of this herbicide was "harmless to humans and animals."[16] Presumably, however, the clearing of the landscape on the border enabled the SADF to harm more effectively any dehumanized, depersonalized enemy that tried to cross the border. In this new ecology of the border, the elimination of hedges was one strategy for reinforcing both the military power of the SADF and the spatial orientation it represented.

The defoliation of the border should not suggest that the older ideal of building walls around a white-controlled world had been abandoned. In the late 1970s, the hedge was replaced by the electrified fence, quite literally a highly charged symbol of protection. On the Angola-Namibia border, an electrified fence was erected to stop guerrillas of the South West African People's Organization (SWAPO). This barrier was part of a larger scheme to put up electric fences along the entire border, constructing a "ring of steel" around South Africa. By 1984, considerable work on a fifteen-foot-high electrified fence around the borders of South Africa had been completed. In 1985, Magnus Malan explained that the purpose of constructing walls and electrified fences along the Limpopo River was "to facilitate more effective border control where necessary." Three years later, he reported to Parliament that fifty-two people had died as a result of contact with electrified fences on the northern and eastern borders of South Africa between August 1985 and February 1988. Nearly a hundred people had died by 1990.[17] Whatever its practical effects in protecting South Africa, the electrified fence represented the persistence of military world-making in the reinforcement of a symbolic orientation. In that spatial orientation, security itself depended upon the construction of clearly defined borders.

But a different definition of borders also operated in the South

African military orientation. In this second definition, borders were much more fluid, appearing, disappearing, and reappearing in the mobile reinforcement of security interests. This was suggested early on by Jan Christian Smuts in the 1940 Senate debates over South Africa's entry into the Second World War. Advocating military support on behalf of Britain, Prime Minister Smuts argued for a fluid definition of the boundaries and borders that symbolized South Africa's security. "Our northern boundary cannot be held," Smuts warned. "If you want to defend this country you will have to proceed a great distance beyond it. Those who know this continent know that the proper line of defence is in the highlands of Kenya."[18] Not the Limpopo River, but the highlands of Kenya, three thousand miles away, represented the borderline of military security in this symbolic reconstruction of South Africa's borders.

To be sure, Smuts was advancing a rhetorical argument for a military alliance with Britain. Nevertheless, he revealed an important aspect of South African military world-making. Borders were not only maintained by fences; they were also established in the states of mind that represented South Africa's power and place in the world. Although this flexible interpretation of South Africa's borders was often reflected in cross-border military operations, it was also acted out through symbolic displays of military power. Reminiscent of the ways in which sacred war in the history of religions has ritually enacted a particular sense of cosmic order in the world, South African Defence Force exercises sometimes assumed the proportions of ritual drama.

For example, between 26 August and 14 September 1984, the army and air force combined in the largest military exercise ever conducted in South Africa. Held in the northwestern Cape, this exercise involved over 11,000 troops. But military power was perhaps most spectacularly demonstrated in the display of sophisticated military technology, hardware, and tactical maneuvers. As a symbolic display of sacred power, this combined exercise even carried a name that evoked a powerful military transcendence over the world—"Exercise Thunder Chariot."

Declaring the exercise a military success, Magnus Malan suggested ways in which Thunder Chariot could also be understood to confirm South Africa's position in the world. First, the exercise sent a clear message to South Africa's enemies. As a maneuver in the ongoing violent negotiations against those enemies, Thunder Chariot, Malan declared, would "make them think twice" about testing South Africa's borders. In this respect, Thunder Chariot was a ritual that reinforced the clearly defined borders of the country. Malan also demonstrated an understanding of the exercise consistent with a sense of South Africa's borders as ever-changing. In its symbolic display of transcendent power, Malan enthusiastically declared, Thunder Chariot proved that the South African Defence Force "could go right through to Cairo."[19] The ritual display of military power in Thunder Chariot was thus interpreted by the minister of defence as having performed two symbolic functions: It demonstrated South Africa's power to reinforce its borders, but it also demonstrated South Africa's capacity to transcend its borders by extending its military power throughout the entire continent of Africa.

In defense of the border in Namibia, the South African Defence Force was deployed in a war that lasted nearly twenty-three years. According to government sources, the war cost the lives of 715 security force soldiers, 1,087 Namibian civilians, and 11,291 SWAPO and Angolan soldiers. Although South Africa's occupation of Namibia had been condemned by the United Nations and declared illegal by the International Court of Justice, the SADF persisted in conducting its border war. In official ideology, the war was justified as a defense of legitimate borders against the incursions of terrorists and the threat of communism. In particular, SWAPO was combated as part of a larger campaign against communism in southern Africa, a campaign that crossed the Namibian border into Angola. However, the ideological borderline became somewhat confused in the early phases of the war when SWAPO leader Herman Toivo ja Toivo, accused during his trial in 1967–68 of making communist statements in official SWAPO documents, could point out that many of those same documents "finish with an appeal to the Almighty to guide us in our struggle for freedom."[20]

SADF military action against SWAPO intensified in the 1970s, its troop commitment increasing from 16,000 in 1975 to over 50,000 in 1976. Whatever strategic and economic interests might have been at stake—including an interest in becoming one of the world's foremost arms dealers in "battle-tested" weapons—South Africa used the war in Namibia to pursue certain symbolic interests. The "Official SADF Border Song," as published in *Paratus,* suggests the symbolism of power and place that was being reinforced among South Africa's soldiers on the border.[21] In part, the song ran

> Dauntless our will to survive and to prosper
> Here in our Southern land—
> Free as the winds o'er our plains and our mountains
> Free from oppressor's hand.
> Dark are the forces that menace our country—
> Frontier and city and farm.
> Ours is the courage triumphant to crush them—
> Ruthless the strength of our arm.

Although the official border song contained patriotic and martial imagery that could be found in military anthems of many countries, it nevertheless can be interpreted as speaking directly to the South African military situation on the border. Consistent with the government's total strategy, the song celebrated a military idealism. It affirmed the idea that spiritual strength—"will" and "courage"—were the prerequisites for military triumph. It also reinforced a particular orientation by claiming symbolic ownership of the entire world of southern Africa. This recurring claim to ownership—"our plains," "our mountains," "our country," "our Southern land"—asserted a personal and collective investment. The song effectively appropriated the discourse of the opposition that was struggling for freedom from South African oppression by taking over the very terms "freedom" and "oppression" and cleverly inverting them. South Africa's enemies were dehumanized and demonized as "dark forces" of "menace," with the unavoidable hint of racial classification in the image of the "dark" forces of opposition. Finally, the song conveyed potent body imagery. While the enemy had a hand, the SADF had the whole arm, ruthless in its crushing strength. In the immediacy of that body symbolism, the official border song celebrated the obvious conclusion that soldiers in the SADF incarnated the transcendent power of the ruthless military arm of the South African government on the border.

During the 1980s, the long arm of the South African Defence Force also extended across borders other than the Namibian border. The government was frequently accused of a concerted policy of destabilization in the region of southern Africa. Cross-border raids into neighboring countries were the most publicized demonstrations of the fluid borders of South African security interests. For example, in May 1986, SADF forces attacked the alleged headquarters of the African National Congress almost simultaneously in Botswana, Zimbabwe, and Zambia. Once again, the official military ideology explained the cross-border raids in terms of body symbolism: "The long arm of the SADF reached into the Southern African countries of Botswana, Zimbabwe and Zambia on Monday 19 May 1986 to smash facilities used by the Moscow-backed terrorist organisation, the African National Congress."[22]

Demonstrating a coordinated, total strategy in these operations, the "long arm" of the SADF not only "smashed" alleged terrorist bases, it also conducted ideological warfare. In Botswana, leaflets were delivered addressed to the Botswana Defence Force, specifying that "our only objective is to eliminate these ANC gangsters." After stating this intention, the leaflet concluded: "Greetings to our fellow-soldiers!" In addition to this message of martial solidarity in the work of eliminating evil enemies, other leaflets were targeted at the general public in Botswana and Zimbabwe. Also referring to the ANC as gangsters, these leaflets warned the people of those neighboring countries that the SADF had "no choice but to remove them from their nests wherever they may be." In this assertion, the SADF informed countries on the South African borders that there were—symbolically, actually—no recognized boundaries in the war against the ANC. Nevertheless, the leaflet closed, "Greetings to Our Neighbours!"[23]

Townships

In the 1980s, military force was redirected from the borders to the townships. As Michael Evans and Mark Phillips noted, "the lines of battle shifted from the borders of Namibia to the black townships of South Africa . . . in which the SADF was deployed for the first time in South Africa's history on an ongoing and national basis inside the country."[24] Although borders continued to be defended, a new internal arena for military operations was defined in the suppression of so-called unrest. This mobilization and deployment of troops in the townships not only represented an escalation in the amount of violent force the government was willing to use in suppressing resistance, but the presence of troops in the townships also signaled a profound reorientation in the South African symbolism of space. Put simply, under ordinary conditions, military force was exercised outside, police force inside the country. In principle, the outside could be threatened by military force, but the inside was to be protected by police. Outside and inside therefore represented a particular orientation in which military force and police force were encoded. By deploying military force inside the country, however, the government waged war on its own population and thereby violated any meaningful distinction between an inside (protected by police force) and an outside (threatened by military force) in the South African spatial order. In more conventional terms, the breakdown of an ordinary order in South Africa appeared simply, obviously as civil war.

The level of military involvement within the country that was achieved during the uprisings from 1984 to 1986 was unprecedented in South African history. On 23 October 1984, SADF troops were deployed in the Vaal township of Sebokeng, a site of rent protests during the previous months, in a military engagement called "Operation Palmiet." Ostensibly, the purpose of this operation, according to Minister of Law and Order Louis Le Grange, was to "rid the areas of criminal and revolutionary elements." In defining the purpose of Operation Palmiet, the minister of law and order effectively fused the police and military functions assumed by the SADF in the township. Rather than rooting out revolutionaries, however, the operation resulted in about 350 arrests for various crimes—pass law offenses, influx control violations, and the possession of drugs or pornography.[25]

The operation dramatized the government's commitment to deploy the SADF in the country's black townships, a military commitment that continued to represent government policy throughout the 1980s. During 1985, over 35,000 troops were deployed in ninety-six townships throughout the country. In official government discourse, the SADF troops were in the townships for "the prevention or suppression of the internal disorder." From the perspective of the townships, however, as an editorial in one prominent black newspaper suggested, it was hard not to form the "impression that this part of the country [was] under military occupation."[26]

In response, opposition movements such as the United Democratic

Front and the Azanian Peoples Organization issued public statements claiming that the use of the army in the townships signaled the start of civil war in South Africa. Religious organizations also objected to the deployment of troops in the townships. For example, the Southern African Catholic Bishops Conference published a report on military and police actions in the townships from August to November of 1984. "Instead of acting as protectors of the people," the report alleged, "the police and army are now seen as the aggressors by openly invading the townships." In July of 1985, the South African Council of Churches called upon State President P. W. Botha to withdraw the troops and riot police from the townships. President Botha, however, replied by insisting that the troops were in the townships to protect law-abiding citizens, even ensuring the security that allowed the SACC to voice "whatever irresponsible opinions [it] wished to express under the cloak of religion." Nevertheless, a broad coalition of religious leaders and organizations echoed this call for the removal of troops from the townships.[27]

Troops were eventually deployed in the townships under the special security conditions established by the state of emergency. On 21 July 1985, a limited state of emergency was imposed over thirty-six magisterial districts. It was extended on 25 October 1985 and lifted in March 1986. A few months later, however, on 12 June 1986, a nationwide state of emergency was declared that effectively placed the entire country under martial law. This state of emergency was renewed every subsequent year throughout the decade of the 1980s. In imposing the first state of emergency, President P. W. Botha argued that special measures were necessary to stop violence and to return to normality in the townships. But normal township life was violent; the presence of police and troops merely intensified the violence of life in the townships. Even after security forces had largely succeeded in repressing the "uprising" by 1987, the state of emergency remained in effect because, in the words of Minister of Law and Order Adriaan Vlok, the townships still had a "revolutionary climate."[28]

Emergency regulations were an exercise in symbolic world-making, not only because they authorized the security forces to take any actions deemed necessary to maintain law and order in the world of the townships, but also because they imposed controls on any symbolic discourses or practices that might be regarded as subversive to the world and worldview of the state. Controls were placed on the media and education, but they were also placed on religion. Specifically, restrictions were placed on a ritual practice that became a focus for repression and resistance—the funeral. On 31 July 1985, the commissioner of the South African Police, General P. J. Coetzee, proclaimed the state's policy—actually, since the state was intervening in religious practice, a set of ritual rules—governing the performance of funeral ceremonies, including memorial services, funeral processions, or burials, of any person who had apparently died as a result of "unnatural causes" in areas affected by the state of emergency.[29] The state's ritual rules governing funerals were modified and elaborated, but they remained in effect for the duration of the state of emergency.

Funerals had become sites of ritual mobilization for resistance against the state. Thus the burial ground became one of the battlefields on which the state waged its war against resistance in the townships. As an exercise in ritual politics, government policy on funerals specified rules of discourse and practice enforced by the state. More than mere acts of political repression and control, these regulations entered into a religious struggle over sacred persons, sacred time, sacred space, and sacred objects involved in the ritual.

With respect to sacred persons, emergency regulations specified not only that no one but an ordained minister could officiate, but that only an ordained minister could speak at a funeral. In this, the state sought to silence more overtly political voices during funerals. But even ordained ministers were cautioned to observe ritual rules of silence on matters of current politics. While conducting a funeral ritual, the minister was restrained by emergency regulations from any statement that might be spoken to "defend, attack, criticise, propagate, or discuss any form of government, any principle or policy of a government or a state, any boycott action, the existence of a state of emergency, or any action of a force or member of a force." Where ministers of religion were not condemned to silence, they were commanded to speak softly by the regulation that prohibited the use of any public address system at a funeral.

Two other ritual rules governed persons at a funeral. Emergency regulations specified that any particular funeral must be held for one and only one deceased. By preventing multiple burials, the state devised a way to prevent any recognition of the collective nature of death in the townships under emergency conditions. Funeral rituals had to celebrate individuals rather than the collective sacrifices of a resistance movement. Furthermore, to prevent funeral rituals from being occasions for the mobilization of opposition, emergency regulations in 1986 limited the number of mourners who might be in attendance to no more than two hundred.

With respect to sacred space and time, emergency regulations outlined a pattern of ritual control to be enforced by the state. Outdoor funeral services were entirely prohibited. Within the ritual space demarcated by four walls, funerals were permitted, but all space outside those walls was under the immediate control of the police and army. As an indication of that control, another ritual rule specified that the route of any funeral procession had to be determined by a divisional commissioner of police. Along that prescribed route, mourners were prohibited from walking by yet another regulation, one that required travel by vehicle. In 1986, the sacred time of a funeral was defined by emergency regulations as no more than four hours—reduced to three hours the following year—and in certain areas, funerals could not be timed to coincide with weekends or public holidays.

Finally, the state's ritual rules governing funerals prohibited any symbolic display of certain ritual objects. No flags, banners, placards, pamphlets, or posters were allowed during a funeral service. We can see the seriousness with which these ritual rules were enforced in the funeral service held in 1987 for Ashley Kriel. In the western Cape township of Bonteheuwel, Kriel's funeral was disrupted when police allegedly ripped an ANC flag off the coffin and shot tear gas at mourners and clergy.[30] Although the state enforced its own ritual rules, opposition to the state could be registered with even greater clarity by breaking them. Thus, in the townships, the funeral became a ceremony of struggle and civil war.

In resistance to the control over funerals by emergency regulations and security forces, the toy AK-47 machine gun became a potent ritual object during many services. For the police and army, however, the gun was not merely a ceremonial object; it was the primary instrument of worldview negotiation in the townships. Even before the imposition of general emergency regulations governing funeral rituals, the armed enforcement of law and order had a history of violence in the townships. On the twenty-fifth anniversary of the 1960 Sharpeville massacre, for example, a confrontation between police and township residents recalled this history on the road between the township of Langa and the white town of Uitenhage in the eastern Cape. Blocking a group of as many as a thousand people walking down the road, police in several armored vehicles opened fire, killing twenty, wounding twenty-seven. According to the report of the official commission of inquiry, most of the dead or injured were shot in the back. The police had been armed with shotguns, R1 rifles, and 9mm automatic pistols, not the kind of weapons designed for crowd control but for deadly force. This exercise of force, however, was implicated in powerful forms of ritual.

First, the Uitenhage massacre was implicated in government restrictions on funerals. Although some in the crowd were going to work, many were on their way to a funeral that they thought was being held for several young men killed by the police. Earlier, Security Police Captain Goosen had arranged for the magisterial banning under the Internal Security Act of any funerals held on Saturdays, Sundays, Mondays, or public holidays. When Captain Goosen realized that Thursday, 21 March, was Sharpeville Day, he sought to prevent funerals that might commemorate that police massacre by obtaining a second magisterial order that banned all funerals except those conducted on a Sunday. Obviously, the two orders created an impossible situation, in effect requiring funerals to be performed only on Sunday, but not on Sunday. As the report of the official inquiry noted, this "could only lead to a sense of frustration and resentment among the residents of the townships."[31] Nevertheless, ritual respect for the dead required that a funeral be performed. Recognizing that the ritual rules set by the police were impossible, township residents apparently selected Sharpeville Day for the funeral.

Second, the Uitenhage massacre represented another ritual, a martial ritual of confrontation, reenacting precedents—Sharpeville in 1960, Soweto in 1976—that provided a ritualized format for police violence against township residents. Although the police claimed to have been pelted with stones by the crowd, no stones were later found at the scene in or around the police vehicles. Provocation and danger had assumed the more intangible forms of symbolic gesture: The police imagined that a Rastafarian was the leader of an organized uprising; they imagined that a bare-breasted woman taunted them; they imagined that people singing and dancing in the road were preparing for war; they imagined that a fifteen-year-old-boy on a bicycle, riding by with a clenched fist in the air (on his way to work, as it turned out) was signaling an attack. The police attacked.

Ironically, however, unlike the mobilized, politicized crowds that were massacred in Sharpeville and Soweto, the people at Uitenhage seem to have been disorganized, with many different motives bringing them to that place of confrontation. But the ritualized pattern of such confrontations was already established. Apparently, as the boy riding by on a bicycle raised his fist—in defiance of the police, in solidarity with the crowd, but also trying to get around the armored vehicles to get to work—the police took this gesture as a cue to open fire. At Uitenhage, therefore, violent acts reenacted a confrontation that dramatized, but also reinforced, the ritualized order represented by the presence of the police and army in the townships.[32]

In reinforcing the state's ceremonial control over South African space, emergency regulations also attempted to govern what people could say. Under the term "subversive statements," a long list of prohibited utterances were enshrined in law during the state of emergency. Punishment for making subversive statements was specified in the regulations as imprisonment for ten years or a fine of R20,000. On 11 December 1986, President Botha issued Proclamation R224, which, among other things, clarified the state's definition of a subversive statement. In a list of eleven different types of prohibited statements, the proclamation gave priority in its definition of subversion to any "statement which discredited or undermined compulsory military service."[33]

In particular, this attack upon subversive discourse was targeted at a nationwide organization, the End Conscription Campaign (ECC), which had been mobilizing resistance to conscription and support for conscientious objection to military service. The ECC had been founded in 1983, partly as a response to the Defence Amendment Act of that year, which had changed the term of imprisonment for failure to report for military service from two to six years. Following an initiative by the women's protest movement Black Sash, the ECC began gradually to establish branches in major urban centers around the country. In July 1984, the ECC issued a declaration which asserted that because South Africa was a society that denied basic human rights and was in a state of civil war, involved in the illegal occupation of Namibia, foreign incursions, and the implementation of apartheid at home, it was the "moral right" of people to "exercise freedom of conscience and to choose not to serve in the SADF."[34]

After the deployment of troops in the townships, the ECC embarked on a series of larger-scale public awareness campaigns—"Stop the Call Up," "Working for a Just Peace," and "War is No Solution"—which included festivals, workshops, and public meetings. The ECC projects seemed to coincide with a dropping off of enthusiasm for military service among white South Africans. For example, in the first major call-up after the deployment of troops in the townships, 7,589 conscripts (about 50 percent of the total called) reportedly failed to appear for military service. Although the minister of defence later insisted that his own department's figures had been in error in this account, he refused thereafter to report any statistics on the rates of response to conscription. In addition, during the period from 1984 to 1987, more than 45,000 people left the country. Although certainly not all, many of the young, white males who emigrated apparently left to avoid military service.[35]

The ECC worked to give ideological content to white aversion to serving in the SADF. Often, the arguments for resistance to compulsory military service were formulated in explicitly Christian terms. In a 1985 press statement, for example, the organization argued that "involvement in the ECC is a concrete way for Christians to express their commitment to peace and justice for all people." That commitment to peace and justice, however, took the form of militant ideological warfare against the unjust order of the South African state that was upheld by the SADF. Taking a page from the SADF's own manual of total strategy, as ECC organizer Laurie Nathan noted, "the ECC was engaged in 'warfare in the indirect mode,' that is, at the psychological and ideological levels."[36] Conversely, from the organization's inception, the government regarded it as an enemy of the state because it operated on that ideological level of warfare.

In response to the 1984 ECC declaration, the government expressed its concern that the campaign against conscription went "well beyond the parameters of conscientious objection on religious grounds." Although the government had been prepared since 1982 to recognize a religious commitment to universal pacifism as grounds for conscientious objection to military service, it was not prepared to recognize the type of moral, political, or ideological critique advanced by the ECC, even when the ECC invoked religious authority. In fact, official defence department statements regarding the ECC were consistently framed in terms of symbolic warfare against demonic forces that endangered South African society. In September 1985, Adriaan Vlok, then deputy minister of defence, accused the ECC of being used by the African National Congress to accomplish its "evil goals" in waging a terrorist war against South Africa; in 1986, Defence Minister Magnus Malan ordered the ECC to stop its "devilish onslaught" against the South African Defence Force; and in April 1987, Malan declared the ECC to be the "direct enemy of the SADF."[37]

Under the state of emergency, such rhetoric was easily translated into security actions against the ECC. At least seventy-five leaders were detained under security or emergency legislation, twenty-five were served with restriction orders, and ninety offices and homes were raided by security police. In addition to police action against the ECC, the military waged its own war against the organization. As was revealed in the Supreme Court in Cape Town, the SADF had been conducting a campaign of harassment—publishing documents that smeared the organization, devising and printing derogatory slogans, dropping pamphlets from helicopters at ECC gatherings—which it admitted but defended as "legitimate secret countermeasures" against a dangerous enemy of the state. Furthermore, spokesmen for the SADF argued that these military maneuvers were beyond the jurisdiction of the court because South Africa was in a state of war. As chief of the air force, General Van Loggerenberg insisted, these acts of harassment were "necessary military measures" because the SADF was "on a war footing."[38] Rejecting this argument, the court issued an interdict prohibiting the SADF from harassing or interfering with the organization.

However, this small legal victory in the ideological war came too late for the End Conscription Campaign. The organization had already been banned by proclamation of the government a few days earlier. At the beginning of August 1988, the ECC had organized a press conference for 143 conscripts who refused military service. Out of this group, two claimed solely religious motives; the rest refused to serve in the SADF on political or moral grounds. Almost immediately, the defence minister issued a resounding condemnation of the ECC, warning that the organization was "threatening the security of the state." Malan declared that "the movement was the vanguard of those forces that are intent on wrecking the present dispensation and its renewal." About two weeks later, on 22 August 1988, the government issued a banning order on the ECC. Ironically, for all its attention to the details of controlling discourse, the state had to repeat the banning two days later because the first government gazette had erroneously recorded the name of the ECC as the "End Conscription Committee." By whatever name, however, the government insisted that the ECC had to be suppressed because of the "dangers it [posed] to the safety of the public and the maintenance of public order."[39]

Government, security police, and defence force counterattacks against the ECC suggest that the very existence of an organized ideological challenge to the legitimacy of military service in defense of the South African political order—whether on the borders or in the townships—was perceived by the state as highly dangerous to that order. Although objectors to military service were few in number, their religious, moral, and ideological claims registered as serious threats to the state. Objectors, like Charles Bester, sentenced in December 1988 to six years in prison, invoked a "higher law than apartheid." Many, like David Bruce, also sentenced in 1988 to six years imprisonment, translated appeals to a higher authority into a critique of the role of the military in South Africa, arguing that they were "not prepared to serve in the SADF, which defends a racist system and is involved in what is essentially a civil war."[40] In the ideological warfare waged between conscientious objectors and the government, the state allowed little latitude for such maneuvers. By defining any statement that discredited or even questioned compulsory service as subversive under emergency regulations, the state permitted little space for personal conscience under the domain of the military. Ultimately, in its banning of the End Conscription Campaign, the state indicated that it would allow absolutely no space for any organized ideological, moral, or religious resistance to the military order of South Africa or to its established armed religion.

Organized religious resistance was being mounted nevertheless, often explicitly in terms of sacred space. Although the government had tried to totalize South African space under a single sacred order reinforced by the military and the police, religious leaders in opposition to the government struggled to defend small enclaves of an alternative sacred space in South Africa. For example, on 4 September 1989, Archbishop Desmond Tutu publicly accused the police riot squad of having violated the sanctity of Saint George's Cathedral in Cape Town. The previous day, the riot police had invaded the cathedral to break up a religious service conducted by the archbishop in support of people who had been attacked, beaten, and arrested in downtown Cape Town while peacefully protesting upcoming elections for South Africa's racial parliament. Compounding their flouting of civil liberty, the police riot squad, according to Archbishop Tutu, had also been guilty of "scandalous breaches of religious liberty" when they entered the cathedral and stopped the service. In the highly charged symbolic idiom of sacred space, Archbishop Tutu declared that the police had "desecrated Saint George's Cathedral." The violation was defined by more than the entrance of the police into the cathedral, armed and dangerous. It was also constituted by their utter disregard for the sanctity of that space. "Police broke into the church carrying guns [and] quirts," Archbishop Tutu noted, "and wearing their hats, in this holy place." With their hats on their heads, the police violated the power and purity of the sacred space circumscribed by Saint George's Cathedral.

Focusing on what might seem an incidental detail of police attire, Desmond Tutu captured something important about the symbolic, religious dimensions of the conflict over power, authority, and legitimacy in South Africa. The confrontation between government and opposition was entangled in a dialectic of the sacred and the profane, a contest, in this case, that the police lost—not only, but partly—because they wore hats in church. As Archbishop Tutu insisted, the police had "shown a profane disregard for the sanctity of our churches." In drawing more general conclusions from this incident, Archbishop Tutu enlarged the implications of the police invasion of a Christian space. "This act was performed by those representing a government which claims to be Christian," Tutu observed. Because the government had often invoked the Christian God in its own support, Archbishop Tutu could declare, without hyperbole, "We are appalled that this kind of act is carried out in the name of God."[41]

Although arguably a minor incident in the ongoing confrontations between government security forces and opposition forces, the desecration of Saint George's Cathedral illustrated how conflict in South Africa could be implicated in symbolic and ritual conflicts over sacred space. In her useful analysis of the symbolism of space in Swazi culture, religion, and politics, anthropologist Hilda Kuper argued that political struggles in southern Africa required "not only a redistribution of land and other resources but the creation of new spatial foci (new sites) of national identity." Those new spatial foci were sites of struggle over both the material and the symbolic resources that went into the construction of new orientations, new orders of religious and political significance. In Cape Town, Saint George's Cathedral stood as one such site of struggle. The cathedral was a center in a world of multiple centers. It operated as a sacred site in what Hilda Kuper called "the politics of space."[42] By manipulating the language of that particular site—theological language, political language, and even the apparently minor languages of gesture, manners, and costume—Archbishop Desmond Tutu was able to negotiate a powerful alternative orientation for his congregation. Although the government had tried to define sacred space as the totalization of South Africa under the religious worldview of a total strategy, Archbishop Tutu and other religious leaders opposed to the government struggled to redefine sacred space as liberated space. Indeed, the politics of space in South Africa became increasingly violent in the 1980s because many opponents of the government perceived that time as particularly full of revolutionary potential. In the decade that the African National Congress called the "Decade of Liberation," the space of war was being transformed into a time of revolution.

C H A P T E R 6

The Time of Revolution

•

ON SUNDAY afternoon, 11 February 1990, Nelson Mandela walked out of prison. Later that day, addressing an estimated crowd of 100,000 in Cape Town, Mandela said, "I stand here before you not as a prophet, but as a humble servant of you, the people. Your tireless and heroic sacrifices have made it possible for me to be here today. I therefore place the remaining years of my life in your hands." Referring to specific organizations that had contributed to the liberation struggle, Mandela acknowledged the work of resistance that had been carried out by various religious groups inside and outside of the country. "I pay tribute to the many religious communities," he declared, "who carried the campaign for justice forward when the organisations of our people were silenced." Although this was the only direct reference to religion in Mandela's speech, it might be argued that the entire event carried an aura of the sacred. Restating a vision of redemption from racial oppression in South Africa, Mandela concluded by quoting from the transcript of his 1964 trial: "I have fought against white domination and I have fought against black domination. I have carried the ideal of a democratic and free society in which all persons live together in harmony and with equal opportunity. It is an ideal which I hope to live for and to achieve. But, if needs be, it is an ideal for which I am prepared to die."[1]

Being prepared to die for the cause of liberation signaled an essentially religious commitment to what the psychologist Robert Jay Lifton has called "revolutionary immortality." In revolutionary immortality, an individual's life and death may be absorbed in the ongoing life of a political, social, but also profoundly sacred revolution. In 1964, Nelson Mandela had announced his willingness to merge his own life into that ongoing struggle against oppression in South Africa. In 1990, he restated that commitment. For more than a quarter century, while Mandela was imprisoned, others had committed themselves to a sacrificial entry into revolutionary immortality. Archbishop Desmond Tutu had himself invoked the powerful rhetoric of redemptive sacrifice when he stated in 1987, "For this I am ready to die." Others had in fact made that supreme sacrifice. Reflecting on the upsurge of resistance from 1984 to 1986, theologian Buti Tlhagale remarked that "some of the young people have laid down their lives for the sake of justice—as did Christ."[2]

In South African resistance, the example of Christ was appropriated as a revolutionary model of suffering and death for the sake of liberation. In this respect, the Rev. Jesse Jackson, visiting South Africa at the time of Mandela's release, was not merely engaging in flamboyant rhetoric when he declared in a sermon in Cape Town that Nelson Mandela "was a Christ-like figure" who had "suffered his way into power." Although he went on to describe Mandela's release from prison, "now that the stone [had] been rolled away," as an apocalyptic "second coming," Jackson did not overstate the importance of Nelson Mandela as a symbol of suffering, sacrifice, and the promise of redemption from oppression in South Africa.[3] Not a prophet, Mandela came out of prison as a suffering servant, a redemptive sacrifice, and a living symbol of revolutionary immortality in South Africa.

The invocation of Christ suggests that resistance to the apartheid regime involved symbolic, religious negotiations over superhuman meaning and power. In addition, resistance also entailed renegotiations of space and time in South Africa. As historian William Beinart has observed, "struggles against oppression produce their own historical myths, symbols of resistance and interpretations of the past." Since the 1950s, Mandela had been at the center of the nexus of symbols, myths, and interpretations that have given the struggle against oppression in South Africa a sacred dimension of meaning and power. Mandela himself testified in 1964 that particular interpretations of the past had been important to his own development. As a child, he had listened to the tales of African military heroes of resistance, powerful historical myths about "wars fought by our ancestors in defence of the fatherland." Impressed by those models of resistance, Mandela related in court, "I hoped then that life might offer me the opportunity to serve my people and make my own humble contribution to their freedom struggle."[4]

Historical myths of African culture also provided models for the social and economic reorganization of South Africa. "Today I am attracted by the idea of a classless society," Mandela told the court, "an attraction which springs in part from Marxist reading and, in part, from my admiration of the structure and organisation of early African societies in this country."[5] In those societies, land belonged to the community, with no vast inequalities in wealth and no exploitation. With reference to these historical myths of military resistance and social organization, therefore, Mandela could propose that the way forward for South Africa was also a path that led back to earlier African models. In this sense, revolution was at the same time a work of historical recovery, a vital link between a past and a future in the process of being born. Resistance was simultaneously a commitment to reclaim history and a commitment to radical change in South Africa.

What was the role of violence in this work of resistance, recovery, and social change? As an extension of the political work of the African National Congress, after it was banned in 1960, Mandela had directed the formation of a military wing—Umkhonto we Sizwe, Spear of the Nation—in 1961 to undertake a program of sabotage against the government. Armed struggle was politics by violent means. Mandela argued that the ANC was compelled to resort to violence for two reasons: Its commitment since its founding in 1912 to nonviolent protest had clearly failed, and the government's commitment to violence had to be resisted through armed self-defence. Almost immediately after the armed struggle was initiated, however, its leaders found themselves either in prison or in exile. By the 1980s, Umkhonto we Sizwe had expanded its military organization, training, and operations, conducting a declared war to seize power from the state, but it had achieved little in the way of tangible success. Nevertheless, the ANC and its military wing operated as powerful symbols of resistance and hope for many inside and outside South Africa, as well as symbols of dangerous evil—forces, as Foreign Minister Pik Botha insisted, of "evil design"—in the worldview of the government.[6]

In 1985, President P. W. Botha extended a conditional offer of release to imprisoned members of banned political organizations if they would agree to renounce violence. This offer also applied to Nelson Mandela. As President Botha put it, "All that is required of him now is that he should unconditionally reject violence as a political instrument." Mandela, however, refused to accept any conditions that might be placed by the government on his release. In a statement issued from prison, Mandela turned the invitation to renounce violence back on the government. "I am surprised at the conditions that the government wants to impose on me," Mandela noted. "I am not a violent man." Mandela then went on to explain the ANC's understanding that the cause of violence in South Africa was not the armed struggle but a government that had ignored and violently repressed the political aspirations of the majority of the people.

> My colleagues and I wrote in 1952 to Malan asking for a round table conference. . . . When Strijdom was in power, we made the same offer. Again it was ignored. When Verwoerd was in power we asked for a National Convention for all the people in South Africa to decide on their future. This, too, was in vain. It was only then when all other forms of resistance were no longer open to us that we turned to armed struggle. Let Botha show that he is different to Malan, Strijdom and Verwoerd. Let him renounce violence. Let him guarantee free political activity so that people may decide who will govern them.

In this statement, Mandela represented armed struggle as an alternative form of negotiation forced on the ANC when its attempts at nonviolent negotiations with the government had failed. In addition, by inverting the terms and conditions of President Botha's offer of release, Mandela implied that he would come out of prison only if the government renounced the violence through which it reinforced its oppressive control over South Africa. Not the armed struggle, but state violence needed to be renounced.[7]

Among other things, this exchange between Botha and Mandela revealed how the very term "violence" was being contested in symbolic negotiations over the meaning and power of a world. One front of resistance was therefore the battlefield of discourse. The relation between force and discourse became significant terrain for the conflict between the ANC and the National Party government. The state exercised considerable control over the production and dissemination of language and imagery about force through television, radio, press, and propaganda. But an alternative discourse was never effectively silenced. That alternative was not only a particular way of talking about force that reversed the terms in which violence could be located in South Africa; it was also an alternative in which force itself operated as a type of discourse, as a mode of communication, as a signifying practice that announced a worldview of resistance.

Force and Discourse

On the occasion of the seventy-fifth anniversary of the founding of the ANC, president Oliver Tambo reflected on the role of violence in the work of liberation. Acknowledging that violence was a potentially dehumanizing tactic, Tambo assured his audience that the "need for us to take up arms will never transform us into prisoners of the idea of violence, slaves to the goddess of war." In his rhetorical apotheosis of war, recognizing its power to turn devotees into something less than human, Tambo carved out a symbolic space in which humanity might be maintained even in the conduct of violent resistance against the South African regime. By implication, that regime had become enslaved to the goddess of violence, but the ANC, Tambo argued, would never be so dehumanized. Nevertheless, resistance required military, as well as potently symbolic, strategies of armed struggle. Because the regime was devoted to violence, Tambo concluded, "if the opponents of democracy have their way, we will have to wade through rivers of blood to reach our goal of liberty, justice and peace."[8]

Blood has indeed flowed in that conflict. Intensifying its attacks after 1976, the military wing of the ANC had assumed responsibility for 80 deaths by 1984. Oliver Tambo, however, could point to over 2,000 deaths caused by the South African security forces from 1984 to 1987. Armed struggle against the regime was not measured only in body counts. In its revolution against the state, the ANC also mobilized symbolic instruments of force and discourse, symbols of resistance that were not merely symbolic, but were meaningful, powerful strategies for renegotiating a world. Although the ANC drew increasingly on the support and legitimation provided by religious communities, its own symbolic discourse deployed strategies of classification and orientation that fashioned a compelling worldview.

Founded in 1912 as the South African Natives National Congress, in the 1980s the ANC could claim to be the oldest political organization in Africa. Initially, its leaders engaged in protest against oppressive legislation and exclusion from representation in the recently formed Union of South Africa through petitions, representations, and delegations to the government. Not civil disobedience, but civilized protest was the prevailing strategy. Leaders invoked ideals of Christianity as the moral ground of their protest. The ANC's first president, John Dube, for example—a Congregational minister, American-trained educator, and founder of the Ohlange Institute in Natal, based on Booker T. Washington's model of industrial education—urged the congress toward Christian civilization. "Onward! Upward!" Dube exhorted, "into the higher places of civilisation and Christianity—not backwards into the slump of darkness nor downward into the abyss of antiquated tribal systems." Likewise, ANC president in the 1940s, A. B. Xuma, formulated the initial aims of the organization as an effort to "promote the ideals of Christianity, human decency, and democracy."[9]

As a Christian, mission-educated elite, Dube, Xuma, and other early leaders of the ANC were struck by the incongruity between these ideals and the exclusion they suffered in the Union of South Africa. In addition, however, they claimed to speak on behalf of a wider African constituency that suffered under oppressive legislation, particularly the Natives Land Act of 1913, which dispossessed and displaced so many in laying the foundation for the reserve system. "How can a government policy proclaiming itself Christian perpetrate such cruelties on the inarticulate poor?" Dube asked. "How can a professedly Christian people permit such persecution in their midst and look on unmoved?"[10] In the name of Christianity, therefore, the founders of the ANC sought a hearing for those who had been denied a voice in the Union of South Africa. Although it exposed a profound irony in the policies of a self-professed Christian government, the ANC call for a true Christian civilization resulted in no tangible redress of African grievances.

During the 1920s and 1930s, other political movements mobilized resistance. The Industrial and Commercial Workers Union, the South African Communist Party, and various rural movements drew considerable support.[11] In the 1940s, however, the ANC underwent a kind of revival. At the center of that renewal was the religious nationalist Anton Lembede. Educated as a Roman Catholic, Lembede formulated a nationalist creed—Africanism. In 1946, Lembede identified what he called a condition of "moral degeneration" that "manifests itself in abnormal and pathological phenomena as loss of self-confidence, inferiority complex, a feeling of frustration, the worship and idolization of whitemen, foreign leaders and ideologies." As an antidote to this pathological condition, Lembede looked to a nationalism in which people could "live and move and have their being in the spirit of Africa." This spiritualized African nationalism, Lembede argued, had to be "pursued with the fanaticism and bigotry of religion, for it is the only creed that will dispel and disperse the inferiority complex which blurs our sight and darkens our horizon." This new creed not only promised personal redemption from a dehumanizing sense of inferiority; it promised national liberation from oppression. As Lembede exhorted, "We have a divine mission of unifying and liberating Africa, thus enabling her to occupy her rightful and honorable place amongst the nations of the world."[12]

Anton Lembede negotiated a new classification of persons in which the dehumanized could become human by embodying the superhuman spirit of Africa; he negotiated a new orientation in space in which the land could be reclaimed by its rightful owners; and he negotiated a new orientation in time in which the heroes of military resistance against colonial domination could be imitated in working out the divine destiny of African liberation. Although Lembede died in 1947, the worldview he articulated was appropriated in different ways by two movements within the ANC as a basis for mobilization and concerted action.

One version of African nationalism was developed within the Congress Youth League, proclaiming "Africa for Africans, Africans for humanity, and humanity for God and Africa." Leaders of the Youth League, including Nelson Mandela, Oliver Tambo, and Walter Sisulu, drew up a program of action that resulted in the organized nonviolent civil disobedience of the Defiance Campaign of the early

1950s. Consistent with the religious heritage of the ANC, as Leo Kuper noted, organizers of the Defiance Campaign "stressed the affinity between nonviolent resistance and the ethic of Christianity." President of the ANC Albert Luthuli, in particular, represented the Defiance Campaign in explicitly Christian terms. The contribution of the ANC to the formulation of the Freedom Charter in 1955 affiliated this version of African nationalism with a plural, nonracial, and democratic social order in which the land would belong to all who lived in South Africa, black or white.[13]

In the other version of African nationalism, however, black claims on the land were reasserted, insisting that the "African people have an inalienable claim on every inch of the African soil." Leaders of the Africanist wing of the ANC in the 1950s, like Peter Mda, Victor Sifora, and Robert Sobukwe, claimed to be the true heirs of Lembede, even celebrating an annual memorial service in his honor to reinforce a living connection with African religious nationalism. In 1959, the Africanists broke with the ANC to form the Pan Africanist Congress (PAC). The new organization's first president, Robert Sobukwe, had been a Methodist lay preacher, but by 1949 he had merged Christianity with African nationalism, invoking the "God of Africa" in the cause of liberating African humanity. At the inaugural convention of the PAC, sermons and prayers delivered by African nationalist ministers denounced the "hooligans from Europe who killed our God." In religious idiom, therefore, the violence of white oppression was articulated, but a militant, African resistance was also mobilized.[14]

In its first organized resistance, the anti-pass campaign, the PAC reiterated its commitment to nonviolent civil disobedience. As Robert Sobukwe insisted in a press conference in Johannesburg on 18 March 1960, the PAC was doing everything it could "to make sure that this campaign is conducted in a spirit of absolute nonviolence." However, Sobukwe also noted, in terms that anticipated the violent response of the police to the protest, "If the other side so desires, we will provide them with an opportunity to demonstrate to the world how brutal they can be. We are ready to die for our cause." Three days later, a gathering of about 7,000 people in Sharpeville was confronted by the police. The crowd was ordered to disperse, teargassed, and fired upon, leaving 69 dead and many wounded. The following day, the black townships around Cape Town erupted in protests, demonstrations, and marches, only to be cordoned off by the police and army. On 28 March, Albert Luthuli was arrested, imprisoned for five months, and then banned to his home for a period of five years. His crime was to have the ANC declare a day of mourning for the victims of Sharpeville. The brutal suppression of dissent throughout the country was followed by the banning of political organizations, making membership in the Pan Africanist Congress or the African National Congress a criminal offense under South African law.[15]

Forced out of South African civil, public space, both political movements responded by going underground and into exile to undertake military campaigns. The military wing of the Pan Africanist Congress assumed the name Poqo—signifying "alone" or "pure," a term apparently first used during the 1930s by African independent churches in the eastern Cape—and embarked on a program of violent action. During the height of its popular support, between 1961 and 1963, Poqo was probably the largest underground African political organization in South Africa. Poqo adopted a strategy of violence to eliminate blacks who were perceived as traitors, to kill white administrators and policemen, and to plan a general violent uprising against the white population of South Africa. PAC National Secretary Potlako Leballo, in exile, formulated the plans for an uprising that would require the indiscriminate, mass slaughter of whites. According to Leballo's announced plan for insurrection, Poqo soldiers would be called upon on the appointed day to attack the "forces of darkness" and kill as many whites as possible for a period of four hours. When the killing stopped, the whites who remained would be invited to join in the formation of a new government. Before this plan could be carried out, however, the police raided Leballo's hiding place, discovered a list of about 10,000 names of Poqo supporters, and began arresting anyone suspected of affiliation with the movement.

Although a few, highly publicized attacks on whites were carried out, Poqo's general uprising never materialized. Yet Poqo played an important role in South African resistance, as Tom Lodge has noted, as "the first African political movement in South Africa to adopt a strategy that explicitly involved killing people." Analyses of Poqo have tended to see its tactics in the light of the celebration of anticolonial violence found in the work of Frantz Fanon. In struggles against colonial domination, Fanon argued, violence could be purifying, liberating, and redemptive—exercised as it was by those who suffered under oppression. But the violence planned and exercised by Poqo can be read even more directly as a religious symbolism of redemption. Its religious symbols fused elements of Christian and traditional African religious discourse and practice. Although the name Poqo might have been derived from separatist Christian churches, it also suggested the ritualized, sacrificial killing of animals for purification in traditional African religious practice. The movement formed its own church—Qamata, both a traditional and mission name for God—but also engaged in ritual practices, such as ceremonial initiations, war-doctoring for immunity from bullets, and invoking the ancestors, the gods of Africa, or the God of Africa, that carried the aura of a traditional African religion. In the end, however, these symbolic instruments of power were mobilized in an apocalyptic battle against the "forces of darkness." Weaving together Christian and traditional symbols, Poqo—like other movements that have been called "revitalization movements" or movements of "primary resistance"—was not an atavistic, "tribal" regression, but a modern innovation in the field of religious symbols of redemption.[16]

The African National Congress also formed a military wing. In April 1961, Nelson Mandela went underground to prepare plans for military action, culminating in the formation of Umkhonto we Sizwe in December of that year. As Mandela later explained in a prepared statement during the "Rivonia Trial" in 1964, Umkhonto had been formed to engage in acts of sabotage against government installations for the purpose of getting the attention of the white electorate in South Africa. "Our first actions will awaken everyone to a realisation of the disastrous situation to which the Nationalist policy is leading. We hope that we will bring the Government and its supporters to their senses before it is too late, so that both Government and its policies can be changed before matters reach the desperate stage of civil war."

In court statements delivered during trials in 1962 and 1964, Mandela provided three fundamental justifications for the ANC's recourse to acts of violence. First, military organization and leadership were necessary to channel the anger of the people into disciplined acts of resistance. Without control, Mandela argued, anger promised to erupt into terrorism that would only intensify hostility in the country. Second, Mandela argued that the government had initiated the conflict by its brutal suppression of peaceful protest. The government had "set the scene for violence by relying exclusively on violence to answer our people and their demands." As a result, the violence of the state had bred the counterviolence of resistance. Third, Mandela reminded the government that since political organizations dedicated to peaceful protest had been banned, no nonviolent avenues of protest or resistance remained open. "It was only when all else had failed, when all channels of peaceful protest had been barred to us," he noted, "that the decision was made to embark on violent forms of political struggle." In this respect, armed struggle against the government was a course of last resort, "solely because the Government," Mandela concluded, "had left us with no other choice."[17]

In contrast to Poqo, the military program of the ANC was justified, not in terms of religious symbols of sudden redemption, but in terms of a pragmatic, rational justification of means and ends. The ANC had a long tradition of commitment to the objective of a unified, nonracial, democratic political order, and it had pursued that objective through nonviolent means. When nonviolent means of political action were closed, however, the ANC was forced to resort to violence as an alternative means for achieving the same objective. This explanation of the ANC's turn to armed struggle was still repeated in the 1980s. Addressing the conference "Peace and Development in Frontline States," in June 1988, Oliver Tambo argued that the armed struggle had been forced on the liberation movement by the government. "It came not because we had any love of violence," Tambo argued, "but because the path of non-violence was closed by the Pretoria regime." Mandela reiterated this position in a statement drawn up for a meeting with P. W. Botha in July 1989. Identifying the government as the source of violence, Mandela argued that in the early 1960s the state "took advantage of our commitment to a nonviolent struggle and unleashed the most violent form of racial oppression this country has ever seen. It stripped us of all basic human rights, outlawed our organisations and barred all channels of peaceful resistance. It met our just demands with force and, despite the grave problems facing the country, it continues to refuse to talk to us. There can only be one answer to this challenge: Violent forms of struggle."[18]

In their justifications of violent forms of struggle, leaders of the ANC drew an implicit contrast between the use of force on the one hand and forms of discourse on the other. Violence was reluctantly adopted as a substitute for talk to awaken, to gain a hearing, to bring the government to the negotiating table. But it became as well a strategy in its own right, sometimes referred to as "armed propaganda," that empowered the African National Congress and Umkhonto we Sizwe as symbols of resistance in South Africa. In spite of the minimal success achieved during twenty-five years of armed struggle, the ANC's discourse about force and, more important, its exercise of force as a symbolic discourse were essential to building mass support, international recognition, and even the eventual acknowledgment by the government that the organization was central to any political solution for South Africa.

In a January 1989 article that appeared in the official publication of the African National Congress, *Sechaba,* the Rev. John Lamola insisted that the term "violence" should not be used to describe the armed struggle of liberation. Lamola argued that any ruling class tends to constitute the meaning of terms. "In our experience and epoch," he observed, "no other concept has been so successfully manipulated by the reactionary imperialist forces as that of 'violence.'" The South African government and its supporters had succeeded in manipulating the term so that it only applied to actions by the liberation movement; the violence of the state disappeared, only to appear in official discourse as legitimate force. Illustrating the importance of symbolic discourse in the conflict over South Africa, words themselves became part of the contest between the government and its opposition. The government insisted on a distinction between its legitimate use of force to maintain law and order and the illegitimate violence employed by the military wing of the ANC.

Maneuvering in this contest of symbols, Lamola adopted the same definitional strategy but reversed its terms of reference. The apartheid regime was violence (in the sense of a systematic violation of human rights, dignity, and well-being) maintained by violence (in the sense of direct, coercive force). Lamola asked, "Wouldn't defence of a brutal and dehumanizing system like apartheid constitute violence?—a violent defence of violence by further violence?" In answer to his own inquiry into the nature of violence, Lamola concluded, "in essence and reality, South Africa is violence."

Supplementing his discussion with a theological reading, Lamola argued that violence could only be understood against a standard of peace, a peace that was not merely the absence of conflict, but the presence of the material and spiritual well-being among the people embodied in the Hebrew term *shalom*. "From a theological point of view," Lamola suggested, "when victims of an aggressive, shalom-violating regime rise up in defence of their humanity, they are doing so not necessarily in their personal, or nationalistic, interests. They are essentially making a concrete proclamation that seeks to have God's will of justice, peace and righteousness done and preserved on earth. They are fighting for a manifestation and extension of shalom." In this sense, the armed struggle could be viewed as a religious enterprise, a struggle to work out divine will in the world.

Whether in religious, political, or moral terms, the thrust of Lamola's argument about violence was that the term must only be applied to the violations of humanity and the illegitimate exercise of force by the South African government: "To engage in military acts of struggle for the liberation of the oppressed from a political system as vicious as apartheid is not to engage in what can be called 'violence,' nor even 'revolutionary violence,' since wrongness and immorality is implied in the word, 'violence.'" Although he recommended alternative terms—armed struggle, armed revolution, or people's defence—Lamola's primary intent seemed to be to exonerate the liberation movement from any implication in the immorality represented by violence. In this respect, he outlined a definition of violence that became a consistent factor in the ANC's armed propaganda.[19]

As already noted, however, discourse about force was only one aspect of the symbolism of violence in the armed propaganda of the ANC. Force itself had become a powerful language of negotiation. First, it was a language that had to be used by the ANC in order for the political aspirations it represented to receive a hearing in South Africa. To be seen and heard, to be recognized, acknowledged, and taken seriously, the ANC had to speak in a particularly forceful voice. In a statement issued by the National Executive Committee of the ANC in 1987, the leadership of the movement observed, "Our people have only been taken seriously, whether in Pretoria, London, Washington or Bonn, because of our armed activity." Without the armed struggle spearheaded by Umkhonto we Sizwe, the NEC statement concluded, "our people and the leader of our revolution, the African

National Congress, would be a voice without force." In reviewing the history of Umkhonto, Cassius Mandla noted that the armed struggle was intended in the beginning as "a language of communication with the enemy." This symbolic orientation toward the exercise of force as message, communication, language, and voice was certainly held by the founders of Umkhonto. As Wilton Mkwayi observed at his sentencing in 1964, the act of sabotage was not a declaration of war, "but a letter of invitation to the government and the white minority of South Africa to come to [a national] convention." Their demands ignored, their voices silenced by banning, the founders of Umkhonto turned to a louder voice, as Mandla recalled, "as a tactic of pressuring the oppressors to open their ears and hearts to the demands of the oppressed."[20]

Second, force was represented as the only possible way to communicate with the government because force was the dominant and perhaps sole idiom of state power. As Nelson Mandela noted in 1964, the government's response to the language, the message, the invitation that had been signified by the sabotage campaign was "characteristically violent." Instead of entering negotiations, Mandela observed, the government "responded to our call by suggesting the laager." In some cases, the ANC argued, violence was the state's preferred discourse. In his annual president's message in 1985, for example, Oliver Tambo announced that armed struggle was necessary "to talk to the enemy in the language he understands best." Under more extreme provocation, however, the ANC concluded that force was the only language that the government could comprehend. After the assassination of two ANC members in Swaziland in July 1987, the ANC executive concluded that such an incident, like many others, was "a clear indication that the South African racist regime, in its desperation, is at all times bent on terror and cold-blooded murder against its opponents who are dedicated to the ending of the hated and evil system of apartheid." Interpreting the violence of the government as discourse, the ANC stated, "We for our part pledge to answer these brutal assassinations of our comrades with the only language which Botha and his regime understand, the language of escalating armed struggle and intensified mass resistance."[21]

Third, force represented a type of spiritual discourse that effected self-understanding within the ANC. Force clarified, inspired, unified, and expanded the liberation movement. In an interview about the history of the armed struggle, Umkhonto leader Ronnie Kasrils described military action as a kind of spiritual politics. At the beginning, the sabotage campaign was designed to strike a blow at the government. In addition, however, and perhaps of greater significance, the use of force "was meant to inspire our people, and build our forces, the nucleus of a people's army to be." Force therefore sent a message not only to the government but also to the oppressed people of South Africa. In this respect, force was an inspirational message. "This was a period of armed propaganda," Kasrils recalled, "propaganda by force," a forceful discourse that communicated not only with the oppressor but also with the oppressed.

As Kasrils continued his narrative of the history of the armed struggle, its next stage was marked by the Zimbabwe campaign of 1967–68 in which Umkhonto soldiers in the Luthuli Detachment fought alongside the rebels against Rhodesian and South African troops. Although they did not succeed in getting home to start a guerrilla war in South Africa, these soldiers underwent "a true baptism of fire" in the spiritual politics of the armed struggle. Not only a martial ritual of initiation, the presence of Umkhonto soldiers in the field sent the message to the South African government that the military wing of the ANC was ready and willing to confront its forces in battle.

A third stage in this narrative was reached with the brutal suppression of peaceful protest associated with Soweto in 1976. Soweto, Kasrils recalled, was "a flash of lightning that showed an entire generation the need for arms." As a revelation in the spiritual politics of the armed struggle, Soweto signified the righteousness of armed actions against the forces of evil represented by the government. Although armed struggle might not immediately achieve victory over that enemy, it did promise to broaden the cause of liberation. As one ANC theorist put it, "The more we fight, the more we grow." In the 1980s, force continued to be exercised and understood as an inspiring discourse. Reflecting on the impact of more than two hundred Umkhonto attacks in 1986, the editors of *Sechaba* concluded that "these acts inspire our people, give them new confidence in their strength and mobilize them to greater acts of heroism and sacrifice."[22]

During the second half of the 1980s, the relation between the ANC and religious communities within South Africa changed dramatically. Some impression of that change can be gained by comparing Oliver Tambo's annual presidential addresses in 1986 and 1990. In his 1986 message, Tambo urged the religious community to assume its responsibilities in the struggle for liberation: "The religious community has an immense and urgent responsibility to act in defence of life itself, and accordingly, to fight for justice and peace." Four years later, however, the ANC president no longer had to exhort the religious community to join the fight. He was able to pay tribute to a high degree of religious involvement in furthering the aims of the liberation movement: "Prominent religious figures have played an outstanding role in the fight against injustice. We salute these great patriots." Prominent religious leaders, such as Archbishop Desmond Tutu, the Rev. Allan Boesak, and the Rev. Frank Chikane, had made important contributions to resistance in South Africa. In paying tribute to these religious leaders, Tambo measured their religious integrity in terms of their sacrificial commitment to the struggle. "They have been prepared to sacrifice even their lives," he noted, "to remain true to their beliefs." But these high-profile religious leaders were joined by many others at grassroots level in the religious community, who by being true to their religious beliefs, "help shorten the lifespan of this system and bring life where death was the order of the day."[23]

Oliver Tambo's personal religious history reflected the experience of many of the older generation of leaders in the ANC. Tambo's religious training and background provided a persistent spiritual and moral frame of reference throughout his life. His Christian disposition during the 1940s has been described as puritanical. In the 1950s, Tambo condemned the oppressive South African regime as essentially anti-Christian. This dissonance between a self-professed Christian government and its oppressive political policies contributed to a certain disillusionment with the Christian religion. In an anecdote recalled for a biographical profile, Tambo remembered being told by a white priest during a Good Friday service in an Anglican cathedral, "Would you please go to the back of the cathedral, because this section is reserved for Whites?" As long as the church incorporated apartheid within its own practice, many black leaders despaired of the liberating potential of a Christian faith. By the 1980s, however, Oliver Tambo and the ANC were in a position to reappropriate the religious community as a site of struggle for liberation.[24]

In 1987, Tambo described the ANC's strong ties to the religious community. Although the government had tried to portray the organization as made up of "ungodly, irreligious atheists," the history of the ANC revealed its long association with the church: "Our founders were church men and women. Throughout our 75 years that link has never been broken." If in the past ANC leaders had been disappointed in their relations with religious institutions, their common history began to witness significant breakthroughs. In 1976, for example, the resolution of the Christian Institute to support the political objectives of the ANC and the Freedom Charter was an advance in religious support for the liberation movement. In 1977, however, the Christian Institute was banned by the government, its leaders banned, imprisoned, or in exile. Direct support of the ANC was discouraged by such government intervention.[25]

In the 1980s, the major obstacle faced by religious institutions in their relations with the ANC was the armed struggle. As South African churches began to reestablish contacts with the ANC in the second half of the decade, the question of violence was foremost in their deliberations. In April 1986, for example, a delegation from the Southern African Catholic Bishops Conference met with the ANC in Lusaka. The joint statement issued after that meeting affirmed a common purpose, but disagreed on the role of violence in resistance. The ANC accepted "the Catholic Church and the religious community in general as an important force in the struggle against apartheid, for justice and peace." For its part, however, the Catholic delegation insisted that, "though it understood the reasons why the ANC resorted to force, it felt it could not identify with this aspect of ANC strategy." Other churches drew similar conclusions, expressing solidarity with the ANC's political objectives, but reservations about the use of violence.[26]

A turning point in Christian reflections on violence in South Africa was initiated in 1985 by the group of theologians who produced the *Kairos Document*. The document distinguished between a state theology that supported the current South African regime, a church theology that, in its professed neutrality and commitment to nonviolence, actually supported the perpetuation of the regime, and a prophetic theology that demanded resistance to and replacement of the unjust rule of the South African government. It was the document's discussion of violence that achieved the greatest clarity, as well as generated the greatest controversy, in the relations between the church and the liberation struggle. The document asked, "Is it legitimate, especially in our circumstances, to use the same word violence in a blanket condemnation to cover the ruthless and repressive activities of the State and the desperate attempts of people to defend themselves?"[27] In the South African situation, Christian condemnations of all violence did not represent what the *Kairos Document* regarded as a biblically mandated differentiation between the illegitimate violence of oppression and legitimate self-defense against aggression and injustice. In that distinction between illegitimate violence and legitimate force, the kairos theologians concluded that under extreme conditions force might not only be understandable, but also permitted within Christian ethics. Although this theological reading was certainly consistent with ANC discourse on violence, even such a cautious recognition that the use of force in the liberation struggle might be warranted met with rejection by most South African churches.

In May 1987, another breakthrough in the ANC's relations with the religious community was marked by the meeting of representatives from South African, Namibian, and international church organizations for a consultation in Lusaka sponsored by the World Council of Churches. The issue of violence was central to the consultation. The joint statement that emerged from this meeting concluded that the ANC had been compelled to use force in the struggle against oppression. First, the *Lusaka Statement* identified the context for theological deliberations about violence as the "anguish, suffering, unimaginable pain and heroic resistance" that were "the hallmarks of the struggle against injustice in Southern Africa." Out of that context, the *Lusaka Statement* outlined a political theology that read Romans 13:1 to indicate that "civil authority is instituted of God to do good, and that under biblical imperative all people are obliged to do justice and show special care for the oppressed and the poor." In the light of this reading, the civil authority of the South African regime was condemned as illegitimate, an illegitimacy that required the church "to work for the removal of the present rulers who persistently usurp the stewardship of God's authority."

By stark contrast, liberation movements in southern Africa represented authentic vehicles for the political aspirations of the majority of the people. Although it reaffirmed a Christian commitment to peace, the *Lusaka Statement* issued the strongest church support for the ANC's recourse to force in the liberation struggle. "While remaining committed to peaceful change," the statement concluded, "we recognize that the nature of the South African regime, which wages war against its own inhabitants and neighbours, compels the movements to the use of force along with other means to end oppression." In solidarity with the liberation movements in Namibia and South Africa, the *Lusaka Statement* called on all Christian churches and the international community to support the regional struggle for liberation.[28]

Some churches and church leaders who adopted the *Lusaka Statement* did seek to strengthen ties with the ANC and other liberation movements. After the banning of eighteen anti-apartheid organizations in February 1988, church leaders assumed an even more prominent role in resistance to the government. Finding themselves in the same position as the ANC and PAC had been in 1960, as the Rev. Frank Chikane noted, they were met by a government saying, in effect, "No peaceful, nonviolent political activity and resistance against apartheid is going to be allowed. Instead, we want you on the battlefield." For Chikane, and for other religious leaders, the suppression of nonviolent avenues of protest raised once again the moral question of whether the religious community could "still accuse the liberation movement of violence if the government has itself openly resorted to violence."[29]

This increasingly active involvement of religious leaders and organizations in the struggle, while welcomed, was also criticized by the ANC. Theologians of the movement's "religious committee" sought to clarify the relation between religion and the liberation struggle from the ANC's perspective. In a cautionary critique, John Lamola warned that the new, radical involvement of organized Christianity might create the illusion that the church was leading the revolution. If the church were to be regarded as a leading force in the struggle, then church leaders might set their own agendas, people might think that all they had to do was to support the church, and the church would appear as the "ANC at prayer," the exclusive, privileged expression of the spiritual politics of the liberation movement. However, Lamola argued, the church was not a force of struggle, but a site of struggle, like schools, factories, and other arenas of South African public life, both a gathering point for people and a target to be captured and liberated. As another ANC theologian, Cedric Mayson, observed, "The Church is not an army but a battlefield. It is one of the places where the struggle is being waged, and it is necessary to analyse the forces involved in the conflict in relation to the revolution." From this perspective, the religious community did not necessarily provide spiritual forces for resolving the South African conflict; it constituted an important battlefield on which the conflict in South Africa—particularly the contest over the legitimate ownership of sacred symbols—was being fought.[30]

In his analysis of the relations between Christian churches and liberation, John Lamola identified three critical points to bear in mind. First, Christian theology was by nature contested theology, "one of the most disputed among human areas of enquiry." As a result, Christian theology, even a prophetic theology, did not provide a firm basis from which to derive political principles and practice.

Second, Christian churches represented only one among many religious constituencies in South Africa. Recognizing the vitality of religious pluralism in the country, the liberation movement had to be a broad-based, national movement that could "draw people from all religious persuasions," maintain multifaith religious support, protect "freedom of religion," and ensure that any future South Africa would not be a Christian state, but "a state that will take into account Christian values, just as it will those of other religions." In particular, Christians had to recognize the involvement of Muslims in the liberation struggle. In a joint statement, the ANC, the Natal Indian Congress, and the Transvaal Indian Congress, with a strong representation of Muslims, reaffirmed a commitment to religious freedom, recognizing that "all religions are fundamentally opposed to the apartheid system." Even the South African Communist Party had affirmed the importance of religious pluralism and freedom. "The ideology of the South African Communist Party is based on scientific materialism," the SACP noted. "But we recognize the right of all people to adopt and practice religious beliefs of their choice." In these affirmations of pluralism, the ANC suggested that no single religious constituency could enjoy privileged access to the spiritual truth of the struggle.[31]

Finally, Lamola suggested that the spiritual politics of the liberation movement were determined by the movement itself and not by the Christian churches or other religious organizations. In that regard, he argued, the religious community ultimately had to be accountable to the people, their struggle, and their liberation movement. Accountability, Lamola maintained, required "consultation between the religious structures and the people's political structures," so that, in partnership, religion could be deployed to supplement the political work of the liberation movement. In the end, he concluded, although the Kairos and Lusaka statements were steps in the right direction, the church would have to identify with the spiritual politics of the ANC in order to become a "servant of the revolution."[32]

Person

The spiritual politics of the African National Congress did not depend upon the legitimation provided by religious leaders or organizations in South Africa. Rather, the ANC's spiritual politics was grounded in a detailed, coherent, and compelling worldview in which politics and religion overlapped. Remarking on the Lusaka consultation, Jim Thompson, a British bishop, noted this convergence of religion and politics in the ANC. Recalling the "profound influence of theism, and especially Christianity" on the movement, Bishop Thompson also observed what he referred to as "the spiritual content of politicians' speeches."[33] Thus the place to look for links between religion, revolution, and armed struggle was not in the relations between the religious community and the ANC. The political discourse and practice of the liberation movement itself was the primary locus in and through which a religious worldview that located violence was worked out.

Like any worldview, the religious worldview of the ANC negotiated a human identity within a symbolic classification of persons. In particular, the armed religion of the ANC was represented as a counterforce that broke the classification of persons imposed by the apartheid regime. One dimension of that counterforce was a spiritual recovery from the depths of dehumanization. In the racist ideology of the state, dehumanization had been supported by religious legitimation. The armed struggle of the ANC required not legitimation but liberation, a rising up that promised to invert the prevailing order in South Africa, turning apartheid dreams into nightmares, and nightmares of oppression into dreams of a restored humanity.

Reflections on superhuman meaning and power in many South African worldviews have exhibited a distinct dualism. Theologian James Cochrane, for example, noted that there were "two Gods in South Africa, both served by people who claim Christ." Dividing these superhuman beings between the forces of popular liberation and the interests of state legitimation, Cochrane specified that "one is visible in the poor man of Galilee who, with his motley crowd, marched upon Jerusalem, the centre of religious, political, and economic power, to give his body that life might be served. The other serves the national security state—an idol who, like all idols, demands blood sacrifice."[34] Although Cochrane sought to emphasize the bloodthirsty, idolatrous, and sacrificial nature of the God of the national security state, it is also clear that both gods were sacrificial gods. In this dualism, both superhuman beings—the God of legitimation, as well as the God of liberation—required offerings. To the extent that sacrifice can be regarded as violent, in both cases, divine power was identified with the power of violent death.

Part of the theological work of the ANC was directed at disempowering the superhuman claims that had legitimated the apartheid system. Cedric Mayson approvingly cited the pamphlet *The Road to Damascus* for its dismissal of the transcendent presumptions of oppressive regimes, like the South African state, whose authorities "are like priests of a pseudo-religion," in which "money and property and, above all, security are sacred," and "Whites become a sacred people." Challenging these religious commitments, Mayson argued that "the liberation of religion is part of our struggle," an important element in liberating human beings "from oppression in an inhuman system." As an argument against the pseudo-religion of the state, Mayson recommended the work of the Catholic theologian Albert Nolan, *God in South Africa,* as "a manual for Christian revolutionaries, a sort of theological [Umkhonto], demolishing the symbols and systems of the oppressor, and revealing the liberating God in the heart of the people's struggle."[35]

In order to reveal the superhuman power in the liberation struggle, Mayson suggested, the religious symbols and systems of the oppressor had to be disempowered. In theological terms, transcendence had to be relocated in the liberation of a human identity. "The idea of an old man in the sky has long ceased to trouble most of us," Mayson observed. In recommending the work of Father Nolan, however, Mayson asserted that God must be seen "in terms of an experience of transcendence at the heart of humanity." For the ANC, that experience of transcendence was located in the struggle for freedom. As Nolan argued, "the practice of the struggle is the practice of faith even when it is not accompanied by an explicit expression of faith in God or Jesus Christ." As a strategy of worldview renegotiation, this relocation of superhuman power at the heart of humanity and its struggle for liberation from a dehumanizing system represented a significant reclassification of persons in South Africa.

Thus the struggle itself generated a power traditionally ascribed in Christian theology to the person of Christ. For theologians like Cedric Mayson and Albert Nolan, the imitation of Christ, and the way of the cross, took on new significance in the South African context. In recalling a Mass in Sebokeng in 1985, Nolan described how the congregants, in ritual procession, presented their bishops with rubber bullets, teargas cannisters, chains, and even rent bills, "the modern crosses," Nolan observed, "the symbols of repression that were being transformed like the cross into sacred symbols of our hope and liberation." Although people in the black townships of South Africa confronted the violence of the cross daily, the spiritual politics of the ANC attributed a special, Christ-like role to the soldiers in the liberation struggle. Mayson, for example, commended revolutionaries who, in taking up arms, were "taking up the cross to follow Jesus, who voluntarily chose the dangerous path of confronting violence himself to open the way for a new society."[36]

In the spiritual politics of the armed struggle, soldiers assumed superhuman significance and power in and through their sacrificial confrontation with violence. As embodiments of the liberating "spirit of revolt," soldiers in Umkhonto we Sizwe combined the roles of heroic warrior and sacrificial martyr. "In the unfolding of our revolution," the National Executive Committee of the ANC noted in 1987, "it became a sacred duty of Umkhonto we Sizwe to revive the spirit of revolt amongst our people." Like heroic African warriors of the past, Umkhonto soldiers were praised for reviving the spiritual politics of armed resistance. Even when they achieved no military victories, the soldiers of Umkhonto we Sizwe kept alive a transcendent spirit. Recalling the generation of Umkhonto soldiers of the 1960s—known as the "torchbearers"—the ANC executives insisted that although they failed in battle, "with superhuman dedication to the cause of our people, they held aloft our dream and lived with only one purpose in mind—to get back into our country and to pursue the revolution."[37]

The superhuman power of the soldier merged into that of the martyr. At the beginning of each annual presidential address, Oliver Tambo paid special tribute to those martyrs who had died in the struggle during the previous year. In 1986, for example, President Tambo saluted those whose deaths represented an entry into revolutionary immortality. "Their example of selfless service to the revolution will live on," Tambo proclaimed, "inspiring us to intensify the struggle until victory."[38] As in any ideology of martyrdom, the role of the martyr represented both a sacred past and a future in the worldview of the ANC. In retrospect, the protomartyr of the armed struggle was Solomon Mahlangu. Arrested in 1977, hanged in 1979, Mahlangu supposedly declared before his death, "My blood will nourish the tree that will bear the fruits of freedom." Looking to the future, the memory and model of Solomon Mahlangu were enshrined in the institution of the ANC school, the Solomon Mahlangu Freedom College (SOMAFCO) in Tanzania. Its mandate for education was described by Oliver Tambo in 1983 explicitly in terms of the spiritual politics of the liberation movement. "SOMAFCO will not be an institution of superhumans," Tambo remarked, setting apart, perhaps, the superhuman martyr for whom the institution was named, "but it will be an institution in which we have developed in our students a profound commitment to our cause." To study there, Tambo concluded, "is to be on a mission." Whether a religious mission or a military mission was intended, the executives of the ANC represented SOMAFCO as a "window on the future" because it kept alive through education the spirit of sacrificial martyrdom for the cause represented by Solomon Mahlangu.[39]

Other martyrs lived on, transcending time through their devotion to the revolution even unto death. Oliver Tambo, in a moving funeral oration in 1986 for Moses Mabhida, secretary-general of the South African Communist Party, member of the National Executive Committee of the ANC, and vice-president of the South African Congress of Trade Unions, indicated that a classification of persons was at stake in the interpretation of Mabhida's life and death. For some, Tambo noted, the enemy appeared as the "brutal armed strength of a superhuman machine," but not for Mabhida, nor, following his example, for the resistance organizations he represented. In this respect, the revolutionary spirit that Mabhida embodied had already succeeded in disempowering any superhuman claims that might be made by the enemy. That freedom of spirit, Tambo suggested, anticipated the ultimate victory over the enemy on "the glorious day of liberation . . . when the voice of the liberation proclaims from the heights of the sign of our land, from the sacred mountains of Ulundi, when it proclaims that the cause for which so many perished has triumphed." On that apocalyptic day of liberation, Tambo promised, the grave of Moses Mbheki Mabhida would be "a place of pilgrimage for lovers of freedom." Like the martyr, the saint, or those historian Peter Brown has called the "special dead," the revolutionary in death joined the company of those who continued to emanate a sacred power that benefited the living and signaled the promise of their redemption. "Moses Mabhida lives," Oliver Tambo concluded. "The struggle continues. Victory is assured."[40]

Not a superhuman machine, the enemy was sometimes characterized as inhuman in the arguments of the ANC. "Let us remind ourselves," the ANC National Executive Committee stated in 1987, "that we face a vicious and inhuman foe."[41] Because the apartheid system of the South African regime failed to recognize the majority of the people as human, upholders of that system had failed in their own humanity. In renegotiating a worldview, the ANC sometimes inverted the classifications of apartheid. Symbolic inversion reassigned the subhuman status to those who had violently dehumanized others. But this strategy was not prominent in the spiritual politics of the ANC. Rather, attention was focused on the system that the enemy had created and reinforced in South Africa. The ANC recognized that any symbolic inversion of the system would perpetuate dehumanization. The systematic subclassification of persons could not be inverted; it had to be completely dismantled.

Founders of the ANC had linked Christianity, democracy, and humanity as standards against which to measure the systematic dehumanization of blacks in South Africa. Exclusion in the religious and political spheres signaled a fundamental denial of humanity. Fifty years later, Albert Luthuli pointed out that, for blacks in South Africa, "strivings after civilized values will not, in the present order, ever earn for them recognition as sane and responsible civilized beings." Exclusion, however, was only one aspect of oppression. A more pervasive dehumanization was found in the perception of black South Africans as objects to be owned, operated, exploited, and manipulated by white interests. In 1910, as Luthuli recalled, the "Act of Union virtually handed the whole of South Africa over to a minority of whites. . . . They had become owners of the new state. The members of other races who found themselves handed over officially, entirely without their consent, were the livestock which went with the estate, objects rather than subjects."[42] As objects rather than human subjects, black South Africans continued to suffer the degradations of the apartheid system.

International law provided the ANC a vocabulary for representing the true nature of apartheid. Ever since South Africa refused to associate itself with the Universal Declaration of Human Rights in 1948, the United Nations had increasingly provided support for a definition of apartheid as a "crime against humanity." Representing apartheid as not merely criminal but, more specifically, as a crime against humanity captured the inherently dehumanizing character of the racist system. As Oliver Tambo observed in his 1988 presidential address, "the apartheid regime is an illegitimate creature of an immoral and criminal system which no decent human being can support or tolerate." By implication, support for this system defined the region of the subhuman in the worldview of the ANC. In defence of humanity, President Tambo exhorted the liberation movement forward to fulfill "the historic mission we have to carry out—the destruction of the apartheid crime against humanity."[43]

In many modern worldviews, the region of the subhuman has been defined by two institutions of exclusion from society through confinement—the prison and the asylum. Most modern metaphors of exclusion have recourse to the figures of criminality and madness to represent those seen as not belonging in human society. In the worldview of the ANC, South Africa appeared as a prison that was being run by the criminals. "This criminal regime has reduced our country to a huge prison," Oliver Tambo remarked in his 1989 presidential address, "its administration, courts and regulations tailored to maintain and intensify White domination by every conceivable means." South Africa could also be seen as an asylum run by madmen. The maniacal dreams of the apartheid ideologues and architects, turned into nightmares by the armed resistance of the liberation movement, nevertheless continued to reproduce an insane reality in South Africa. An editorial in *Sechaba* captured this imagery of madness as a metaphor for the subhuman in South Africa. "Those whom the gods wish to destroy," the editors suggested, "they first make mad." In between the gods and the mad rulers of South Africa destined for destruction, the spiritual politics of the ANC carved out a space for human beings.[44]

Negotiating within the symbolic imagery of subclassification, confinement, and bondage, the spiritual politics of the ANC required action to recover a human identity. If the subhuman was defined by bondage, the human was recovered in the forceful freedom represented by the armed struggle. For a new, free human identity to be created, old patterns of dehumanization had to be destroyed. "Prospects of a bloodbath and the reduction of South Africa to a wasteland will not stop this struggle," Oliver Tambo insisted in 1986. Not destruction for its own sake, however, the armed struggle was a reluctant requirement for liberation from bondage in South Africa. "We would much rather that no blood was lost, that the country was left intact," Tambo observed, "but not at the expense of our continued enslavement." Freeing a human identity from the subhuman condition of slavery entailed a passage through violence, and that violent passage meant more than a willingness to be martyred for the cause of freedom. "We shall not only die for freedom," the editors of *Sechaba* announced in 1986, "we shall kill for freedom."[45]

This ultimate commitment to kill and be killed in order to free a fully human identity was framed in a context of ostensible reforms in the apartheid system during the 1980s. The tricameral parliament that drew Coloureds and Indians into the national government, promising further reforms of the apartheid system, was absolutely rejected by the ANC, as well as by the coalition of resistance organizations that came together in the formation of the United Democratic Front. Government promises of reform appeared as a disingenuous effort to maintain white power and privilege, while meliorating some of the harsher features of apartheid.

Apartheid, however, as the ANC, UDF, and other extra-parliamentary opposition movements argued, could not be reformed; it had to be abolished. This appeal for the total destruction of apartheid was a recurring theme in the international mission of the ANC. In an address to British trade unionists in 1988, for example, the secretary-general of the ANC, Alfred Nzo, argued that reform of the apartheid system in South Africa was unimaginable because it was impossible to "humanize something that is inherently evil, violent and inhuman." Echoing this reading of the South African situation, an African leader such as Julius Nyerere could argue that apartheid could not be humanized because it was absolutely inhuman. "There can be no such thing as 'apartheid with a human face,'" Nyerere observed, "for apartheid is based on the denial of man's common humanity." Therefore, he concluded, apartheid was "totally inhuman and has to be totally abolished." In recovering humanity from a dehumanizing system, reform of that system was not negotiable. That which was inherently inhuman had to be destroyed before a fully human identity could emerge in South Africa.[46]

In a 1986 appeal for international support, Oliver Tambo called upon world governments to "intervene on our side, on the side of humanity." This invocation elevated the ANC's appeal for support above the political, or more accurately, it linked support for the ANC with a moral or spiritual politics of human liberation. Above ordinary political interests, that liberation promised redemption for all human beings. As President Tambo announced in 1988, the ANC was prepared to make "further advances in the new year in the interests of all humanity."[47] In this respect, the spiritual politics of the ANC negotiated a human identity that was specific to the South African situation but, at the same time, invested with more general meaning and power for the entire world. The human was at once a particular and a universal promise of liberation.

This link between the particular and the universal, especially in the South African situation, raised difficult questions about the saliency of race in a definition of the human. If racism was a synonym for a violation of the promise of human liberation, the worldview negotiations conducted by the ANC had to find some way of coming to terms with racial classifications of persons. Certainly, one way of coming to terms with racial classifications was to abolish them as fundamentally invalid, artificial constructs. In its consistent vision of a nonracial, unified, and democratic South Africa, the ANC seemed to anticipate an elimination of race as a significant feature of human identity. Nevertheless, some ambiguity on this point was evident. When the Freedom Charter, for example, announced that South Africa belonged to all who lived in it, black or white, race lingered as a residual feature of human identity. In the spiritual politics of the ANC, a fully human being demonstrated a love of all humanity, regardless of race. In a 1986 tribute to the "outstanding humanists" in the liberation struggle, for example, Oliver Tambo praised those "who hate racism and love all humanity enough to be prepared to die in the defence of liberty of all persons, regardless of their colour or race."[48] Did this disregard for race, however, subtly retain the concept of race as a constituent trait of humanity?

During the 1970s, the ANC came under renewed criticism on this point from the black consciousness movement. Arguing that the ANC's position on race should be more accurately described as multiracial than nonracial, representatives of the black consciousness movement conducted a more radical deconstruction of racial classifications. As defined by Steve Biko, black consciousness required a rejection of imposed racial classifications in South Africa in the liberation of a "true humanity." As the movement developed, oppression came increasingly to be identified as an issue of socioeconomic class rather than race, a class oppression that had been colored by the contingent, historical formations of racial capitalism in South Africa. In this regard, black was a designation for the oppressed, not a racial classification. As religious reflection on that condition of oppression, black theology emerged, in the words of Basil Moore, as "a theology by which to affirm black humanity," not in racial terms, but as "a theology of the oppressed, by the oppressed, for the liberation of the oppressed." In the 1980s, black consciousness organizations, particularly the Azanian Peoples Organization, continued to provide a vital alternative to the ANC's renegotiation of a humanity for the oppressed in South Africa.[49]

Initially, the ANC resisted the emergence of the black consciousness movement and its redefinition of a black human identity. In 1973, for example, the ANC argued that the formation of a new psychological identity for the oppressed should not be regarded as an end in itself. Psychological emancipation had to be linked to the practice of armed struggle against the apartheid regime. "To be effective," the ANC argued, "a break with the cultural and spiritual mode that the enemy has imposed on us cannot but be sharp and violent."[50] In this claim, it might be argued, the ANC exercised its armed propaganda against the alternative definition of black humanity represented by the black consciousness movement, insisting that without the armed struggle it was, in effect, a psychological discourse without force.

After 1976, however, the ANC increasingly appropriated and adapted elements of black consciousness and black theology in its spiritual politics. By 1977, Oliver Tambo explained black consciousness in such a way that it was subsumed within what he regarded as the larger scope for humanity represented by the ANC. Arguing that the ANC started from a position of black consciousness, Tambo insisted that the liberation movement had moved on "to the position where we expect all the people in South Africa to form part of the movement for the transformation of the social, political and economic situation. Black consciousness, looked at from this point of view, is thus a phase in the struggle. It is not outside the struggle for human rights—on the contrary—it grows into the mainstream which has been set by the African National Congress."[51] In this formulation, the unique contribution of the black consciousness movement—its deconstruction of racial classifications and reconstruction of a black humanity in liberation from class oppression—was absorbed into what its proponents regarded as a universal, multiracial definition of humanity that failed to address the particular historical situation of oppression under racial capitalism in South Africa.

In its spiritual politics, therefore, the ANC sought to speak for the populist interests of a humanity drawn from all sections of South African life. Consistently, the ANC invoked "the people" as its mandate for resistance to the South African regime. In one catalog drawn up in 1987, the National Executive Committee of the ANC specified the people as workers, women, youth, students, township residents, rural people, teachers and other professionals, progressive whites, and religious congregations and leaders. In placing workers at the top of this list, the ANC executive reflected the increasing importance of union organization and resistance in the liberation movement. "We say to these gallant sons of Africa," the national executive declared a few months later, "Stay united and you will never be defeated!" Invoking the union slogan—"An injury to one is an injury to all"—the ANC suggested something important about what it meant to be a human being within the liberation movement. To be human was to be at the nexus of reciprocal relations between part and whole. Each part existed to serve the whole; the whole existed to serve each part. In that integration, the liberation movement claimed its populist mandate to represent the people. Ultimately, the ANC represented the armed struggle as a "People's War," a war in which the "liberation army becomes rooted amongst the people, who progressively participate actively in the armed struggle both politically and militarily, including the possibility of engaging in partial or general insurrection." A "People's War" was a war of the people, by the people, for the liberation of the people, a war in which Umkhonto we Sizwe was the vanguard.[52]

In attacks carried out by the vanguard of the populist war of resistance against the state, people were sometimes killed. However, the National Executive Committee of the ANC consistently maintained that it was committed to the conduct of humane warfare. In a public statement in 1988, the NEC insisted that "it is contrary to our policy to select targets whose sole objective is to strike at civilians. Our morality as revolutionaries dictates that we respect the values underpinning the humane conduct of war." Nevertheless, as Oliver Tambo pointed out in reaction to the bombing of a supermarket in 1986, although "there is nothing in the ANC policy or strategy which calls for attacks on civilians," people had to realize that "the South African situation is one of violence. There is a war going on there."[53] The war of resistance was not only targeted at forcibly liberating a revolutionary humanity; it was also conducted in and through the tangible, material, and profoundly symbolic coordinates of space and time in South Africa.

Place

The dystopian design of apartheid had quite literally left the ANC no place in South Africa. From exile, its leadership sought to recover a place through violent and nonviolent negotiations that recast the world of South Africa as one in which both space and time belonged to the liberation movement. The leadership of the ANC might have found itself outside of South Africa, in exile in foreign lands. But through the armed struggle, it could claim in a more profound sense to be truly inside—underground, central, and even, in a recurring assertion, everywhere—because it was alive in the hearts of the people. Not land masses, but popular masses formed the foundation for a spatial reorientation in the worldview represented by the ANC. Mass action, combined with armed attacks, defined a space in which the pressure of the liberation movement promised to crush the forces of oppression inside South Africa. As a result, a new order would be created, a new orientation in which the enemy would have no place.

That new order, however, was a matter of time. South Africa was in a time of crisis, a revolutionary situation unprecedented in history. The ANC positioned itself to seize the moment of victory. Negotiating with time itself, the ANC designated the 1980s as the "Decade of Liberation." Although unprecedented, the revolutionary situation was felt to have had historical antecedents in the resistance of heroic warriors against colonial forces. In an important sense, seizing the future involved recovering a past that had been stolen by the European conquerors, aided by administrators, missionaries, and educators, who continued to erase the heroic past of African military resistance to conquest. In 1979, for example, the ANC began its practice of marking each year by a theme. Nineteen seventy-nine marked the centenary of the Zulu victory over British troops at Isandhlwana, hence its designation as the "Year of the Spear." Symbolically, the ANC thus claimed to be the heirs of that Zulu victory, celebrating Umkhonto we Sizwe as the modern incarnation of the African spirit of resistance. That spirit of resistance, however, was clearly embodied in a new orientation in time and space.

In an important discussion of spatial orientation, historian of religion Jonathan Z. Smith has argued that the attempts of alternative religious movements to create a utopian space have often appeared subversive from the vantage point of those who maintain and control order in public, civil space.[54] These three types of space—civil, subversive, and utopian—were oddly transposed in the South African public order. As we have seen, the apartheid order had been intentionally created as utopian space, a public order in which the majority of the population had been excluded from the civil right of full participation. As an alternative movement in this imposed "utopia," the ANC imagined a civil space of nonracial, unified, and democratic public order. In this peculiar historical situation, the aspiration toward a civil space registered as subversive from the vantage point of those who upheld the apartheid utopian order in South Africa.

In a 1987 statement, the ANC National Executive Committee outlined the four pillars of the liberation movement's program of action. The ANC was engaged in concerted efforts to build an underground network, to mobilize mass action, to expand military operations inside South Africa, and to gain the support of the international community in isolating the South African regime. Each of these pillars represented a fundamental spatial reorientation of the world of South Africa. Their cumulative effect promised the destruction of the old order. As one ANC theorist observed, "In the new order, and in the efforts to construct it, the enemy has no role." In the meantime, however, the ANC sought to negotiate an alternative orientation to the order that dominated South Africa.[55]

That alternative orientation began underground. As a symbol of subversion, the underground represented resources that had the potential to undermine the order, the space, of domination. The underground took on a mythic quality in the worldview of the ANC, recalling the original emergence of human beings from beneath the earth in traditional African creation myths. As Ronnie Kasrils noted, the underground was the original source of Umkhonto we Sizwe. "After all," Kasrils recalled, "it was the underground that created Umkhonto we Sizwe in the first place!" Nevertheless, the potential of the underground within South Africa remained unfulfilled. In 1988,

Kasrils pointed to the "lack of such an underground at home." As a high priority, therefore, the ANC was committed to awakening subversive forces beneath the dominant order of South Africa. "A strong underground presence at home would help solve all the problems we face," Kasrils concluded, envisioning an underground that "can bring the masses into action, that can work for a nation-wide general strike, that can help build and lead the revolutionary armed forces."[56]

The underground would have a significant role in the second pillar of the ANC's program of action, the mobilization of the masses to exert pressure on the government. In a recurring image, South African space was symbolized as a region squeezed between mass resistance and armed struggle. In a message from Robben Island, for example, Nelson Mandela announced that "between the anvil of united mass action and the hammer of armed struggle we shall crush apartheid racist rule." Since South Africa was experienced as oppressive space, resistance required the counterpressure of mass action. With its hammer and anvil, the ANC would forge a place in which the oppressed would exert the pressure and the popular masses would destroy the apartheid laager: "We, and we alone, the democratic forces, are the only force which can smash the White laager of apartheid. It is our own armed struggle, mass mobilization and resistance that will bring down apartheid and bring fundamental change in South Africa."[57]

As the third pillar of the ANC program of action, the armed struggle was conducted by revolutionary forces in exile. The armed struggle thus seemed to be initiated and pursued from outside the geographical boundaries of South Africa. This was certainly the position that the South African Defence Force took against the ANC in defending and crossing borders in pursuit of its war against what official rhetoric portrayed as an external enemy. From the perspective of the ANC, however, the revolution was not outside; it was omnipresent. "Wherever we are," Oliver Tambo insisted in 1985, "we must transform our locality into a mass revolutionary base." Transcending the limitations imposed by exile, ANC leadership announced that "the ANC is everywhere." By 1990, one ANC theorist observed that attacks in different locations in South Africa confirmed "the fact that armed struggle waged by Umkhonto we Sizwe takes place throughout the country." Therefore, he could conclude, Umkhonto "is everywhere." As a strategic renegotiation of spatial symbolism, the ANC positioned itself not in exile, not outside, not even underground, but everywhere, evoking a spiritual, revolutionary transcendence of ordinary spatial limits.[58]

Finally, the fourth pillar of the program of action recognized the importance of the international arena for the struggle conducted by the liberation movement. In its appeals for international support, the ANC attempted to negotiate a particular spatial orientation that would isolate the South African government from the rest of the world. In this respect, the ANC's call to "impose comprehensive and mandatory sanctions against apartheid South Africa" was profoundly symbolic. This is not to say that sanctions were "merely symbolic," as economist Merle Lipton suggested in a 1988 report for the London-based Economic Intelligence Unit. Nor is this to say that the ANC proposed sanctions as a nonviolent alternative to the armed struggle, as advocated by Archbishop Desmond Tutu or the Commonwealth report on South Africa. Sanctions were represented by the ANC as a military weapon in the struggle, a supplement to the armed campaign to weaken the enemy and quicken the pace of victory. As Oliver Tambo insisted in 1988, sanctions were "an important weapon in the struggle to end the apartheid system and therefore eliminate the source of violence, war and instability in Southern Africa."[59]

Nevertheless, that weapon did have far-reaching implications for the symbolic position of the apartheid government. Beyond the economic, military, and cultural isolation of South Africa, the international sanctions campaign attempted to enforce a symbolic isolation that would remove the country from the moral community of nations. If that total, multivalent isolation of the South African government were to be completely enforced, some ANC leaders anticipated that a transfer of power would quickly follow. In March 1987, for example, Joe Slovo suggested that sanctions could have a dramatic effect upon the political transition in South Africa. "In fact," Slovo said, "I venture to guess that in six months of mandatory international sanctions being introduced, Botha or his successor will be sitting round the table."[60] Whether achieved through a violent seizure or a peaceful transfer of power, ANC leaders were convinced that a fundamental spatial reorientation in South Africa was only a matter of time.

In the mid 1980s, South Africa was obviously in a time of crisis. The government certified this perception of crisis by declaring and renewing a state of emergency. As Frank Kermode once observed, "Crisis, however facile the conception, is inescapably a central element in our endeavors toward making sense of the world." In the worldviews of many South Africans, the country had reached a turning point. From the government's perspective, the crisis had to be managed, contained, or repressed. For resistance movements, however, this time of crisis was a situation of unique opportunity. Crisis was given a distinctly spiritual content by the kairos theologians when they observed that "this is the KAIROS, the moment of grace and opportunity, the favorable time in which God issues a challenge to decisive action." The ANC had its own ways of making sense out of a world in crisis. Nevertheless, like the kairos theologians, the ANC saw the South African crisis as sacred time, a time outside of ordinary time, in which the crucial moment had arrived.[61]

The spiritual politics of the ANC made sense of the world by identifying the crisis as a unique revolutionary situation. In 1986, for example, Oliver Tambo announced that the South African government was "in a crisis moment which is without precedent in the history of southern Africa." Reading that crisis as the promise of revolutionary redemption, President Tambo declared "that death is for us but a renewal of life, that death is for us a defeat in battle, a rehearsal for a victorious war." During the following year, Tambo reinforced his interpretation of the spiritual dimensions of the South African crisis, observing that "a new spirit is abroad. Something outside of our experience is approaching." Both oppressor and oppressed, Tambo concluded, were "very close to the moment of decision."[62]

This sacred, decisive, critical time promised to activate the potential of the people, who, as one ANC theorist noted, "in times of revolution are capable of mind-defying miracles." This was a time in which the cultivation of "revolutionary impatience" among the people was regarded as a virtue. It was a moment that had to be grasped because, as Ronnie Kasrils observed, "history does not often present revolutionary situations." In short, the South African crisis represented the sacred time in the spiritual politics of the ANC within which the liberation movement would realize its historical destiny.[63]

This theme of historical destiny, linking the past with the creation of a future, was a recurring motif in the political speeches of Oliver Tambo. In his president's message in 1985, for example, Tambo claimed that "history has entrusted us with the destiny of our country." In the Decade of Liberation, the task of the ANC was "to carve out the path to our historically determined destination." The fulfillment of that historical destiny depended upon the armed struggle of resistance waged by Umkhonto we Sizwe. As one ANC theorist declared, "Umkhonto has the advantage of being an army fighting to bring an order decreed by the objective march of history. Its victory is assured." Although often represented as "a struggle for a future," the armed resistance conducted by the military wing of the ANC also had an important relation to the past. In the spiritual politics negotiated by the ANC, the historical destiny not only promised to create a future but also to recover the heroic past of African military resistance. Coming full circle, it was that past that was felt to hold the key to the future because, as the ANC National Executive Committee reflected in 1987, "through centuries of White domination our people have learnt how to die for a future."[64]

As an editorial in *Sechaba* recalled in 1987, the first recorded armed resistance to white encroachment in South Africa was conducted by the Khoisan in the Cape in May 1659. Khoisan resistance began what the ANC regarded as 250 years of armed struggle throughout South Africa, "fought by our people," culminating in the Bambatha rebellion in the region of Natal in 1906. The military wing of the ANC, the editors concluded, "continued the struggle waged by our forefathers," keeping alive the spirit of resistance represented by those armed African ancestors. Ancestral heroes of armed resistance were celebrated: The Xhosa chief Hintsa, who was "martyred under nefarious circumstances in a war of resistance against foreign marauders"; the Sotho chief Moshoeshoe, who "waged a principled struggle on the diplomatic and military levels to defend our independence"; and the Zulu chief Shaka, who was a "military genius," even though he was "born of a small tribe, the Zulus." In each case, armed resistance represented "an immediate link between the fighters of modern times and their forefathers who fought the colonialists.[65]

That historical linkage between ancestral warriors and modern freedom fighters had to be carefully negotiated in the worldview represented by the ANC. Underscoring what they regarded as the primary lesson to be drawn from the history of African resistance, ANC theorists argued that armed struggle had failed for lack of unity.

History was therefore claimed by the ANC in such a way that it could not be claimed in the interests of parochial, "tribal" politics that threatened to divide unity. For example, one theorist declared that the ANC's armed struggle signified that a "new generation of Black South Africans had now taken the torch, as heirs of that great tradition of resistance." Although this ANC historian declared that Makhanda, a nineteenth-century Xhosa prophet and rebel, had passed his torch to (Xhosa) Oliver Tambo, he carefully crossed, and symbolically erased, tribal lines by suggesting that (Sotho) Moshoeshoe had passed his torch to (Zulu) Luthuli, while the Zulu King Cetshwayo had passed his torch on to (Xhosa) Nelson Mandela.[66] Ultimately, this sacred history of the ANC suggested that "tribal" designations—Xhosa, Zulu, Sotho, which were arguably arbitrary constructs of apartheid design—were irrelevant in the unified armed struggle led by modern warriors for South Africa's future.

More specifically, the sacred history of the ANC symbolically undermined the claims to tribal or ethnic particularism that had been advanced by Chief Mangosuthu Gatsha Buthelezi and his Inkatha movement. Not only was the spiritual mantle of Zulu royalty attributed to the populist leader Nelson Mandela, but the heroic Zulu past that formed such an important part of Inkatha ideology was also renegotiated in the sacred history of the ANC. Thus the ANC claimed to have inherited the spirit of resistance demonstrated by Zulu regiments at Isandhlwana. "Not since the battle of Isandhlwana in 1879," the ANC National Executive Committee declared, "had our rulers been so shaken by our fighting formations." Similarly, the ANC claimed the legacy of the Zulu rebellion associated with Bambatha, which in ANC ideology represented the climax of two and a half centuries of armed resistance. Arguing that Bambatha had failed to elicit Zulu royal support for the rebellion and had gone instead "to the people themselves," the ANC historian underscored the organization's own appeal to a populist, rather than a "tribal," mandate. The ANC was formed only six years after the Bambatha rebellion. As heir to "this glorious tradition," Umkhonto we Sizwe revived its populist spirit in armed resistance. "For the first time since 1906, the time of Bambatha in Natal," another ANC historian observed, "the colonial forces of South Africa were met with fire-power from the oppressed community." In such strategic renegotiations of history, the worldview of the ANC appropriated historical models from the African past for a united, nationwide resistance against the apartheid state.[67]

The temporal orientation of the ANC also required the renegotiation of a sacred calendar for South Africa. In the 1980s, the decade, the years, and even the days of the months assumed a definite spiritual significance. As Oliver Tambo pointed out in January 1989, the liberation movement was "entering the last 12 months of the Decade of Liberation." During that decade, each year had been designated by a theme. For many, this practice of marking the years had become habit, whereas, according to ANC theorist Cassius Mandla, "the purpose is to galvanize the entire liberation movement and the masses into action and thought that will demonstrate anew that we are meritorious custodians and continuers of the unflagging courage and determination of our forefathers." In this respect, marking the years became a sacred revitalization of time, a renewal of the spirit of resistance represented by the ancestors. Recommending seminars, public meetings, celebrations, and the critical examination of attitudes and contributions during the course of each year, Mandla advised that it "is only in this way that the intended renewal of our spirits and escalation of the struggle can be achieved."[68]

As in many religious and national traditions, the ANC marked the annual renewal of time by means of a calendar that commemorated crucial events of a sacred past. In the ANC's sacred calendar, the course of each year was punctuated by holy days: 8 January, the founding of the ANC; 21 March, Sharpeville Day; 1 May, Workers' Day; 16 June, Soweto Day; 26 June, South African Freedom Day, recalling the adoption of the Freedom Charter; 9 August, International Solidarity Day, paying particular attention to the role of women in the struggle; 11 October, Political Prisoners' Day; and 16 December, one of the more highly charged holy days in South Africa, celebrating Heroes' Day on the anniversary of the founding of Umkhonto we Sizwe in 1961.

As a calendar for an emergent religious nationalism, this cycle of holy days emphasized what might be called a patriotism of pain. In particular, 21 March and 16 June commemorated the profound losses of the 1960s and 1970s. By contrast, the sacred calendar of Afrikaner nationalism celebrated what could be called a patriotism of power, especially the power of conquest over African resistance symbolized by the Battle of Blood River, 16 December 1838, the holiest of the Afrikaner holy days. It was "not by accident," as the ANC National Executive Committee noted in 1987, that the liberation movement had chosen that day on which to launch Umkhonto we Sizwe: "White South Africa observes that day as the triumph of its military might over our people. The violence that they celebrate is the violence of a minority aimed at subjugating the majority of the people of our country. It is a celebration of injustice and the inhumanity of man against man." On the battlefield of symbols, therefore, the ANC condemned the holiest day of the Afrikaner nationalist calendar as a celebration of violent inhumanity. Taking that day as their own, the ANC executive argued, "We chose that day to show how different we were. We celebrate December 16, our Heroes' Day, to underline our commitment that we are waging a just war in pursuit of freedom, democracy and peace."[69] In renegotiating the significance of that holy day, the ANC symbolically transformed its pain into the spiritual power represented by a heroic, liberated humanity.

During the Afrikaner nationalist celebrations of 1988, this contest over sacred symbols continued to be negotiated by political leaders of the ANC. In his presidential address in January 1988, for example, Oliver Tambo noted that the government and Afrikaner cultural organizations were preparing to celebrate their sacred anniversaries. "In their celebrations," Tambo maintained, "the racists will seek once more to assert the permanence and legitimacy of White minority domination." Tambo exhorted the ANC to continue its "own implacable opposition to the colonial, racist and fascist legacy which all these anniversaries represent." The previous month, Thabo Mbeki, at the time ANC director of information and publicity, had dramatically announced his opposition to what he referred to as the "obscene anniversaries" the regime planned to celebrate in 1988. At a cultural conference in Amsterdam, Mbeki exhorted his audience to remember what King Dingane had said when he faced the enemy: "*Bulala abathakathi!*—Kill the sorcerers!" By implication, the leaders of the South African government were identified as witches and sorcerers, as evil persons manipulating supernatural instruments of power to perform violent harm. In their "obscene anniversaries," Mbeki suggested through the metaphor of sorcery, the government and Afrikaner cultural organizations were manipulating symbolic resources to perpetuate their violent, illegitimate domination of South Africa. Also by implication, the only legitimate response to those celebrations of sacralized violence was forceful resistance.[70]

As we have noted, the battlefield of symbols associated with the commemoration of 16 December 1988 was also contested among different factions of Afrikaner nationalism. Divisions in Afrikanerdom did not go unnoticed by the ANC. As the January 1989 editorial of *Sechaba* observed, "Even the December 16th celebrations—a perverted historical memory—were characterised by divisions, fear and uncertainty about the future." To the ANC, the apparent conflicts over the celebration of the most sacred time of the year for Afrikaner nationalists meant one thing: "Surely the future does not belong to them."[71] In the process of stealing sacred symbols back and forth, the ANC had appropriated 16 December as its own celebration of the armed struggle of resistance. In this symbolic negotiation of sacred time, the ANC asserted that not only the holy day, but the entire future of South Africa belonged to the liberation movement.

CHAPTER 7

Violent Negotiations

•

THE CLAIM that the future belonged to the liberation movement led by the African National Congress was contested on a number of different fronts. Obviously, the ANC pursued this contest along a military front against the government. In addition, however, the ANC asserted its claims on the future against other black political movements. In the spiritual politics of South Africa, the ANC might have represented, as journalist Joseph Lelyveld noted, "the broad, true church of black politics," but other movements mobilized spiritual and material support.[1] The discourse of the ANC in the 1980s revealed little concern with any competition from the Pan Africanist Congress or black consciousness organizations, even though these movements challenged any exclusive, privileged claims on a black future made by the ANC. Rather, ANC polemic against alternative black political alignments in the 1980s was addressed almost exclusively at undermining the position of homeland leader Mangosuthu Gatsha Buthelezi.

As noted in chapter 1, the chief minister of KwaZulu led a cultural and political organization that claimed to represent six million Zulus, not only determining their present position in the grand apartheid system of South Africa, but also trying to control any claims on their past or future. As a homeland leader, Buthelezi attempted to consolidate his power through the creation and promotion of a particularist Zulu ethnic identity, culture, and worldview. Along with other grievances, the ANC and affiliated organizations such as the United Democratic Front and the Congress of South African Trade Unions came into conflict with Buthelezi's Inkatha organization at the symbolic level of worldview formation. These symbolic negotiations by 1990 were reflected in the endemic violence of the region of Natal.

Strained Relations

Operating within the particularist cultural idiom of Zulu ethnic identity, Buthelezi succeeded in restructuring the symbolism of a Zulu nation within the framework of apartheid homeland politics. From its inception in 1975, Inkatha was tied to the ethnic politics of the KwaZulu homeland. Although maintaining an ambiguous posture of resistance—working within the apartheid system, yet refusing to accept full independence for KwaZulu—Buthelezi often claimed to have the support of the ANC. However, his opposition to ANC policy and affiliated organizations, evident in his condemnation of the armed struggle, his campaigns against economic sanctions, his creation of a rival trade union in competition with the Congress of South African Trade Unions, and his engagement in conflict with supporters of the United Democratic Front, suggested to many in the ANC that Chief Buthelezi was a collaborator with the government in the apartheid system.[2]

A letter to the editors of *Sechaba* observed that "every revolution produces its heroes, leaders, martyrs" but also exposes "opportunists and 'committed' servants of the enemy (the racist regime)." The correspondent's case in point was Buthelezi and his Inkatha organization, whose tribal vigilantes were perceived to be oppressing the people of KwaZulu and Natal as "an extension of the regime's army and police." This impression was consistent with ANC discourse about Buthelezi and Inkatha throughout the second half of the "Decade of Liberation." While the ANC struggled to mobilize a revolution, government, media, and business, according to ANC theorist Mzala, had marshaled a "huge political marketing operation advertising Chief Buthelezi's virtues as the prophylactic against violent revolution in South Africa."[3] Provided with remarkable access to domestic and foreign media, Chief Buthelezi frequently spoke out against violence. However, militant Inkatha followers, allegedly with the support of the South African police and military, were said to enforce Buthelezi's ethnic politics in KwaZulu and the region of Natal.

The rise of armed vigilantes in different regions of the country became a prominent feature of violence in South Africa after 1986. Appearing in the media under the racist designation "black on black violence," the action of vigilante groups—in the Transvaal, the Cape, and Natal—served the interests and apparently received the support of the government. In the squatter community of Crossroads near Cape Town, for example, during three weeks in May and June 1986, hundreds of armed vigilantes, known as *witdoeke* ("white headbands"), with apparent police support, destroyed four squatter camps, causing over 100 deaths and the removal of over 70,000 people. In can therefore be said that vigilante action achieved the aims of government policy in suppressing resistance and relocating residents of Crossroads.[4]

In its front against Buthelezi, the ANC maintained that Inkatha's vigilantes, known as *amabutho,* were also doing the work of the government. Arguing that the *amabutho* were the surrogates of apartheid, the ANC pointed to "the atrocities committed on a vast scale by Gatsha Buthelezi's Inkatha vigilantes." In 1988, ANC Secretary-General Alfred Nzo told a meeting of British trade unionists that in the region of Natal "more than 1,000 people have been killed by vigilante groups with the connivance of the state." Two years later, the body count in that conflict was over 3,000, as the region was engulfed in a devastating, apparently interminable, state of war between Inkatha forces and supporters of the UDF, COSATU, and the ANC. A United States diplomat called the region the "most violent place on earth."[5] While that conflict brought death and destruction to the townships and throughout the countryside of the region, the battle was also fought on the level of symbols, particularly in and through symbols of authenticity in the spiritual politics of the two rival political movements.

Claiming a common purpose with the ANC, Chief Buthelezi had consistently called for the release of Nelson Mandela. However, a 1988 editorial in *Sechaba* asked, "Can he genuinely be for Mandela's release when his thugs are killing Mandela's followers, when the UDF members are being harassed?" Denying Inkatha's claim to be an authentic liberation movement, the editorial argued that "Gatsha has nothing in common with Nelson Mandela." Insisting that Inkatha employed ethnicity as a substitute for politics, the editors maintained that Chief Buthelezi was working to reinforce the apartheid system in South Africa. "Gatsha's vigilantes are not engaged in armed struggle," the editorial concluded, "but in doing Botha's job."[6]

Employing the cultural symbolism of Zulu royalty and religious nationalism, Buthelezi had carved a space for himself within the apartheid system. An ANC critic condemned Buthelezi's "pretentious claims to Zulu royalty." But the point was not merely Buthelezi's authority, but his deployment of that authority to appropriate the sacred history of African resistance. "While actually engaged in acts of collaboration with the fascists of South Africa, and with capitalism in general, in the suppression of the African people," his ANC critics noted, "Gatsha Buthelezi drapes himself in the finery of the glorious traditions of resistance which were the hallmark of the great patriots of the past, whose attributes, victories and titles he appropriates by a process of usurpation, and for a different cause." In a polemical study of Buthelezi, Mzala sought to disempower the symbolic claims represented by the symbols, myths, and rituals of Zulu royalty that had been adopted by Inkatha. According to Mzala, "The true link between the wars of resistance of earlier times and modern endeavours to grapple with the enemy is symbolised, not by the leopard-skin regalia often worn by those whom the apartheid regime allows to address meetings, even during a state of emergency, but by continued loyalty to the ideals of the total and genuine liberation of South Africa and all the sacrifices that such a stand entails." Reclaiming those sacred symbols of African integrity, ANC critics of Buthelezi argued that the past was alive in the sacrifices made by the soldiers in the liberation movement. Following in the footsteps of their ancestors, Umkhonto soldiers were "engaged in a real struggle, not a phony one, not a bogus, dumb charade."[7]

Authenticity was thus negotiated in terms of the spiritual politics of a sacred history. But it was also contested through the violent negotiations of killing and being killed in the intense conflicts that swept through the region of Natal. As the violence intensified in 1990, symbolic negotiations in the idiom of spiritual politics continued to be pursued. After the unbanning of the ANC in February 1990, Inkatha changed the colors of its flag. To the traditional ANC colors—

green, yellow, and black—that Inkatha had taken in 1975 for its own flag were added white (representing peace) and red (representing the blood of those killed in the struggle for liberation). As blood continued to flow in the conflict, a meeting between Buthelezi and an ANC delegation for the purpose of working out a peaceful resolution was proposed. Buthelezi insisted that the meeting take place at Ulundi, the capital of KwaZulu. When the ANC suggested an alternative site, however, Buthelezi canceled the meeting on the grounds that the ANC had "insulted" the Zulu monarch, King Goodwill Zwelithini, by refusing to meet in Ulundi. In his 1986 funeral oration for Moses Mabhida, Oliver Tambo had declared that the day of victory would be announced "when the voice of liberation proclaims from the heights of the sign of our land, from the sacred mountains of Ulundi, when it proclaims that the cause for which so many perished has triumphed." In 1990, however, Ulundi was not a symbolic site of victory, but the center of a rival political organization that sought legitimation through the authority of a religious, royal, ethnic nationalism. After a subsequent meeting was canceled because Buthelezi insisted that it be held in another Inkatha stronghold, Mandela and Buthelezi toured the war zone. Mandela visited the devastated townships, while Buthelezi flew over the area in a helicopter with the South African minister of police. Both leaders insisted that the violence had to stop; yet the violence continued.[8]

Journalists covering the conflict struggled to explain its causes. Like the racist dismissal "black on black violence," an ethnic description, explaining the conflict as the result of tribal feuds that had been going on in the region for generations, obscured the specific historical, social, economic, and political conditions that had generated violence. In this light, emphasis on the extreme poverty of the region at least recognized that the violence emerged within a specific context of severe economic and social deprivation. But as a functionalist theory of violence, deprivation—or relative deprivation—has had limited explanatory power, if for no other reason than the fact that not all people who experience deprivation resort to violence. Furthermore, the socioeconomic explanation of the violence in KwaZulu and Natal also masked the political interests at stake. For this reason, Inkatha and its supporters pointed to the poverty of the region as the sole explanation for the violence, thus deflecting attention from their attempt to establish a coercive hegemony in the region as an important political factor in the conflict.

Yet when we turn to political analysis, most explanations seem to be reduced to the casting and recasting of blame. The government blamed the ANC, particularly pointing to its continued commitment to the armed struggle as having created conditions of violent revolt against authority. Government policy in the 1980s itself could be faulted, particularly for its practice of arresting and detaining the leadership of opposition organizations, so that disciplined, nonviolent resistance degenerated into a chaotic, "culture of revolt." Inkatha and the ANC, of course, blamed each other. In most academic analyses, however, at least in those not directly sponsored by Inkatha, the primary cause of the violence was located in the cycle of Inkatha coercion, popular resistance, and Inkatha reactionary repression that perpetuated the spiral of violent conflict in the region.[9]

In all these explanations, the implication of religious symbols, myths, and rituals in violent conflict was completely ignored. Inkatha had proclaimed its leader as "the chief of the Buthelezi tribe, prime minister of the Zulu nation, member of the royal family, and, of late, the leader with prophetic powers." Fusing royal and religious symbols, Buthelezi claimed to speak in a prophetic voice on behalf of six million Zulus. The emergence of the UDF thus threatened not only Buthelezi's political authority, but also his religious power as that authentic prophetic voice. With the force of his voice contested, force itself became a type of discourse that was evident, for example, in the alleged Inkatha massacre of students at Ngoye in 1983 in defense of Buthelezi's name and authority. "Inkatha youth will demonstrate their strength and prowess," Buthelezi declared immediately after that incident. Indicating that Inkatha force should be interpreted as a warning to all South Africa, Buthelezi concluded, "The abuse of me must now cease. Continuing to label me a sell-out is going to have ugly repercussions."[10] In addition to controlling the political, social, and economic life of the region, therefore, Inkatha forced itself into the sphere of worldview negotiations by asserting its domination over all symbolic and ideological discourse within the region.

As royal chief, minister, and prophet, Buthelezi continued to deploy mythic and ritual instruments of symbolic power in reinforcing his political movement. Not as a "prophet," but as a "servant of the people," Nelson Mandela was also engaged in nonviolent and violent symbolic negotiations over a worldview and a world. At a mass rally in Natal, shortly after his release from prison, Mandela called for an end to the violence in the region, exhorting all combatants to throw their weapons into the sea so they could work together for a new, just, and peaceful South Africa. His appeal was ignored. Some commentators saw this rebuff as a measure of Mandela's loss of political authority. At least one journalist saw it as a measure of his loss of symbolic power, noting that the sacred aura surrounding the world's most famous political prisoner had "swiftly fallen away to reveal just another African politician. We are now seeing Mandela the man, not the myth."[11] As the myth of sudden, miraculous redemption disappeared, Mandela was revealed as a mere mortal who was unable to bring an end to the violence of political conflict in South Africa.

It could be argued, on the contrary, that Nelson Mandela retained considerable mythic authority, witnessed not only by the tremendous crowds he continued to draw at ANC rallies throughout the country, but also by the government's attempt to appropriate him as a symbol of peaceful resolution for South Africa in its own symbolic negotiations with domestic and international constituencies. What the continuing conflict in the Natal region revealed, however, was the tendency of myth to assume a life of its own, or, more accurately, to be taken over and mobilized in the lives of people in ways that might not be easily predicted or controlled. While both Mandela and Buthelezi called for an end to the violence, combatants in the conflict on the ground called upon ritual resources—sacred medicines, war-doctoring, powerful chants, martial dancing, and the frenzy of fighting itself—as symbolic instruments of power in the struggle to make myths real.[12] As the ritual practices of the ANC, Inkatha, and the government had already demonstrated, the reality of myths depended upon the strategic, violent negotiation of a real world.

In August and September 1990, the epicenter of violence shifted from Natal to Johannesburg. During a six-week period, over 700 people were killed. Once again, Inkatha was at the center of the violence, continuing to proclaim the armed religion of ethnic nationalism. While media persisted in advancing racist and ethnic stereotypes, real human issues remained obscured. At the very least, the orgy of killing revealed that in the birth pains of a "New South Africa," meaning and power would continue to be violently negotiated in the three basic ways we have considered in this book—ritual killing, dehumanization, and the spiritual politics of armed religion.

Seasons of Violence

As we have seen, ritual killing has been a significant type of violent negotiation in religious worldviews. In October 1990, a sudden, unexpected outburst of violence on the Durban beachfront recalled the ritual killing performed by Afrikaner nationalist Barend Hendrik Strydom two years earlier in Pretoria. On the evening of 8 October, Jeqe Ngcobo gathered a following of about twenty young men for an all-night prayer vigil on the beach. Ngcobo preached a specific religious message. He said that God was black and that God's real name was "Holy John Africa." Ngcobo claimed to be the son of "Holy John Africa," that is, the son of God. The next morning, he led a group of youths on a violent rampage, stabbing white people at random, leaving eight people injured. One of the youths apparently shouted, "We have come to take over this place." Once again, therefore, the symbolic relations of person and place in South Africa were being renegotiated through violent acts.

No act of ritual killing, however, can close those negotiations over sacred meaning and superhuman power, because they are inevitably reopened by another act of ritual killing. That afternoon a group of militant, right-wing, white supremacists machine-gunned a bus, killing seven and wounding twenty of its black passengers. The killers explained their action as revenge for the Durban beachfront stabbings. But it could also be seen as a countermove in the ongoing contest over superhuman power in South Africa. Countering Ngcobo's attempt to make sacrificial offerings to a black God, white supremacists made an offering to their own white, nationalist God. One of the right-wing killers explicitly claimed that the massacre had been "religiously justified." AWB member Eugene Marais had been influenced by a church, variously known as the Community of the Covenant People, the Israeli Vision Church, or the Israelites, to imagine that "all those people who were not Israelites had not been made by God, but by Satan. Blacks were animals of the field, animals that looked like people." Barend Strydom had been influenced by the same church before he performed his sacrifice of black people. As the seasons of violence continued in South Africa, devotees of violent nationalist religions persisted in offering blood sacrifices to violent Gods. We mistake these killings if we understand them merely as acts of vengeance. They were enacted in a sacrificial exchange system, an offering of human victims in the hope of receiving superhuman power in return. As long as superhuman power is implicated in such an exchange system, ritual killing will continue to be exercised as a strategy for making that power real in the world.[13]

Not only a violent offering, ritual killing has also been an act of symbolic elimination. In the cases of Barend Strydom, the collective killing of Lucas Sethwala, and the execution of alleged witches, we have seen instances of ritual killing for the elimination of persons perceived as threatening the symbolic purity of a world. In all these cases, persons were perceived as threatening because they represented anomalies in a symbolic classification system. Barend Strydom experienced black people as threatening because they appeared to him simultaneously as human beings, subhuman animals, and superhuman demons. During 1990, militant, right-wing Afrikaner nationalists persisted in trying to renegotiate the meaning and power of South Africa through violent rhetoric, even defending the violent acts of Strydom. The leader of the Boerestaat Party, Robert van Tonder, insisted that Strydom should be regarded as a political prisoner. Ironically, in attempting to negotiate the release of its own political prisoners, the African National Congress also called for Strydom's release. On the same day in April 1991, the death sentences of Strydom and ANC political prisoner Robert McBride were commuted to life imprisonment. But Strydom was less a political prisoner than a prisoner of a worldview that had classified human beings as subhuman. His acts cannot be regarded merely as political acts. They enacted a violent religious worldview. As long as worldviews generate symbolic systems that classify persons as less than fully human, we can expect to see acts of ritual killing to negotiate the purity of a human identity within those systems.

The deputy leader of the Boerestaat Party, Piet Rudolph, bearing the nickname "Skiet" ("Shoot"), stole a weapons cache from the air force armory and hid out underground for months. From hiding, Piet "Skiet" Rudolph sent a videotaped declaration of war against the government and the ANC that reflected a symbolic classification of persons similar to the one held by Barend Strydom. "I believe in the unquestionable truth of the Bible, in God the three-in-one and the existence of his chosen people here on the southern point [of Africa]," Rudolph declared. Drawing on that superhuman power represented by God, the Bible, and nationalism, Rudolph proclaimed the superiority of a white race and the subclassification of black people in South Africa. Sacrifice was required to make those classifications real. Not only killing, but also being killed, would establish the purity of person and place according to the demands of this sacrificial complex. "All we need are about 500 dedicated Boere who are prepared to lay their lives on the altar of this ideal," Rudolph claimed. "It is better to die gloriously rather than live in humiliation." As we have seen, the scapegoat and the martyr are two sides of the same sacrificial impulse in nationalist religion. In that violent religion, salvation has often been perceived in terms of a single, sacrificial, saving act. On the run, in hiding, Piet Rudolph promised precisely such a sacrificial redemption for the Boerevolk.

Eventually, however, Rudolph was arrested. He made a full confession to a magistrate. From prison, he issued a call to his supporters to renounce violence and turn in their weapons. Almost immediately, militant Afrikaner nationalists denounced his betrayal and placed their former hero under a sentence of death. Apparently, a renegotiation of the purity of their nationalist cause required his elimination. Nearly overnight, Rudolph was transformed from a nationalist hero and potential martyr to a scapegoat who had to be eliminated in order to reestablish the purity and violent unanimity of the Boerevolk. During February 1991, however, Rudolph renegotiated his status as a right-wing martyr by going on a sustained hunger strike in prison. The following month he was granted indemnity by the government and released.[14]

As violence intensified in the black townships of South Africa during 1990, local ritual killings that eliminated and desecrated surrogate victims were occasionally revived. In March 1990, for example, a crowd in the Zola neighborhood of Soweto killed a local gang leader by the name of "Sugar" Nkomo, who had allegedly terrorized the neighborhood and killed several young political activists. According to one participant in the killing, Nkomo had been working for "the system." As in Paballelo, the victim was an anomaly. He was inside the township, but drew power from association with the oppressive system outside. Local residents killed Sugar Nkomo, and his body was beheaded, mutilated, doused with petrol, and set on fire. People danced around the flames and sang, "The dog is dead." As in Paballelo, ritual killing renegotiated the purity and violent unanimity of a black township. Also as in Paballelo, that ritual elimination and desecration of a symbol of "the system" achieved only temporary results. Several hours after the killing, the police arrived, confiscated Nkomo's head for evidence, and proceeded to arrest a random number of participants. Violent contests, therefore, continued to be conducted through the selection and elimination of surrogate victims.[15]

Violent contests in South Africa also continued to be represented in symbolisms of evil. A flurry of newspaper reports alleging Satan worship, child sacrifice, and even satanic rites performed at the Afrikaans-language monument once again filled the popular press. White South Africa's inner demons were reemerging during a time of stress. In June 1990, Minister of Law and Order Adriaan Vlok promised Parliament that the police were doing everything possible to combat this "diabolic phenomenon." The police investigation continued.[16] But the violent conflicts of 1990 also could be represented in the symbolism of witchcraft and ritual murder. In the homeland of Venda in February 1990, a group of youths returning from a political rally celebrating the release of Nelson Mandela accused an old woman from a nearby village of being a witch. After stoning her to death, they burned her body in a hut. This ritual killing to eliminate an alleged witch was one of twenty reported from Venda during the first three months of 1990. Witch eradication practices were linked with the widespread popular perception that the chiefs, headmen, politicians, bureaucrats, and businessmen in the homeland government had been trying to secure their uncertain positions by performing human sacrifices for strong medicine. The brother of the Venda minister of justice had been tried, convicted, and executed for medicine murders in 1984. Many people, however, believed that this judicial execution had merely been a cover-up for ritual murders performed by leaders of the homeland government. Popular anger against the government of President Frank Ravele was channeled through this symbolism of evil. As one Venda resident explained,

"When we say 'away with Ravele,' we say away with his witchcraft." By March 1990, Ravele and his government had been deposed. The leader of the coup promised that one of his first undertakings would be an investigation into the practice of ritual killing for medicine.[17]

In three ways, therefore, ritual killing persisted. It was an offering to a violent God; it was a ritual of elimination to restore purity; it was a ritual of incorporation to gain power. As the seasons of violence recycled in South Africa, ritual killing continued in the violent negotiations over the meaning and power of that world. It remained the central ritual practice of all the violent religions of South Africa. We cannot expect it to end. As long as there are exchange systems in which human sacrifices can be offered to violent gods, classification systems from which persons can be eliminated, and political systems in which people can be incorporated and exploited as symbols of power, ritual killing will be practiced.

In South Africa, as we have seen, the ritualized and institutionalized dehumanization of persons has been reinforced by religion. Most obviously, we have seen dehumanization reinforced by ritual in the violent underworlds of the mines and prisons. During 1990 allegations of slavery and torture continued to be reported. In April 1990, however, those allegations were turned on the African National Congress. Seven former soldiers in Umkhonto we Sizwe told a London newspaper about the enslavement, torture, and killing of "dissidents" by the military wing of the ANC in the early 1980s. Although these former soldiers reported from Kenya that they remained loyal to the political leadership of the ANC, they claimed that at least sixty people had been executed, tortured to death, died in detention, or had disappeared under the direction of Umkhonto leaders in Angola and Tanzania. They recounted being confined in crowded cells, buried in underground containers, and beaten, crushed, burned, and humiliated in the prison camps of Umkhonto we Sizwe. Describing life in those camps, one dissident recalled that "when you enter there you must just forget you are a human being." Once again, slavery and torture were employed as metaphors—and, allegedly, as practices—in negotiations over what it meant to be human.

Like officials of the South African government, ANC leaders initially responded to the claims of these dissidents by invoking a humane code of conduct that in principle prohibited torture. Pointing to a code that had been formalized in 1985, ANC executive Anthony Mongalo countered the accusations by arguing that the organization had "a very strong policy which outlaws all forms of torture and physical coercion under any circumstances." According to Mongalo, this code had been rigorously applied. Unlike the official position of the government, however, the ANC soon confirmed that instances of torture had in fact occurred. They admitted that brutal methods had been used at camps operated by Umkhonto. However, they explained the creation of those camps in the context of the armed struggle in the 1980s. Although proclaimed the "Decade of Liberation," the early 1980s was a time of tension, as Umkhonto leaders tried to identify South African agents who had infiltrated their camps. While Umkhonto was involved in a military campaign in Angola in 1984, dissident soldiers mutinied and captured one of the camps, killing five officers in the process. After that camp was retaken, seven leaders of the mutiny were executed, while dissidents, regarded as traitors, were consigned to prison camps in northern Angola and Tanzania. Soldiers who had participated in the mutiny were held in those camps for four years, until they were pardoned and freed in 1988.[18]

Confronted with allegations of enslavement and torture, ANC leadership acknowledged their truth and insisted that measures had been taken to prevent their recurrence. Although they had occurred under extreme military conditions, these violent rites of dehumanization still had to be resisted. They had long been employed to reinforce the superhuman power of the state and capital in South Africa. They could not be perpetuated by any movement committed to human liberation because they defined the very reality of dehumanization. Although intended to discredit the ANC, the reports of abuse in 1990 provided the movement an opportunity to pursue its symbolic negotiations against the South African government. While the ANC was willing to admit and correct any violations of humanity that might have been committed in its name in the past, the government, as Nelson Mandela argued, continued to enslave, torture, and kill black people in South Africa.

The new era that followed the unbanning of South African political organizations did not bring an immediate end to the war over South Africa. In his speech of 2 February 1990, President De Klerk announced that the ANC's justifications for pursuing violent forms of struggle against a government that had prevented peaceful protest no longer applied. In a recurring metaphor, De Klerk insisted that his door was open; no one had to break it down. Upon his release from prison a week later, however, Nelson Mandela called for the extension and intensification of the armed struggle. Although the ANC was prepared to enter peaceful negotiations, it was not prepared to relinquish the forceful discourse of its military wing. As preparations were underway for talks between ANC and government delegations, Archbishop Desmond Tutu called upon the ANC to end its armed struggle. In response, senior ANC information officer Tom Sebina replied that the liberation movement would continue to fight "until the grievances which caused people to take up arms have been removed."[19] As representatives of the ANC argued, this had not happened, apartheid remained intact, and the armed forces of the government continued to wage war against the people of South Africa. Since the government persisted in reinforcing its power through violence, the ANC would maintain its armed struggle.

Ironically, on the same day that Archbishop Tutu was calling for an end to the ANC's armed struggle, an incident occurred in the Vaal township of Sebokeng that confirmed the perception that violent negotiations were still being conducted by the armed forces of the state. Protesting high rents and poor living conditions in the townships, a crowd of about 50,000 marched to a local police station to present a memorandum to be passed on to the government. They were blocked by police. As community leaders restrained the crowd, Vaal Community Association representative Bavumile Vilakazi met with the police station commander midway between marchers and the police. After presenting the commander with the petition, Vilakazi returned to instruct the marchers to turn back and go home. Without warning, police opened fire on the crowd, leaving perhaps 20 dead and nearly 450 wounded by birdshot. Once again, a ritual confrontation reinforced the presence and power of the state's armed religion.[20]

According to the police account, shooting people in the streets had been justified because "the crowd which acted in a threatening manner, surged forward. Police were attacked and opened fire in self-defence." During a time in which crowds in the streets and town squares of eastern Europe were celebrated on South African television, the crowd in the streets of Sebokeng was represented by both state-controlled media and the police as threatening and dangerous. Although the official police report claimed self-defense, eyewitnesses and newspapers reported that the shooting had been unprovoked, a finding confirmed by a commission of inquiry months later. Not merely another example of the ritualized defense of the South African order by the police, however, the shooting in Sebokeng could be interpreted in the context of the pending talks between the ANC and the government. In that context, police action could be construed as an intervention in the negotiations, as itself a violent act of negotiation. Indeed, a spokesperson for the UDF interpreted the shootings as a violent entry into the talks by members of the police force who were "trying to derail the negotiating process." By preventing peaceful protest, the police seemed to be pushing the ANC away from the table and back to the battlefield. That the ANC took this view of the shootings at Sebokeng was indicated by Nelson Mandela's breaking off the scheduled talks with the government. Although peaceful negotiations were soon resumed, the police action at Sebokeng demonstrated that violence remained very much part of the process of negotiation in South Africa.[21]

While preparations for peaceful discussions in the midst of violence were underway, alternatives to the position represented by the ANC were being voiced. The Pan Africanist Congress rejected the proposed talks with the government. After being imprisoned for twenty-seven years, PAC leader Jafta Masemola came out strongly against dealing with those who had oppressed the people of South Africa. "To negotiate with people who are stronger than yourself," Masemola observed, "is not negotiation but collaboration." Noting that even if apartheid were removed the oppressors would still be in power, Masemola concluded, "We say away with the oppressors." Similarly, representing the position of the black consciousness movement, the president of the Azanian Peoples Organization, Itumeleng Mosala, insisted that "negotiations should take place among resistance organizations of the black people, not with the ruling class." In spite of their general agreement in opposing any settlements with the government, however, members of the PAC and Azapo were occasionally involved in violent confrontations with each other, indicating the priority of Mosala's call for negotiations among resistance organizations.[22]

Eager to enter discussions with the government, Chief Mangosuthu Gatsha Buthelezi was one of only two homeland leaders who accepted President De Klerk's invitation for talks in Cape Town in early April 1990. While the war continued to rage in Natal, Buthelezi pursued his symbolic negotiations with the government as leader of an ethnic Zulu nationalism. Contesting Buthelezi's claims in 1990, however, the Congress of Traditional Leaders of South Africa (Contralesa) aligned itself with the ANC. At a meeting of the International Commission of Jurists, Contralesa representative Chief Mhlabunzima Maphumulo challenged the authenticity of Buthelezi's ethnic nationalism. "He is not the leader of all the Zulus," Maphumulo argued, "only of the Buthelezi clan and of the apartheid-created KwaZulu, which does not have the support or mandate of the majority." Chief Maphumulo presented an interim report in Geneva on a study of the conflict in Natal that had been funded by the South African Council of Churches. Although the study was being conducted by an independent researcher, Chief Buthelezi and Inkatha had refused to cooperate because they identified the South African Council of Churches with the political aims of the ANC, UDF, and COSATU. The interim report explained the violence in Natal as a result of aggressive Inkatha recruitment drives in the mid 1980s in which "unconventional tactics, like intimidation and duress, were employed." By 1990, the report concluded, Inkatha coercion in the region had resulted in a devastating, escalating "civil war."[23]

Clearly, religion was involved in that conflict. By this I mean not only the sponsorship by the South African Council of Churches of research that found Inkatha to be the cause of the violence in Natal. In addition, the Zulu nationalism promoted by Chief Buthelezi must be regarded as a religious movement. Representing a different religious orientation, a delegation of religious leaders, including Desmond Tutu, Allan Boesak, and Frank Chikane, met with President De Klerk in April 1990 to present a peace plan for Natal. The government, however, had already initiated its own peace plan by sending its police and troops into the region. As bearers of the armed religion of the state, those forces allegedly entered the conflict in support of the armed religion of Inkatha. In multiple, multiplying ways, religion continued to be implicated in armed conflict in South Africa.

Conversely, armed conflict also informed religion. Religion was a force, a power, a strategy—often a violent strategy—for negotiating person and place in South Africa. At a 1990 memorial service held in Alexandra township for as many as forty-five people who had been killed there by police during six days in 1986, ministers from several Christian denominations delivered sermons to mark the occasion. That memorial service did not stand outside of the conflict it commemorated. Ritual was part of the conflict, a mobilization of forces in and through religious symbols in action. As ministers on the platform looked through their Bibles, journalist Thami Mkhwanazi noted, "They were gearing themselves for war. After locating the right pages, they kept their fingers in the relevant chapters, ready to pull the trigger. They were armed to the teeth—with the word of God." Reverend Mokobane of the Zion Christian Church drew upon the classic biblical symbolism of victory over an apparently overwhelming enemy force. "The enemy will be destroyed by the weaker oppressed," he declared, "in the same way Goliath was destroyed by David."[24] As the people of Alexandra commemorated their dead, they could also anticipate victory over their oppressors in the potent symbols of an armed religion.

The fact that violent force permeated the very character of religion should not be surprising. Violence, in all the forms we have considered in this book, permeated South Africa, from politics, through social and economic relations, to the rhythms of everyday life. As South Africa entered the 1990s, however, a new prospect of relatively peaceful, negotiated change unexpectedly appeared. De Klerk's government promised the removal of basic pillars of apartheid, including racist legislation governing public schools, public amenities, residential areas, land ownership, and population registration. A future South Africa depended upon a more inclusive process of political negotiation. But all of the prospective negotiators had just lived through a decade in which politics was not about dialogue, cooperation, compromise, or democratic participation. Rather, politics was about essentially religious strategies for achieving sudden salvation, redemptive sacrifice, sacred purity, and superhuman power. As we have seen, none of these strategies was innocent, because all were directly implicated in the seasons of violence in South Africa. The future therefore depended not merely upon opening the door and setting the table for political negotiations but upon finding new ways to negotiate. Those new strategies would somehow have to diminish the violence of South Africa's ongoing, inherently violent symbolic negotiations of person and place.

More explicit attention to the potency of religious worldviews might help in the search for new ways to negotiate. If we reject the racist, ethnic, or nationalist assumption that worldviews are "things" attached to particular "peoples," then a new awareness of the dynamic and contested processes of worldview negotiation might be possible. As I have tried to show in this book, worldviews in which religion, politics, and violence were interwoven played a significant role in the violent negotiations over South Africa during the 1980s. In those negotiations, contenders made conflicting claims on South African sacred symbols, often, especially in the case of the government, making privileged claims to the symbolic ownership of South Africa. Sacred symbols were constantly at stake, symbols associated with God, the Bible, and nationalism, the scapegoat and the martyr, the witch and the witchdoctor, the demon and the exorcist, the land, the past, and the future, and all the many rituals of purity and power that negotiated and renegotiated a human world. Although all these symbols were "symbolic," they were at the same time "real," because people had real investments in them. These symbols were not sacred in and of themselves, I would suggest, because the sacredness of symbols tends to be directly related to the energy generated when people appropriate them, invest in them, and fight over them in the always contested struggles over ownership. In this respect, South Africa during the 1980s must certainly have been one of the most sacred places on earth, with so much energy generated by conflicting, mutually exclusive claims on its sacred symbols.

Would South Africa somehow be a less sacred place if, to paraphrase the Freedom Charter, its symbols belonged to all who live in it, black and white? While renegotiating the terms and conditions of political, social, and economic empowerment, what would it mean to negotiate a redistribution of the wealth of symbols? In the prospect of a "New South Africa," political analysts in 1990 occasionally called for the creation of new symbols of national identity. Since nationalism, that most potent, violent religion of the modern world, has done so much damage, it is hard to be enthusiastic about the creation of new national symbols. Is it possible to forge national symbols of purity without exclusion or symbols of power without domination? That is the challenge. Although I conclude with no formula for the future, intending my final remarks as analytic, rather than prescriptive, I do propose that attention to worldview negotiations suggests at least two basic considerations about new symbols in South Africa.

First, regardless of their content, new national symbols will inevitably give rise to intense, even violent, conflict as long as symbolic negotiations are directed toward underwriting claims on their legitimate, authentic ownership. What is required for a "New South Africa," therefore, is not any specific, particular symbolism, but a new style of symbolic negotiation based, not on the privileged appropriation, but on the availability of symbols. This would represent a dramatic reorientation toward sacred symbols. Rather than asserting, "You don't own them, we do," a new negotiating style would have to maintain, "You don't own them, no one does." No one can claim exclusive, privileged ownership of sacred symbols because, as we have seen throughout this book, no negotiated claim on symbols has ever been final. Privileged claims to the ownership of symbols are always contested. The only way to diminish the violence of such conflict would be to achieve a renunciation of all exclusive symbolic claims.

Second, again irrespective of content, new national symbols will result in conflict if the more fundamental issue of access to the means of symbolic production is not addressed. With more open access to the media of symbolic production—which, of course, includes electronic and print media, but also the government, police, military, schools, workplace, and other arenas of worldview negotiation we have examined—a new style of symbolic negotiation might be possible. That new style would most likely not produce a unified, orthodox set of national symbols, but a plural, varied, and open field of symbolic production. A more open field of symbolic production, distribution, and exchange might better allow human beings, in all their diversity, to be seen, heard, and recognized as human. As we have seen, where peaceful symbolic negotiations of humanity become impossible, violent negotiations become inevitable. A more open access to the means of symbolic production might diminish violent assertions of humanity, broaden the scope of peaceful negotiation, and facilitate mutual human recognition in a "New South Africa."

Both these requirements—availability of symbols and access to the means of symbolic production—must appear hopelessly utopian. But the challenge of creating a new, just, and democratic South Africa implies nothing less than the negotiation of a new world. Inevitably, worldview negotiations will be interwoven in the political, social, and economic struggles over a "New South Africa." If history has taught us anything, it is that those symbolic negotiations will often be violent. If the recent, ancient history of religion and violence in South Africa has taught us anything, it is that a new era will depend upon new ways of negotiating person and place in that world. Otherwise, if new strategies are not found, the "New South Africa" will be engulfed in the same war of the worldviews that has animated the old.

Notes

Preface

1. C. Wright Mills, *The Power Elite* (New York: Oxford University Press, 1956), 71.

2. A good introduction to South African historiography, especially for an American reader, is found in Colin Bundy, "An Image of Its Own Past? Towards a Comparison of American and South African Historiography," *Radical History Review* 46/47 (1990): 117–43. An accessible overview of South African history is provided by Leonard Thompson, *A History of South Africa* (New Haven: Yale University Press, 1990). A comparative history of religions in South Africa is available in David Chidester, *Religions of South Africa* (London: Routledge, 1992).

3. For a definition of violence as direct physical harm, see Robert B. Miller, "Violence, Force, and Coercion," in Jerome A. Schaffer, ed., *Violence* (New York: David McKay, 1971), 25. For a discussion of political violence as collective acts causing direct physical harm, see Perry Mars, "The Nature of Political Violence," *Social and Economic Studies* 24 (1975): 221–38. Among other problems, "minimalist" definitions of violence have ignored the variability of cultural constructions of what counts as harm. See Paul Heelas, "Anthropology, Violence, and Catharsis," in Peter Marsh and Anne Campbell, eds., *Aggression and Violence* (New York: Saint Martin's Press, 1982), 47–61. For important contributions to an emerging anthropology of violence, see M. Estellie Smith, "Cultural Variability in the Structuring of Violence," in Thomas R. Williams, ed., *Psychological Anthropology* (The Hague: Mouton, 1975), 333–51; Natalie Zemon Davis, "Rites of Violence," in *Society and Culture in Early Modern France: Eight Essays* (Stanford: Stanford University Press, 1976), 152–87; Randall Collins, "Three Faces of Cruelty: Toward a Comparative Sociology of Violence," in *Sociology since Midcentury* (New York: Academic Press, 1981), 133–60; Paula Brown and Ilsa Schuster, eds., "Culture and Aggression, Special Issue," *Anthropological Quarterly* 59, no. 4 (1986); Georges Balandier, "An Anthropology of Violence and War," *International Social Science Journal* 38 (1986): 499–511; and David Riches, ed., *The Anthropology of Violence* (Oxford: Basil Blackwell, 1986).

4. Probably the most influential statements of a "maximalist" definition of violence, incorporating the violation of humanity in the definition, have been Newton Garver, "What Violence Is," in A. K. Bierman and James A. Gould, eds., *Philosophy for a New Generation* (London: Macmillan, 1970), 353–64; and the work of Johan Galtung, for example, *The True Worlds: A Transnational Perspective* (New York: Free Press, 1980). In similar terms, violence has been defined as anything "infringing upon or disregarding or abusing or denying [a person], whether physical harm is involved or not" (Robert McAfee Brown, *Religion and Violence: A Primer for White Americans* [Philadelphia: Westminster Press, 1973], 7); anything that violates the humanity and dignity of persons (Robert L. Holmes, "Violence and Nonviolence," in Shaffer, *Violence,* 110); or anything that destroys the "ethical substance" of a person (Ninian Smart, "René Girard: *Violence and the Sacred,*" *Religious Studies Review* 6 [1980]: 175). For critiques of this approach, see Joseph Betz, "Violence: Garver's Definition and a Deweyan Correction," *Ethics* 87 (1976/77): 339–51; and William Maley, "Peace, Needs, and Utopia," *Political Studies* 33 (1985): 578–91.

5. For Dewey's distinction between violence and force, see John Dewey, "Force, Violence, and Law," in Joseph Ratner, ed., *Intelligence in the Modern World* (New York: Modern Library, 1939), 488. In this distinction between illegitimate violence and legitimate force, the normalized, institutionalized violence of the state disappears, whether that violence is defined in Weber's terms as the state's claim to be the "exclusive source of the right to use violence," or defined in Lenin's terms as the state's existence as a "creation of order" based on the "oppression of one class by another." See Max Weber, "Politics as a Vocation," in H. H. Gerth and C. Wright Mills, eds., *From Max Weber: Essays in Sociology* (London: Routledge and Kegan Paul, 1970), 78; V. I. Lenin, *The State and Revolution* (London: Allen and Unwin, 1917), 154. Arguably, the "establishment violence" of the state also disappears in explanations of political violence based on a theory of "relative deprivation," most clearly formulated in Ted Gurr, *Why Men Rebel?* (Princeton: Princeton University Press, 1970). For a useful discussion of these issues, see Rasheeduddin Khan, "Violence and Socioeconomic Development," *International Social Science Journal* 30 (1978): 814–57.

6. A strong appeal for a return to the "minimalist" definition and standards of ethical evaluation is made in Gerald Runkle, "Is Violence Always Wrong?" *Journal of Politics* 38 (1976): 367–89. The classic celebrations of violence as a liberating force from class or colonial oppression are Georges Sorel, *Reflections on Violence* (1908; reprinted, New York: Macmillan, 1961); and Frantz Fanon, *The Wretched of the Earth,* trans. Constance Farrington (1961; reprint, New York: Grove Press, 1968).

7. For recent comparative analysis of violent conflict in South Africa, Northern Ireland, and Israel, see Hermann Giliomee and Jannie Gagiano, eds., *The Elusive Search for Peace: South Africa, Israel, and Northern Ireland* (Cape Town: Oxford University Press, 1990). Symbolic dimensions of violent conflict

have been explored from a comparative perspective in Bruce Kapferer, *Legends of People, Myths of State: Violence, Intolerance, and Political Culture in Sri Lanka and Australia* (Washington, D.C.: Smithsonian Institution Press, 1988). Useful resources for the analysis of religion and violence in America have been collected in Michael Newton and Judy Ann Newton, eds., *Racial and Religious Violence in America* (New York: Garland, 1990).

Chapter 1: White Wolves

1. All citations of Barend Hendrik Strydom's testimony have been taken from accounts in the local press: *Cape Argus,* 17 November 1988, 18, 19, 20, 23 May 1989; *Cape Times,* 20 May 1989.

2. Jacques Derrida, "Racism's Last Word," in Henry Louis Gates, Jr., ed., *"Race," Writing, and Difference* (Chicago: University of Chicago Press, 1985), 330. On apartheid as Calvinism, see W. A. de Klerk, *Puritans in Africa* (Harmondsworth: Penguin, 1976), but also see the cautionary critique provided in the work of André du Toit: "No Chosen People: The Myth of the Calvinist Origins of Afrikaner Nationalism and Racial Ideology," *American Historical Review* 88 (1983): 920–52; "Captive to the Nationalist Paradigm: Prof. F. A. van Jaarsveld and the Historical Evidence for the Afrikaner's Ideas on His Calling and Mission," *South African Historical Journal* 16 (1984): 49–80; and "Puritans in Africa? Afrikaner 'Calvinism' and Kuyperian Neo-Calvinism in Late Nineteenth-Century South Africa," *Comparative Studies in Society and History* 27 (1985): 209–40. On apartheid as civil religion, see T. Dunbar Moodie, *The Rise of Afrikanerdom: Power, Apartheid, and Afrikaner Civil Religion* (Berkeley: University of California Press, 1975). On apartheid as an ideological class alliance, see Dan O'Meara, *Volkskapitalisme: Class, Capital, and Ideology in the Development of Afrikaner Nationalism, 1934–1948* (Cambridge: Cambridge University Press, 1983). On apartheid and the "awakening" of an ethnic nationalism, see F. A. van Jaarsveld, *The Awakening of Afrikaner Nationalism, 1868–1881* (Cape Town: Human and Rousseau, 1961). On apartheid and the "mobilization" of an ethnic nationalism, see Heribert Adam and Hermann Giliomee, *The Rise and Crisis of Afrikaner Power* (Cape Town: David Philip, 1979). On apartheid and the "invention" of an ethnic nationalism, see Hermann Giliomee, "The Beginning of Afrikaner Ethnic Consciousness, 1850–1915," in Leroy Vail, ed., *The Creation of Tribalism in Southern Africa* (Berkeley: University of California Press, 1989), 21–54. On apartheid as political mythology, see Leonard Thompson, *The Political Mythology of Apartheid* (New Haven: Yale University Press, 1985).

3. The apartheid study of worldviews is most obvious in the academic discipline of *volkekunde,* which passes for anthropology at Afrikaans-speaking universities. See John Sharp, "The Roots and Development of Volkekunde in South Africa," *Journal of Southern African Studies* 8 (1981): 16–36; Brian M. Du Toit,

"Missionaries, Anthropologists, and the Politics of the Dutch Reformed Church," *Journal of Modern African Studies* 22 (1984): 617–32; and Robert Gordon, "Apartheid's Anthropologists: The Genealogy of Afrikaner Anthropology," *American Ethnologist* 15 (1988): 535–53.

4. This definition of "worldview" is a modified version of categories developed in David Chidester, *Salvation and Suicide: An Interpretation of Jim Jones, the Peoples Temple, and Jonestown* (Bloomington: Indiana University Press, 1988). I propose here again that "worldview" be reconceptualized as a set of discursive, practical, and social strategies, rather than "beliefs," in keeping with the multidimensional definition of religion—theoretical, practical, and social—found in Joachim Wach, *Sociology of Religion* (Chicago: University of Chicago Press, 1944), 17–34.

5. For similar usage of the term "negotiation," see T. O. Beidelman, "Sacrifice and Sacred Rule in Africa," *American Ethnologist* 14 (1987): 546; W. B. Gallie, *Philosophy and the Historical Understanding* (New York: Schocken Books, 1968), 157–91; and Lawrence Rosen, *Bargaining for Reality: The Construction of Social Relations in a Muslim Community* (Chicago: University of Chicago Press, 1984), 185–86. For the classic statement in the study of religion on the creation of "life worlds," see Peter L. Berger and Thomas Luckmann, *The Social Construction of Reality: A Treatise in the Sociology of Knowledge* (Garden City, N.Y.: Doubleday, 1967). However, my emphasis on discursive, practical, and social strategies is more consistent with the idea of *habitus* developed in Pierre Bourdieu, *Outline of a Theory of Practice,* trans. Richard Nice (Cambridge: Cambridge University Press, 1977). For a useful, accessible application of the concept of plural worlds in religious studies, see William Paden, *Religious Worlds: The Comparative Study of Religion* (Boston: Beacon Press, 1988).

6. The best introduction to South African churches remains John de Gruchy, *The Church Struggle in South Africa* (Grand Rapids, Mich.: Eerdmans, 1979). On the Dutch Reformed Church and apartheid, see Susan Rennie Ritner, "The Dutch Reformed Church and Apartheid," *Journal of Contemporary History* 2, no. 4 (1967): 17–37; Ritner, "Salvation through Separation: The Role of the Dutch Reformed Church in South Africa in the Formulation of Afrikaner Race Ideology" (Ph.D. dissertation, Columbia University, 1977); J. H. P. Serfontein, *Apartheid, Change and the N. G. Kerk* (Emmarentia: Taurus, 1982); Ken Jubber, "The Prodigal Church: South Africa's Dutch Reformed Church and the Apartheid Policy," *Social Compass* 32 (1985): 273–85; J. A. Loubser, *The Apartheid Bible: A Critical Review of Racial Theology in South Africa* (Cape Town: Maskew Miller Longman, 1987); and Cecil Ngcokovane, *Demons of Apartheid: A Moral and Ethical Analysis of the N.G.K., N.P., and Broederbond's Justification of Apartheid* (Braamfontein: Skotaville, 1989). For an argument that English-speaking churches have not been immune from entanglements with apartheid, see Charles Villa-Vicencio, *Trapped in Apartheid* (Maryknoll, N.Y.: Orbis, 1988).

7. *Cape Argus,* 17 May 1986; See Franci Henny, "The AWB Prepares for Armageddon," *Scope,* 6 May 1986, 27–34; and David Welsh, "South Africa's Ultra-Right," *Patterns of Prejudice* 22, no. 4 (1988): 13–23 (part 1); 23, no. 1 (1989): 3–15 (part 2).

8. S. W. Pienaar, *Believe in Your People: D. F. Malan as Orator, 1908–1954* (Cape Town: Tafelberg, 1964), 128–29.

9. Thompson, *The Political Mythology of Apartheid,* 187.

10. Albert Grundlingh and Hilary Sapire, "From Feverish Festival to Repetitive Ritual? The Changing Fortunes of Great Trek Mythology in an Industrializing South Africa, 1938–1988," *South African Historical Journal* 21 (1989): 19–37.

11. Frank Manuel, ed., *The Enlightenment* (Englewood Cliffs, N.J.: Prentice-Hall, 1965), 59; Jean Bethke Elshtain, "Citizenship and Armed Civic Virtue: Some Critical Questions on the Commitment to Public Life," in Charles H. Reynolds and Ralph V. Norman, eds., *Community in America: The Challenge of Habits of the Heart* (Berkeley: University of California Press, 1988), 51.

12. *Cape Argus,* 18 November 1988; Orlando Patterson, *Slavery and Social Death: A Comparative Study* (Cambridge: Harvard University Press, 1982).

13. Deborah Posel, "The Meaning of Apartheid before 1948: Conflicting Interests and Forces within the Afrikaner Nationalist Alliance," *Journal of Southern African Studies* 14 (1987): 130.

14. F. W. Reitz, *A Century of Wrong* (London: Review of Books, 1900), 13; *Cape Argus,* 28 April 1983.

15. *Cape Times,* 12 October 1987.

16. David Chidester, "Published by Authority: Religion in the President's Council Report on Youth," *Journal of Theology for Southern Africa* 61 (1987): 73–79. *The Naked Communist* was apparently also used by the South African Defence Force in formulating "Youth Preparedness" courses for the public schools. See Robert Gordon, "'Ethnological Knowledge is of Vital Importance': The Martialization of South African Anthropology," *Dialectical Anthropology* 12 (1988): 446. For further evidence of the treatment of communism as a subhuman or antihuman force in South Africa, see the assertion that communists are "not human . . . in the selective and optimistic sense in which we habitually use the word," in Henry Pike, *A History of Communism in South Africa* (Germiston: Christian Mission International, 1986), 290.

17. Shamil Jeppe, "I. D. du Plessis and the 'Reinvention' of the 'Malay,' c. 1935–1952" (Paper, University of Cape Town, Centre for African Studies, 1988); Surendra Bhana and Joy B. Brain, *Setting Down Roots: Indian Migrants in South Africa, 1860–1911* (Johannesburg: Witwatersrand University Press,

1990), 66; Riva Krut, "The Making of a South African Jewish Community in Johannesburg, 1886–1914," in Belinda Bozzoli, ed., *Class, Community, and Conflict: South African Perspectives* (Johannesburg: Ravan Press, 1987), 135–59.

18. Gerhard Maré, "The Past, the Present, and Negotiation Politics: The Role of Inkatha" (Paper, University of Cape Town, Centre for African Studies, 1989), 4. On Buthelezi's ethnic nationalism, see Gerhard Maré and Georgina Hamilton, *An Appetite for Power: Buthelezi's Inkatha and the Politics of "Loyal Resistance"* (Johannesburg: Ravan Press, 1987); and Mzala, *Gatsha Buthelezi: Chief with a Double Agenda* (London: Zed Books, 1988).

19. De Klerk, *Puritans in Africa,* 246–47.

20. Oliver Tambo, "The Ideology of Racism," *Sechaba,* July 1986, 3; Tambo, "Advance to People's Power," *Sechaba,* February 1987, 3.

21. Manas Buthelezi, "The Christian Presence in Today's South Africa," *Journal of Theology for Southern Africa* 16 (1976): 7. For general introductions to African and black nationalist movements, see Peter Walshe, *The Rise of African Nationalism in South Africa: The African National Congress, 1912–1952* (Berkeley: University of California Press, 1970); Gail M. Gerhart, *Black Power in South Africa: The Evolution of an Ideology* (Berkeley: University of California Press, 1978); and Tom Lodge, *Black Politics in South Africa since 1945* (Johannesburg: Ravan Press, 1983).

22. "Inside South Africa: A New Movement Is Formed," *Sechaba,* March 1973, 5; Robert Fatton, Jr., *Black Consciousness in South Africa: The Dialectics of Ideological Resistance to White Supremacy* (Albany: State University of New York Press, 1986), 138; Tom Lodge, "The African National Congress in South Africa, 1976–1983: Guerrilla War and Armed Propaganda," *Journal of Contemporary African Studies* 3 (1983/84): 153–80; Lodge, "State of Exile: The African National Congress of South Africa," in Philip Frankel, Noam Pines, and Mark Swilling, eds., *State, Resistance, and Change in South Africa* (London: Croom Helm, 1988), 229–58. These themes will be dealt with in more detail in chapter 6.

23. Charles Villa-Vicencio, ed., *Between Christ and Caesar* (Grand Rapids, Mich.: Eerdmans, 1986), 259.

24. Cassius Mandla, "Umkhonto we Sizwe: Let Us Move to an All-out War," *Sechaba,* November 1986, 26; "Obituary: Cassius Make and Paul Dikeledi," *Sechaba,* September 1987, 30; Oliver Tambo, "Umkhonto we Sizwe, Born of the People," *Sechaba,* March 1987, 18; John Dewey, "Force, Violence, and Law," in Joseph Ratner, ed., *Intelligence in the Modern World* (New York: Modern Library, 1939), 488–89.

25. Mircea Eliade, *The Myth of the Eternal Return,* trans. Willard R. Trask (Princeton: Princeton University Press, 1954), ix.

Chapter 2: Black Sheep

1. Harriet Ngubane, *Body and Mind in Zulu Medicine* (London: Academic Press, 1977), 119.

2. Axel-Ivar Berglund, *Zulu Thought Patterns and Symbolism* (London: C. Hurst, 1976), 55; Luc de Heusch, *Sacrifice in Africa: A Structuralist Approach*, trans. Linda O'Brien and Alice Morton (Bloomington: Indiana University Press, 1985), 39–43.

3. *Cape Argus*, 12 July 1989.

4. *Cape Argus*, 14 February 1989. On "mob hysteria," see Elias Canetti, *Crowds and Power*, trans. Carol Stewart (Harmondsworth: Penguin, 1984). For background on the theory of "deindividuation," see Ed Diener, "Deindividuation: The Absence of Self-Awareness and Self-Regulation in Group Members," in P. B. Paulus, ed., *Psychology of Group Influence* (Hillsdale, N.J.: Erlbaum, 1980), 209–42.

5. *Cape Argus*, 17 July 1989.

6. *Cape Argus*, 7 June 1989. See Desirée Hansson and Derrick Fine, "Expert Testimony on Community Attitudes to Sentencing: The Case of the Upington 26," in Desirée Hansson and Dirk van Zyl Smit, eds., *Towards Justice? Crime and State Control in South Africa* (Cape Town: Oxford University Press, 1990), 173–94.

7. The best general introduction to René Girard's work is Burton Mack, "Introduction: Religion and Ritual," in Robert Hamerton Kelly, *Violent Origins: Walter Burkert, René Girard, and Jonathan Z. Smith on Ritual Killing and Cultural Formation* (Stanford: Stanford University Press, 1987), 1–72. For criticism and appreciation, see Ninian Smart, "René Girard: *Violence and the Sacred*," *Religious Studies Review* 6 (1980): 173–77; James G. Williams, "The Innocent Victim: René Girard on Violence, Sacrifice, and the Sacred," *Religious Studies Review* 14 (1988): 320–26; Department of French and Italian, Stanford University, *To Honour René Girard* (Saratoga, CA: ANMA Libri, 1986); and the special issues of *Diacritics* (1978); *Sciences Religieuses/Studies in Religion* (1981); and *Semeia* (1985).

8. *Cape Times*, 16 February 1989.

9. *Cape Argus*, 14 July 1989.

10. *Cape Argus*, 13 July 1989.

11. *Cape Argus*, 14 July 1989.

12. Ibid.

13. René Girard, *Violence and the Sacred*, trans. Patrick Gregory (Baltimore: Johns Hopkins University Press, 1977), 79. For Girard's subsequent work on

"generative scapegoating," see *The Scapegoat,* trans. Yvonne Freccero (Baltimore: Johns Hopkins University Press, 1986); *Job: The Victim of His People,* trans. Yvonne Freccero (Stanford: Stanford University Press, 1987); and "Generative Scapegoating," in Hamerton-Kelly, *Violent Origins,* 73–85.

14. Girard, *Violence and the Sacred,* 271.

15. Ibid., 266.

16. Ibid., 81.

17. Ibid., 14, 17.

18. Ibid., 26–27.

19. Ibid., 199–200, 269.

20. Ibid., 23, 16.

21. Ibid., 23–24.

22. Hansard (A) 7 col. 2161, 18 March 1986.

23. *Johannesburg Star,* 25 March 1986.

24. *Johannesburg Star,* 7 November 1977. See Jerold Taitz, "The Steve Biko Affair," *Medico-Legal Journal* 54 (1986): 119–30; and Mary Rayner, *Turning a Blind Eye? Medical Accountability and the Prevention of Torture in South Africa* (Washington, D.C.: Committee on Scientific Freedom and Responsibility, American Association for the Advancement of Science, 1987).

25. *Weekly Mail,* 16 March 1990; *Cape Argus,* 29 March 1990; Nico Steytler, "Policing Political Opponents: Death Squads and Cop Culture," in Hansson and Van Zyl Smit, *Towards Justice?* 112. For a discussion of violence against "enemies" of the South African state, see J. D. van der Vyver, "State Sponsored Terror Violence," *South African Journal on Human Rights* 4 (1988): 55–75. For a useful, general discussion of relations between religion and political terrorism, see two works by David C. Rapoport: "Fear and Trembling: Terrorism in Three Religious Traditions," *American Political Science Review* 78 (1984): 658–77; and "Messianic Sanctions for Terror," *Comparative Politics* 20 (1988): 195–213.

26. Centre for Applied Legal Studies, *Focus on the Death Penalty,* May 1988; Amnesty International, *When the State Kills: The Death Penalty v. Human Rights* (London: Amnesty International, 1989). For statistics on the application of the death penalty in South Africa during the 1980s, see Christina Murray and Julia Sloth-Nielsen, "Hangings in South Africa: The Last Ten Years," *South African Journal on Human Rights* 5 (1989): 490. In 1990 the government placed a one-year moratorium on judicial executions while undertaking a review of the state's position on capital punishment.

27. John Dugard, "Training Needs in Sentencing in South Africa," *South*

African Journal on Human Rights 1 (1985): 93–105; *Johannesburg Star,* 7 August 1987; *Cape Argus,* 25 May 1989. See C. R. M. Dlamini, "The Influence of Race on the Administration of Justice in South Africa," *South African Journal on Human Rights* 4 (1988): 37–54.

28. Mphunki, "Capital Punishment: Towards a New Approach," *Sechaba,* September 1989, 25; Centre for Applied Legal Studies, *Human Rights Update,* April 1988; Sonia Bunting, "Prisoner of War Status and Our MK Fighters," *Sechaba,* May 1988, 2. See Christina Murray, "The ANC in Court: Towards International Guidelines in Sentencing," *Journal of Southern African Studies* 14 (1987): 140–46.

29. Mervyn E. Bennun, "The Sharpeville Six and the Law in Context," *Sechaba,* October 1988, 3–9.

30. Hansard (D) 12 col. 3086, 3 September 1987. Nevertheless, sentencing in so-called necklace cases showed considerable variation, as three cases decided in 1987 suggest: A case in the eastern Cape resulted in one fourteen-year sentence, two two-year sentences, and one acquittal; a similar case, also in the eastern Cape, decided three months later resulted in six death sentences, with one twenty-year sentence; a filmed and highly publicized case in the Transvaal resulted in three life imprisonments, with six other prison sentences of varying terms (*Weekly Mail,* 25 June 1987). On people's courts, see Jeremy Seekings, "People's Courts and Popular Politics," in South African Research Services, *South African Review Five* (Johannesburg: Ravan Press, 1990), 119–35; and Wilfried Schärf and Baba Ngcokoto, "Images of Punishment in People's Courts of Cape Town, 1985–1987: From Prefigurative Justice to Populist Violence," in N. Chabani Manganyi and André du Toit, eds., *Political Violence and the Struggle in South Africa* (London: Macmillan, 1990), 341–71.

31. Lloyd Vogelman, "The Living Dead: Living on Death Row," *South African Journal on Human Rights* 5 (1989): 195; Arthur Goldstuck, *The Rabbit in the Thorn Tree: Modern Myths and Urban Legends in South Africa* (Harmondsworth: Penguin, 1990), 28–30.

Chapter 3: Witches and Demons

1. Witchcraft has been defined as "the power to exert supernatural harm upon another person or his possessions, that power depending upon inherent evil qualities in the evil person himself/herself," while sorcery has been defined as "the supernatural power to cause another person or that person's possessions harm through the use of various substances or acts," but in either case the aspect of harm identifies both as acts of violence (T. O. Beidelman, *The Kaguru* [New York: Holt, Rinehart, and Winston, 1971], 131–32).

2. J. C. Warner, "Mr. Warner's Notes," in John Maclean, ed., *A Compendium*

of Kafir Laws and Customs (Mount Coke: Wesleyan Mission Press, 1858), 81. See J. B. Peires, *The House of Phalo: A History of the Xhosa People in the Days of Their Independence* (Johannesburg: Ravan Press, 1981), 39; and *The Dead Will Arise: Nongqawuse and the Great Xhosa Cattle-Killing Movement of 1856–1857* (Johannesburg: Ravan Press, 1989), 62.

3. Monica Hunter (Wilson), *Reaction to Conquest: Effects of Contact with Europeans on the Pondo of South Africa,* 2d ed. (London: Oxford University Press, 1961), 108; cited in Donovan Williams, *When Races Meet: The Life and Times of William Ritchie Thomson, Glasgow Society Missionary, Government Agent, and Dutch Reformed Church Minister, 1794–1891* (Johannesburg: A.P.B. Publishers, 1967), 83; and in R. L. Cope, "Christian Missions and Independent African Chiefdoms in South Africa in the Nineteenth Century," *Theoria* 52 (1979): 8.

4. Adam Kuper, *South Africa and the Anthropologist* (London: Routledge and Kegan Paul, 1987), 167–96. For the classic, skeptical critique of theories of cannibalism, see W. Arens, *The Man-Eating Myth: Anthropology and Anthropophagy* (Oxford: Oxford University Press, 1979).

5. François Laydevant, "Remédes magiques ou meurtes rituels," *Bulletin des missions* 24, no. 2 (1950): 134–41.

6. *Cape Argus,* 17 November 1971.

7. *Cape Argus,* 23 December 1971; *Cape Argus,* 28 February 1984.

8. *Cape Times,* 13 January 1977; *Cape Argus,* 24 January 1977.

9. R. Niven, 24 August 1837, *Caffrarian Messenger,* October 1837 (cited in Peires, *House of Phalo,* 206 n. 83).

10. *Sunday Times,* 16 January 1977.

11. H. C. Temple, "Witchcraft or Worship?" *Nongqai* 17, no. 5 (1926): 342, 356.

12. W. Wanger, "Samen- und Felderweihe bei den Zulusprechen Völkern," *Völkerkunde* 2, nos. 4–6 (1926): 121–24; Otto Prozesky, "Die Heilsbotschaft im Swasilande," *Berliner Missions-Berichte* 1 (1926): 2–3; P. Ramseyer, "Le Solaboea," *Journal des missions évangéliques de Paris* 89, no. 1 (1914): 130–34.

13. Baumbach, "Heidengraüel," *Berliner Missions-Berichte* 5/6 (1874): 84–85.

14. W. L. Speight, "Human Sacrifice in South Africa," *Nongqai* 26, no. 2 (1935): 152, 164. See also Speight, "Ritual Murder in South Africa," *Nongqai* 32, no. 1 (1941): 54–55.

15. H. Dieterlen, "Paganisme concentré," *Journal des missions évangéliques de Paris* 87, no. 2 (1912): 168–73; "Ou le paganisme peut aboutir," *Journal des*

missions évangéliques de Paris 71 (1896): 263–66; H. Dieterlen, "La médicine et les médecins du Lessouto," *Les Cahiers Missionaires* 17 (1930): 1–73.

16. François Laydevant, "La sorcellerie en Basutoland," *Études Missionaires* 7, no. 2 (1937): 209–17; M. C. van Straaten, "Ritual Murders Still Continue in Basutoland and There Is 'Muti' Made from Human Flesh," *Nongqai* 39, no. 2 (1948): 146–49; Laydevant, "Remédes magiques ou meurtes rituels," 135–36.

17. G. I. Jones, *Basutoland Medicine Murder* (London: H. M. Stationery Office, 1951), 21; M. D. W. Jeffreys, "Review: G. I. Jones, *Basutoland Medicine Murder*," *Bantu Studios* 11 (1952): 194–96.

18. *Cape Argus*, 30 July 1951.

19. Harriet Ngubane, "The Predicament of the Sinister Healer: Some Observations on 'Ritual Murder' and the Professional Role of the Inyanga," in Murray Last and G. L. Chavunduka, eds., *The Professionalization of African Medicine* (Manchester: Manchester University Press, 1986), 203. See Ngubane, "Some Notions of 'Purity' and 'Impurity' among the Zulu," *Africa* 46 (1976): 274–84, and *Body and Mind in Zulu Medicine* (London: Academic Press, 1977).

20. Ngubane, "The Predicament of the Sinister Healer," 196–97, 202.

21. *Sunday Times*, 16 January 1977.

22. *Cape Argus*, 30 July 1981, 26 May 1982; *Sunday Times*, 16 January 1977.

23. *Cape Argus*, 8 June 1978; *Sunday Times*, 16 January 1977.

24. *Sunday Times*, 17 February 1974. For versions of modern satanisms, see Anton LaVey, *The Satanic Bible* (New York: Avon Books, 1969); Arthur Lyons, *The Second Coming: Satanism in America* (New York: Dodd, Mead, and Co., 1970); and H. T. Rhodes, *The Satanic Mass: A Sociological and Criminological Study* (New York: Citadel Press, 1955).

25. *Sunday Times*, 17 February 1974. The suggestion that such a demonology is based on a projection of a society's inner demons is developed in Norman Cohn, *Europe's Inner Demons* (New York: New American Library, 1975).

26. *Sunday Times*, 17 February 1974; *Cape Times*, 4 September 1975.

27. *Johannesburg Star*, 19 July 1975.

28. *Cape Argus*, 28 May 1977.

29. *Cape Argus*, 30 March 1974.

30. *Cape Argus*, 28 March 1976.

31. *Cape Argus*, 26 September 1978, 2 October 1978.

32. *Cape Argus*, 18 November 1953.

33. Hansard, *House of Assembly Debates,* 73 col. 9378, 19 June 1950.

34. Leo Kuper, *Passive Resistance in South Africa* (New Haven: Yale University Press, 1957), 117.

Chapter 4: Tours of Hell

1. E. B. Tylor, *Primitive Culture* (London: John Murray 1876), 1:424; Emile Durkheim, *The Elementary Forms of the Religious Life,* trans. Joseph Ward Swain (New York: Free Press, 1965), 62.

2. Karl Marx, *Grundrisse,* trans. Martin Nicolaus (London: Penguin and New Left Books, 1973), 325–26.

3. Orlando Patterson, *Slavery and Social Death: A Comparative Study* (Cambridge: Harvard University Press, 1982), 13.

4. James Motlatsi, "1987—The Year Mineworkers Take Control," *South African Labour Bulletin* 12, no. 3 (1987): 39–47.

5. Frederick A. Johnstone, *Class, Race, and Gold* (London: Routledge and Kegan Paul, 1976), 29; Luli Callinicos, *Gold and Workers* (Johannesburg: Ravan Press, 1980), 23. See also Wilmot G. James, "From Segregation to Apartheid: Miners and Peasants in the Making of a Racial Order, South Africa, 1930–1952" (Ph.D. dissertation, University of Wisconsin-Madison, 1982).

6. James R. Cochrane, *Servants of Power: The Role of English-speaking Churches in South Africa* (Johannesburg: Ravan Press, 1987), 113.

7. *Christian Express* 7, no. 95 (1 August 1878): 1–2.

8. Cochrane, *Servants of Power,* 152, 139.

9. Ray Phillips, *The Bantu Are Coming* (London: SCM Press, 1930), 31, 58, 139, 147–50; Tim Couzens, "'Moralizing Leisure Time': The Transatlantic Connection and Black Johannesburg, 1918–1936," in Shula Marks and Richard Rathbone, eds., *Industrialization and Social Change in South Africa* (London: Longman, 1982), 314–37.

10. Philip Bonner, "The Transvaal Native Congress, 1917–1920: The Radicalisation of the Black Petty Bourgeoisie on the Rand," in Marks and Rathbone, *Industrialization and Social Change in South Africa,* 296. For a more recent attempt to analyze worldviews from the bottom of the mines, see James V. Leatt, "Astride Two Worlds: Religion and Values among Black Migrant Mineworkers on South African Gold Mines," *Journal of Theology for Southern Africa* 38 (1982): 59–82, with a response from John Sharp and Martin West, "Dualism, Culture, and Migrant Mineworkers: A Rejoinder from Anthropology," *Journal of Theology for Southern Africa* 39 (1982): 64–69. On the ideology and culture of mineworkers, see T. Dunbar Moodie, "Mine Culture and Miner's Identity on a South

African Goldmine," in Belinda Bozzoli, ed., *Town and Countryside in the Transvaal* (Johannesburg: Ravan Press, 1983), 176–97.

11. Callinicos, *Gold and Workers,* 102. On "fictive kinship," see David Brion Davis, *Slavery and Human Progress* (Oxford: Oxford University Press, 1984), 32–101.

12. René de Villiers, "Afrikaner Nationalism," in Monica Wilson and Leonard Thompson, eds., *The Oxford History of South Africa* (Oxford: Oxford University Press, 1973), 2:407.

13. H. P. Junod, *Bantu Heritage* (Johannesburg: Hortors, for the Transvaal Chamber of Mines, 1938), 92. H. P. Junod was the son of South Africa's pioneer ethnographer, H-A. Junod. See Patrick Harries, "The Anthropologist as Historian and Liberal: H-A. Junod and the Thonga," *Journal of Southern African Studies* 8 (1981): 37–50. William Gemmill continued to argue that low wages and migrant labor were justified by the "nature" or the "tradition" of the "Bantu" worker. See *Report of the Witwatersrand Mine Native Wages Commission* (Pretoria: Government Printers, U.G. 21, 1944); cited in James, "From Segregation to Apartheid," 144. These arguments were still used by Gemmill's son James, who served as general manager of the Native Recruiting Corporation and the Witwatersrand Native Labour Association. See Alan H. Jeeves, *Migrant Labour in South Africa's Mining Economy: The Struggle for the Gold Mine's Labour Supply, 1890–1920* (Kingston: McGill Queen's University Press; Johannesburg: Witwatersrand University Press, 1985), 115.

14. Robert Gordon, *Mines, Masters, and Migrants* (Johannesburg: Ravan Press, 1977), 95; Bernd Heine, *Status and Use of African Lingua Francas* (Munich: Weltforum, 1970), 50.

15. Callinicos, *Gold and Workers,* 45; Jeeves, *Migrant Labour in South Africa's Mining Economy,* 22; James, "From Segregation to Apartheid," 100–1. The anthropology of mining has provided other examples of the association of the mine with death, demons, and the underworld: June Nash, *We Eat the Mines* (New York: Columbia University Press, 1979); Michael Taussig, *The Devil and Commodity Fetishism in South America* (Chapel Hill: University of North Carolina Press, 1980); and Ricardo Godoy, "Mining: Anthropological Perspectives," *Annual Review of Anthropology* 14 (1985): 199–277. For a religiohistorical perspective on the symbolism of mining, see Mircea Eliade, *The Forge and the Crucible: The Origins and Structures of Alchemy,* 2d ed., trans. Stephen Corrin (Chicago: University of Chicago Press, 1978).

16. Christopher Pycroft and Barry Munslow, "Black Mine Workers in South Africa: Strategies of Cooptation and Resistance," *Popular Struggles in Africa: The Review of African Political Economy* (Liverpool: Centre for African Studies, 1986), 3:39.

17. *Weekly Mail,* 12 April 1990.

18. *Cape Argus,* 3 September 1988.

19. Martha Himmelfarb, *Tours of Hell: An Apocalyptic Form in Jewish and Christian Literature* (Philadelphia: Fortress Press, 1985).

20. D. P. Walker, *The Decline of Hell: Seventeenth-Century Discussions of Eternal Torment* (Chicago: University of Chicago Press, 1964).

21. Steven Gregory and Daniel Timerman, "Rituals of the Modern State: The Case of Torture in Argentina," *Dialectical Anthropology* 11 (1986): 63. For important discussions of torture as ritual, see Talal Asad, "Notes on Body Pain and Truth in Medieval Christian Ritual," *Economy and Society* 12 (1983): 287–327; and Michael Taussig, "Culture of Terror—Space of Death: Roger Casement's Putumayo Report and the Explanation of Torture," *Comparative Studies in Society and History* 26 (1984): 467–97. More generally on the history of torture, see Edward Peters, *Torture* (Oxford: Basil Blackwell, 1985). For deep background, see Michel Foucault, *Discipline and Punish: The Birth of the Prison,* trans. Alan Sheridan (New York: Random House, 1977).

22. On the 1982 report and its denial, see South African Institute of Race Relations, *Survey* (Johannesburg: SAIRR, 1982), 253. On the 1985 report and its denial, see Don Foster, with Dennis Davis and Diane Sandler, *Detention and Torture in South Africa: Psychological, Legal, and Historical Studies* (Cape Town: David Philip, 1987). For the 1986 report and its denial, I have relied on the *Johannesburg Star,* 29 September 1986.

23. Minister of Law and Order Louis Le Grange's directive cited in Harold Rudolph, *Security, Terrorism, and Torture: Detainees' Rights in South Africa and Israel: A Comparative Study* (Cape Town: Juta, 1984), 207; his candid observation was reported in *Rand Daily Mail,* 11 August 1982.

24. *Johannesburg Star,* 8 April 1987; *Weekly Mail,* 5 June 1987.

25. Breyten Breytenbach, *The True Confessions of an Albino Terrorist* (Cape Town: Taurus, 1984); *Sunday Express,* 29 April 1984.

26. *Citizen,* 20 June 1984; *Johannesburg Star,* 2 July 1984.

27. Hilda Bernstein, *South Africa: The Terrorism of Torture* (London: International Defence and Aid Fund, Christian Action Publications, 1972), 3. See Gordon Winter, *Inside Boss: South Africa's Secret Police* (Harmondsworth: Penguin, 1981).

28. Elaine Scarry, *The Body in Pain: The Making and Unmaking of the World* (New York: Oxford University Press, 1985).

29. Joseph Lelyveld, "South Africa's Bishop Tutu," *New York Times Magazine,* 14 March 1982, 42; Bernstein, *South Africa,* 11; Ken Flower, *Serving Secretly* (Johannesburg: Galago, 1987), 156.

30. Nico Steytler, "Policing Political Opponents: Death Squads and Cop Culture," in Desirée Hansson and Dirk van Zyl Smit, eds., *Towards Justice: Crime and State Control in South Africa* (Cape Town: Oxford University Press, 1990), 121; M. D. Dippenaar, *Die Geskiedenis van die Suid Afrikaanse Polisie* (Silverton: Promedia, 1988), 246; Republic of South Africa, *White Paper on the Organisation and Functions of the South African Police* (Pretoria: Government Printers, 1990), 64–65. On the history and expansion of the South African security system, see, in addition to other works cited, Kenneth Grundy, *The Rise of the South African Security Establishment: An Essay on the Changing Locus of State Power* (Johannesburg: South African Institute of International Affairs, 1983); and Simon Baynham, ed., *The South African Security Establishment* (London: Routledge and Kegan Paul, 1988).

31. Bonner, "The Transvaal Native Congress," 293, 305.

32. Robert Edgar, "Garveyism in Africa: Dr. Wellington and the American Movement in the Transkei," *Ufahamu* 6, no. 3 (1976): 31–57; William Beinart and Colin Bundy, *Hidden Struggles in Rural South Africa* (Berkeley: University of California Press, 1987): 222–69; Helen Bradford, *A Taste of Freedom: The ICU in Rural South Africa, 1924–1930* (New Haven: Yale University Press, 1987), 213–45.

33. Cyril Ramaphosa, "Interview," *South African Labour Bulletin* 12, no. 4 (1987): 45–55; Father Smangaliso Mkhatshwa cited in Raymond Suttner and Jeremy Cronin, eds., *Thirty Years of the Freedom Charter* (Johannesburg: Ravan Press, 1986), 222–23. On the Freedom Charter, see Peter Hudson, "Images of the Future and Strategies in the Present: The Freedom Charter and the South African Left," in Philip Frankel, Noam Pines, and Mark Swilling, eds., *State, Resistance, and Change in South Africa* (London: Croom Helm, 1988), 259–77.

34. Technical Advice Group, Johannesburg, "Kinross: Health and Safety in the Mines," *South African Labour Bulletin* 12, no. 1 (1987): 14; Motlatsi, "1987—The Year Mineworkers Take Control," 45.

35. Hansard (A) 2 q col. 24, 10 February 1987.

36. *Weekly Mail,* 17 February 1989; *Cape Times,* 14 February 1989.

37. *Cape Argus,* 11 April 1989, emphasis added.

38. *Cape Times,* 14 February 1989, 22 February 1989, 11 March 1989; *Business Day,* 7 March 1989; *Weekly Mail,* 21 April 1989, emphasis added.

Chapter 5: The Space of War

1. David Chidester, *Patterns of Power: Religion and Politics in American Culture* (Englewood Cliffs, N.J.: Prentice-Hall, 1988), 194–96.

2. James Aho, *Religious Mythology and the Art of War: Comparative Religious Symbolisms of Military Violence* (Westport, Conn.: Greenwood Press, 1981).

3. Republic of South Africa, *White Paper on Defence, 1973* (Pretoria: Department of Defence, 1973).

4. *Cape Times,* 6 December 1979; *Rand Daily Mail,* 25 September 1984; *Weekly Mail,* 3 October 1986.

5. G. W. Stow, *The Native Races of South Africa* (London: Swan Sonnenschein and Co., 1905), 233–35; G. M. E. Leistner, "Change in Afrikaner National Life," *Africa Insight* 10, no. 2 (1980): 75–77.

6. Republic of South Africa, *White Paper on Defence, 1977* (Pretoria: Department of Defence, 1977), 1, 4, 8. On the militarization of South Africa, see, in addition to other works cited in this chapter, Kenneth Grundy, *The Militarization of South African Politics* (London: Taurus, 1986); Annette Seegers, "The Military in South Africa: A Comparison and Critique," *South Africa International* 16 (1986): 192–200; and André du Pisani, *Beyond the Barracks: Reflections on the Role of the SADF in the Region* (Cape Town: South African Institute of International Affairs, 1988).

7. Marcel Mauss, *The Gift* (New York: Free Press, 1954), 1.

8. Philip Frankel, *Pretoria's Praetorians: Civil-Military Relations in South Africa* (Cambridge: Cambridge University Press, 1984), 24. Reportedly, the "total strategy" relied heavily on the theoretical work of André Beaufre, *An Introduction to Strategy,* trans. R. H. Barry (London: Faber and Faber, 1963), and *Strategy of Action,* trans. R. H. Barry (London: Faber and Faber, 1967); and of J. J. McCuen, *The Art of Counter-Revolutionary War: The Strategy of Counter-Insurgency* (London: Faber and Faber, 1966).

9. J. Dutton, "Military Aspects of National Security," in H. H. Louw, ed., *National Security: A Modern Approach* (Pretoria: University of Pretoria, Institute for Strategic Studies, 1977), 105, 113.

10. *Citizen Training,* 25 April 1975; Gavin Cawthra, *Brutal Force: The Apartheid War Machine* (London: International Defence and Aid Fund for Southern Africa, 1986), 42–43.

11. Harald E. Winkler and Laurie Nathan, "Waging Peace: Church Resistance to Militarisation," in Jacklyn Cock and Laurie Nathan, eds., *War and Society: The Militarisation of South Africa* (Cape Town: David Philip, 1989), 335; *Paratus,* March 1985, 22; Peter G. Moll, "A Theological Critique of the Military Chaplaincy of the English-speaking Churches" (M.A. thesis, University of Cape Town, 1984), 304.

12. *Daily News,* 13 June 1979.

13. Willem Steenkamp, *South Africa's Border War, 1966–1989* (Gibralter:

Ashanti, 1989), 212; Shula Marks, "The Zulu Disturbances in Natal," in R. I. Rotberg, ed., *Rebellion in Black Africa* (Oxford: Oxford University Press, 1971), 59. See John Ellis, *The Social History of the Machine Gun* (Baltimore: Johns Hopkins University Press, 1975), 101.

14. Julie Frederikse, *South Africa: A Different Kind of War: From Soweto to Pretoria* (Johannesburg: Ravan Press, 1986), 9. On the militarization of South African public schools, see Gavin Evans, "Classrooms of War: The Militarisation of White South African Schooling," in Cock and Nathan, eds., *War and Society,* 283–97.

15. Gerrit Schutte, "Company and Colonists at the Cape, 1652–1795," in Richard Elphick and Hermann Giliomee, eds., *The Shaping of South African Society, 1652–1840* (Cape Town: Maskew Miller Longman, 1989), 292.

16. Hansard (A) 18 q col. 1666, 4 June 1985.

17. James Adams, *The Unnatural Alliance* (London: Quartet Books, 1984), 93; Hansard (A) 8 q col. 742, 19 March 1985; Hansard (A) 3 q col. 104, 24 February 1988.

18. Senate of South Africa, *Debates, Official Report* (Cape Town: Nasionale Pers, 1940–41), col. 13.

19. *Eastern Province Herald,* 10 April 1984.

20. Steenkamp, *South Africa's Border War,* 18.

21. *Paratus,* February 1981, 49.

22. *Paratus,* June 1986, 17.

23. *Paratus,* June 1986, 17–18. On the South African military role in the "destabilization" of the region, see Joseph Hanlon, *Beggar Your Neighbors: Apartheid Power in Southern Africa* (Bloomington: Indiana University Press, 1986); and Victoria Brittain, *Hidden Lives, Hidden Deaths: South Africa's Crippling of a Continent* (London: Faber and Faber, 1988).

24. Michael Evans and Mark Phillips, "Intensifying Civil War: The Role of the South African Defence Force," in Philip Frankel, Noam Pines, and Mark Swilling, eds., *State, Resistance, and Change in South Africa* (London: Croom Helm, 1989), 117.

25. *Johannesburg Star,* 24 October 1984; *Financial Mail,* 26 October 1984.

26. Hansard (A) 13 q cols. 1638–1641, 6 May 1986; *Sowetan,* 26 April 1985.

27. *Financial Mail,* 26 October 1984; *Rand Daily Mail,* 7 November 1984; *Citizen,* 2 July 1985.

28. South African Institute of Race Relations, *Survey* (Johannesburg: SAIRR, 1987/88), 559.

29. *Government Gazette,* no. 9884, notice 1746, 31 July 1985.

30. *Cape Times,* 18 July 1987.

31. D. D. V. Kannemeyer, *Report of the Commission Appointed to Inquire into the Incident Which Occurred on 21 March 1985 at Uitenhage* (Pretoria: Government Printers, 1985), para. 1.2, part 5.

32. See Robert J. Thornton, "The Shooting at Uitenhage, South Africa, 1985: The Context and Interpretation of Violence," *American Ethnologist* 17 (1990): 217–36. For a discussion of South African funerals as ritual, based on their extensive British and American press coverage, see David I. Kertzer, *Ritual, Politics, and Power* (New Haven: Yale University Press, 1988), 171–73.

33. *Government Gazette,* no. 10541, proclamation R224, 11 December 1986. By suggesting that government restrictions on discourse should be regarded as ritual, I adapt insights from the work of Maurice Bloch. In ritual, Bloch has noted, the "formalization of speech . . . dramatically restricts what can be said, so that speech acts are either all alike or all of a kind and thus if this mode of communication is adopted there is hardly any *choice* of what can be said" ("Symbols, Song, Dance, and Features of Articulation: Is Religion an Extreme Form of Traditional Authority?" in Maurice Bloch, *Ritual, History, and Power* [London: Athlone Press, 1989], 27).

34. ECC, *A Declaration to End Conscription,* July 1984. See Michael Graaf, ed., *Hawks and Doves: The Pro- and Anti-Conscription Press in South Africa* (Durban: University of Natal, Contemporary Cultural Studies Unit, 1988).

35. *Cape Times,* 13 March 1985; *Weekly Mail,* 27 April 1987.

36. Winkler and Nathan, "Waging Peace," 335; Laurie Nathan, "'Marching to a Different Beat': The History of the End Conscription Campaign," in Cock and Nathan, *War and Society,* 319.

37. *Citizen,* 13 August 1984, 10 September 1985, 14 April 1987.

38. *Citizen,* 3 September 1988; *Sunday Star,* 4 September 1988.

39. *Johannesburg Star,* 3 August 1988, 4 August 1988; Nathan, "'Marching to a Different Beat,'" 308.

40. *Business Day,* 6 December 1988, 26 July 1988.

41. *Cape Argus,* 5 September 1989.

42. Hilda Kuper, "The Language of Sites in the Politics of Space," *American Anthropologist* 74 (1972): 422, 411.

Chapter 6: The Time of Revolution

1. *Cape Argus,* 12 February 1990; Nelson Mandela, *The Struggle Is My Life* (New York: Pathfinder Press, 1986), 181.

2. Robert Jay Lifton, *Revolutionary Immortality: Mao Tse-tung and the Chinese Cultural Revolution* (New York: W. W. Norton, 1968); Desmond Tutu, "Freedom Fighters or Terrorists?" in Charles Villa-Vicencio, ed., *Theology and Violence: The South African Debate* (Johannesburg: Skotaville, 1987), 78; Buti Tlhagale, "Christian Soldiers," in Villa-Vicencio, *Theology and Violence,* 88. On relations between religion and revolution more generally, see Bruce Lincoln, ed., *Religion, Rebellion, Revolution* (New York: Saint Martin's Press, 1985).

3. *Cape Times,* 17 February 1990.

4. William Beinart, "Review Article: History of the African People," *South African Historical Journal* 18 (1986): 228; Mandela, *Struggle Is My Life,* 161.

5. Mandela, *Struggle Is My Life,* 175.

6. *Business Day,* 10 April 1987.

7. *Cape Times,* 1 February 1985; *Weekly Mail,* 15 February 1985; Mandela, *Struggle Is My Life,* 195–96.

8. *Cape Argus,* 25 April 1987. On the ANC in the 1980s, see Tom Lodge, "The African National Congress in South Africa, 1976–1983: Guerilla War and Armed Propaganda," *Journal of Contemporary African Studies* 3 (1983/84): 153–80; "The ANC in 1982," in South African Research Services, *South African Review One* (Johannesburg: Ravan Press, 1983), 50–54; "The Second Consultative Conference of the ANC," *South Africa International* 16 (1985): 80–97; "Mayehlome!—Let Us Go to War! From Nkomati to Kabwe, the ANC January 1984–June 1985," in South African Research Services, *South African Review Three* (Johannesburg: Ravan Press, 1986), 226–47; "The ANC, Kabwe, and After," *International Affairs Bulletin* 10 (1986): 80–97; "State of Exile: The African National Congress of South Africa," in Philip Frankel, Noam Pines, and Mark Swilling, eds., *State, Resistance, and Change in South Africa* (London: Croom Helm, 1988), 229–58.

9. Peter Walshe, *The Rise of African Nationalism in South Africa* (Berkeley: University of California Press, 1970), 38, 341. On Dube, see R. Hunt Davis, "John L. Dube: A South African Exponent of Booker T. Washington," *Journal of African Studies* 2 (1975): 497–528; and W. Manning Marable, "African Nationalist: The Life of John Langalibalele Dube" (Ph.D. dissertation, University of Maryland, 1976). On Xuma, see Richard D. Ralston, "American Episodes in the Making of an African Leader: A Case Study of Alfred B. Xuma (1893–1962)," *International Journal of African Historical Studies* 6 (1973): 72–93.

10. Shula Marks, "The Ambiguities of Dependence: John L. Dube of Natal," *Journal of Southern African Studies* 1 (1975): 176.

11. See Helen Bradford, *A Taste of Freedom: The ICU in Rural South Africa, 1924–1930* (New Haven: Yale University Press, 1987); Martin Legassick, *Class and Nationalism in South African Protest: The South African Communist Party and the "Native Republic," 1928–1934* (Syracuse: Syracuse University Press, 1973); and William Beinart and Colin Bundy, *Hidden Struggles in Rural South Africa: Politics and Popular Movements in the Transkei and Eastern Cape, 1890–1930* (Johannesburg: Ravan Press, 1987).

12. Gail M. Gerhart, *Black Power in South Africa: The Evolution of an Ideology* (Berkeley: University of California Press, 1978), 58–62.

13. Leo Kuper, *Passive Resistance in South Africa* (New Haven: Yale University Press, 1957), 117; Albert Luthuli, *Let My People Go* (New York: McGraw Hill, 1962). See Edward Callan, *Albert John Luthuli and the South African Race Conflict* (Kalamazoo: Western Michigan University Press, 1962); Mary Benson, *Chief Albert Lutuli of South Africa* (London: Oxford University Press, 1963); and Dorothy Woodson, "The Speeches of Albert J. Luthuli," *Africana Journal* 13 (1982): 41–49.

14. Gerhart, *Black Power in South Africa,* 147; Thomas G. Karis and Gwendolen M. Carter, eds., *From Protest to Challenge: A Documentary History of African Politics in South Africa, 1882–1964* (Stanford: Hoover Institution Press, 1972–77), 2:331–36; Peter Rodda, "The Africanists Cut Loose," *Africa South* 3, no. 4 (1959): 23.

15. Karis and Carter, eds., *From Protest to Challenge,* 3: 566–67. See Ambrose Reeves, *Shooting at Sharpeville: The Agony of South Africa* (London: Victor Gollancz, 1960).

16. Poqo has been generally neglected by historians, with the exception of Tom Lodge, "Insurrectionism in South Africa: The Pan-Africanist Congress and the Poqo Movement" (Ph.D. dissertation, University of York, 1984). On Poqo's unique policy of killing people, see Tom Lodge, "'Izwe-Lethu' (The Land Is Ours): Poqo, The Politics of Despair," in Anne V. Akeroyd and Christopher R. Hill, eds., *Southern African Research in Progress, Collected Papers* (York: University of York, Centre for Southern African Studies, 1977), 3:109; and *Black Politics in South Africa since 1945* (Johannesburg: Ravan Press, 1983), 27. The link between Poqo and Fanon was made in Gerhart, *Black Power in South Africa,* 14–15. See John Alan and Lou Turner, *Frantz Fanon, Soweto, and American Black Thought* (Chicago: News and Letters, 1986). For a discussion of the recurring sacrificial killing of white pigs in the 1920s as a ritual of resistance, see Bradford, *A Taste of Freedom,* 213–45. The role of African religion was recalled by a PAC activist: "At times we would say this struggle of ours is entirely depending on the trust we have to our gods. . . . We didn't mean God; we meant

the gods. . . . that the ancestors are watching" (Gerhart, *Black Power in South Africa*, 204). In Cape Town, PAC leader Philip Kgosana invoked the "Gods of Africa" in launching the anti-pass campaign. Monica Wilson and Archie Mafeje, *Langa: A Study of Social Groups in an African Township* (Cape Town: Oxford University Press, 1963), 112. For comparison, see Michael Adas, *Prophets of Rebellion: Millenarian Protest Movements against the European Colonial Order* (Chapel Hill: University of North Carolina Press, 1979).

17. Karis and Carter, *From Protest to Challenge*, 3: 717, 772, 740, 777.

18. Oliver Tambo, "Peace and Development in Our Region," *Sechaba*, August 1988, 5; Nelson Mandela, *Argus*, 26 January 1990.

19. Lamola, "The Concept of 'Violence' in the Language of the Struggle," *Sechaba*, January 1989, 15–21.

20. NEC, "Umkhonto we Sizwe, Born of the People," *Sechaba*, March 1987, 18; Cassius Mandla, "Umkhonto we Sizwe: Let Us Move to an All-out War," *Sechaba*, November 1986, 26.

21. Mandela, *Struggle Is My Life*, 168–69; Oliver Tambo, "President's Message," *Sechaba*, March 1985, 12; "Obituary: Cassius Make and Paul Dikeledi," *Sechaba*, September 1987, 30.

22. Ronnie Kasrils, "Interview: People's War, Revolution, and Insurrection," *Sechaba*, May 1986, 3; Alex Mashinini, "Preparing the Fire before Cooking the Rice inside the Pot: Some Burning Questions of Our Revolution," *Sechaba*, April 1985, 25; Editorial, "January 8th—An Historic Occasion," *Sechaba*, February 1987, 1.

23. Oliver Tambo, "President's Message" (1985), 5; Tambo, "President's Message," *Sechaba*, February 1990, 11.

24. *Bantu World*, 18 March 1950 (cited in Walshe, *Rise of African Nationalism*, 343); Francis Meli, "President O. R. Tambo: Political Profile on the Occasion of his 70th Birthday," *Sechaba*, October 1987, 3.

25. Cited in Cedric Mayson, "Christianity and Revolution: A Battle Fought on Many Fronts," *Sechaba*, October 1987, 12. See Peter Walshe, *Church versus State in South Africa: The Case of the Christian Institute* (Maryknoll, N.Y.: Orbis, 1983).

26. "Joint Communique of the Southern African Catholic Bishops Conference and the African National Congress, 16 April 1986," *Sechaba*, August 1986, 24. See, for example, "Communique from the Meeting between the ANC and the Northern Diocese of the Evangelical Lutheran Church in Southern Africa, 12–13 November 1986," *Sechaba*, January 1987, 11.

27. "Kairos Document," in Charles Villa-Vicencio, ed., *Between Christ and Caesar* (Grand Rapids, Mich.: Eerdmans, 1986), 259. See Brian M. du Toit,

"Theology, Kairos, and the Church in South Africa," *Missiology* 16 (1988): 57–71; and Willis H. Logan, ed., *The Kairos Covenant: Standing with South African Christians* (New York: Friendship Press, 1988); and Mayson, "Christianity and Revolution," 13.

28. John Lamola, "Churches Identify with Peoples in Struggle," *Sechaba,* July 1987, 21–23.

29. Frank Chikane, "Church and State in Apartheid South Africa," *Sechaba,* June 1988, 4.

30. Cedric Mayson, "The Comradeship of Marx and Jesus," *African Communist* 110 (1987): 54.

31. "ANC Meets with Indian Leaders," *Sechaba,* November 1988, 10; SACP cited in Cedric Mayson, "Converting Christian Subversives," *Sechaba,* September 1989, 29.

32. John Lamola, "Does the Church Lead the Struggle? A Caution," *Sechaba,* June 1988, 7–11.

33. Mayson, "Christianity and Revolution," 12.

34. *The Times* (London), 17 July 1989 (cited in *Sechaba,* September 1989, 27).

35. Mayson, "Converting the Christian Subversives," 29; Mayson, "A Sort of Theological MK," *Sechaba,* February 1989, 31–32.

36. Albert Nolan, *God in South Africa* (Cape Town: David Philip, 1988), 178, 59; Mayson, "Christianity and Revolution," 15.

37. NEC, "Umkhonto we Sizwe, Born of the People," 12.

38. Oliver Tambo, "NEC message, 8 Jan 1986," *Sechaba,* March 1986, 5.

39. Oliver Tambo, "Advance to People's Power," *Sechaba,* February 1987, 2; *Sechaba,* July 1989, 16; Oliver Tambo, 1983 speech, cited in Teacher Freda and Teacher Anna, *Sechaba,* April 1987, 13–14.

40. Oliver Tambo, "Moses Mabhida," *Sechaba,* May 1986, 32. On the "special dead," see Peter Brown, *The Cult of the Saints: Its Rise and Function in Latin Christianity* (Chicago: University of Chicago Press, 1981).

41. NEC, "Umkhonto we Sizwe, Born of the People," 18.

42. Luthuli, *Let My People Go,* 42–43, 88.

43. Oliver Tambo, "Forward to United Action for People's Power," *Sechaba,* March 1988, 11, 5. See John Dugard, "Human Rights and the Rule of Law, 1," in Jeffrey Butler, Richard Elphick, and David Welsh, eds., *Democratic Liberalism in South Africa* (Cape Town: David Philip, 1987), 272.

44. Oliver Tambo, "Mass Action for People's Power," *Sechaba,* February 1989, 3; Editorial, *Sechaba,* August 1986, 1.

45. Oliver Tambo, "We Have Decided to Liberate Ourselves," *Sechaba,* August 1986, 6; Editorial, *Sechaba,* August 1986, 1.

46. Alfred Nzo, "Address to British Trade Unionists," *Sechaba,* October 1988, 15; Mwalimu Julius K. Nyerere, "Address in Arusha," *Sechaba,* January 1988, 5.

47. Tambo, "We Have Decided to Liberate Ourselves," 6; Tambo, "Forward to United Action for People's Power," 15.

48. Oliver Tambo, "The Ideology of Racism," *Sechaba,* July 1986, 2.

49. Steve Biko, "Black Consciousness and the Quest for a True Humanity," in Aelred Stubbs, ed., *I Write What I Like* (San Francisco: Harper and Row, 1986): 87–98; Basil Moore, Preface to Basil Moore, ed., *The Challenge of Black Theology in South Africa* (London: C. Hurst and Co., 1973; Atlanta: John Knox, 1974), ix. On black consciousness, see Robert Fatton, Jr., *Black Consciousness in South Africa: The Dialectics of Ideological Resistance to White Supremacy* (Albany, N.Y.: State University of New York Press, 1986). On black theology, see Itumeleng J. Mosala and Buti Tlhagale, eds., *The Unquestionable Right to be Free: Essays in Black Theology* (Johannesburg: Skotaville, 1986); Louise Kretzschmar, *The Voice of Black Theology in South Africa* (Johannesburg: Ravan Press, 1986); and Itumeleng J. Mosala, *Biblical Hermeneutics and Black Theology in South Africa* (Grand Rapids, Mich.: Eerdmans, 1989). On the relation between African theology and black theology, see Matthew Schoffeleers, "Theology and Relations of Production: The Case of Southern Africa," *Journal of Theology for Southern Africa* 61 (1987): 14–26; and "Black and African Theology in Southern Africa: A Controversy Re-examined," *Journal of Religion in Africa* 18 (1988): 99–124.

50. "Inside South Africa: A New Movement Is Formed," *Sechaba,* March 1973, 5.

51. Oliver Tambo, "ANC President Explains the Struggle," *Sechaba,* fourth quarter 1977, 11.

52. NEC, "Umkhonto we Sizwe, Born of the People," 15; Sara, "A Worker's Victory, the Sarhwu Strike," *Sechaba,* August 1987, 13; Second National Consultative Conference of ANC Commission on Strategy and Tactics, 1985 (cited in Mzala, "Towards People's War and Insurrection," *Sechaba,* April 1987, 6).

53. *Sechaba,* September 1988, 15; Jean Middleton, "The Judicial Murder of Andrew Sibuyiso Zondo," *Sechaba,* August 1986, 29.

54. Jonathan Z. Smith, *Imagining Religion: From Babylon to Jonestown* (Chicago: University of Chicago Press, 1982), 112–17.

55. Mandla, "Umkhonto we Sizwe: Let Us Move to an All-out War," 26. See NEC, "Umkhonto we Sizwe, Born of the People," 15.

56. Ronnie Kasrils, "The Revolutionary Army," *Sechaba,* September 1988, 7.

57. Nelson Mandela cited in Mzala, "Umkhonto we Sizwe: Building People's Forces for Combat War and Insurrection, Part 2," *Sechaba,* January 1987, 26; Editorial, "Democratic Forces Smashing the White Laager," *Sechaba,* April 1987, 1.

58. Oliver Tambo, "President's Message" (1985), 13; Nyawuza, "Response to Comrade Mzala," *Sechaba,* April 1985, 18; Mark Guthrie, "Political Trials Still Continue," *Sechaba,* January 1990, 19.

59. Tambo, "Forward to United Action for People's Power," *Sechaba,* March 1988, 14; Editorial, "Sanctions and Armed Struggle," *Sechaba,* December 1988, 1; Oliver Tambo, "Peace and Development in Frontline States" (June 1988), *Sechaba,* August 1988, 4. See Merle Lipton, *Sanctions and South Africa: The Dynamics of Economic Isolation,* special report no. 119 (London: Economic Intelligence Unit, 1988) (reviewed in *Sechaba,* April 1988, 29); Eminent Persons Group, *Mission to South Africa* (London: Penguin, 1986); and Mark Orkin, ed., *Sanctions against Apartheid* (Johannesburg: Case, 1990).

60. Joe Slovo (3 March 1987), cited in Alex Mashinini, "People's War and Negotiations: Are They Fire and Water?" *Sechaba,* August 1988, 25.

61. Frank Kermode, *The Sense of an Ending: Studies in the Theory of Fiction* (New York: Oxford University Press, 1967), 29; *The Kairos Document: Challenge to the Church,* 2d ed. (Johannesburg: Skotaville, 1986), 1.

62. Tambo, "Moses Mabhida," 32; Tambo, "Advance to People's Power," 2.

63. Alex Mashinini, "Dual Power and the Creation of People's Committees," *Sechaba,* April 1986, 29; Nyawuza, "Response to Comrade Mzala," *Sechaba,* 19; Kasrils, "Interview: People's War, Revolution, and Insurrection," 9.

64. Tambo, "President's Message" (1985), 3; Mandla, "Umkhonto we Sizwe: Let Us Move to an All-out War," 28; NEC, "Umkhonto we Sizwe, Born of the People," 18.

65. Editorial, "ANC—75 Years Old, But Younger than Ever," *Sechaba,* January 1987, 3; Ralph Mzamo, "Hintsa the Great," *Sechaba,* January 1990, 23–25; Sello Moeti, "The Legacy of Moshoeshoe," *Sechaba,* October 1986, 9; Ralph Mzamo, "Shaka, a Military Giant," *Sechaba,* August 1987, 11; the last quotation is from Mzamo, "Hintsa the Great," 23. See Shula Marks, "Khoisan Resistance to the Dutch in the Seventeenth and Eighteenth Centuries," *Journal of African History* 13 (1972): 55–80. The classic, accessible survey of South African resistance is Edward Roux, *Time Longer than Rope: A History of the Black Man's*

Struggle for Freedom in South Africa 2d ed. (1948; reprinted Madison: University of Wisconsin Press, 1966). For a more recent survey, see Charles Villa Vicencio, *Civil Disobedience and Beyond: Law, Resistance, and Religion in South Africa* (Grand Rapids, Mich.: Eerdmans; Cape Town: David Philip, 1990): 14–37.

66. Mzala, "Umkhonto we Sizwe: Building People's Forces for Combat War and Insurrection, Part 1," *Sechaba,* December 1986, 26.

67. NEC, "Umkhonto we Sizwe, Born of the People," 10; "ANC—75 Years Old, But Younger than Ever," 1; Sello Moeti, "Uyadela wena Osulapho," *Sechaba,* April 1986, 15; Mzala, "Umkhonto we Sizwe: Building People's Forces for Combat War and Insurrection, Part 1," 23. On Bambatha, see Shula Marks, *Reluctant Rebellion: The 1906–08 Disturbances in Natal* (Oxford: Clarendon Press, 1970)

68. Tambo, "Mass Action for People's Power," 2; Mandla, "Umkhonto we Sizwe: Let Us Move to an All-out War," 24.

69. NEC, "Umkhonto we Sizwe, Born of the People," 18.

70. Tambo, "Forward to United Action for People's Power," 11; Thabo Mbeki cited in Mandla Langa, "The Quiet Thunder: Report on the Amsterdam Cultural Conference," *Sechaba,* March 1988, 27.

71. Editorial, "History and Time Not on Their Side," *Sechaba,* January 1989, 1.

Chapter 7: Violent Negotiations

1. Joseph Lelyveld, *Move Your Shadow: South Africa, Black and White* (New York: Random House, 1986), 328.

2. Gerhard Maré and Georgina Hamilton, *An Appetite for Power: Buthelezi's Inkatha and the Politics of "Loyal Resistance"* (Johannesburg: Ravan Press, 1987). In addition to using the name of a nineteenth-century ritual object of Zulu royalty, Buthelezi appropriated the name Inkatha from a Zulu royalist movement of the 1920s. See Nicholas Cope, "The Zulu *Petit Bourgeoisie* and Zulu Nationalism in the 1920s: Origins of Inkatha," *Journal of Southern African Studies* 16 (1990): 431–51; and, for broader background, Shula Marks, *The Ambiguities of Dependence in South Africa: State, Class, and Nationalism in Early Twentieth-Century Natal* (Johannesburg: Ravan Press, 1984).

3. *Sechaba,* July 1987, 27; Mzala, "Review: *Appetite for Power,*" *Sechaba,* March 1988, 31.

4. *Weekly Mail,* 12 June 1987; Alex Callinicos, *South Africa between Reform and Revolution* (London: Bookmarks, 1989), 145; Josette Cole, *Crossroads: The Politics of Reform and Repression, 1976–86* (Johannesburg: Ravan Press, 1987),

131. See Nicholas Haysom, *Mabangalala: The Rise of Right-Wing Vigilantes in South Africa* (Johannesburg: University of the Witwatersrand Press, 1986); and "Vigilantism and the Policing of African Townships: Manufacturing Violent Stability," in Desirée Hansson and Dirk van Zyl Smit, eds., *Towards Justice? Crime and State Control in South Africa* (Cape Town: Oxford University Press, 1990), 63–84.

5. Kgomotso Bapela, "Vigilantes: Apartheid's Violent Surrogates," *Sechaba,* August 1986, 26; Alfred Nzo, "Address to British Trade Unionists," *Sechaba,* October 1988, 15; U.S. Consul General Tex Harris cited in *Cape Times,* 13 July 1990.

6. Editorial, "Nelson Mandela and Gatsha Buthelezi," *Sechaba,* November 1988, 1.

7. Mzala, "Review: *Appetite for Power,*" 31; Livingstone Mqotsi, "Review: Mzala, *Gatsha Buthelezi: Chief with a Double Agenda,*" *Sechaba,* September 1988, 29. For an earlier, laudatory biography, see Ben Temkin, *Gatsha Buthelezi: Zulu Statesman* (Cape Town: Purnell, 1976). For an expression of Buthelezi's own position, see Mangosuthu Gatsha Buthelezi, *South Africa: My Vision for the Future* (London: Weidenfeld and Nicolson, 1990). For an insightful investigation of the "authenticity" of Zulu royal symbols appropriated by Buthelezi, see Sandra Klopper, "Mobilizing Cultural Symbols in Twentieth-Century Zululand" (Paper, University of Cape Town, Centre for African Studies, 1989).

8. *Cape Times,* 26 March 1990; Oliver Tambo, "Moses Mabhida," *Sechaba,* May 1986, 32.

9. See Heather Hughes, "Violence in Inanda, August 1985," *Journal of Southern African Studies* 13 (1987): 331–54; Michael Sutcliffe and Paul Wellings, "Inkatha versus the Rest: The Black Opposition to Inkatha in Durban's African Townships," *African Affairs* 87 (1988): 325–60; and, especially, Nkosinathi Gwala, "Political Violence and the Struggle for Control in Pietermaritzburg," *Journal of Southern African Studies* 15 (1989): 506–24.

10. Maré and Hamilton, *Appetite for Power,* 197.

11. *Cape Argus,* 3 April 1990.

12. *Weekly Mail,* 23 March 1990.

13. *Cape Times,* 10 October 1990; *Weekly Mail,* 12 October 1990; *Sunday Times,* 17 March 1991.

14. *Cape Argus,* 22 June 1990; *Johannesburg Star,* 24 June 1990; *Cape Argus,* 23 March 1991.

15. *Weekly Mail,* 23 March 1990.

16. *Cape Argus,* 13 June 1990.

17. *Weekly Mail,* 23 March 1990. On witch-eradication movements as political movements, see Karen Fields, *Revival and Rebellion in Colonial Central Africa* (Princeton: Princeton University Press, 1985).

18. *Cape Argus,* 9 April 1990; *Weekly Mail,* 12 April 1990; *Cape Times,* 9 April 1990.

19. *Cape Times,* 28 March 1990.

20. *Cape Times,* 27 March 1990.

21. *Cape Times,* 2 April 1990; *Weekly Mail,* 30 March 1990.

22. *Cape Argus,* 22 March 1990; *Weekly Mail,* 9 March 1990. Shortly after being released from prison, Jafta Masemola was killed in a car crash.

23. *Cape Times,* 7 April 1990. In February 1991, Chief Maphumulo was machine-gunned to death outside his home. No suspects were arrested.

24. *Weekly Mail,* 5 April 1990.

Index